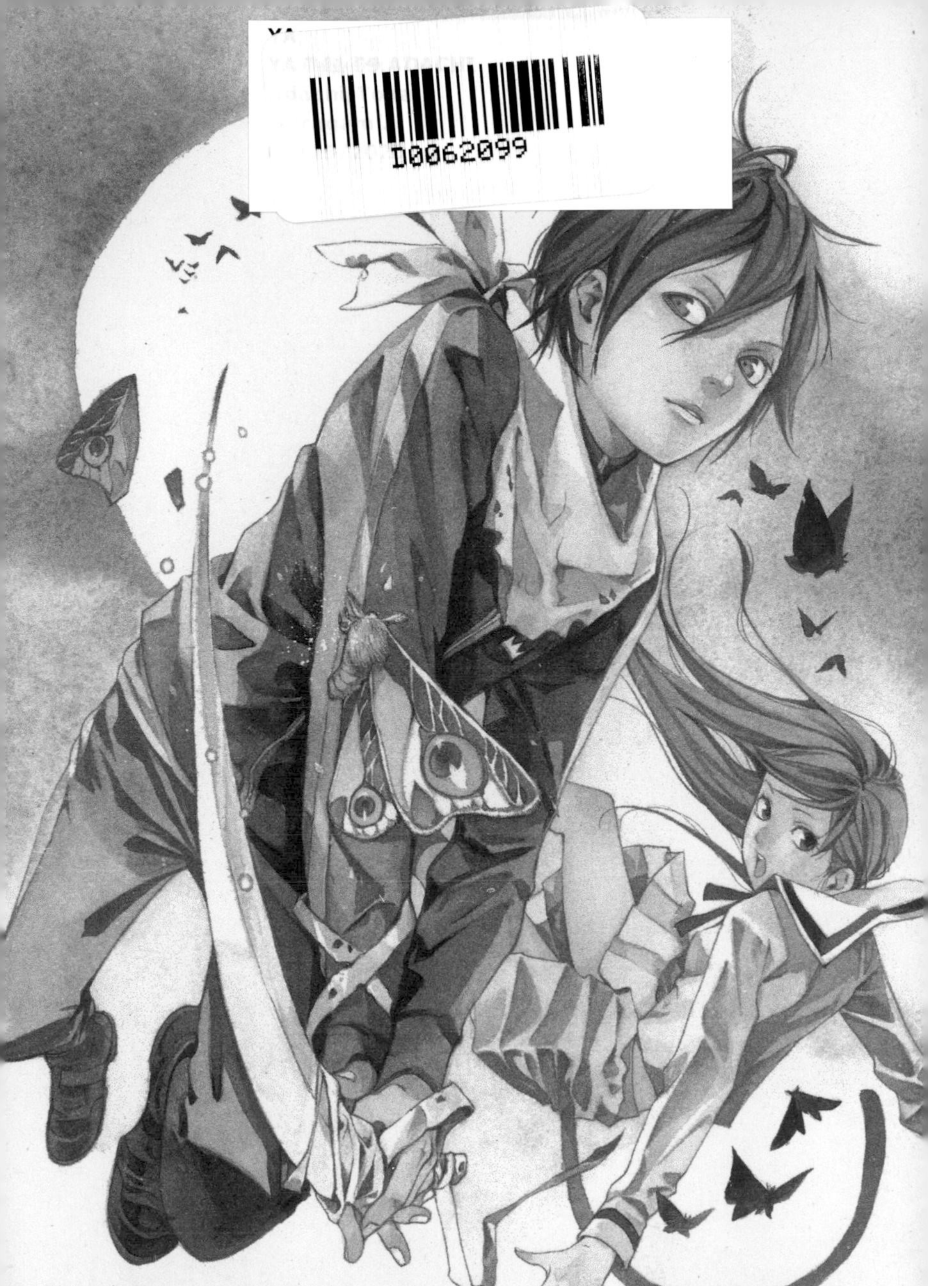

NORAGAMI
STRAY GOD

ADACHITOKA

characters

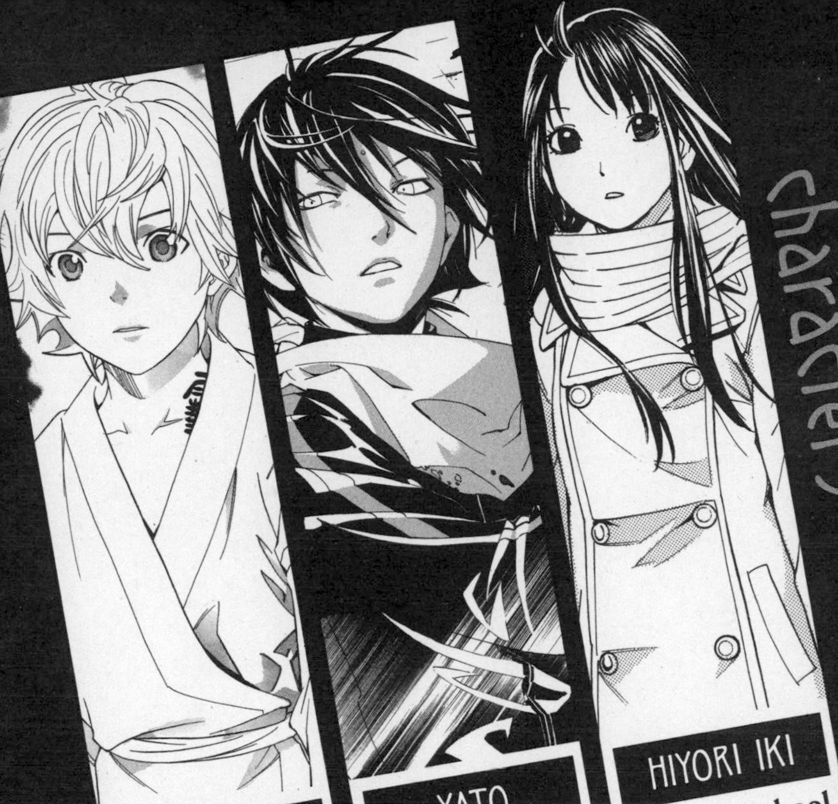

HIYORI IKI

A middle school student and proper young lady who nevertheless loves wrestling. She was in an accident trying to save Yato, and developed a condition that causes her spirit to leave her body.

YATO

A minor-league deity without a single shrine devoted to his worship. He goes around solving people's problems, dreaming of one day having many followers who revere and respect him.

YUKINÉ

A young boy who was wandering around as a ghost when Yato found him and made him a shinki. When Yato calls for Sekki, he becomes a silver blade.

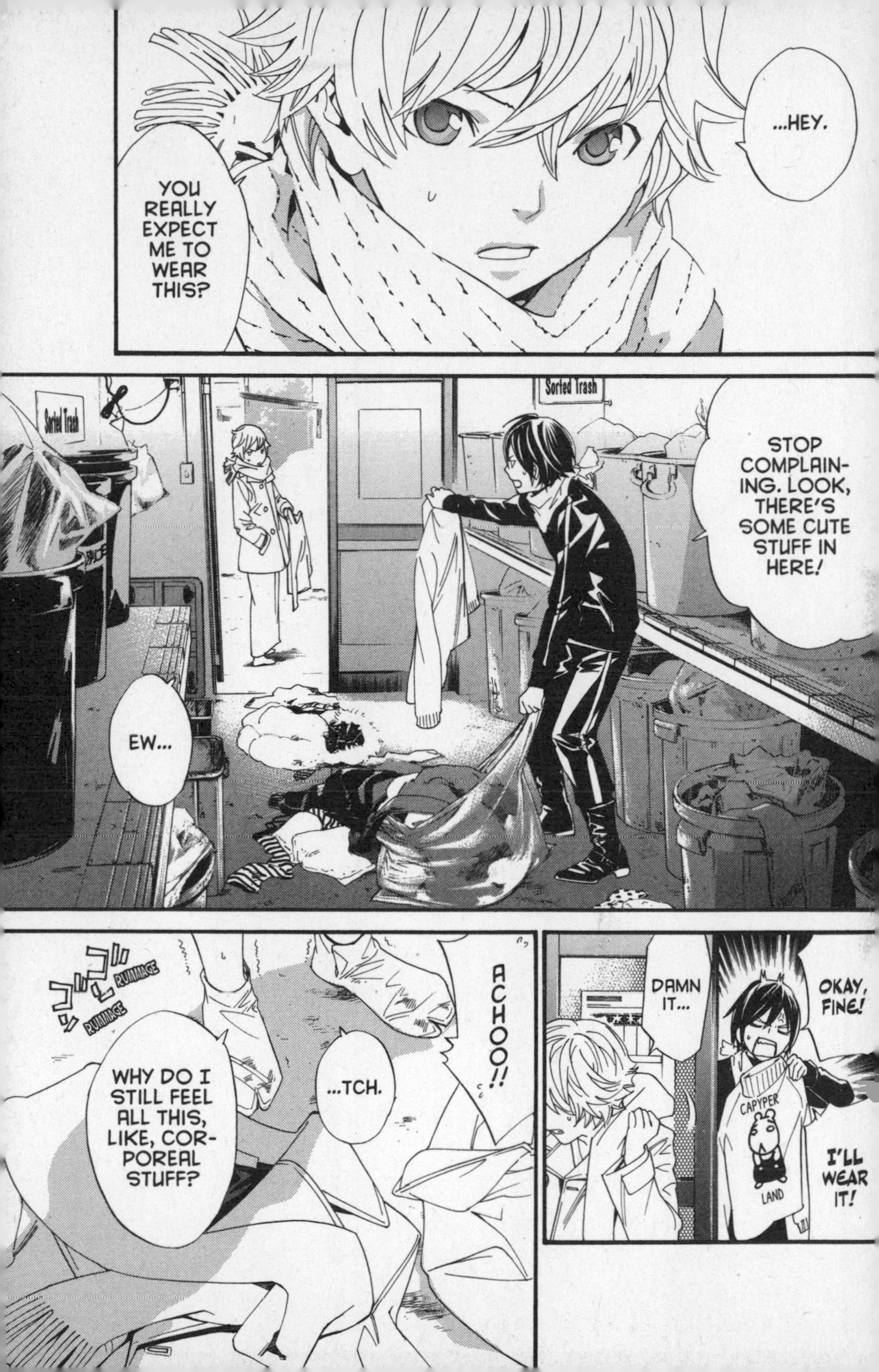
...HEY.
YOU REALLY EXPECT ME TO WEAR THIS?
Sorted Trash
STOP COMPLAINING. LOOK, THERE'S SOME CUTE STUFF IN HERE!
Sorted Trash
EW...
OKAY, FINE!
I'LL WEAR IT!
CAPYPER
LAND
DAMN IT...
ACHOO!!
...TCH.
RUMMAGE
RUMMAGE
WHY DO I STILL FEEL ALL THIS, LIKE, CORPOREAL STUFF?

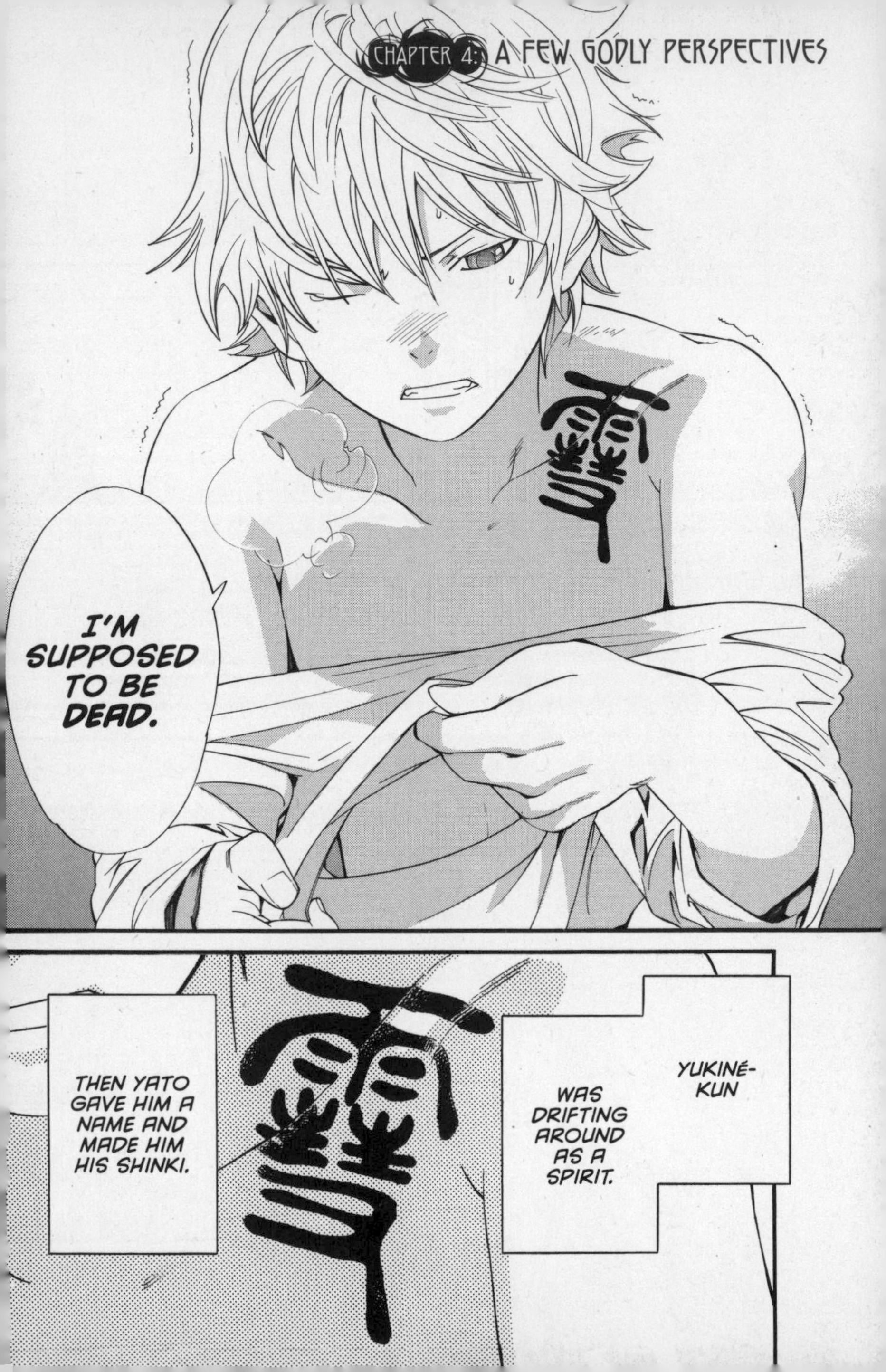
CHAPTER 4: A FEW GODLY PERSPECTIVES
I'M SUPPOSED TO BE DEAD.
YUKINÉ-KUN WAS DRIFTING AROUND AS A SPIRIT.
THEN YATO GAVE HIM A NAME AND MADE HIM HIS SHINKI.

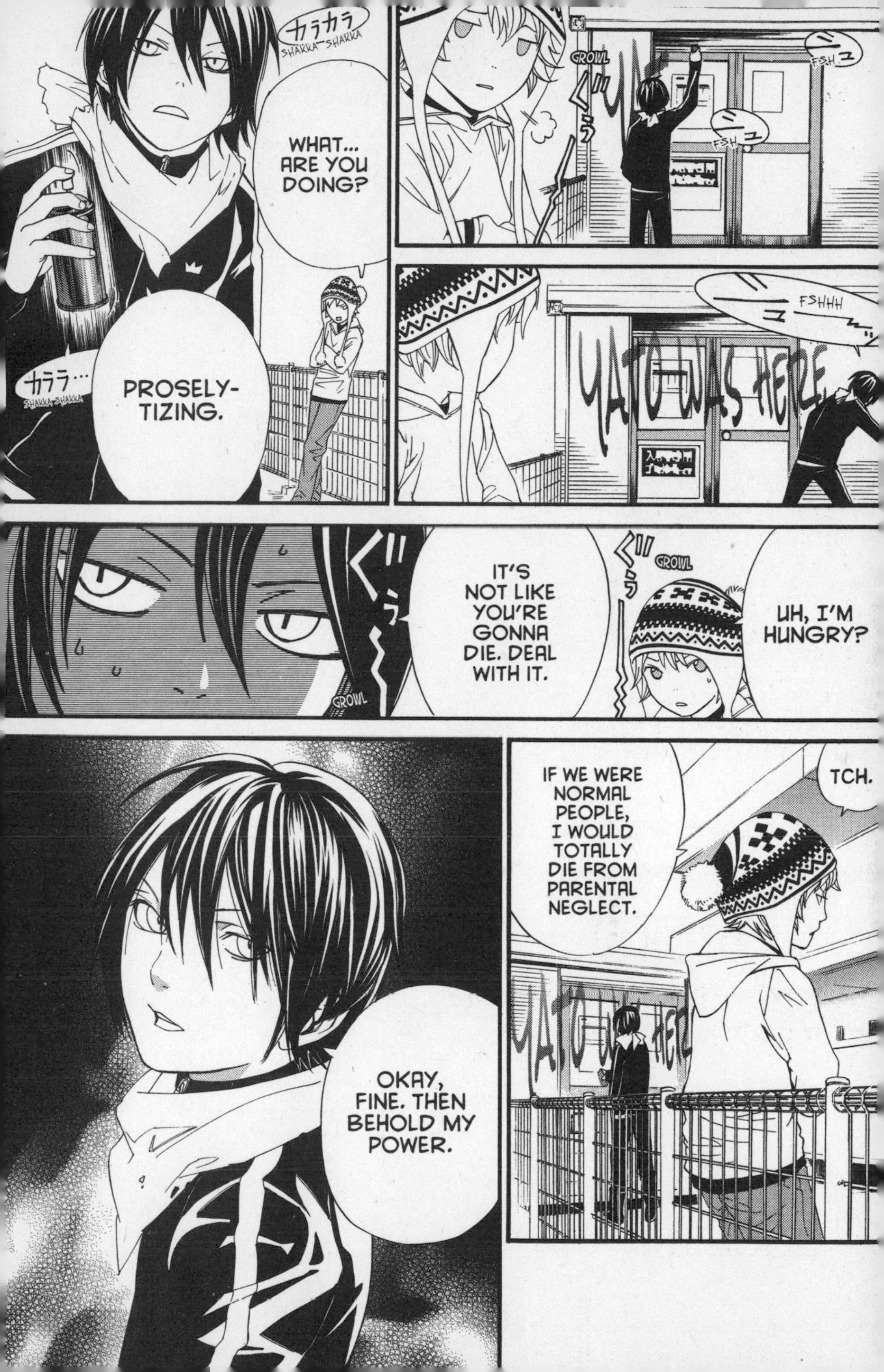

FSH
FSH
GROWL
FSHHH
YATO WAS HERE
カラカラ
SHAKKA SHAKKA
WHAT... ARE YOU DOING?
PROSELY-TIZING.
カララ…
SHAKKA SHAKKA
UH, I'M HUNGRY?
GROWL
IT'S NOT LIKE YOU'RE GONNA DIE. DEAL WITH IT.
GROWL
TCH.
IF WE WERE NORMAL PEOPLE, I WOULD TOTALLY DIE FROM PARENTAL NEGLECT.
OKAY, FINE. THEN BEHOLD MY POWER.

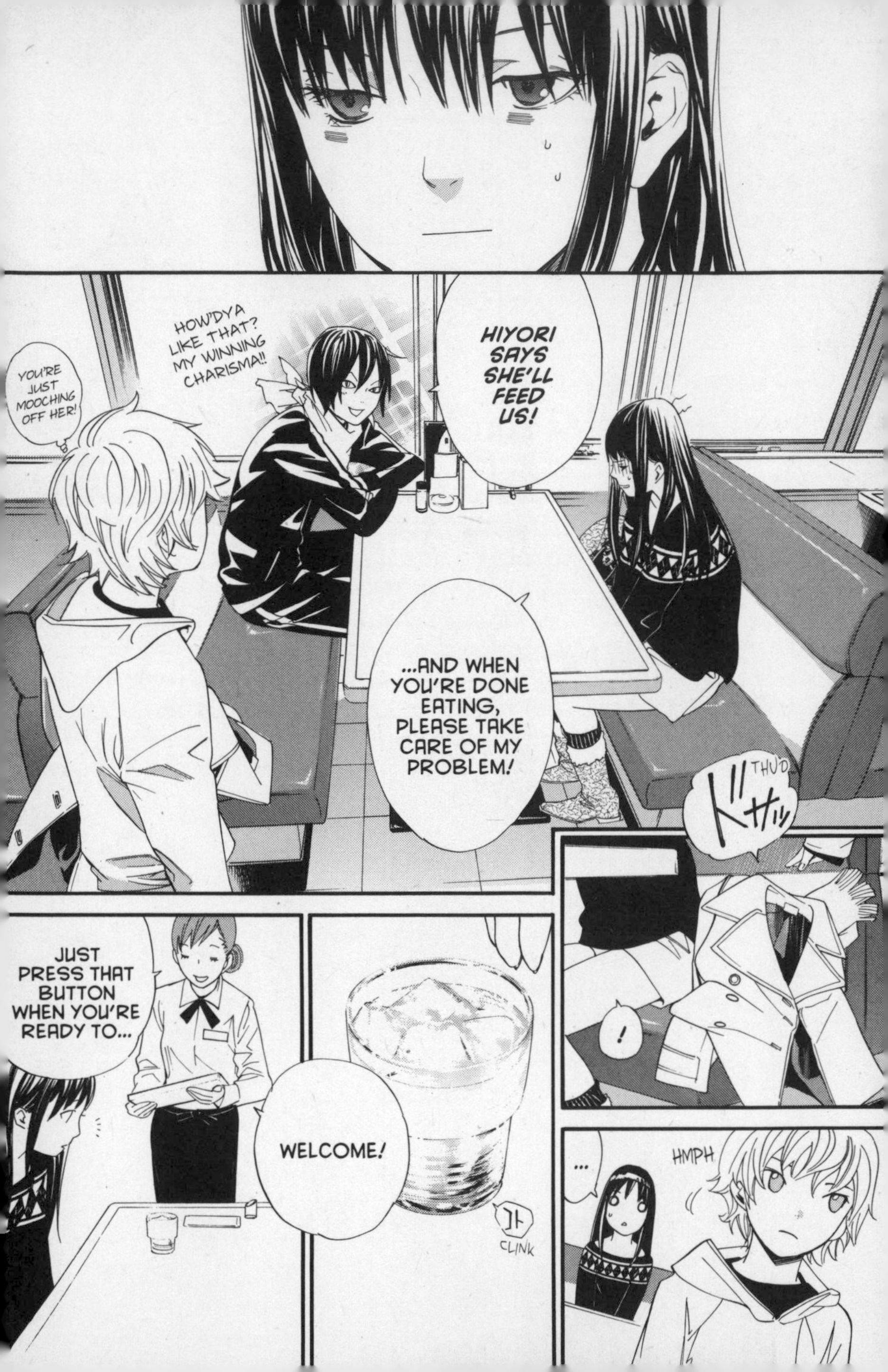
HIYORI SAYS SHE'LL FEED US!
HOW'DYA LIKE THAT? MY WINNING CHARISMA!!
YOU'RE JUST MOOCHING OFF HER!
...AND WHEN YOU'RE DONE EATING, PLEASE TAKE CARE OF MY PROBLEM!
ドサッ THUD
!
HMPH
...
WELCOME!
コト CLINK
JUST PRESS THAT BUTTON WHEN YOU'RE READY TO...

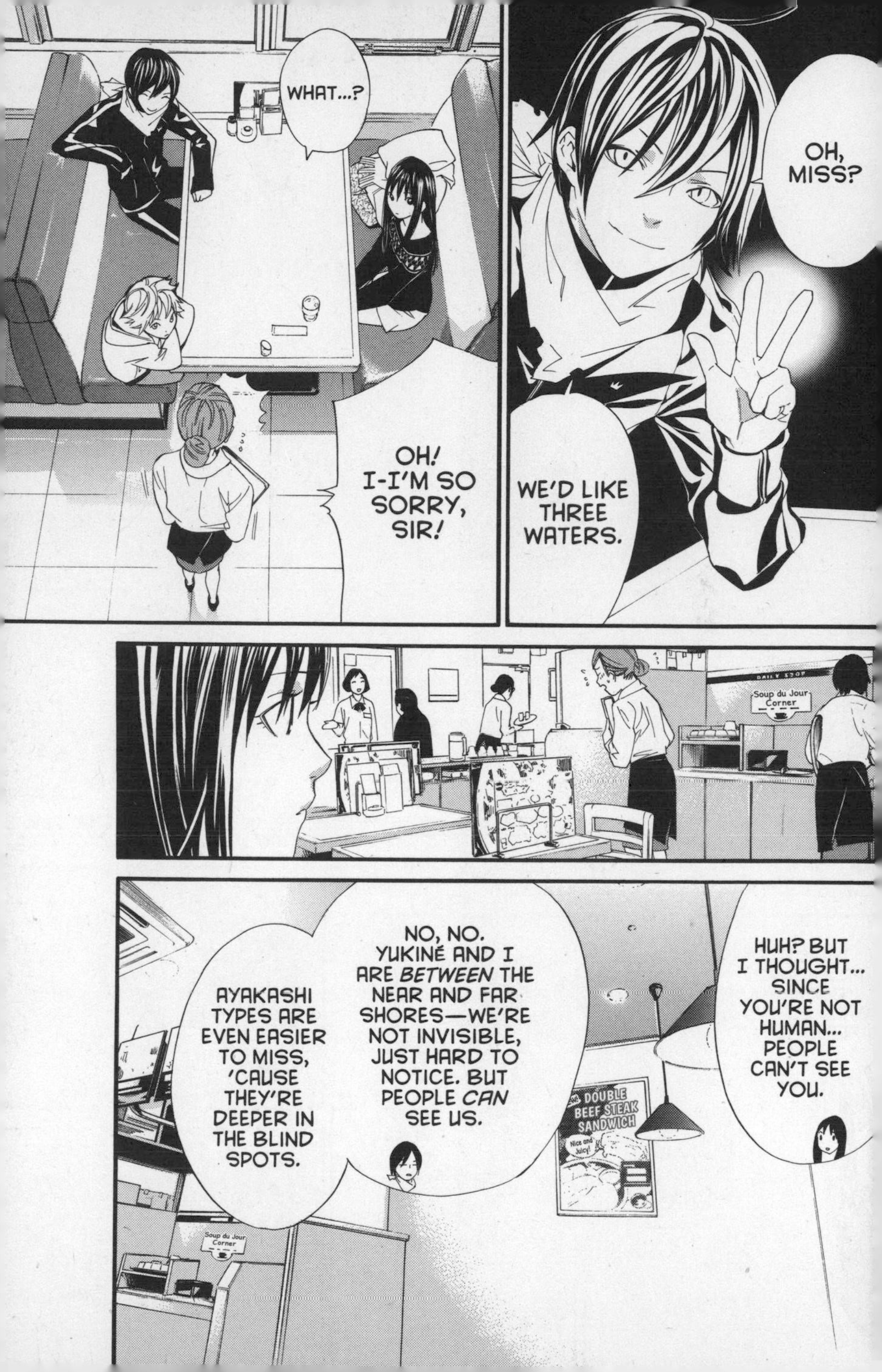
OH, MISS?
WE'D LIKE THREE WATERS.
WHAT...?
OH! I-I'M SO SORRY, SIR!
Soup du Jour Corner
HUH? BUT I THOUGHT... SINCE YOU'RE NOT HUMAN... PEOPLE CAN'T SEE YOU.
NO, NO. YUKINÉ AND I ARE *BETWEEN* THE NEAR AND FAR SHORES—WE'RE NOT INVISIBLE, JUST HARD TO NOTICE. BUT PEOPLE *CAN* SEE US.
AYAKASHI TYPES ARE EVEN EASIER TO MISS, 'CAUSE THEY'RE DEEPER IN THE BLIND SPOTS.
DOUBLE BEEF STEAK SANDWICH
Nice and Juicy!
Soup du Jour Corner

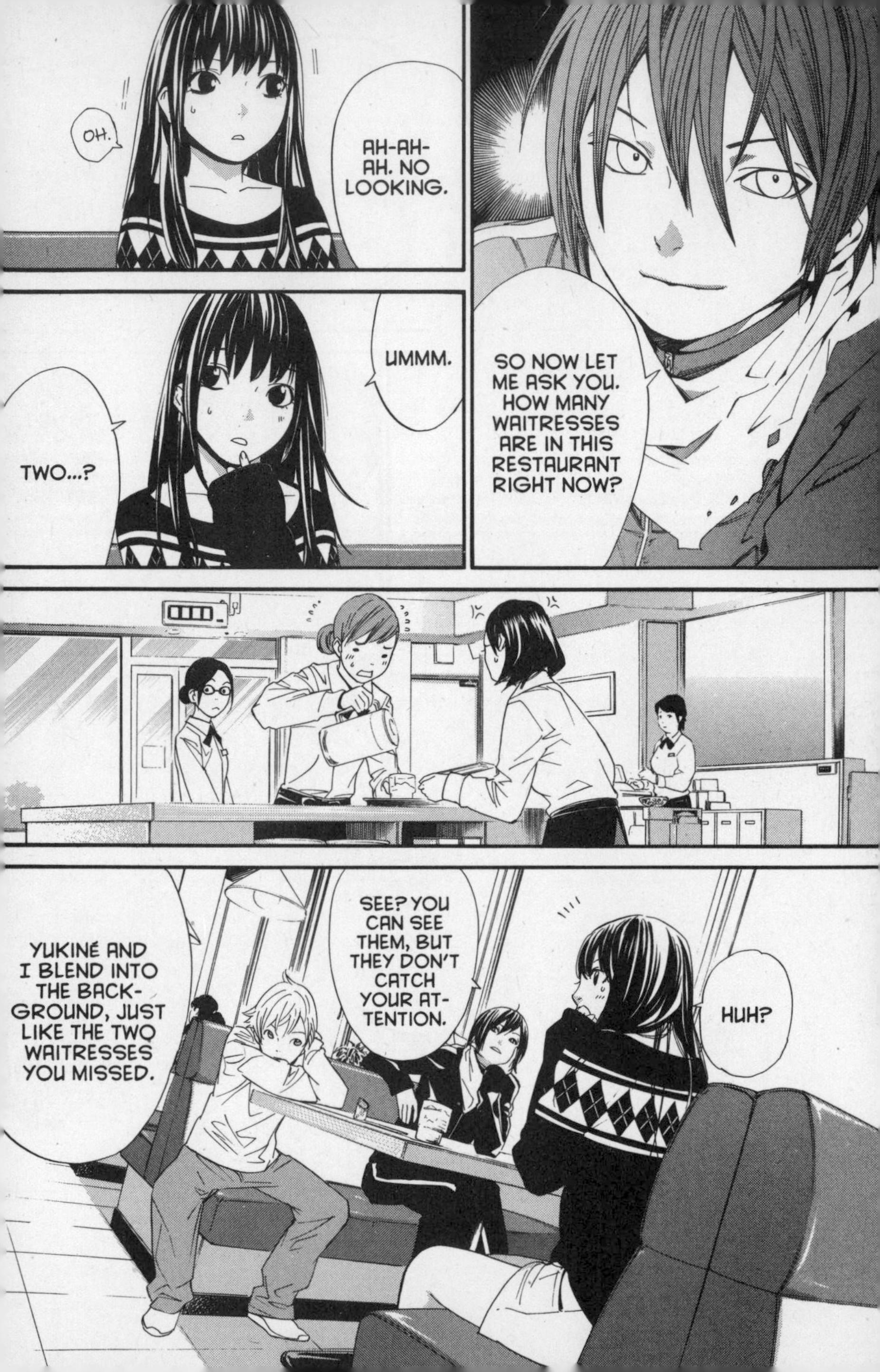
SO NOW LET ME ASK YOU. HOW MANY WAITRESSES ARE IN THIS RESTAURANT RIGHT NOW?
AH-AH-AH. NO LOOKING.
OH.
UMMM.
TWO...?
HUH?
SEE? YOU CAN SEE THEM, BUT THEY DON'T CATCH YOUR AT-TENTION.
YUKINÉ AND I BLEND INTO THE BACK-GROUND, JUST LIKE THE TWO WAITRESSES YOU MISSED.

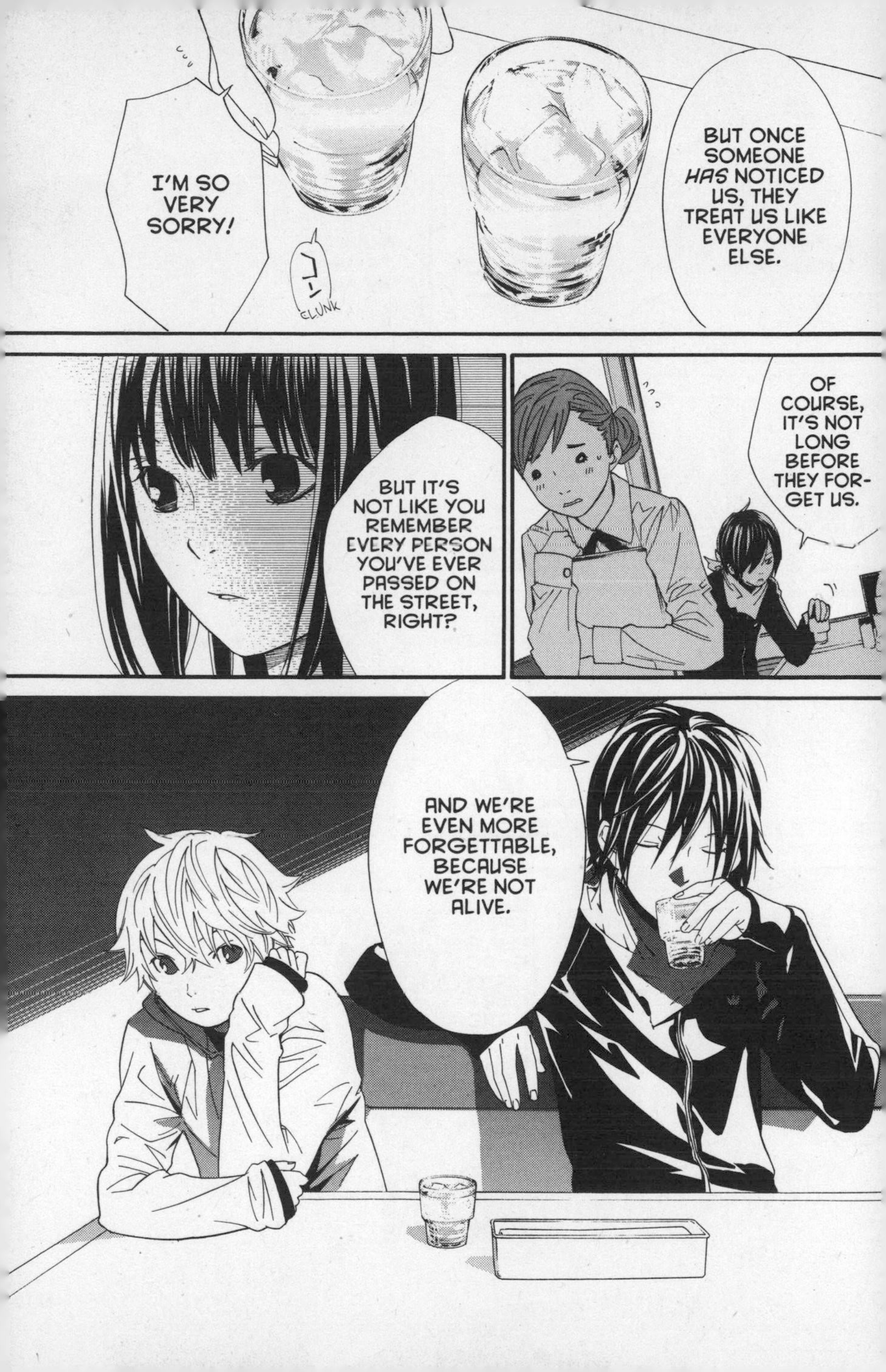
BUT ONCE SOMEONE *HAS* NOTICED US, THEY TREAT US LIKE EVERYONE ELSE.
I'M SO VERY SORRY!
CLUNK
OF COURSE, IT'S NOT LONG BEFORE THEY FOR-GET US.
BUT IT'S NOT LIKE YOU REMEMBER EVERY PERSON YOU'VE EVER PASSED ON THE STREET, RIGHT?
AND WE'RE EVEN MORE FORGETTABLE, BECAUSE WE'RE NOT ALIVE.

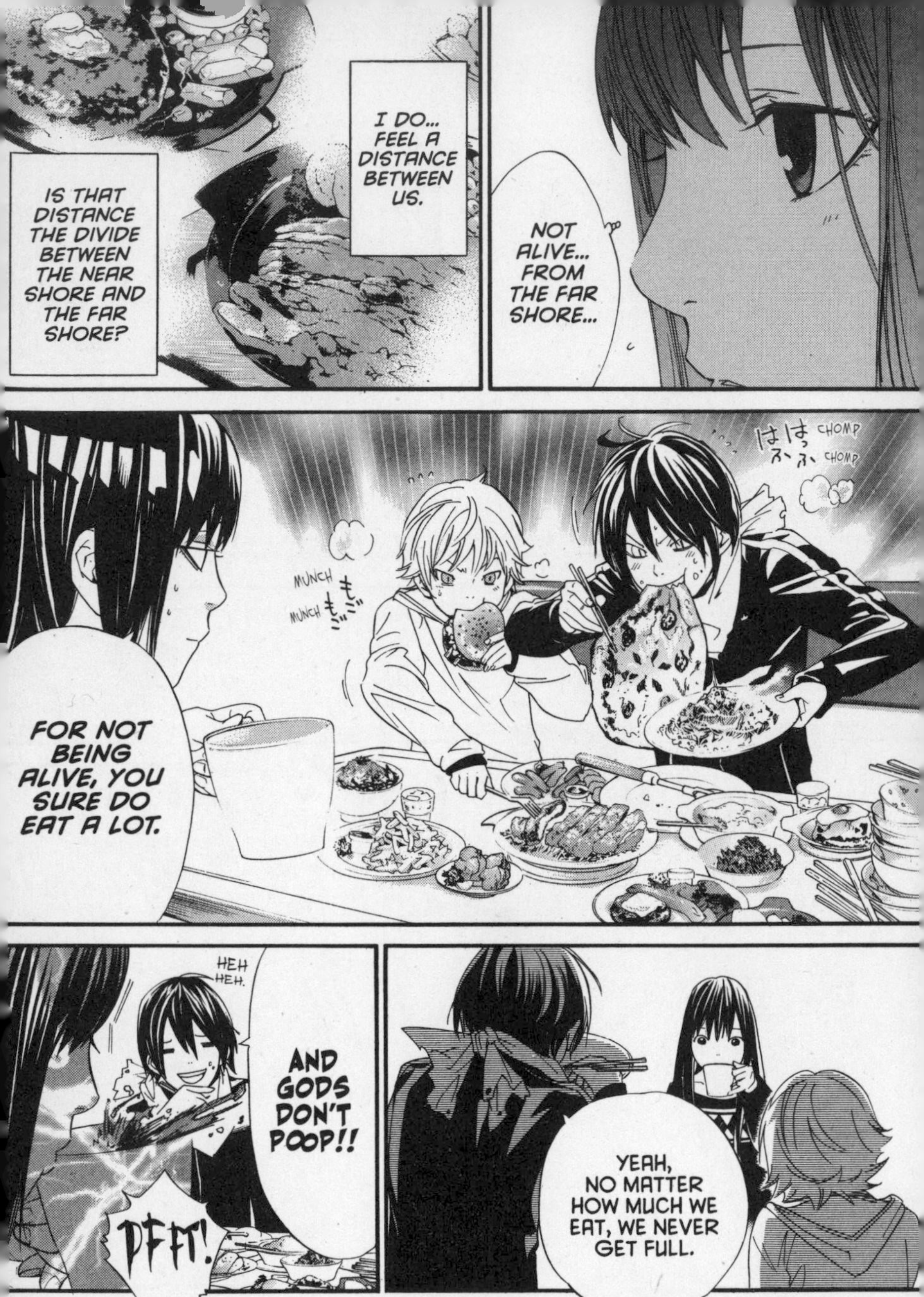
NOT ALIVE... FROM THE FAR SHORE...
I DO... FEEL A DISTANCE BETWEEN US.
IS THAT DISTANCE THE DIVIDE BETWEEN THE NEAR SHORE AND THE FAR SHORE?
はふはふ
CHOMP CHOMP
もぐもぐ
MUNCH MUNCH
FOR NOT BEING ALIVE, YOU SURE DO EAT A LOT.
YEAH, NO MATTER HOW MUCH WE EAT, WE NEVER GET FULL.
HEH HEH.
AND GODS DON'T POOP!!
PFFT!

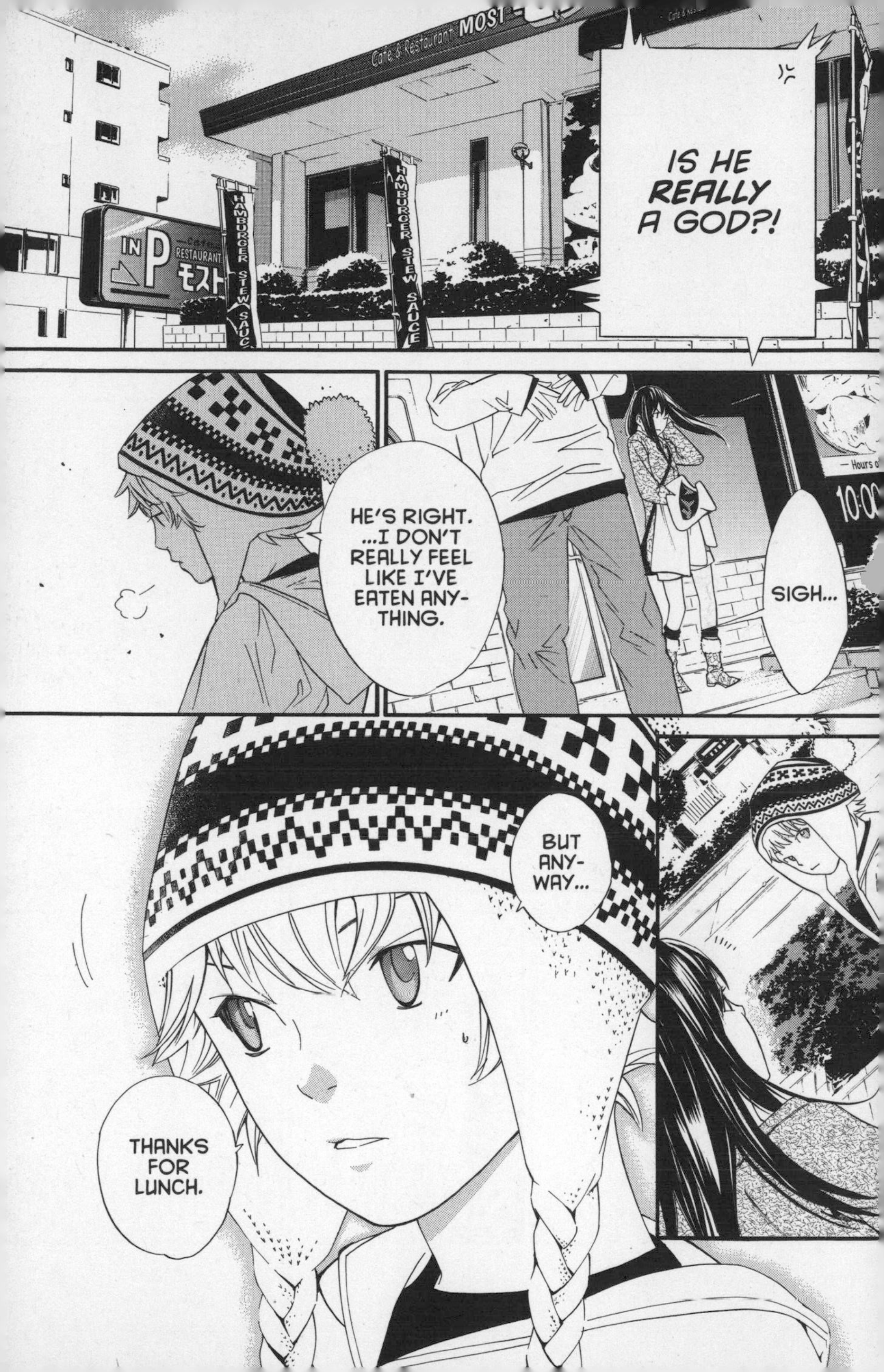
Cafe & Restaurant MOST
IN P
RESTAURANT モスト
HAMBURGER STEW SAUCE
HAMBURGER STEW SAUCE
IS HE REALLY A GOD?!
SIGH...
HE'S RIGHT. ...I DON'T REALLY FEEL LIKE I'VE EATEN ANY-THING.
BUT ANY-WAY...
THANKS FOR LUNCH.

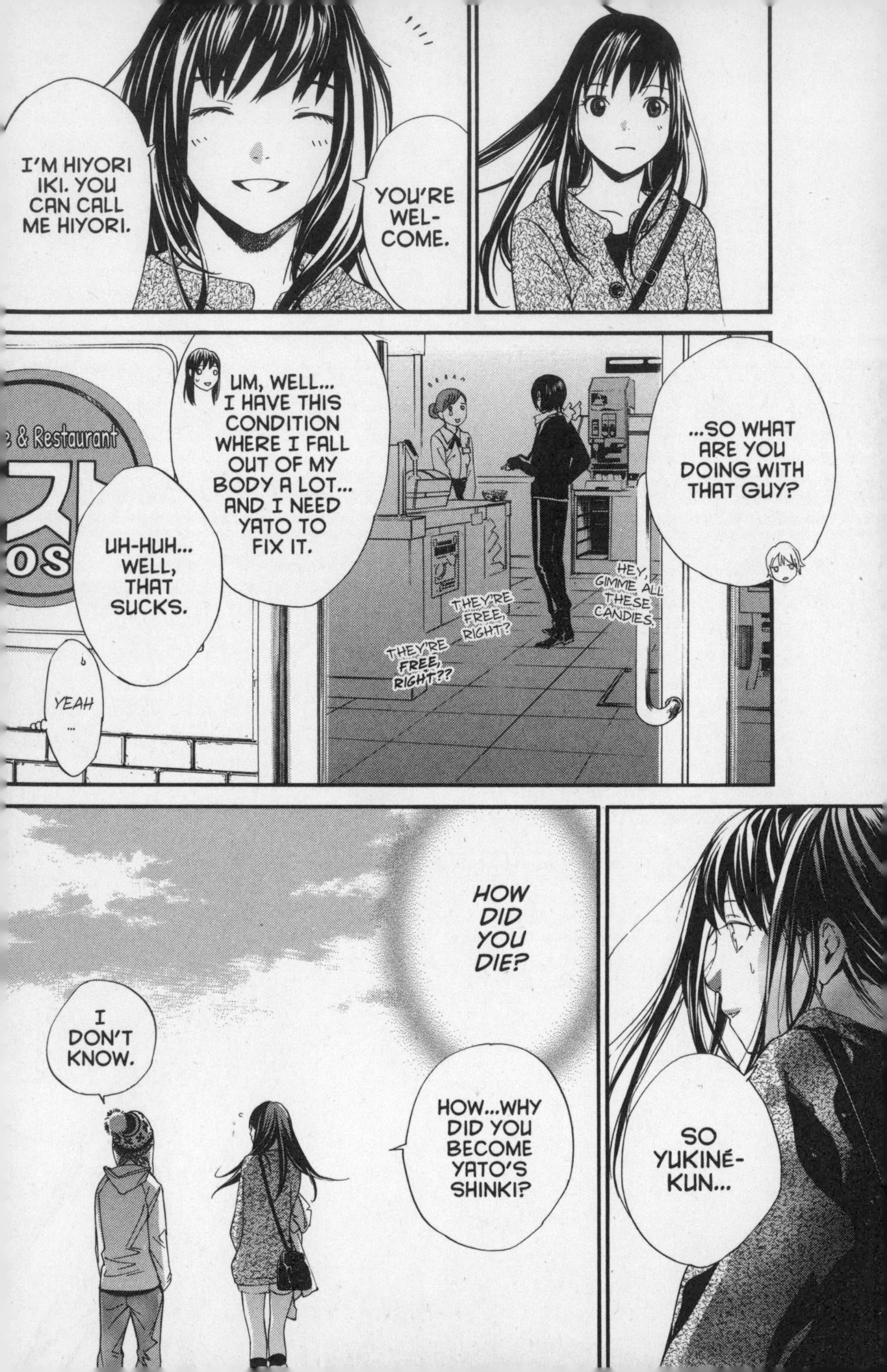
YOU'RE WEL-COME.
I'M HIYORI IKI. YOU CAN CALL ME HIYORI.
...SO WHAT ARE YOU DOING WITH THAT GUY?
HEY, GIMME ALL THESE CANDIES.
THEY'RE FREE, RIGHT?
THEY'RE FREE, RIGHT??
UM, WELL... I HAVE THIS CONDITION WHERE I FALL OUT OF MY BODY A LOT... AND I NEED YATO TO FIX IT.
& Restaurant
UH-HUH... WELL, THAT SUCKS.
YEAH...
SO YUKINÉ-KUN...
HOW DID YOU DIE?
HOW...WHY DID YOU BECOME YATO'S SHINKI?
I DON'T KNOW.

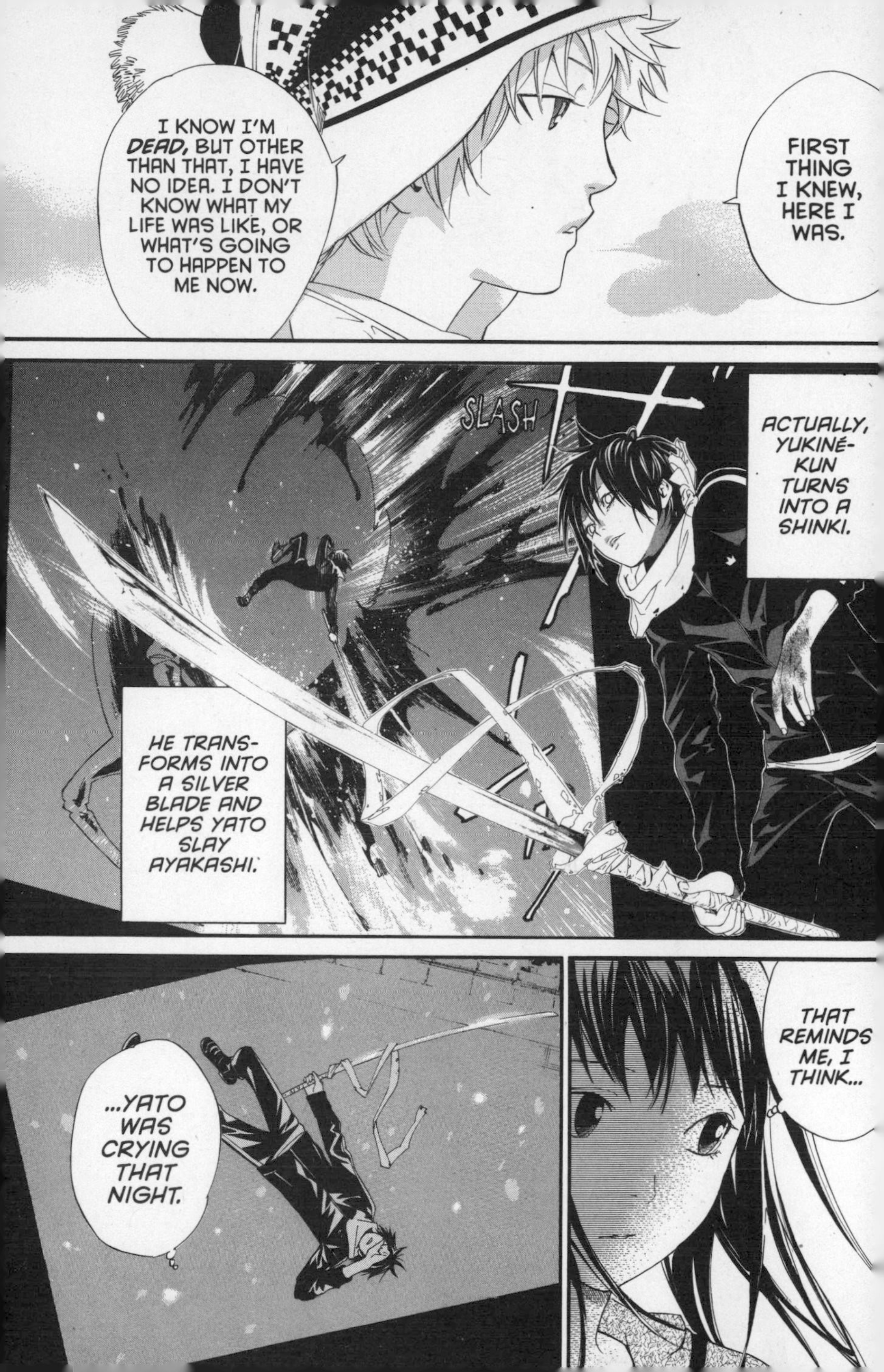
FIRST THING I KNEW, HERE I WAS.
I KNOW I'M DEAD, BUT OTHER THAN THAT, I HAVE NO IDEA. I DON'T KNOW WHAT MY LIFE WAS LIKE, OR WHAT'S GOING TO HAPPEN TO ME NOW.
ACTUALLY, YUKINÉ-KUN TURNS INTO A SHINKI.
SLASH
HE TRANSFORMS INTO A SILVER BLADE AND HELPS YATO SLAY AYAKASHI.
THAT REMINDS ME, I THINK...
...YATO WAS CRYING THAT NIGHT.

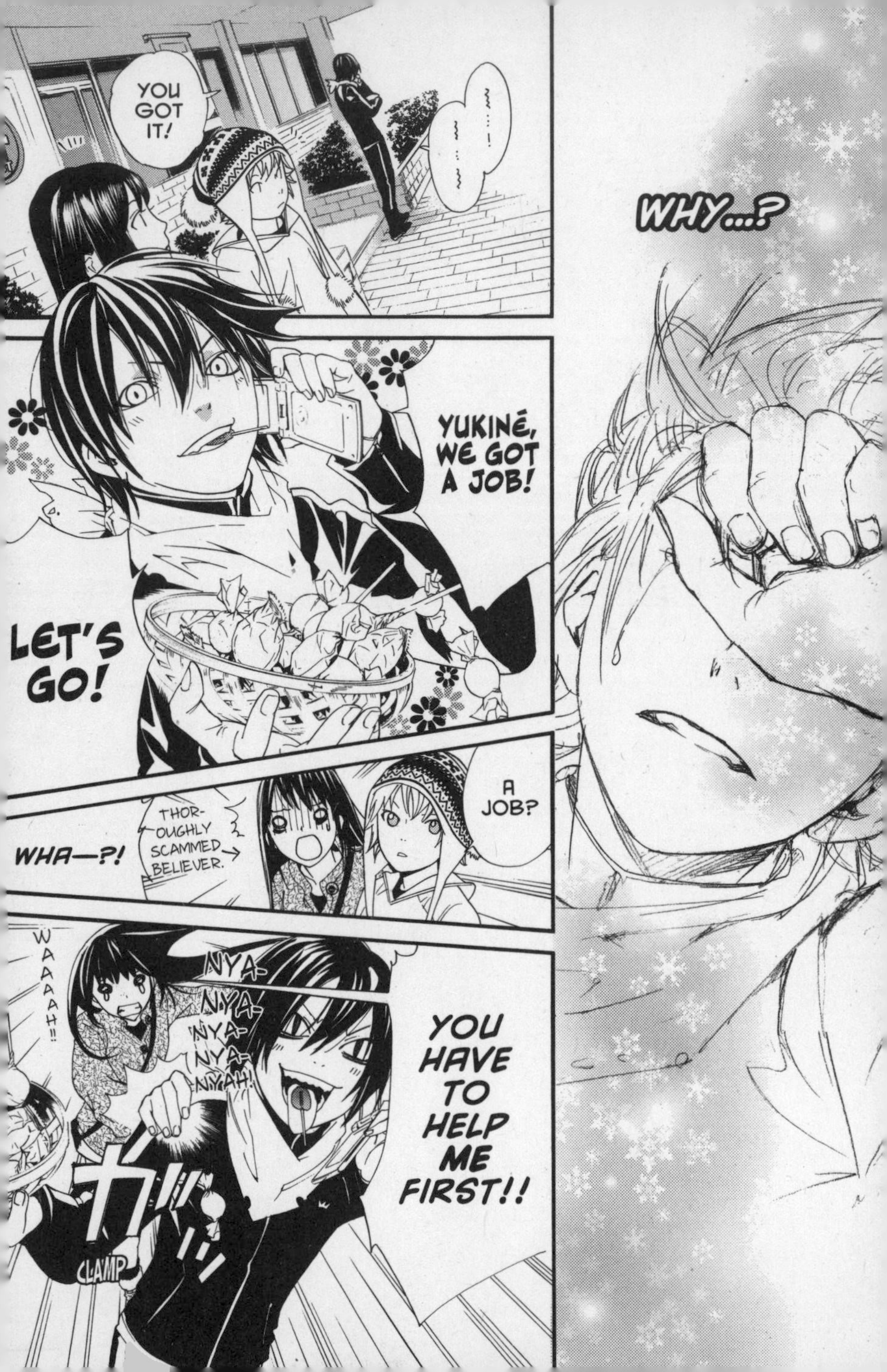
WHY...?
YOU GOT IT!
~...!
~...~
YUKINÉ, WE GOT A JOB!
LET'S GO!
A JOB?
THOROUGHLY SCAMMED BELIEVER.
WHA—?!
YOU HAVE TO HELP ME FIRST!!
NYA-NYA-NYA-NYA-NYAH!
WAAAAAH!!
CLAMP

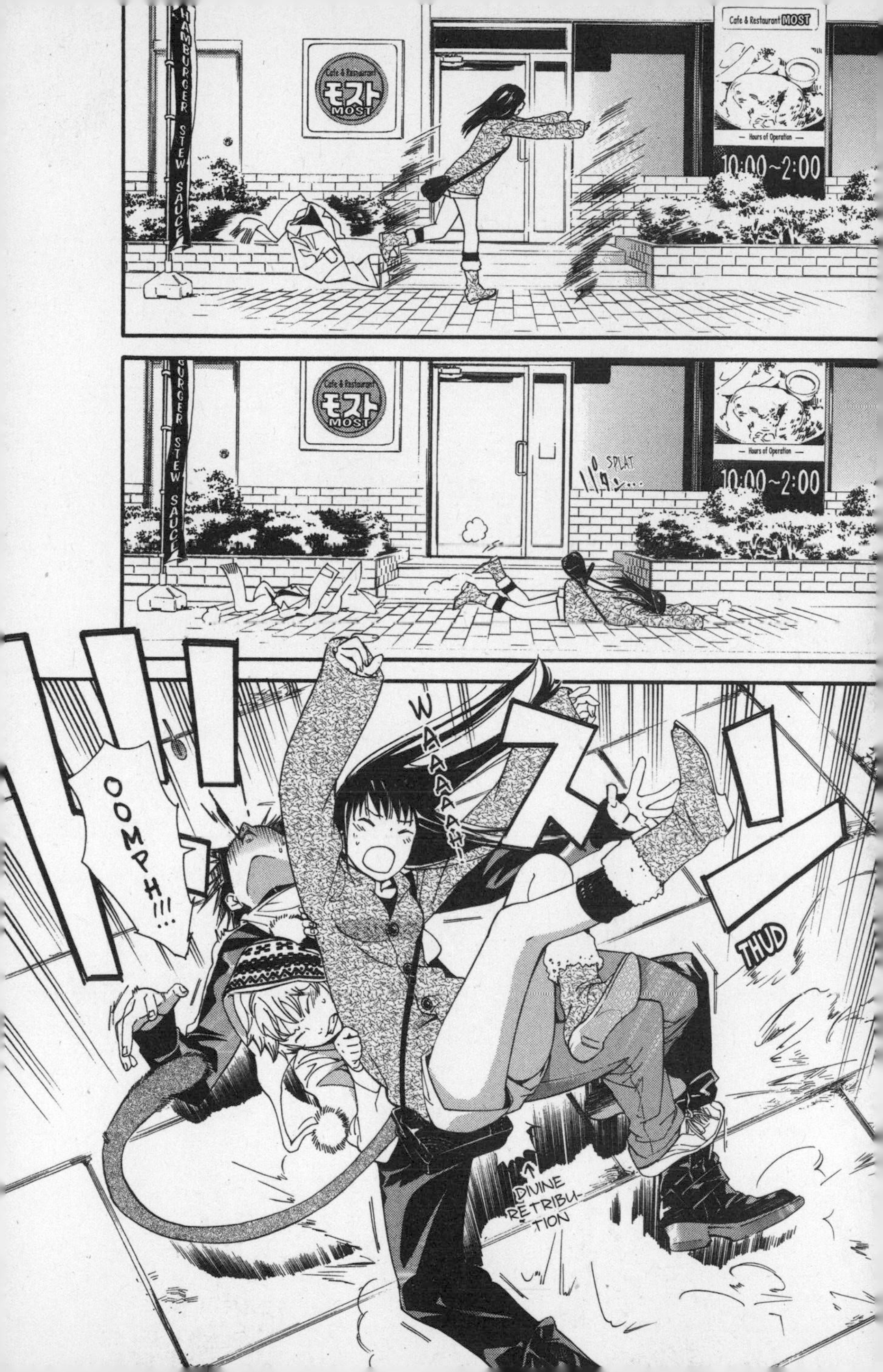
HAMBURGER STEW SAUCE
Cafe & Restaurant モスト MOST
Cafe & Restaurant MOST
Hours of Operation
10:00~2:00
SPLAT
OOMPH!!!
WAAAAAH!
THUD
↑ DIVINE RETRIBUTION

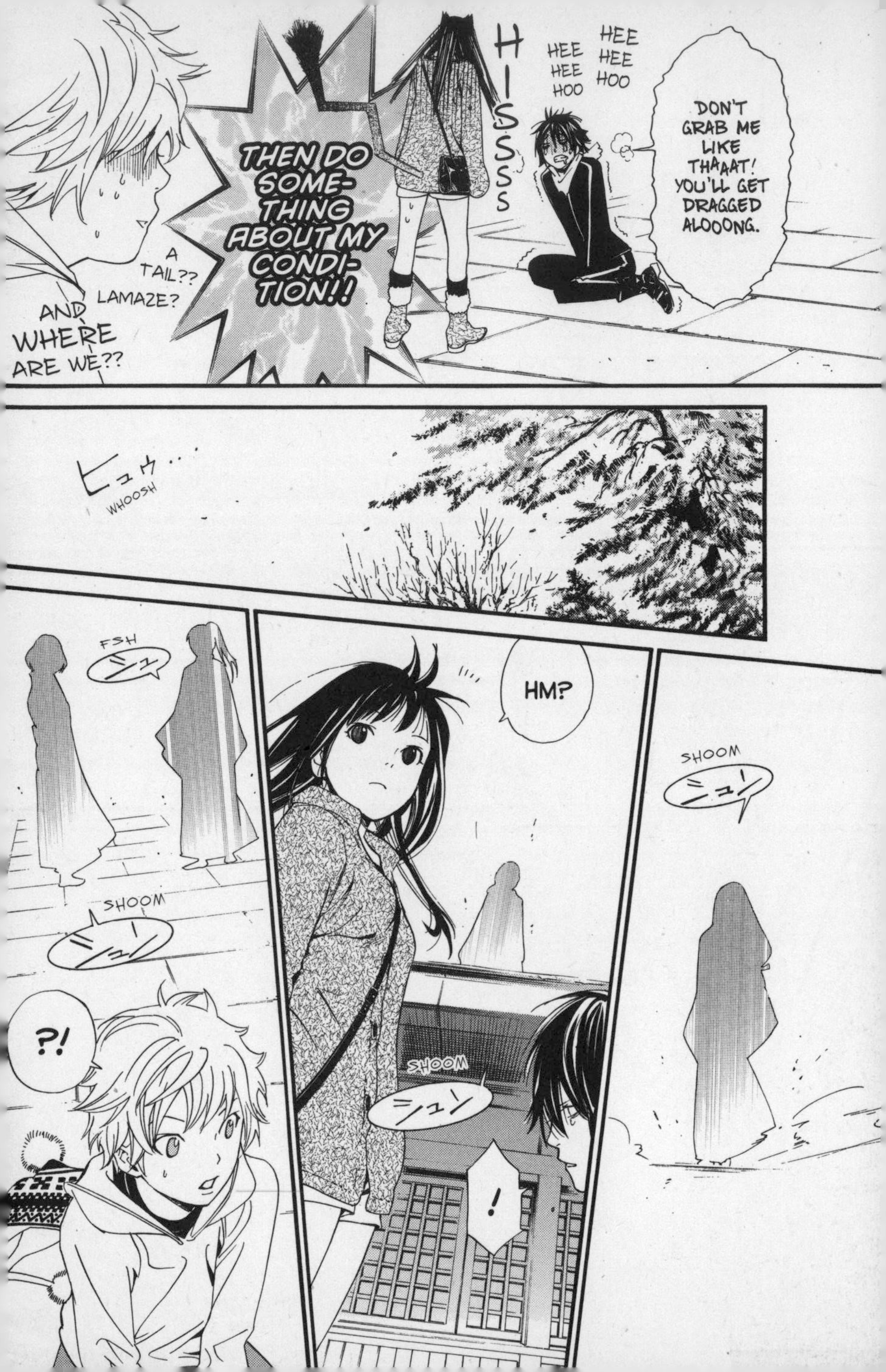

DON'T GRAB ME LIKE THAAAT! YOU'LL GET DRAGGED ALOOONG.
HEE HEE HOO
HEE HEE HOO
HISSS
THEN DO SOME-THING ABOUT MY CONDI-TION!!
A TAIL??
LAMAZE?
AND WHERE ARE WE??
ヒュゥ…
WHOOSH
シュン
SHOOM
HM?
シュン
SHOOM
!
シュ
FSH
シュン
SHOOM
?!

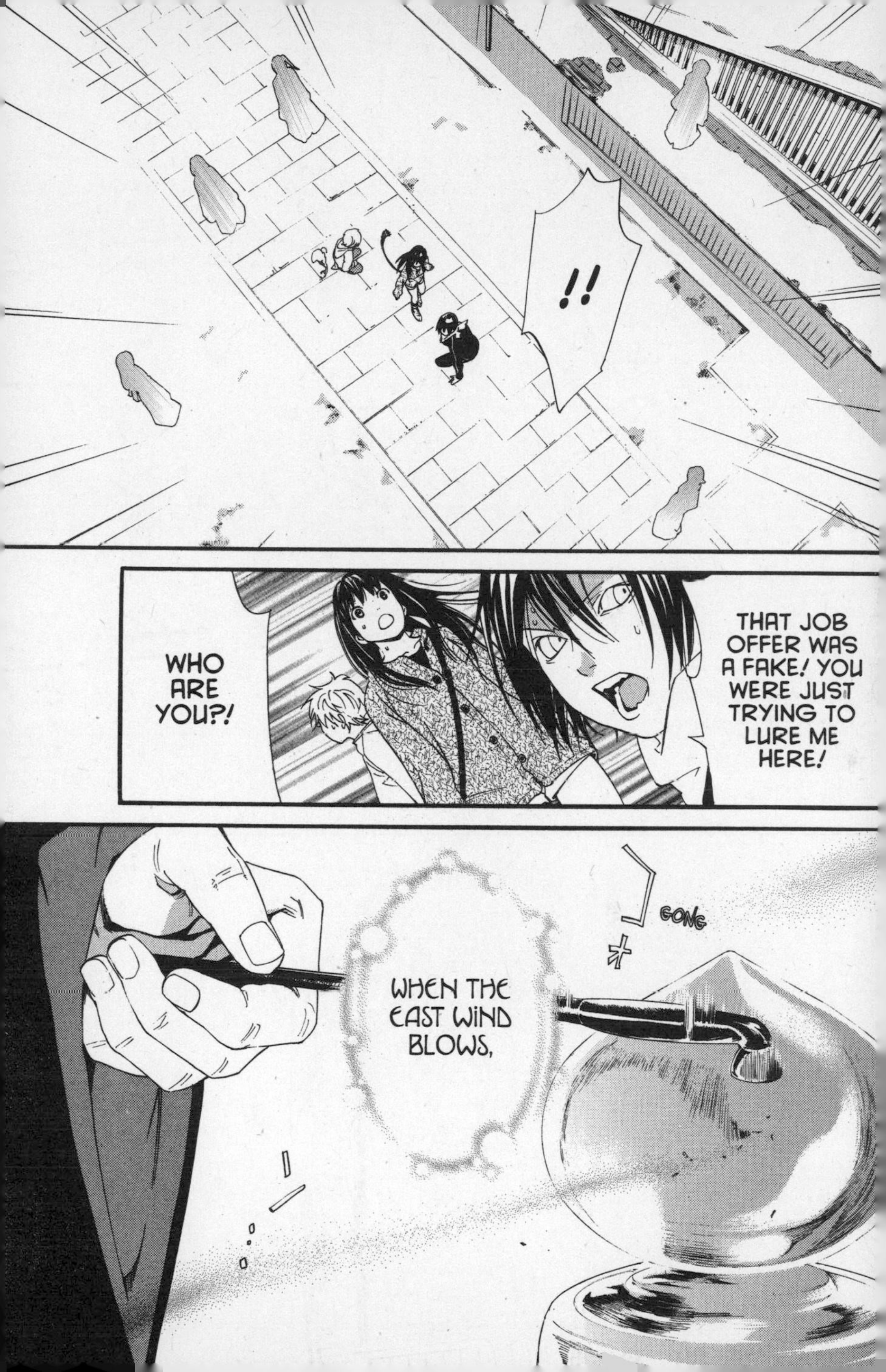
!!
THAT JOB OFFER WAS A FAKE! YOU WERE JUST TRYING TO LURE ME HERE!
WHO ARE YOU?!
GONG
WHEN THE EAST WIND BLOWS,

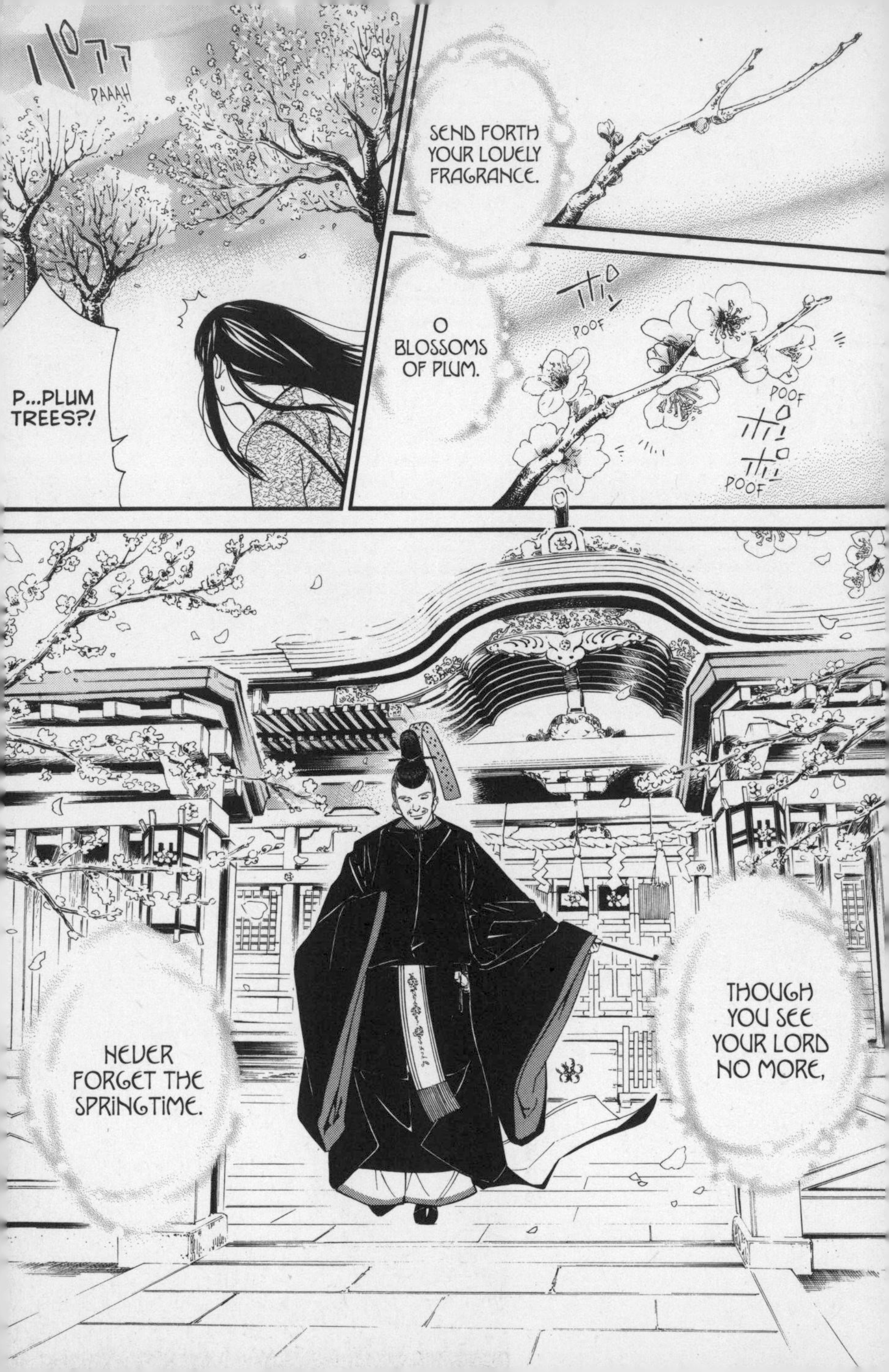
SEND FORTH YOUR LOVELY FRAGRANCE.
POOF
POOF
POOF
O BLOSSOMS OF PLUM.
PAAAH
P...PLUM TREES?!
THOUGH YOU SEE YOUR LORD NO MORE,
NEVER FORGET THE SPRINGTIME.

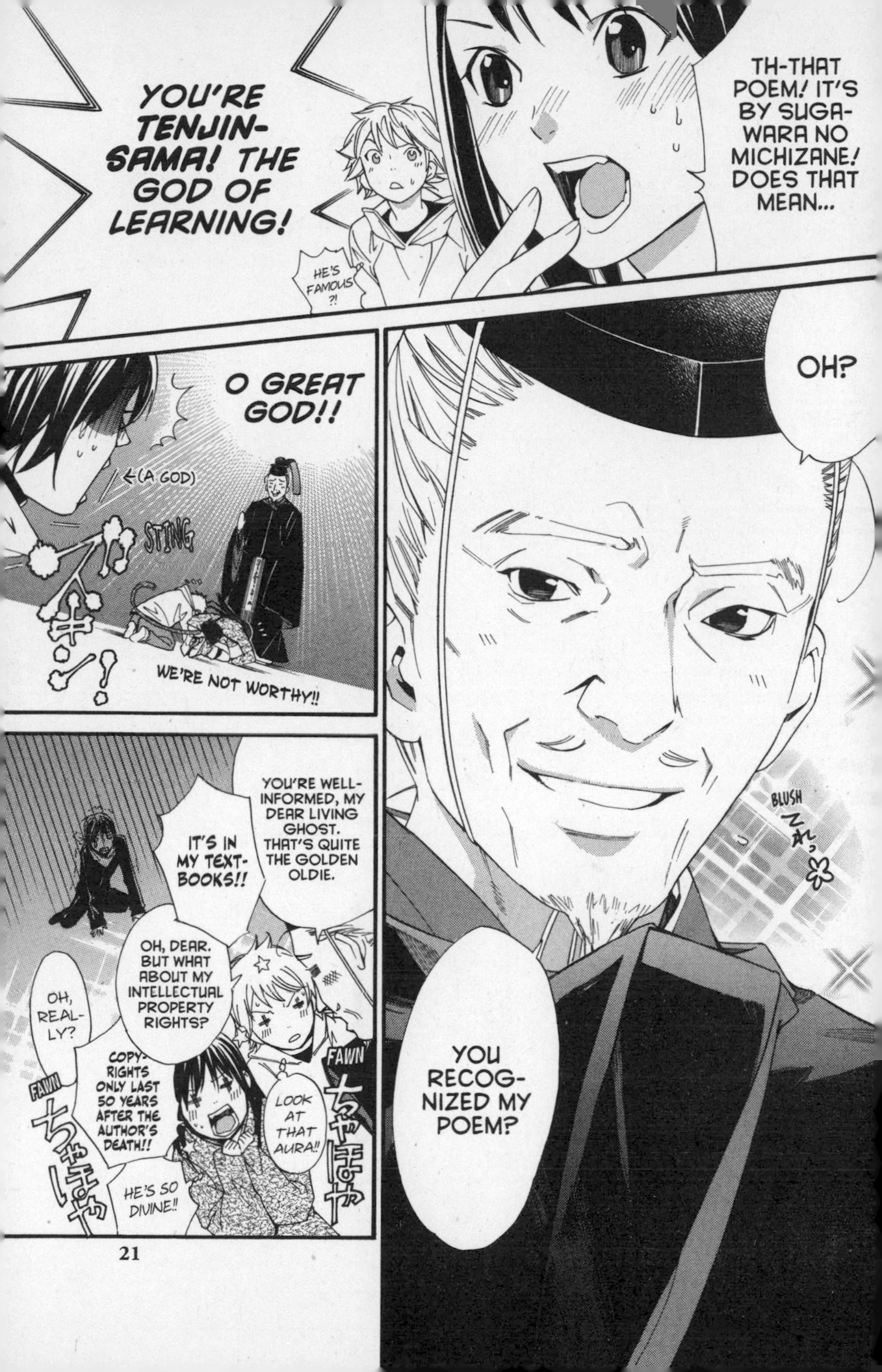
TH-THAT POEM! IT'S BY SUGAWARA NO MICHIZANE! DOES THAT MEAN...
YOU'RE TENJIN-SAMA! THE GOD OF LEARNING!
HE'S FAMOUS?!
OH?
YOU RECOGNIZED MY POEM?
BLUSH
O GREAT GOD!!
←(A GOD)
STING
WE'RE NOT WORTHY!!
YOU'RE WELL-INFORMED, MY DEAR LIVING GHOST. THAT'S QUITE THE GOLDEN OLDIE.
IT'S IN MY TEXTBOOKS!!
OH, DEAR. BUT WHAT ABOUT MY INTELLECTUAL PROPERTY RIGHTS?
OH, REALLY?
FAWN
LOOK AT THAT AURA!!
COPYRIGHTS ONLY LAST 50 YEARS AFTER THE AUTHOR'S DEATH!!
FAWN
HE'S SO DIVINE!!

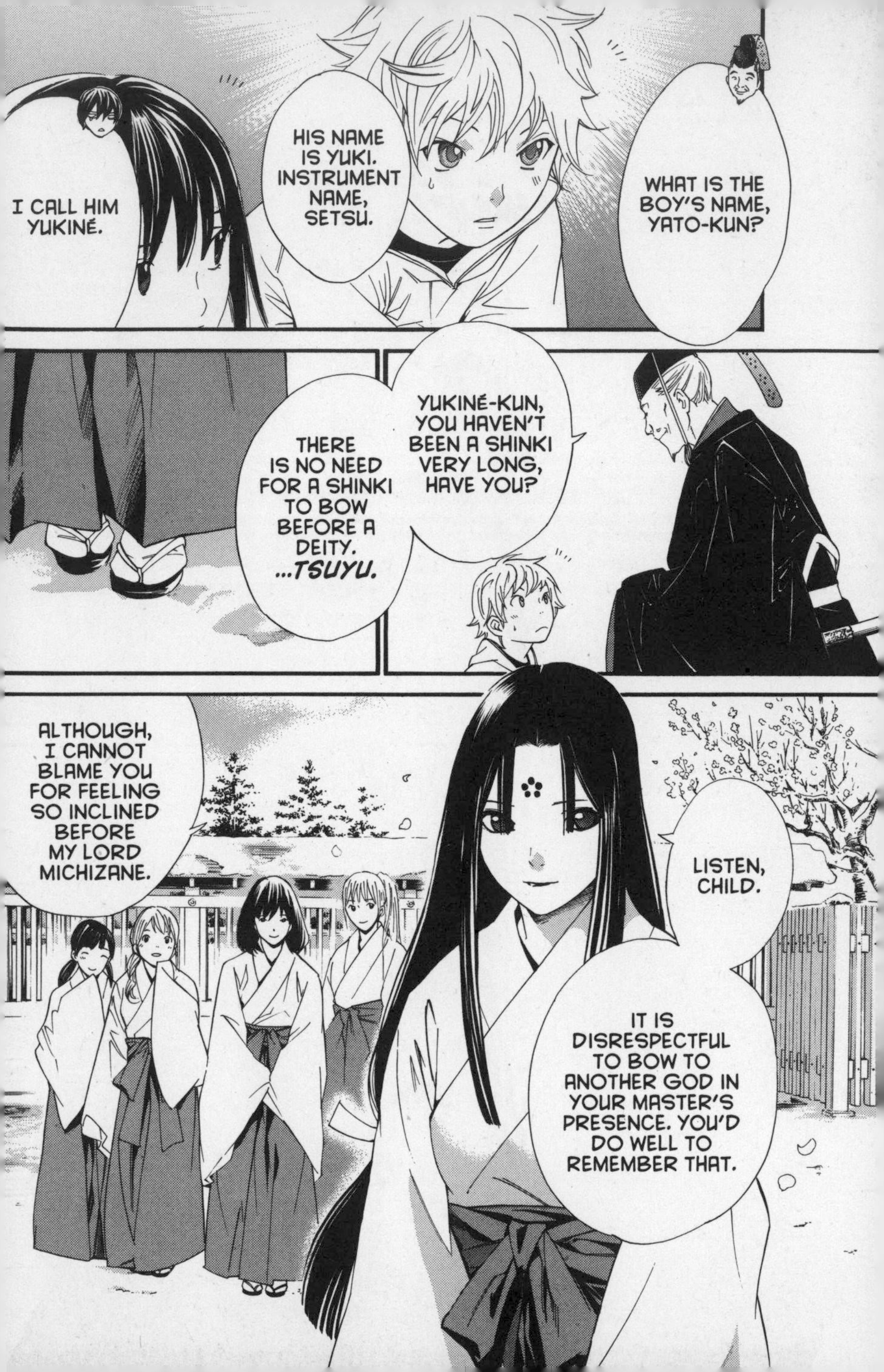
WHAT IS THE BOY'S NAME, YATO-KUN?
HIS NAME IS YUKI. INSTRUMENT NAME, SETSU.
I CALL HIM YUKINÉ.
YUKINÉ-KUN, YOU HAVEN'T BEEN A SHINKI VERY LONG, HAVE YOU?
THERE IS NO NEED FOR A SHINKI TO BOW BEFORE A DEITY. ...TSUYU.
LISTEN, CHILD.
IT IS DISRESPECTFUL TO BOW TO ANOTHER GOD IN YOUR MASTER'S PRESENCE. YOU'D DO WELL TO REMEMBER THAT.
ALTHOUGH, I CANNOT BLAME YOU FOR FEELING SO INCLINED BEFORE MY LORD MICHIZANE.

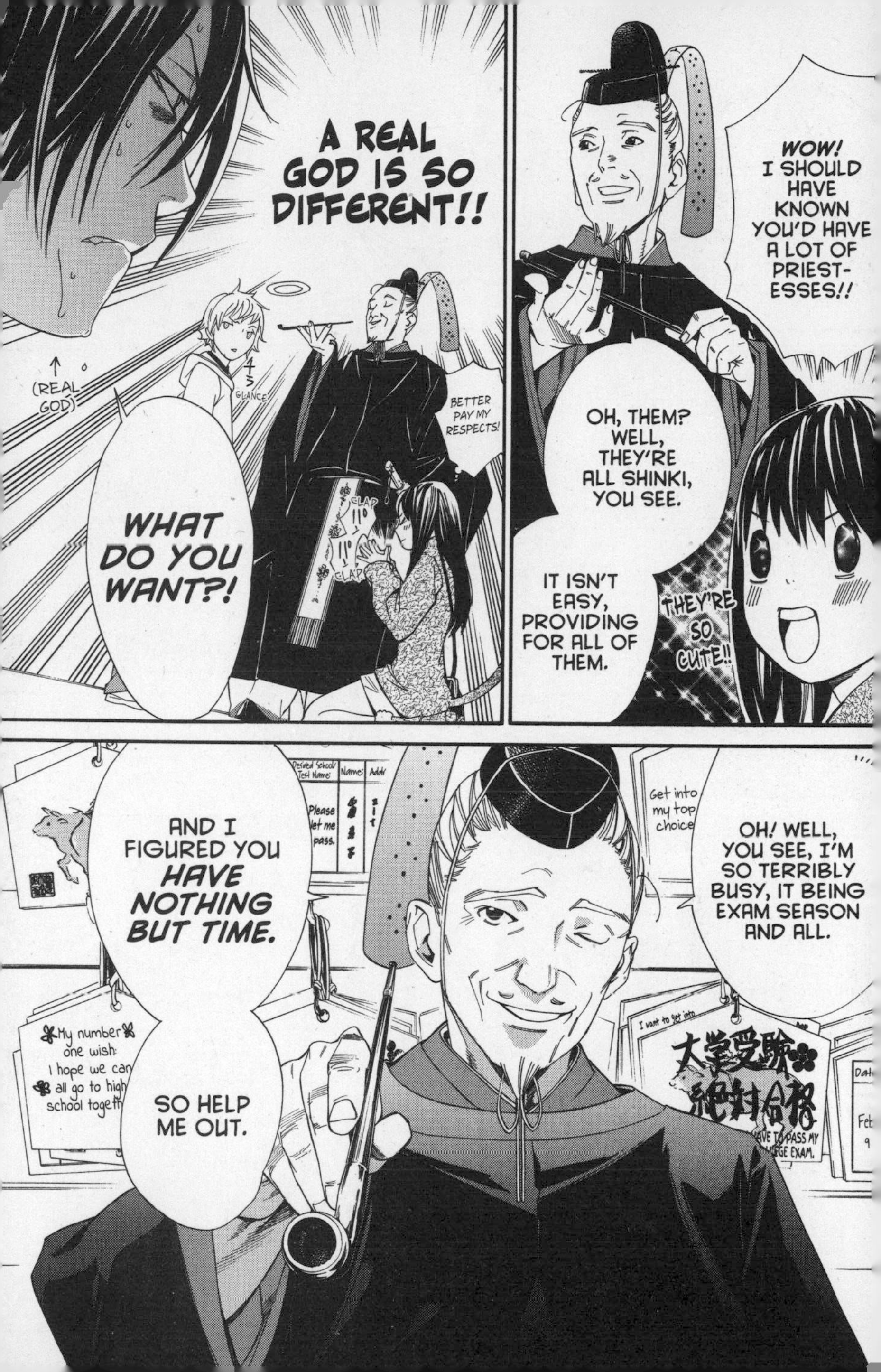
WOW! I SHOULD HAVE KNOWN YOU'D HAVE A LOT OF PRIEST-ESSES!!
OH, THEM? WELL, THEY'RE ALL SHINKI, YOU SEE.
IT ISN'T EASY, PROVIDING FOR ALL OF THEM.
THEY'RE SO CUTE!!
A REAL GOD IS SO DIFFERENT!!
BETTER PAY MY RESPECTS!
GLANCE
CLAP
CLAP
(REAL GOD)
WHAT DO YOU WANT?!
OH! WELL, YOU SEE, I'M SO TERRIBLY BUSY, IT BEING EXAM SEASON AND ALL.
Get into my top choice
I want to get into
大学受験絶対合格
Desired School Test Name:
Name:
Please let me pass.
AND I FIGURED YOU HAVE NOTHING BUT TIME.
SO HELP ME OUT.
My number one wish:

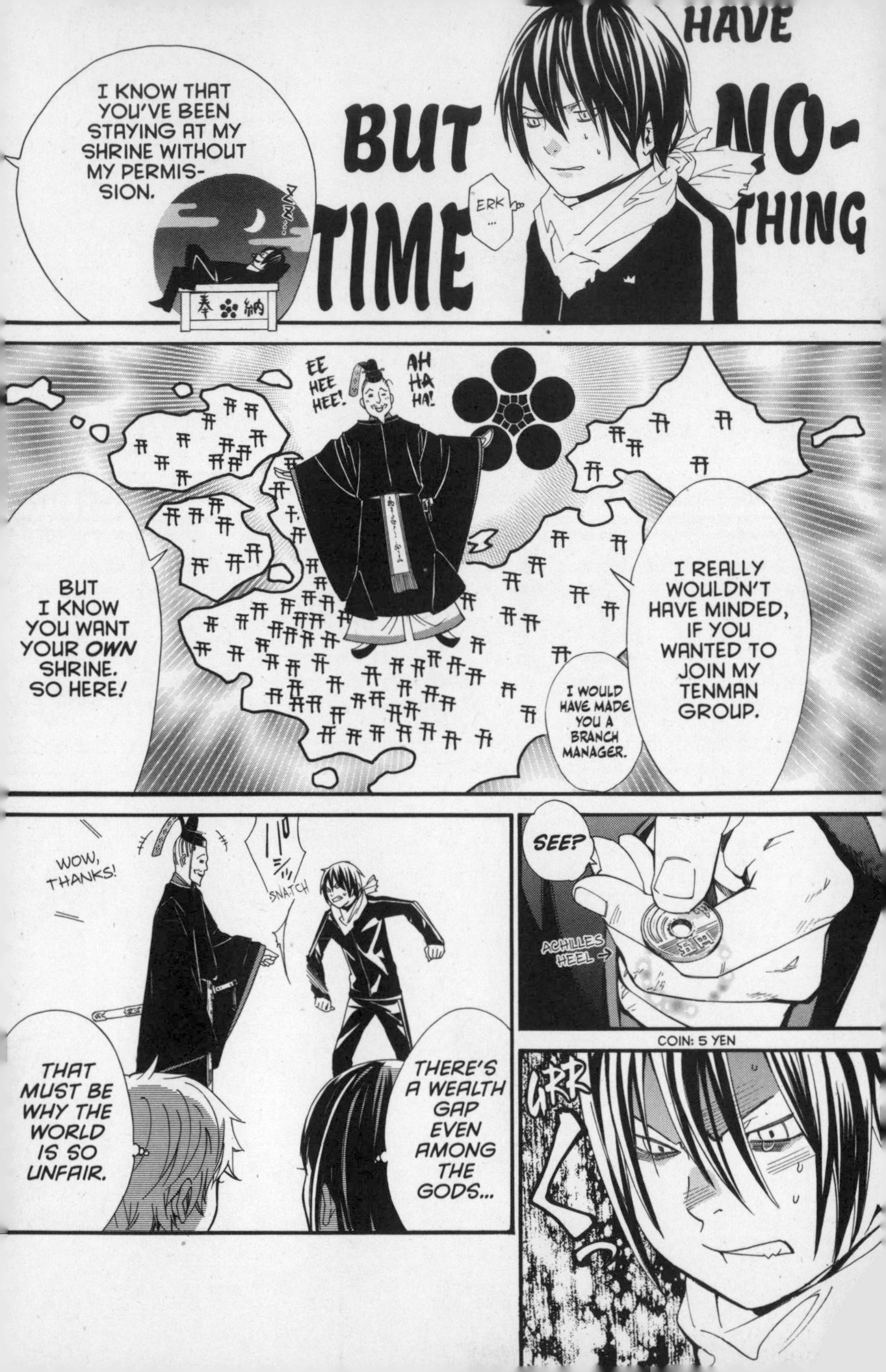
HAVE NO-THING BUT TIME
ERK...
I KNOW THAT YOU'VE BEEN STAYING AT MY SHRINE WITHOUT MY PERMIS-SION.
I REALLY WOULDN'T HAVE MINDED, IF YOU WANTED TO JOIN MY TENMAN GROUP.
I WOULD HAVE MADE YOU A BRANCH MANAGER.
AH HA HA!
EE HEE HEE!
BUT I KNOW YOU WANT YOUR *OWN* SHRINE. SO HERE!
SEE?
ACHILLES HEEL →
COIN: 5 YEN
GRR
SNATCH
WOW, THANKS!
THERE'S A WEALTH GAP EVEN AMONG THE GODS...
THAT MUST BE WHY THE WORLD IS SO UNFAIR.

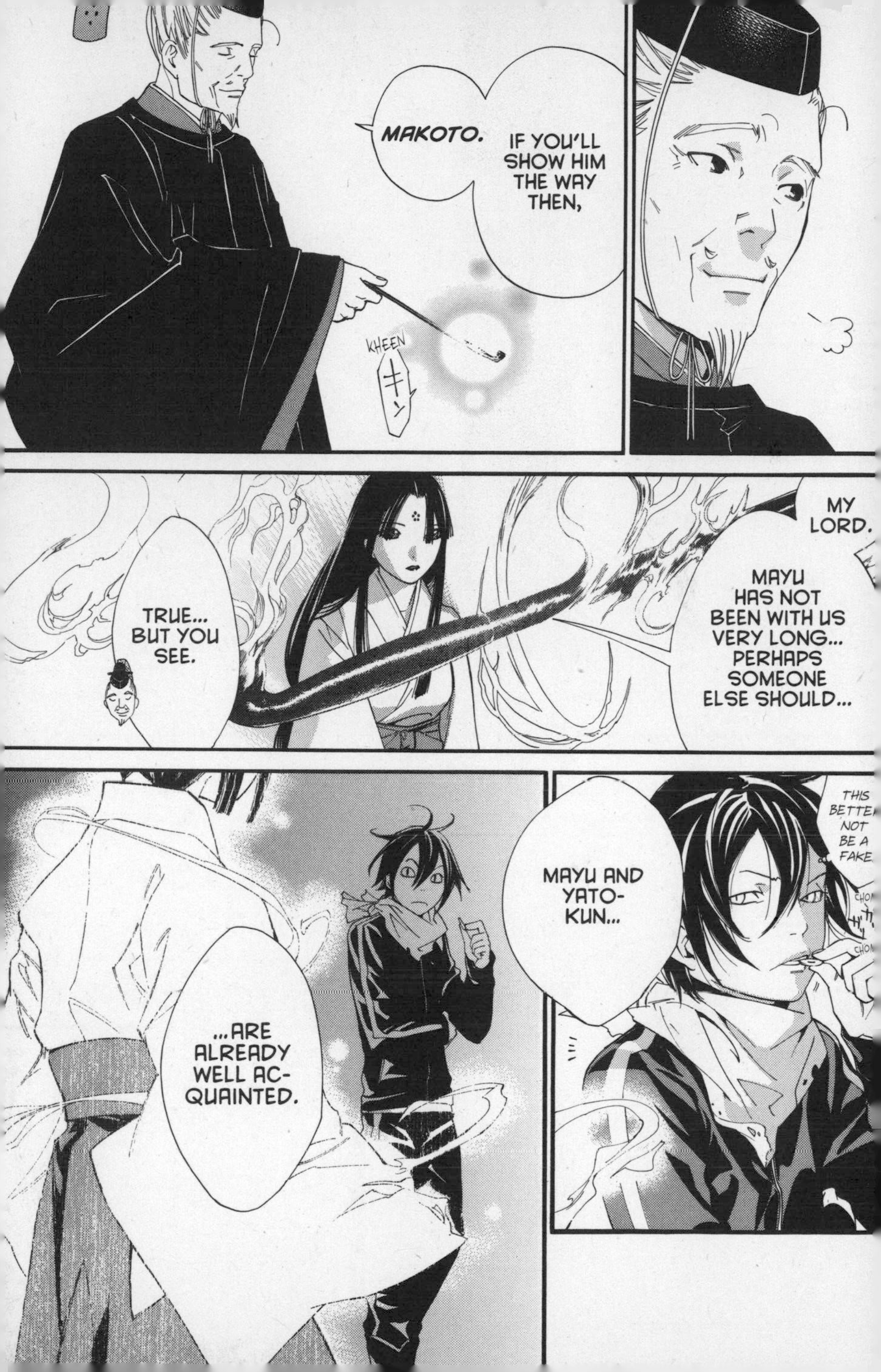
MAKOTO. IF YOU'LL SHOW HIM THE WAY THEN,
KHEEN
MY LORD.
MAYU HAS NOT BEEN WITH US VERY LONG... PERHAPS SOMEONE ELSE SHOULD...
TRUE... BUT YOU SEE.
THIS BETTE NOT BE A FAKE.
CHOM
CHOM
MAYU AND YATO-KUN...
...ARE ALREADY WELL AC-QUAINTED.

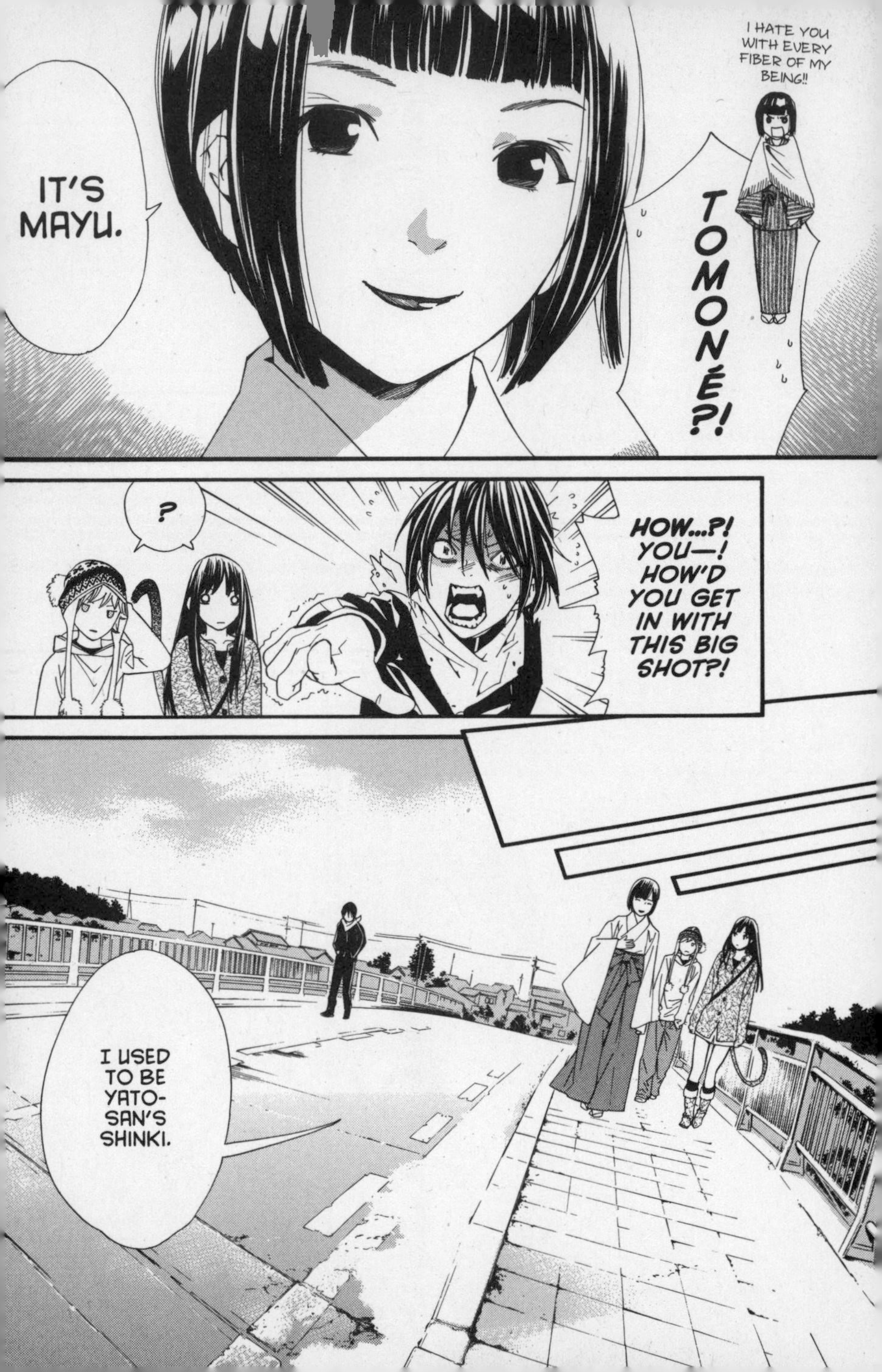
I HATE YOU WITH EVERY FIBER OF MY BEING!!
TOMONÉ?!
IT'S MAYU.
HOW...?! YOU—! HOW'D YOU GET IN WITH THIS BIG SHOT?!
?
I USED TO BE YATO-SAN'S SHINKI.

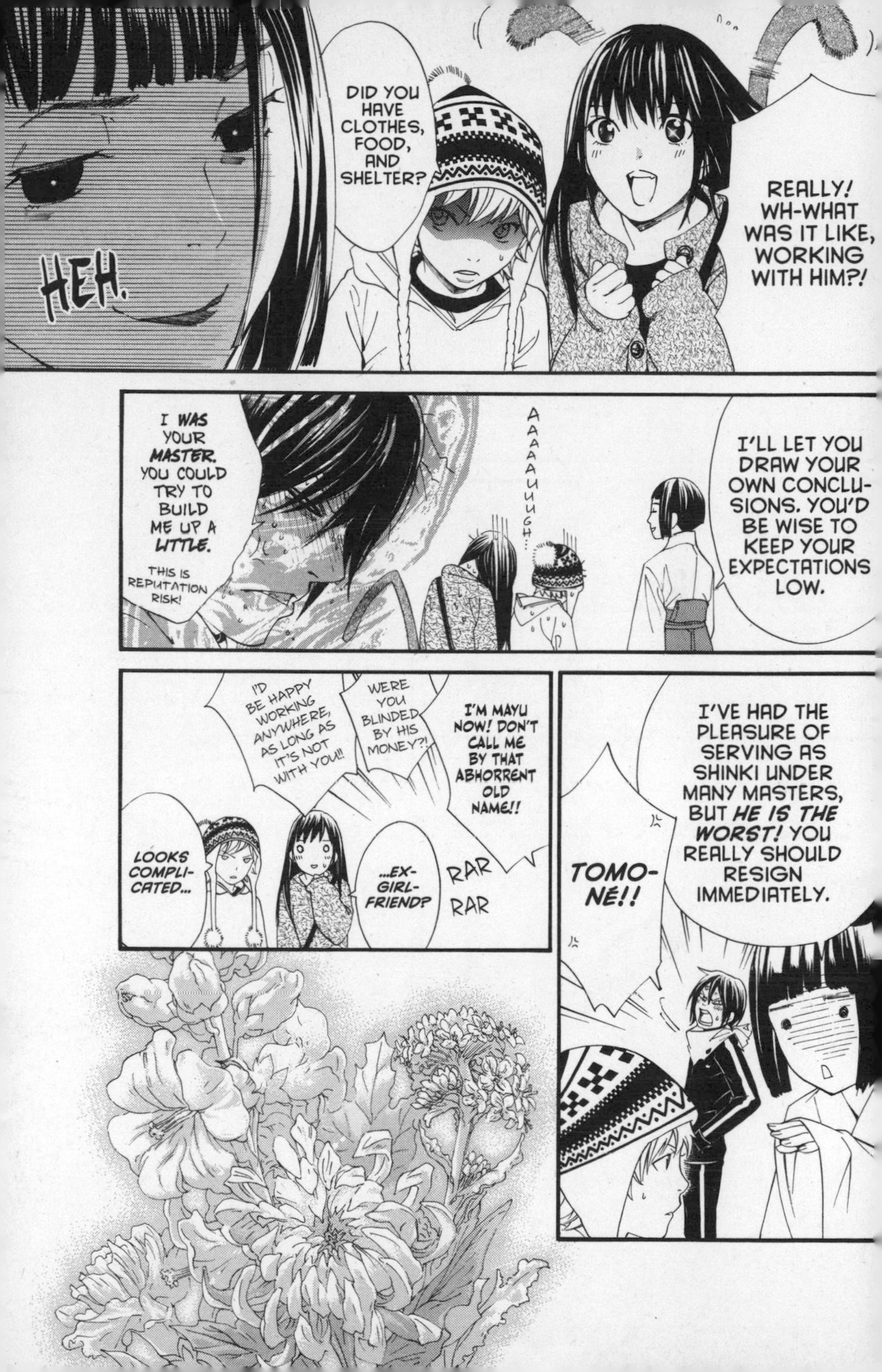
REALLY! WH-WHAT WAS IT LIKE, WORKING WITH HIM?!
DID YOU HAVE CLOTHES, FOOD, AND SHELTER?
HEH.
I'LL LET YOU DRAW YOUR OWN CONCLUSIONS. YOU'D BE WISE TO KEEP YOUR EXPECTATIONS LOW.
AAAAAUUGH...
I WAS YOUR MASTER. YOU COULD TRY TO BUILD ME UP A LITTLE.
THIS IS REPUTATION RISK!
I'VE HAD THE PLEASURE OF SERVING AS SHINKI UNDER MANY MASTERS, BUT HE IS THE WORST! YOU REALLY SHOULD RESIGN IMMEDIATELY.
TOMONÉ!!
I'M MAYU NOW! DON'T CALL ME BY THAT ABHORRENT OLD NAME!!
WERE YOU BLINDED BY HIS MONEY?!
I'D BE HAPPY WORKING ANYWHERE, AS LONG AS IT'S NOT WITH YOU!!
RAR
RAR
...EX-GIRLFRIEND?
LOOKS COMPLICATED...

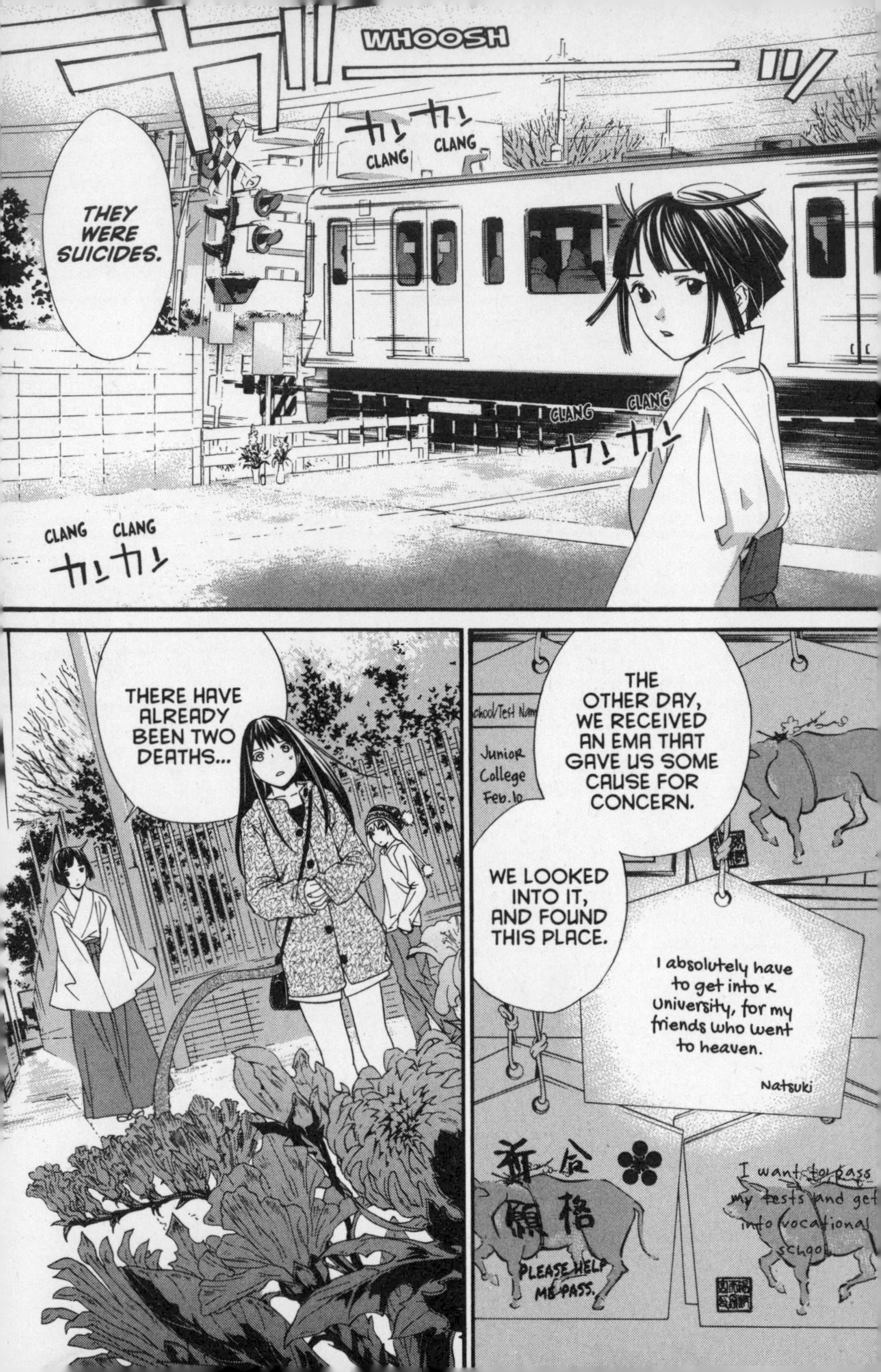
WHOOSH
CLANG CLANG
THEY WERE SUICIDES.
CLANG CLANG
CLANG CLANG
THE OTHER DAY, WE RECEIVED AN EMA THAT GAVE US SOME CAUSE FOR CONCERN.
Junior College Feb.10
WE LOOKED INTO IT, AND FOUND THIS PLACE.
I absolutely have to get into K University, for my friends who went to heaven.
Natsuki
I want to pass my tests and get into vocational school
PLEASE HELP ME PASS.
THERE HAVE ALREADY BEEN TWO DEATHS...

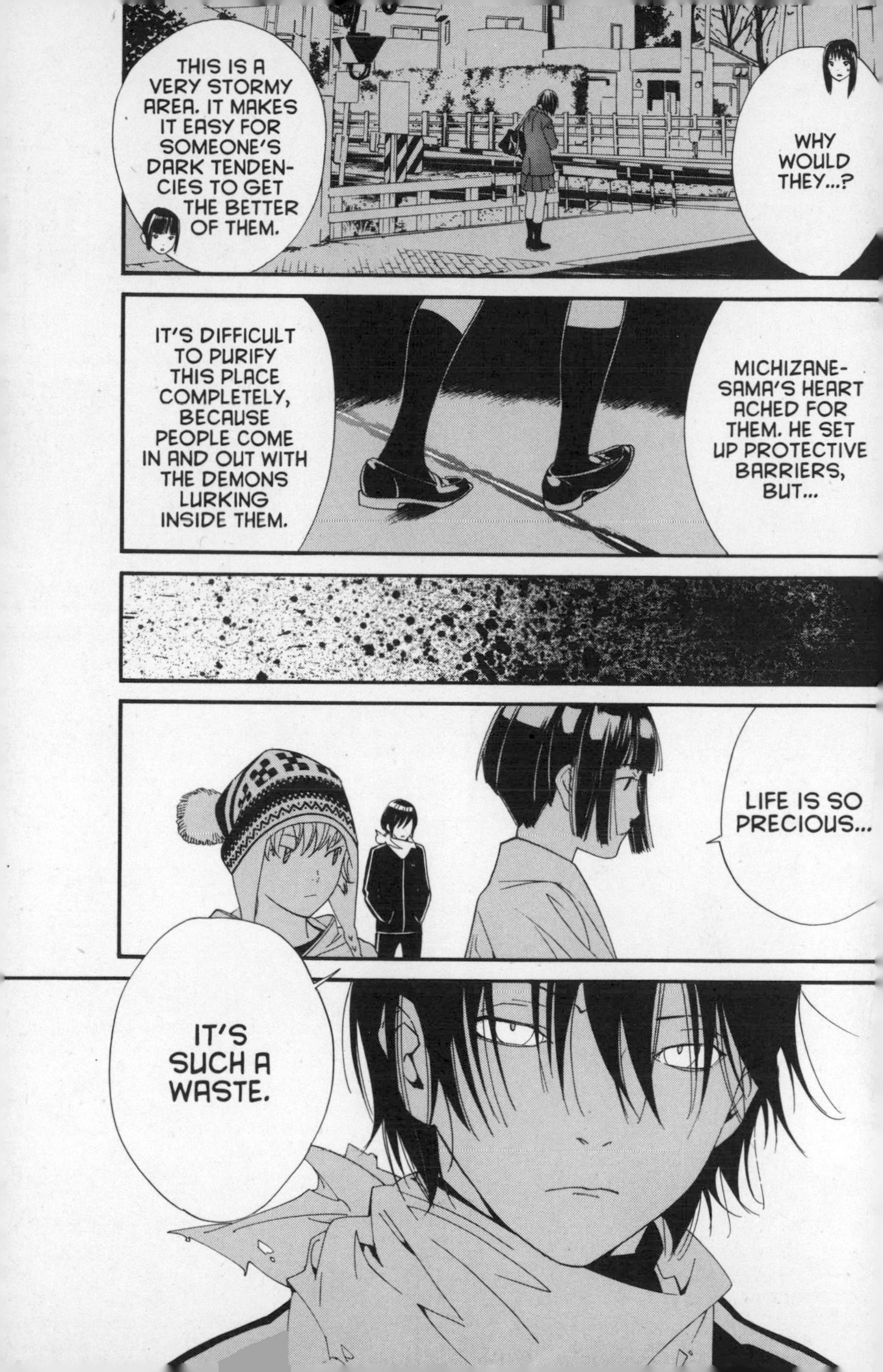
WHY WOULD THEY...?
THIS IS A VERY STORMY AREA. IT MAKES IT EASY FOR SOMEONE'S DARK TENDENCIES TO GET THE BETTER OF THEM.
MICHIZANE-SAMA'S HEART ACHED FOR THEM. HE SET UP PROTECTIVE BARRIERS, BUT...
IT'S DIFFICULT TO PURIFY THIS PLACE COMPLETELY, BECAUSE PEOPLE COME IN AND OUT WITH THE DEMONS LURKING INSIDE THEM.
LIFE IS SO PRECIOUS...
IT'S SUCH A WASTE.

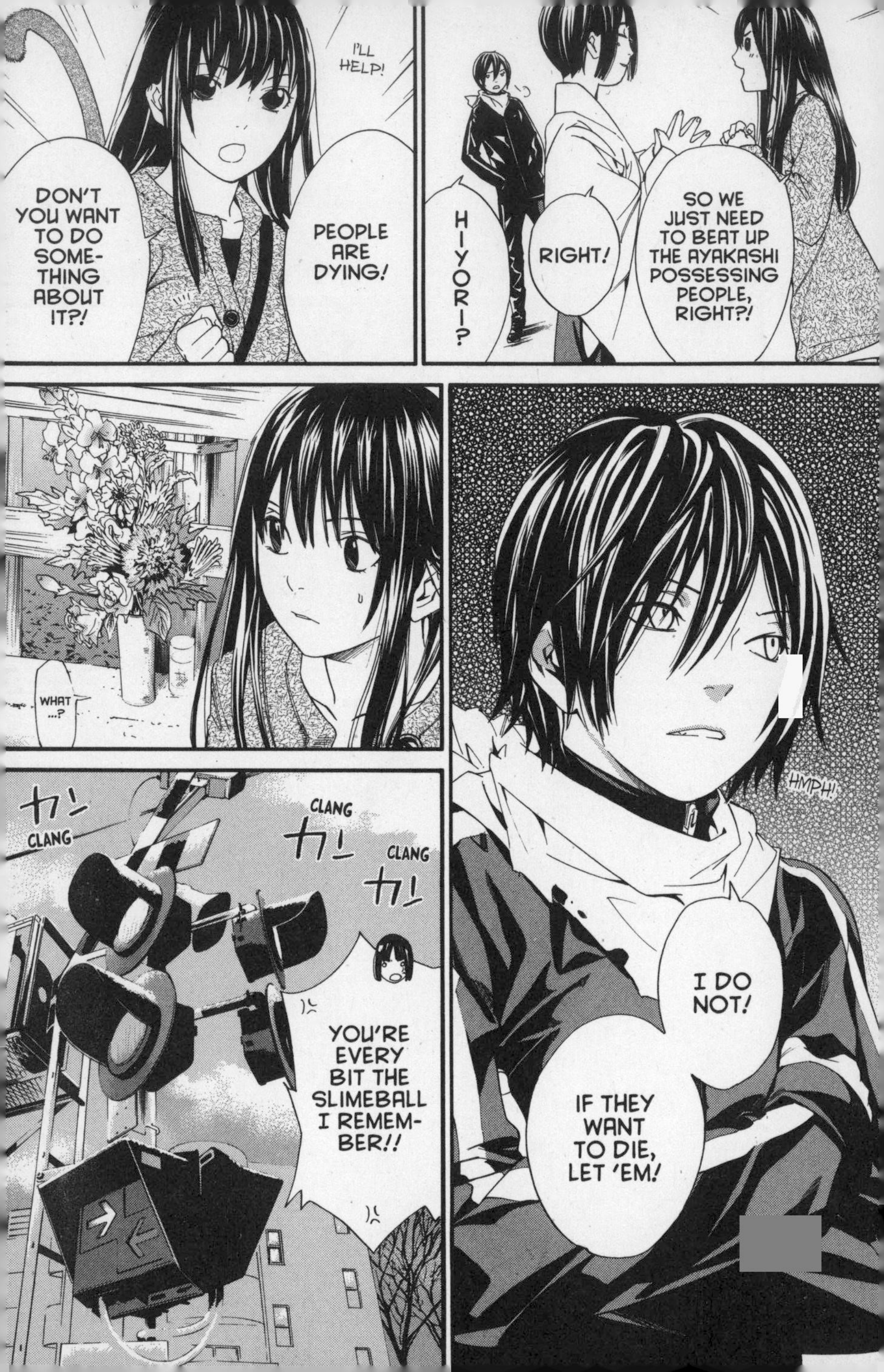
SO WE JUST NEED TO BEAT UP THE AYAKASHI POSSESSING PEOPLE, RIGHT?!
RIGHT!
HIYORI?
I'LL HELP!
PEOPLE ARE DYING!
DON'T YOU WANT TO DO SOMETHING ABOUT IT?!
HMPH!
I DO NOT!
IF THEY WANT TO DIE, LET 'EM!
WHAT ...?
CLANG
CLANG
CLANG
YOU'RE EVERY BIT THE SLIMEBALL I REMEMBER!!

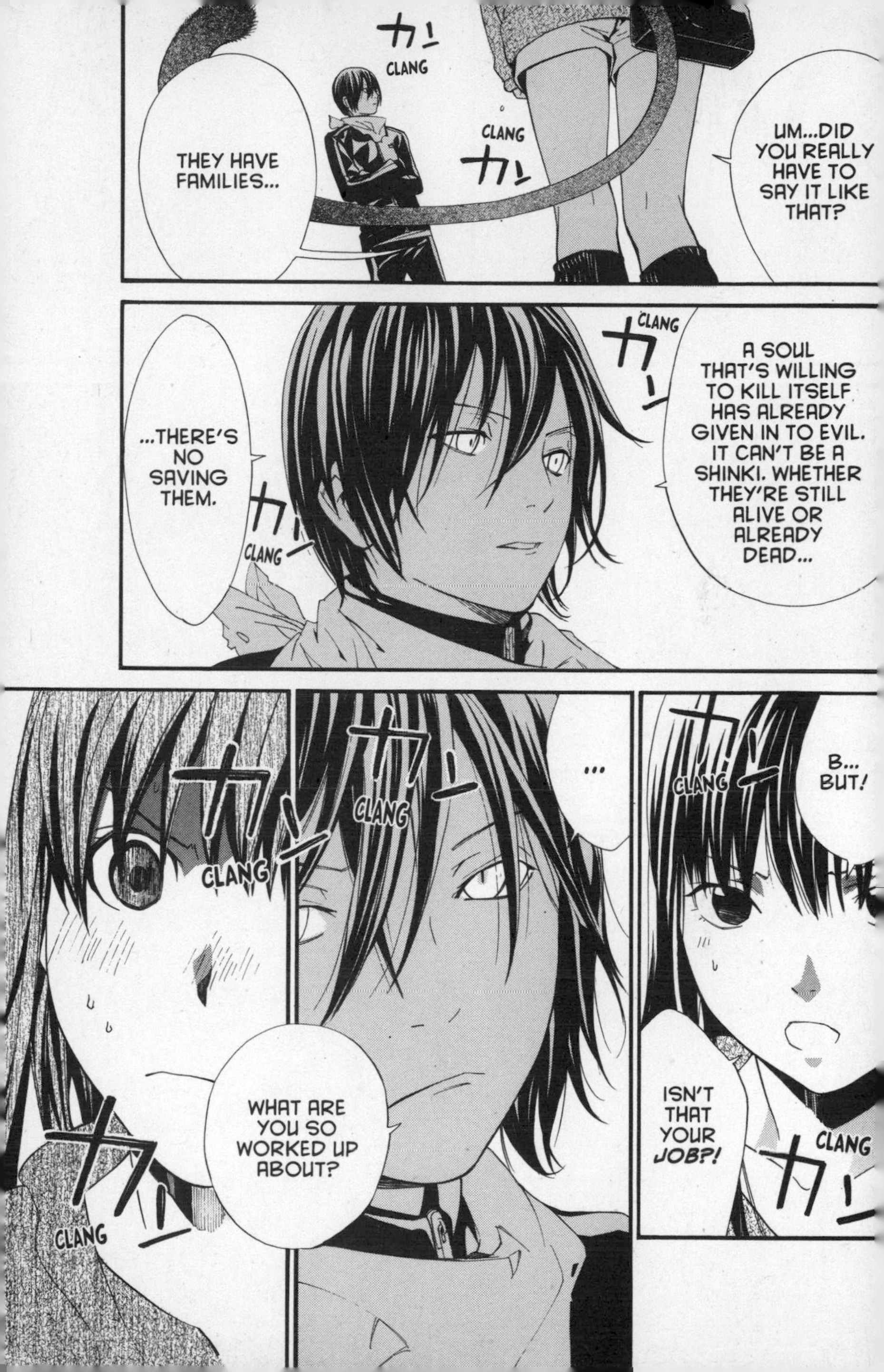
UM...DID YOU REALLY HAVE TO SAY IT LIKE THAT?
CLANG
CLANG
THEY HAVE FAMILIES...
CLANG
A SOUL THAT'S WILLING TO KILL ITSELF HAS ALREADY GIVEN IN TO EVIL. IT CAN'T BE A SHINKI. WHETHER THEY'RE STILL ALIVE OR ALREADY DEAD...
...THERE'S NO SAVING THEM.
CLANG
B... BUT!
CLANG
ISN'T THAT YOUR *JOB?!*
CLANG
...
CLANG
WHAT ARE YOU SO WORKED UP ABOUT?
CLANG
CLANG

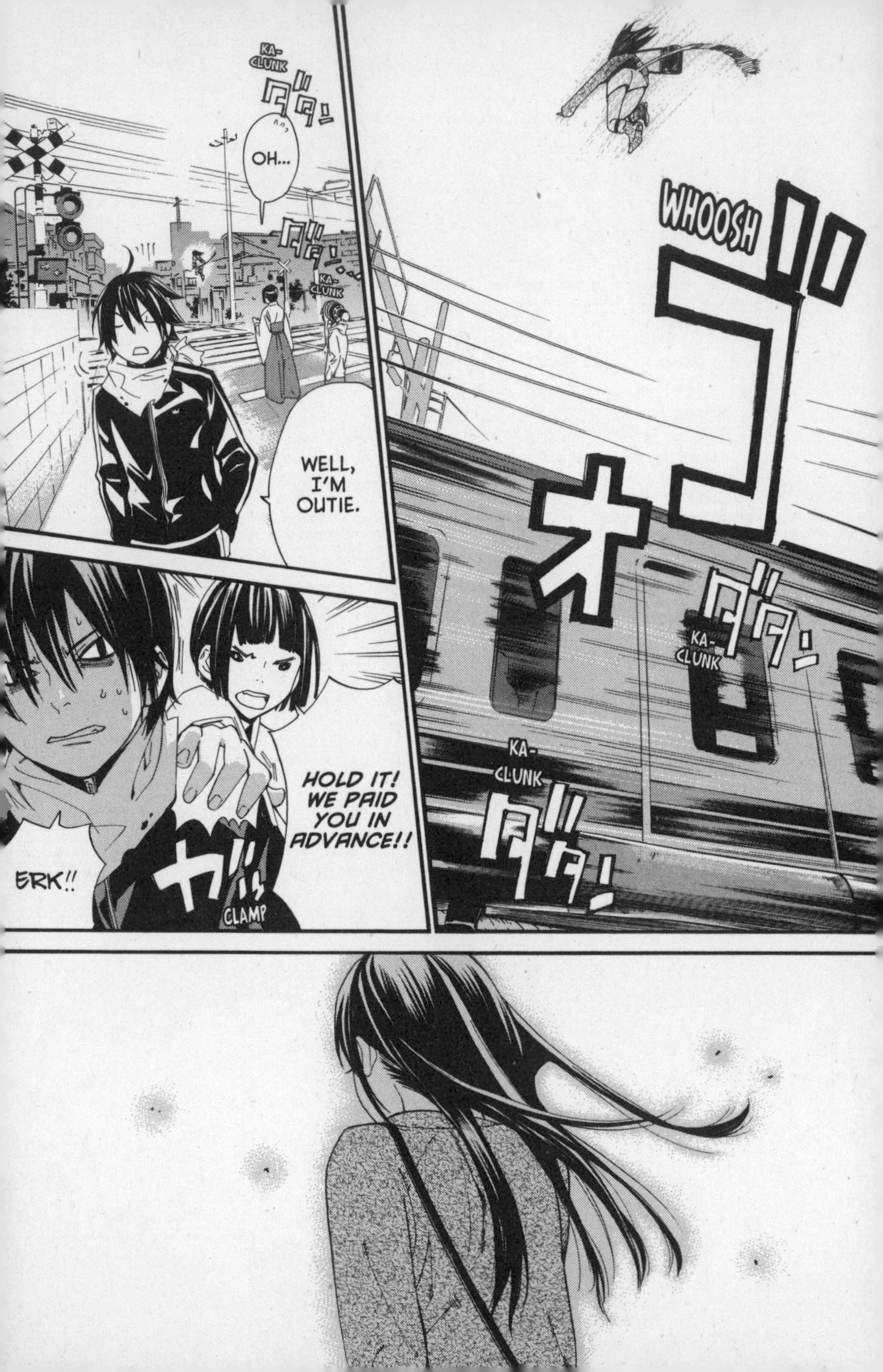
WHOOSH
KA-CLUNK
KA-CLUNK
KA-CLUNK
OH...
KA-CLUNK
WELL, I'M OUTIE.
HOLD IT! WE PAID YOU IN ADVANCE!!
ERK!!
CLAMP

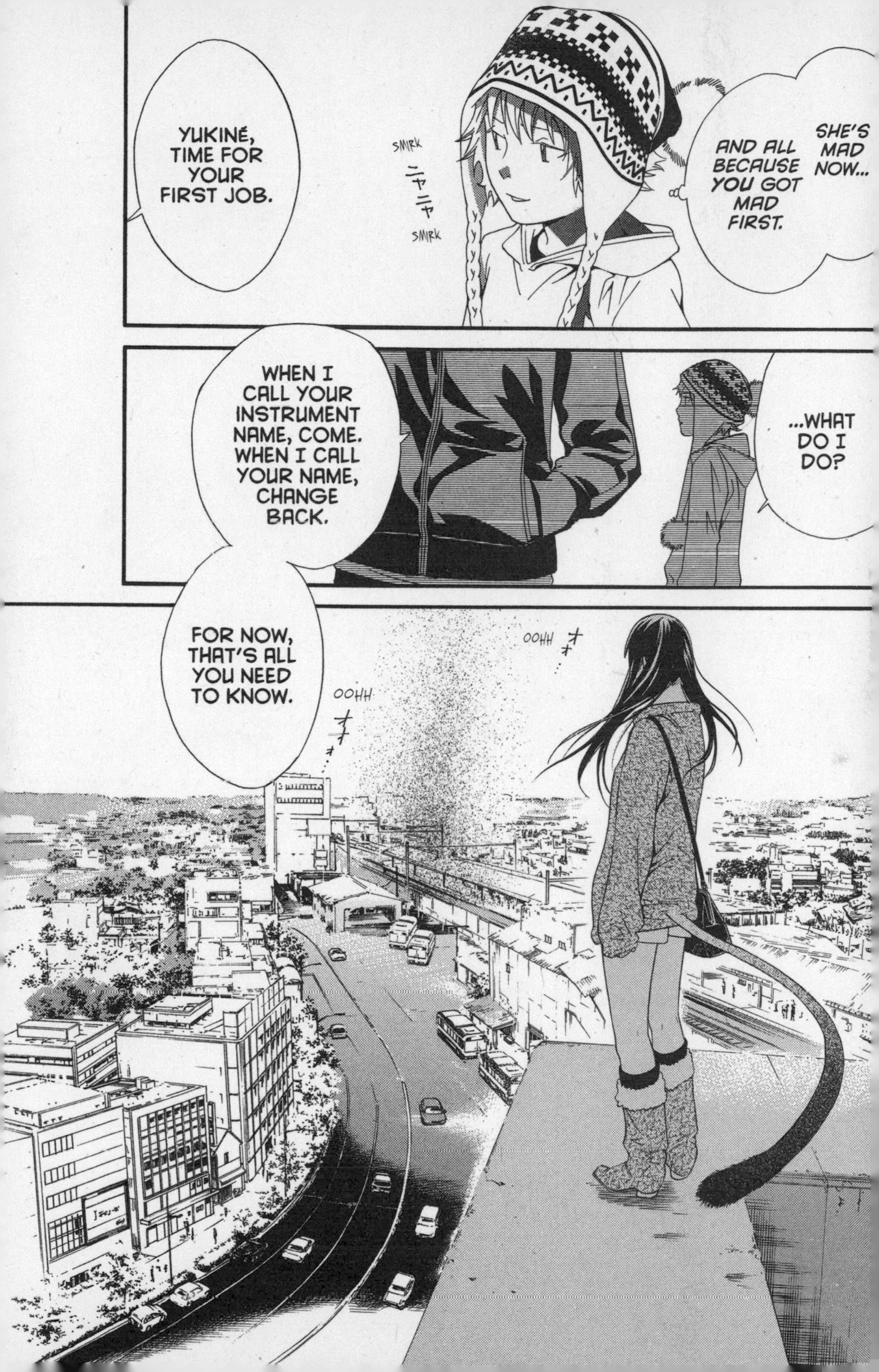
SHE'S MAD NOW...
AND ALL BECAUSE YOU GOT MAD FIRST.
SMIRK
ニヤニヤ
SMIRK
YUKINÉ, TIME FOR YOUR FIRST JOB.
...WHAT DO I DO?
WHEN I CALL YOUR INSTRUMENT NAME, COME. WHEN I CALL YOUR NAME, CHANGE BACK.
FOR NOW, THAT'S ALL YOU NEED TO KNOW.
OOHH
オォ…
OOHH
オォ…

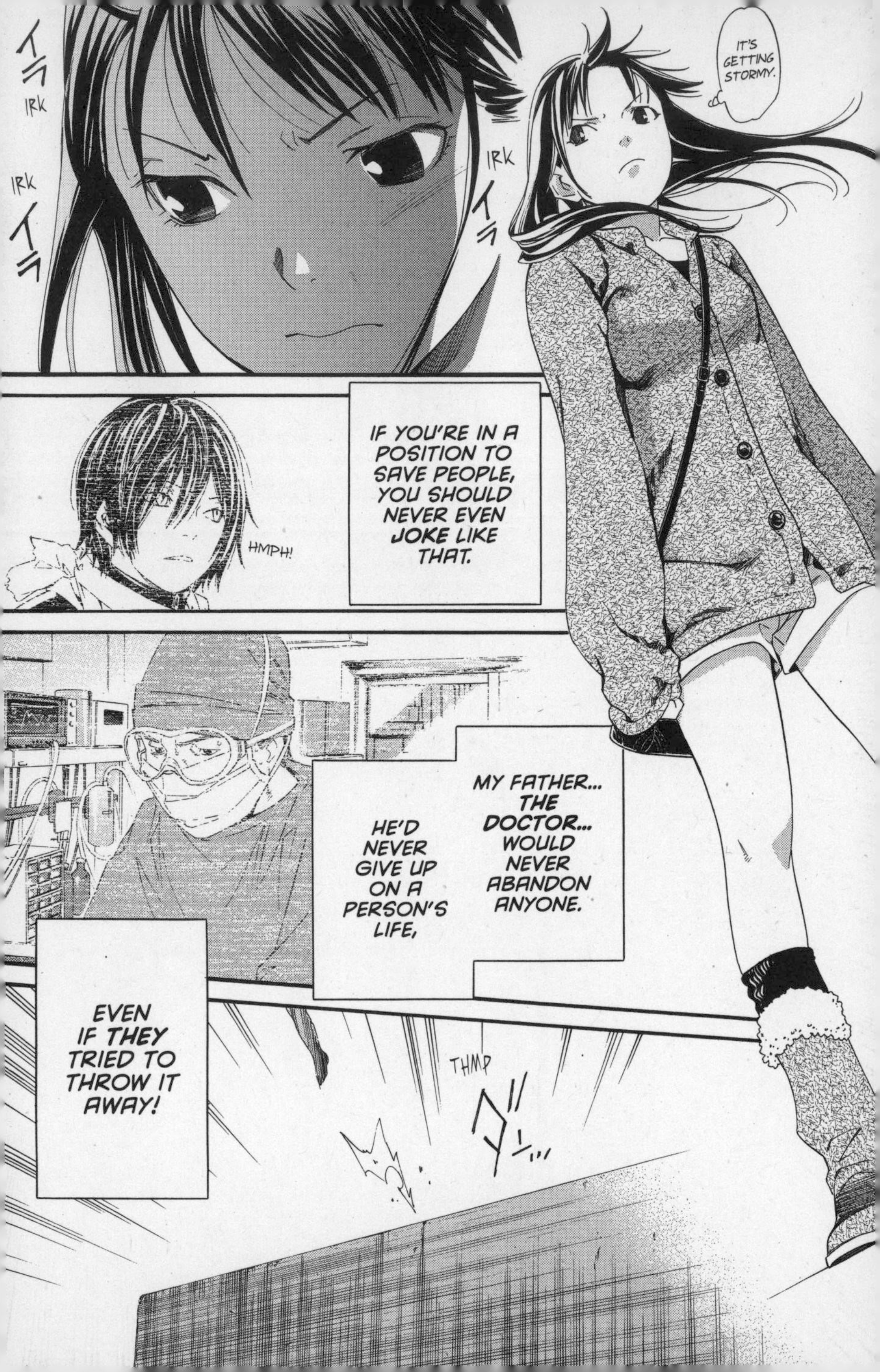
IT'S GETTING STORMY.
IRK
IRK
IRK
IF YOU'RE IN A POSITION TO SAVE PEOPLE, YOU SHOULD NEVER EVEN JOKE LIKE THAT.
HMPH!
MY FATHER... THE DOCTOR... WOULD NEVER ABANDON ANYONE.
HE'D NEVER GIVE UP ON A PERSON'S LIFE,
EVEN IF THEY TRIED TO THROW IT AWAY!
THMP

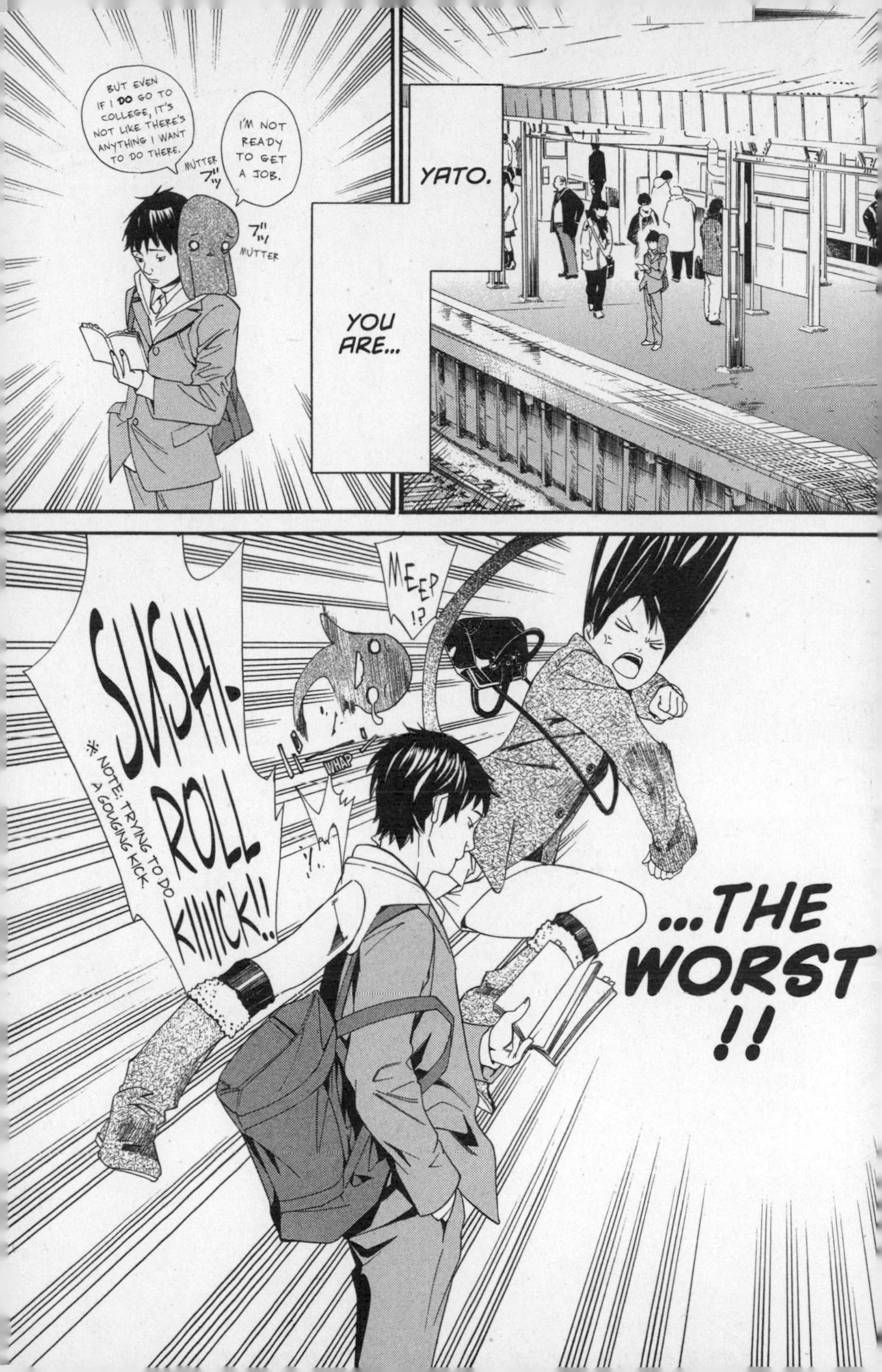
YATO.
YOU ARE...
I'M NOT READY TO GET A JOB.
MUTTER
BUT EVEN IF I DO GO TO COLLEGE, IT'S NOT LIKE THERE'S ANYTHING I WANT TO DO THERE.
MUTTER
MEEP !?
SUSHI-ROLL KIIIICK!!
※ NOTE: TRYING TO DO A GOUGING KICK.
WHAP
...THE WORST !!

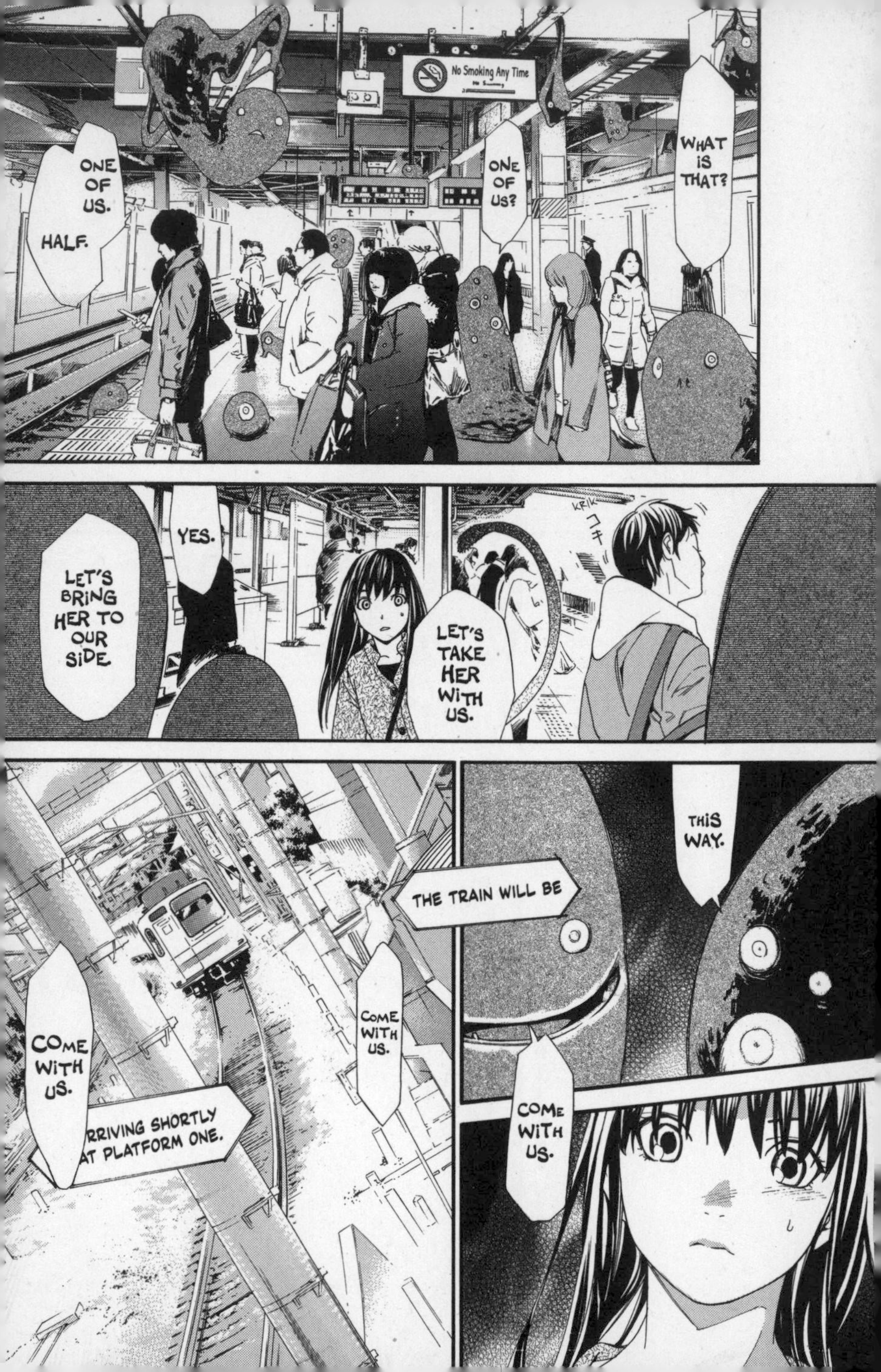
WHAT IS THAT?
No Smoking Any Time
ONE OF US?
ONE OF US.
HALF.
KRIK
コキ
LET'S TAKE HER WITH US.
YES.
LET'S BRING HER TO OUR SIDE
THIS WAY.
COME WITH US.
THE TRAIN WILL BE
COME WITH US.
COME WITH US.
RRIVING SHORTLY AT PLATFORM ONE.

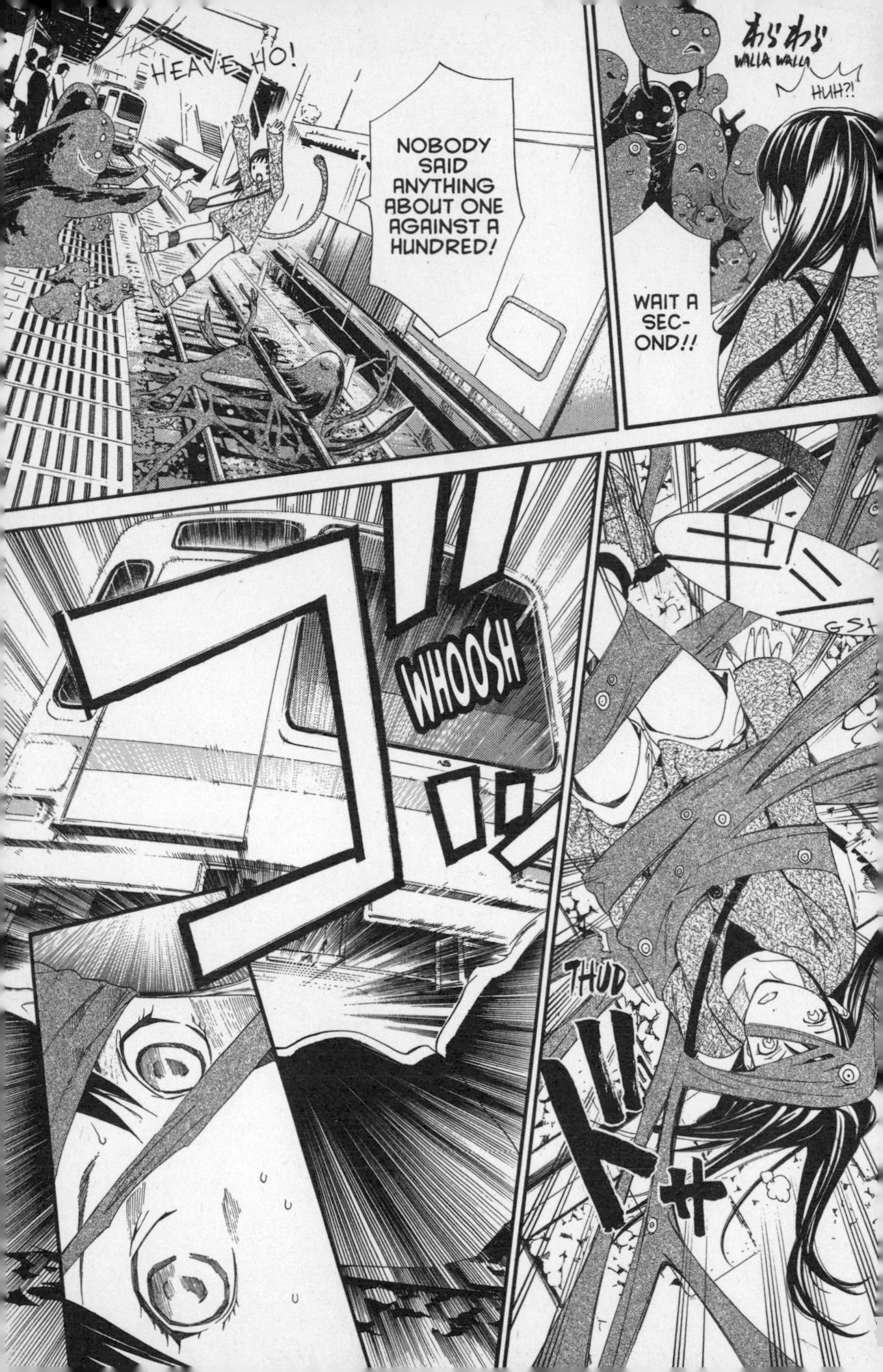

わらわら
WALLA WALLA
HUH?!
WAIT A SEC-OND!!
HEAVE HO!
NOBODY SAID ANYTHING ABOUT ONE AGAINST A HUNDRED!
THUD
WHOOSH

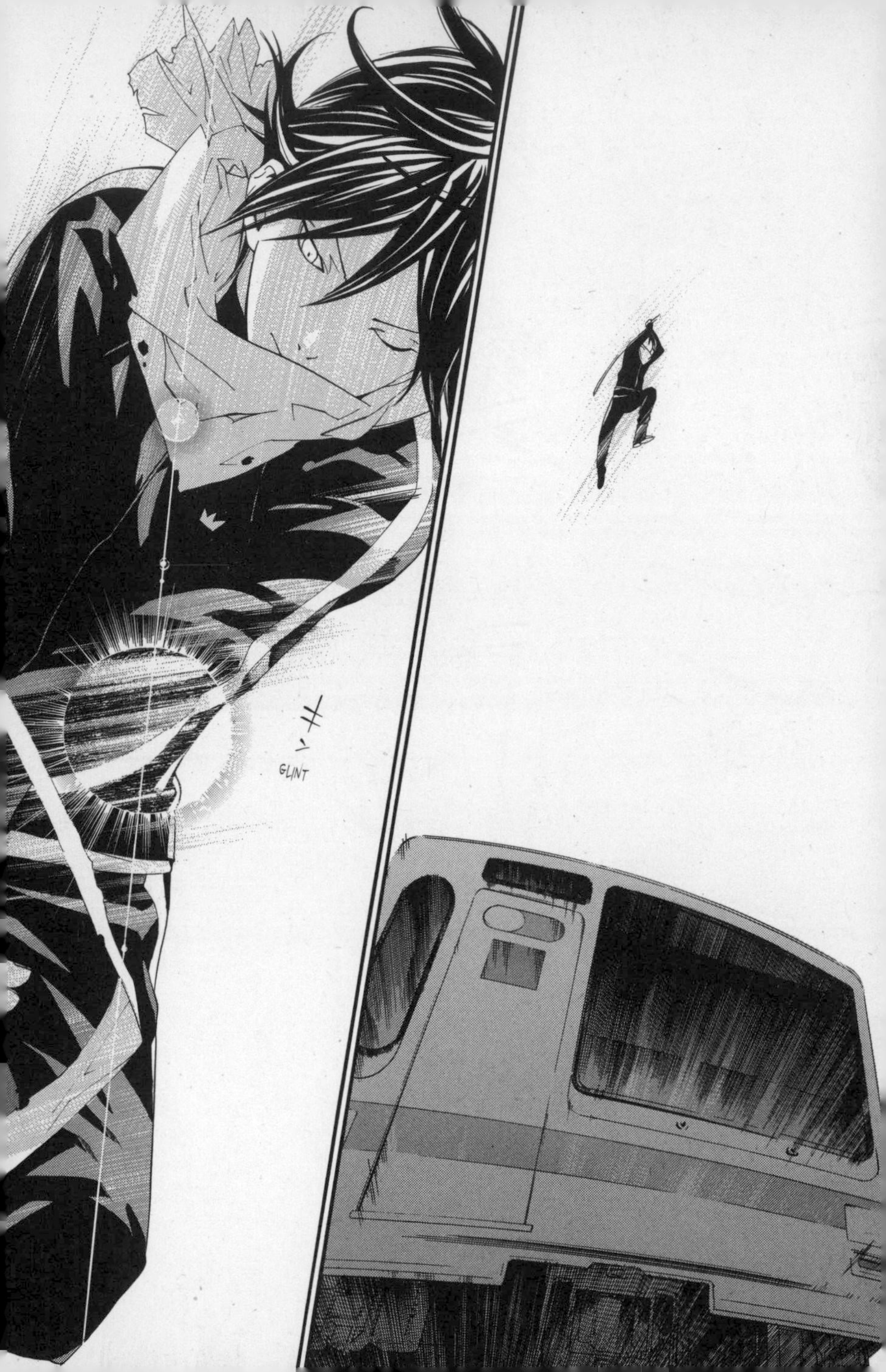
キン
GLINT

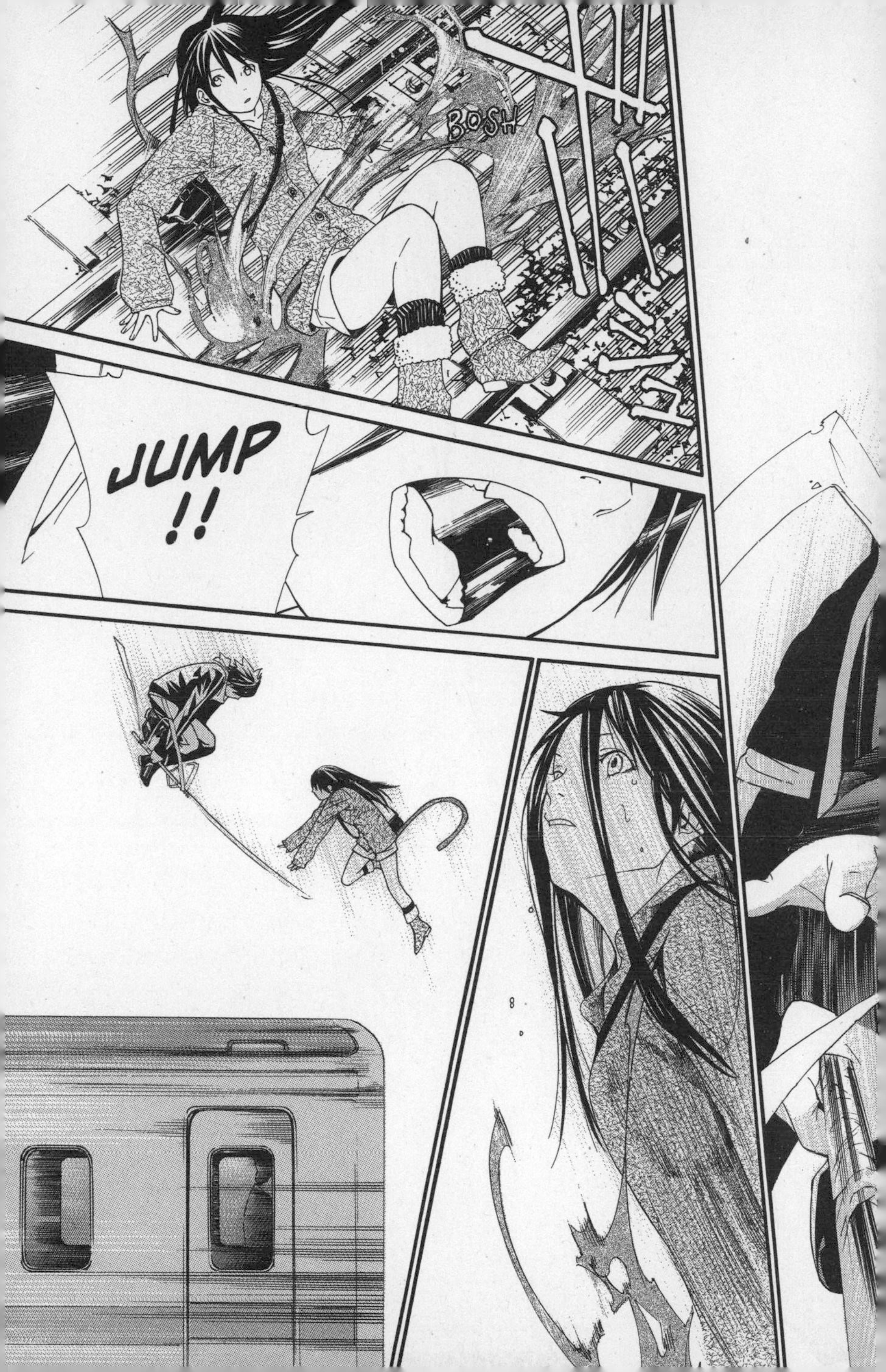
BOSH
JUMP !!

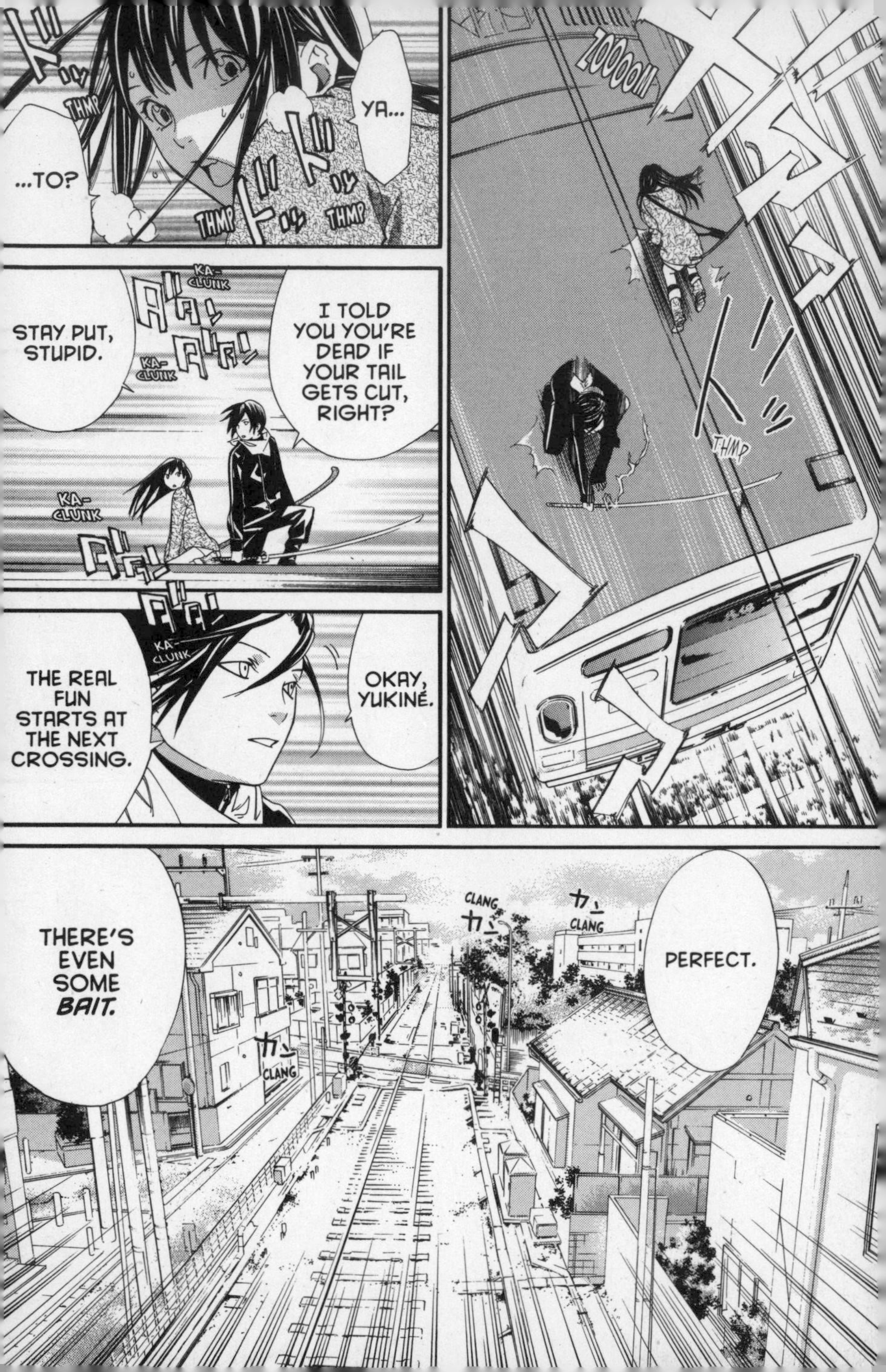
ZOOOOM
THMP
YA...
...TO?
THMP
THMP
THMP
I TOLD YOU YOU'RE DEAD IF YOUR TAIL GETS CUT, RIGHT?
KA-CLUNK
KA-CLUNK
STAY PUT, STUPID.
KA-CLUNK
KA-CLUNK
OKAY, YUKINÉ.
THE REAL FUN STARTS AT THE NEXT CROSSING.
CLANG
CLANG
PERFECT.
CLANG
THERE'S EVEN SOME *BAIT.*

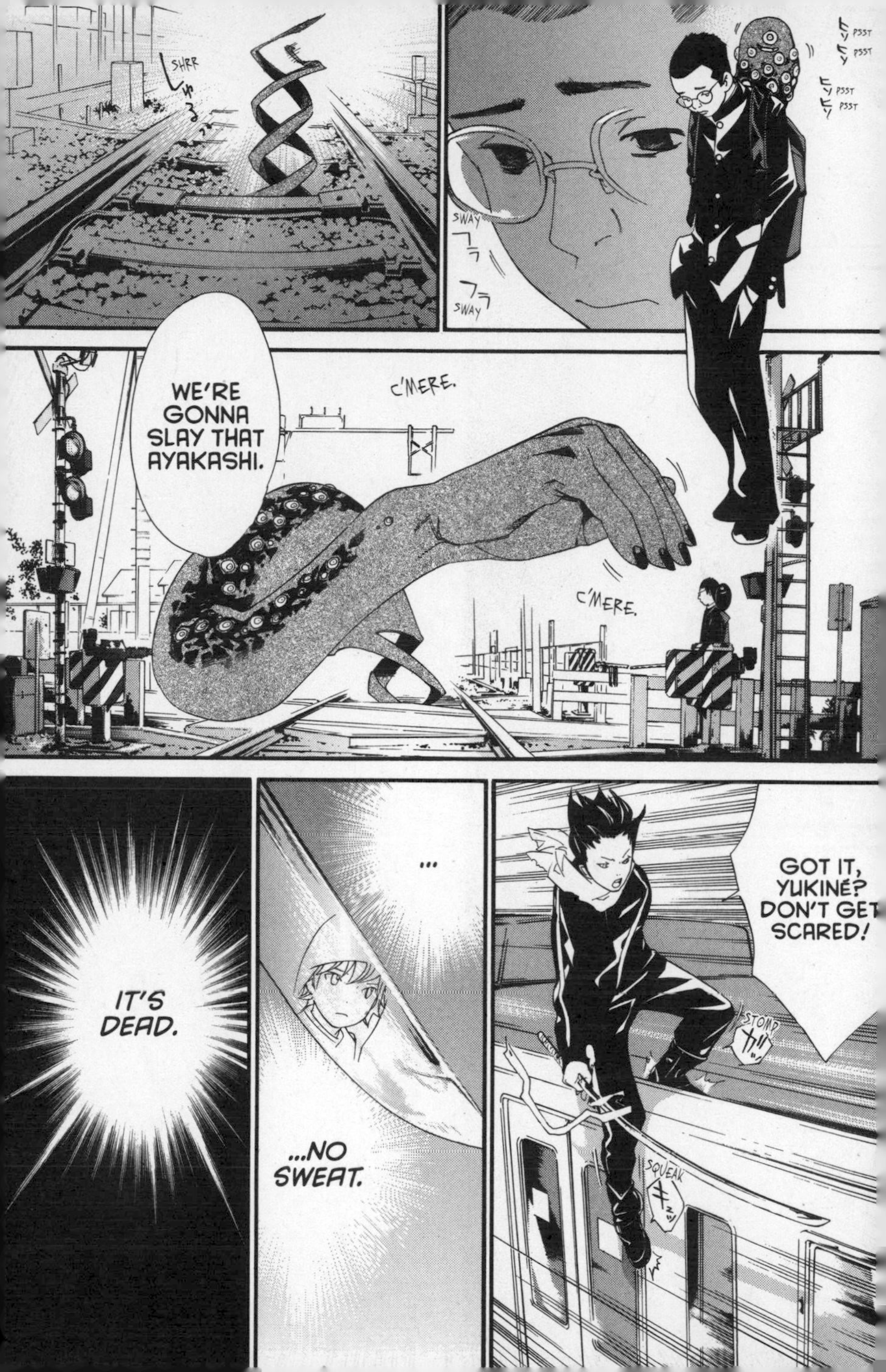
ヒソヒソ PSST PSST
ヒソヒソ PSST PSST
SWAY フラ
フラ SWAY
SHRR しゅる
WE'RE GONNA SLAY THAT AYAKASHI.
C'MERE.
C'MERE.
GOT IT, YUKINE? DON'T GET SCARED!
STOMP ガッ
SQUEAK キュッ
...
...NO SWEAT.
IT'S DEAD.

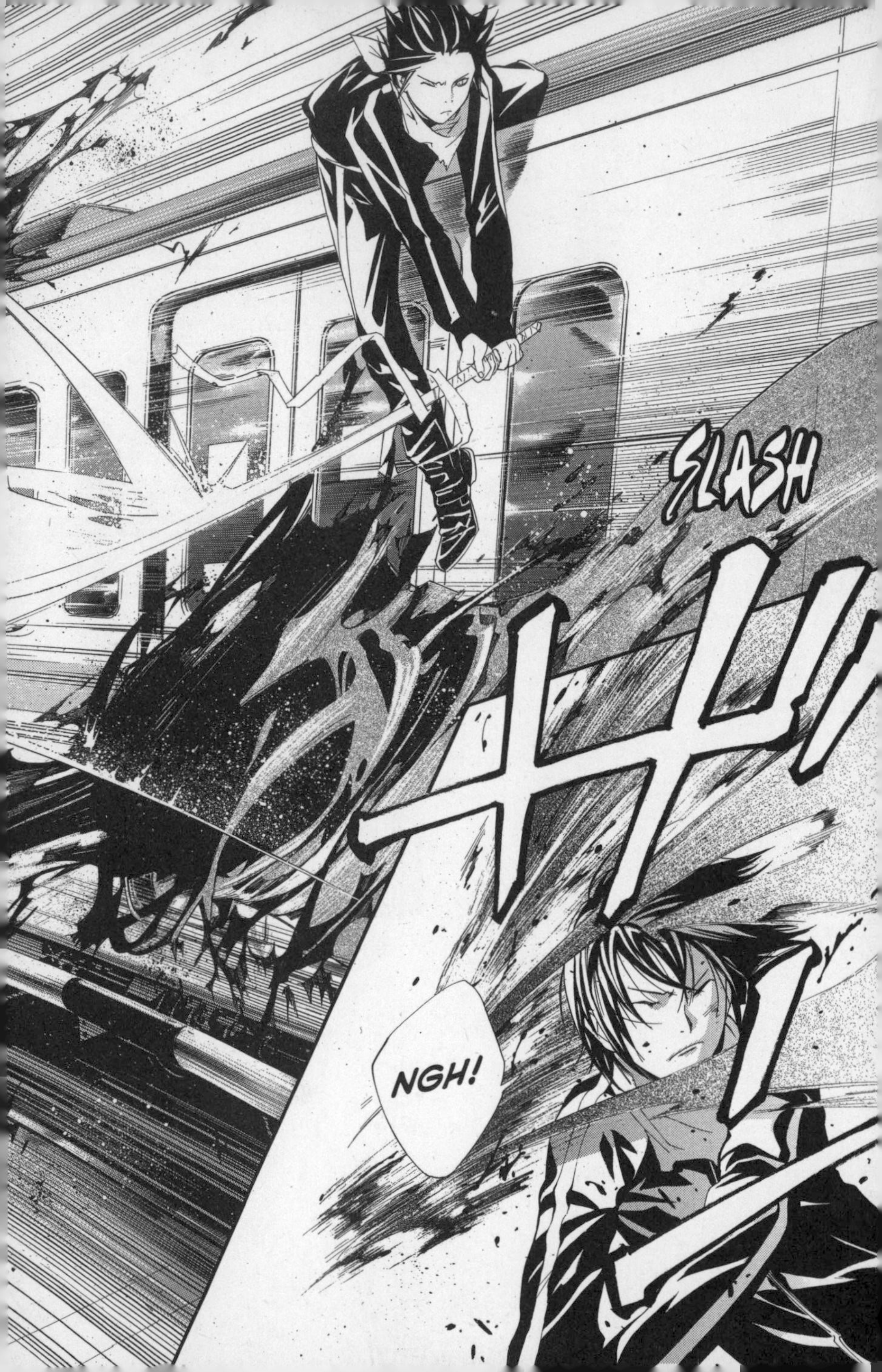
SLASH
NGH!

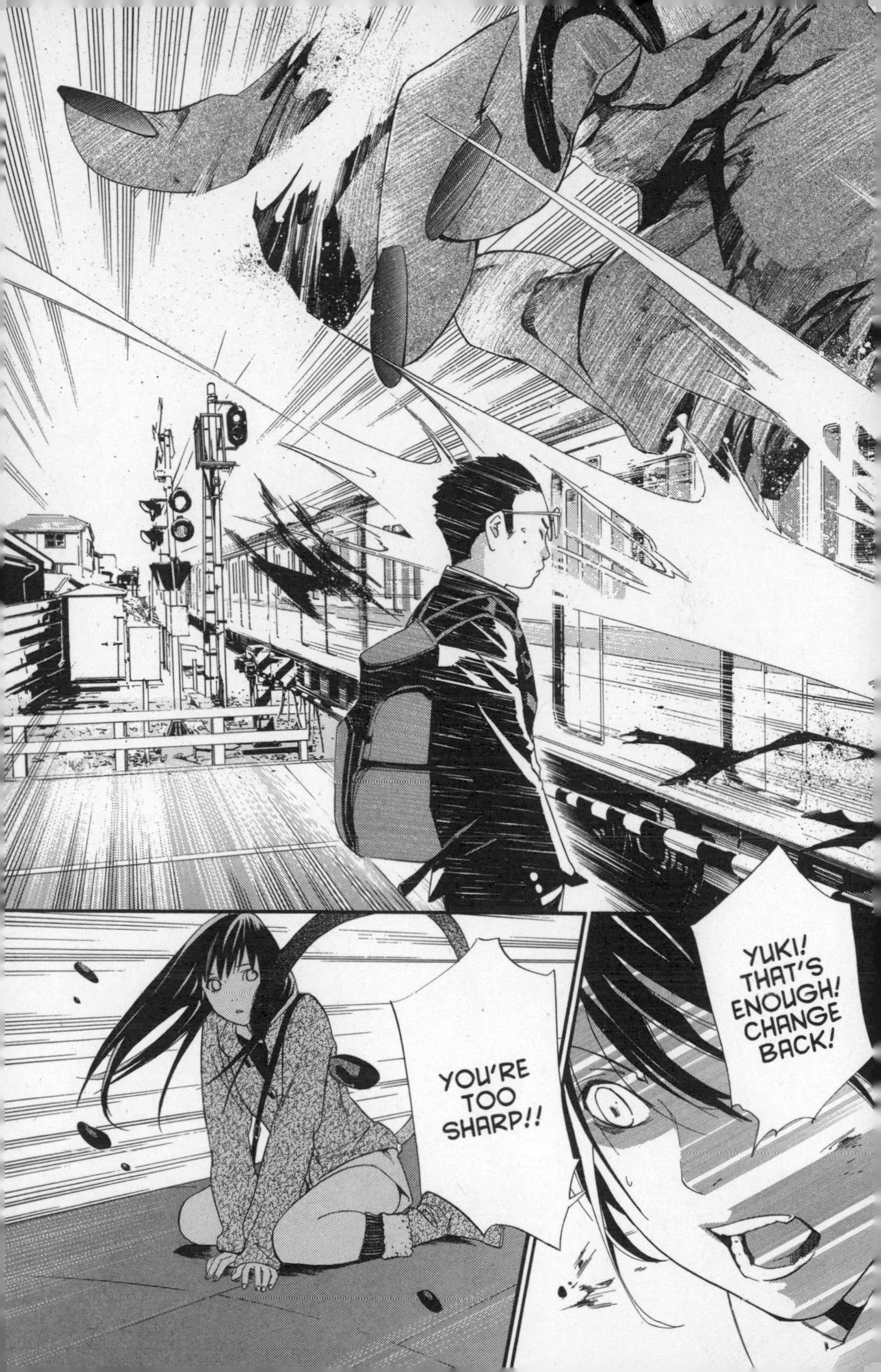
YUKI! THAT'S ENOUGH! CHANGE BACK!
YOU'RE TOO SHARP!!

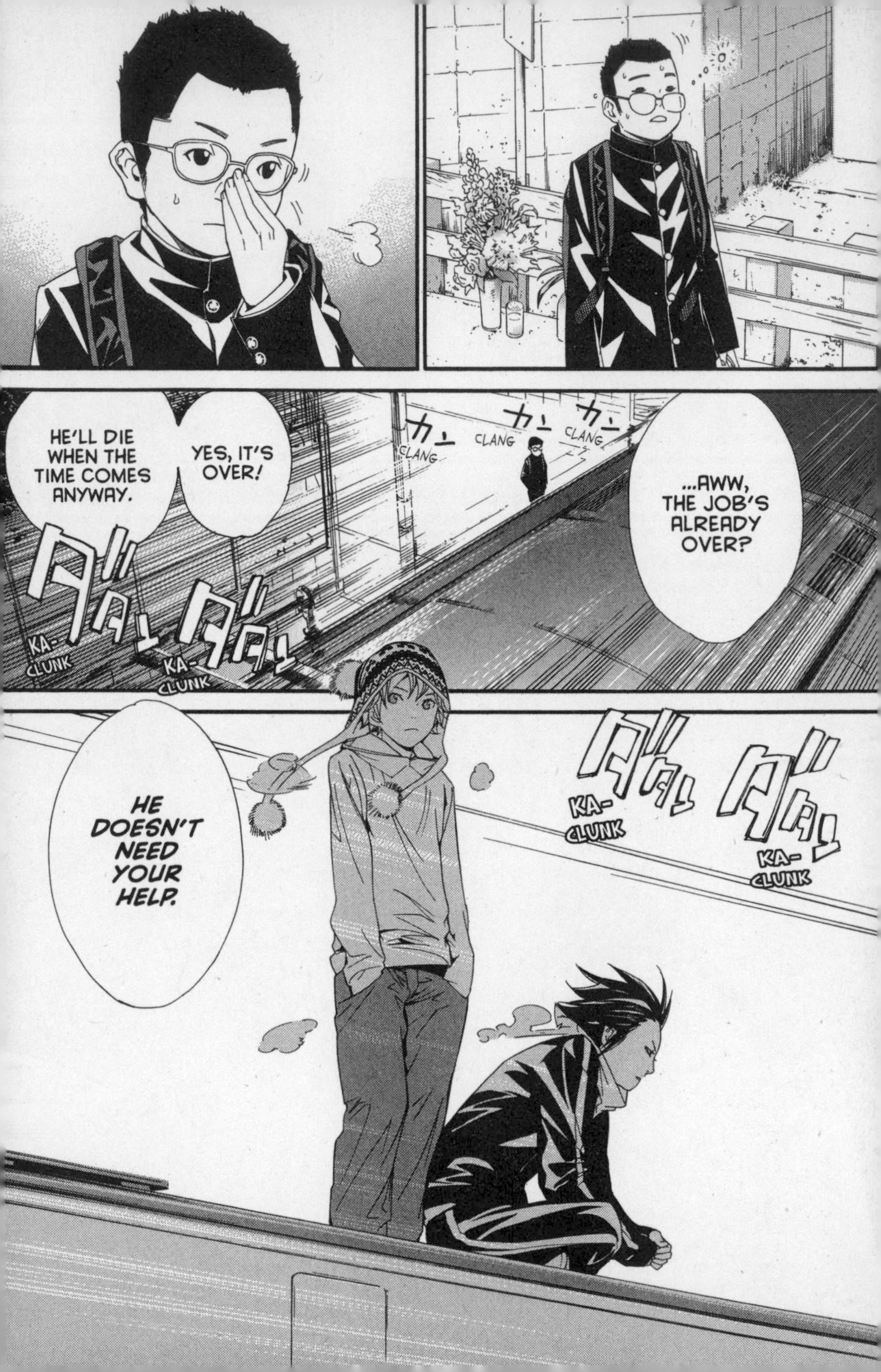
...AWW, THE JOB'S ALREADY OVER?
CLANG
CLANG
CLANG
YES, IT'S OVER!
HE'LL DIE WHEN THE TIME COMES ANYWAY.
KA-CLUNK
KA-CLUNK
KA-CLUNK
KA-CLUNK
HE DOESN'T NEED YOUR HELP.

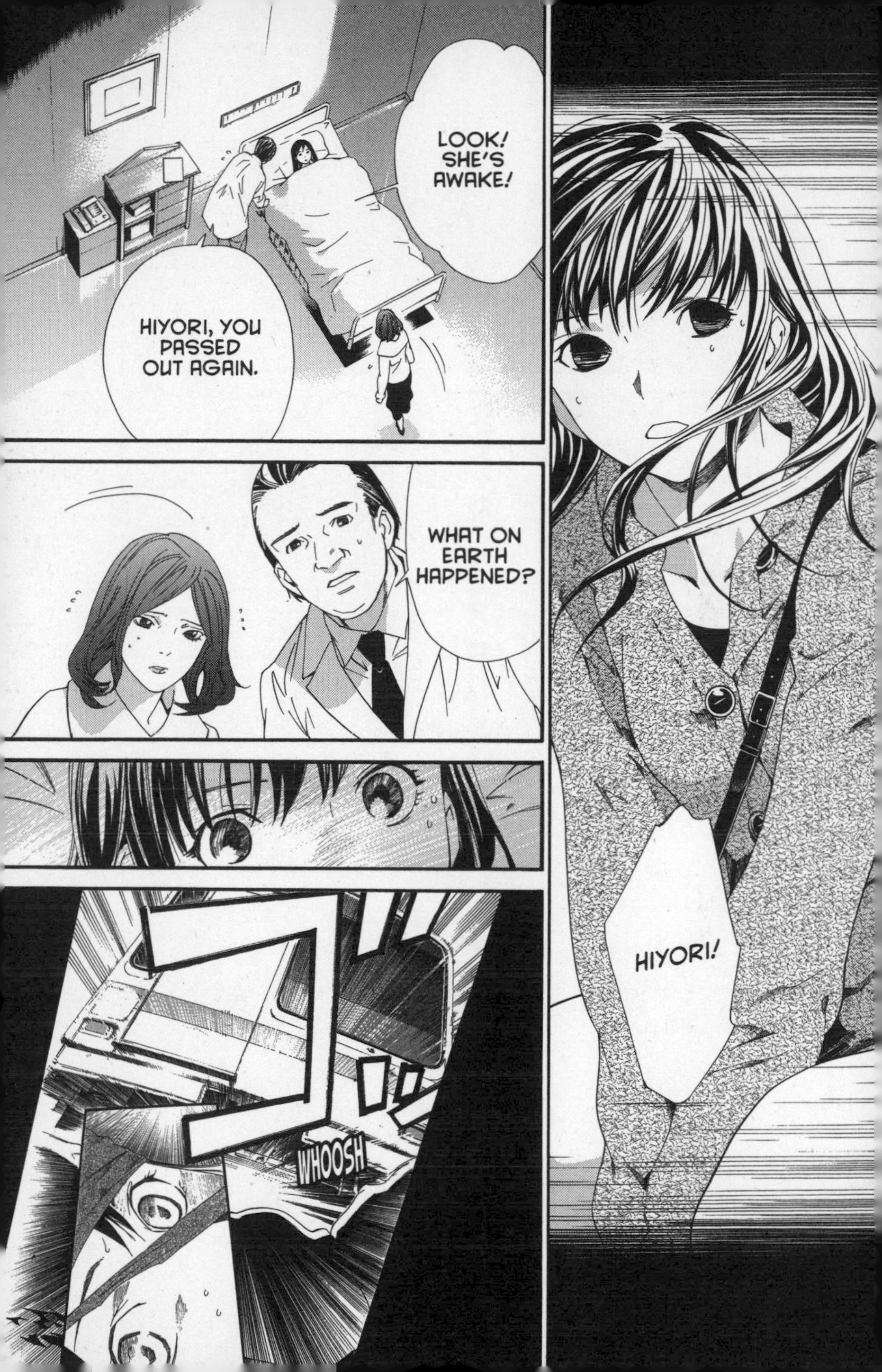
HIYORI!
LOOK! SHE'S AWAKE!
HIYORI, YOU PASSED OUT AGAIN.
WHAT ON EARTH HAPPENED?
WHOOSH

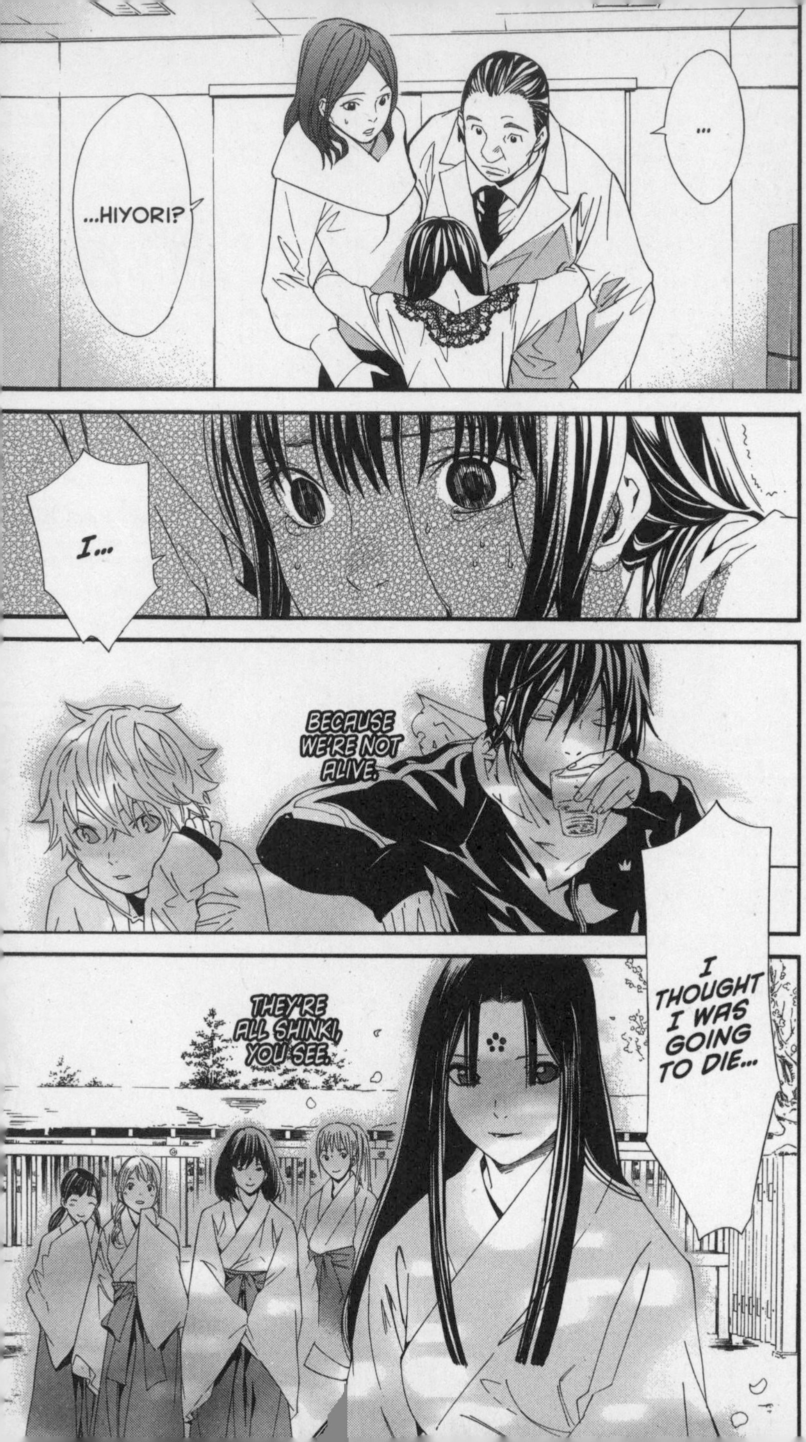
...
...HIYORI?
I...
BECAUSE WE'RE NOT ALIVE.
I THOUGHT I WAS GOING TO DIE...
THEY'RE ALL SHINKI, YOU SEE.

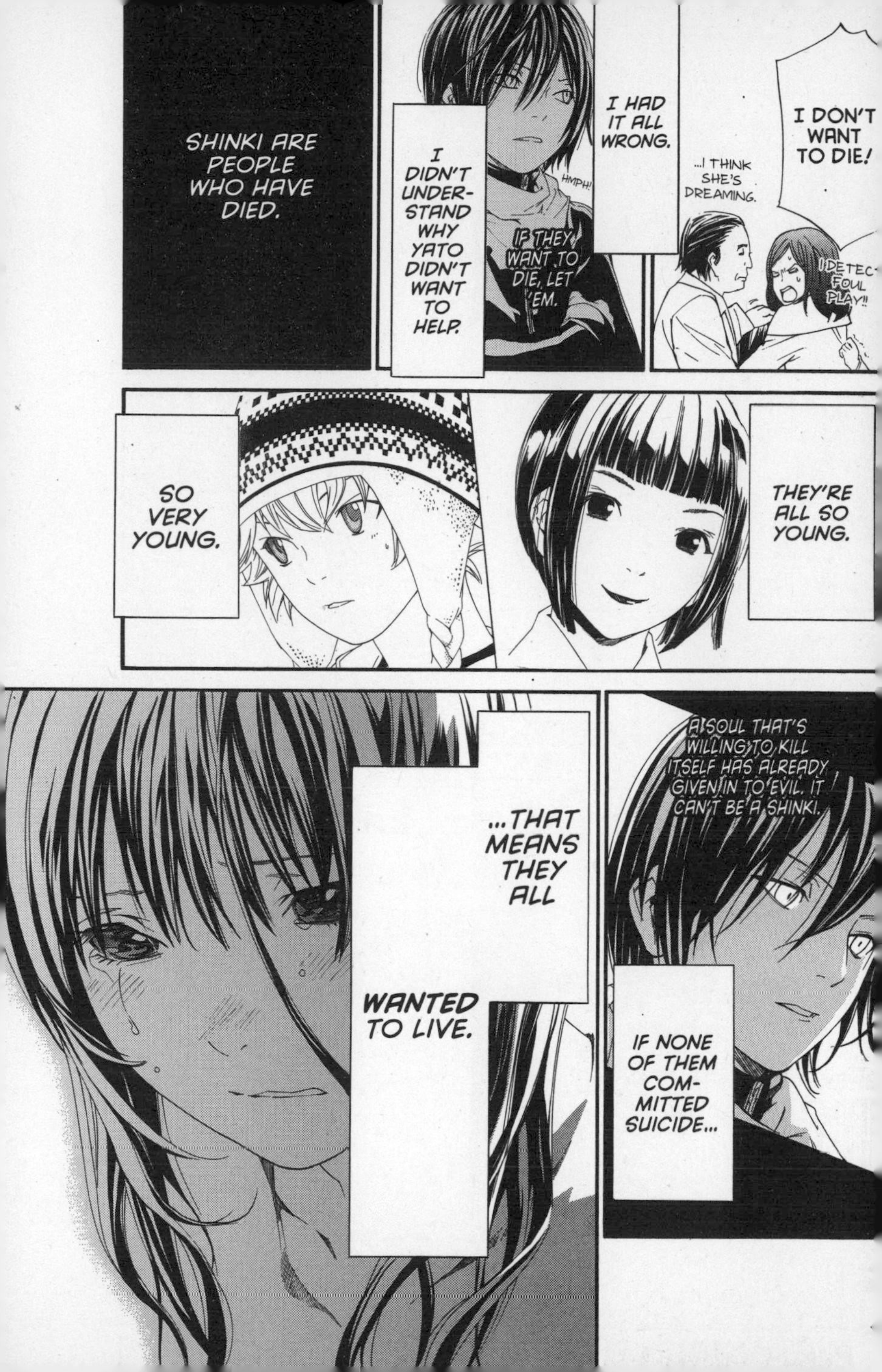
I DON'T WANT TO DIE!
...I THINK SHE'S DREAMING.
I DETECT FOUL PLAY!!
I HAD IT ALL WRONG.
HMPH!
IF THEY WANT TO DIE, LET 'EM.
I DIDN'T UNDERSTAND WHY YATO DIDN'T WANT TO HELP.
SHINKI ARE PEOPLE WHO HAVE DIED.
THEY'RE ALL SO YOUNG.
SO VERY YOUNG.
A SOUL THAT'S WILLING TO KILL ITSELF HAS ALREADY GIVEN IN TO EVIL. IT CAN'T BE A SHINKI.
IF NONE OF THEM COMMITTED SUICIDE...
...THAT MEANS THEY ALL
WANTED TO LIVE.

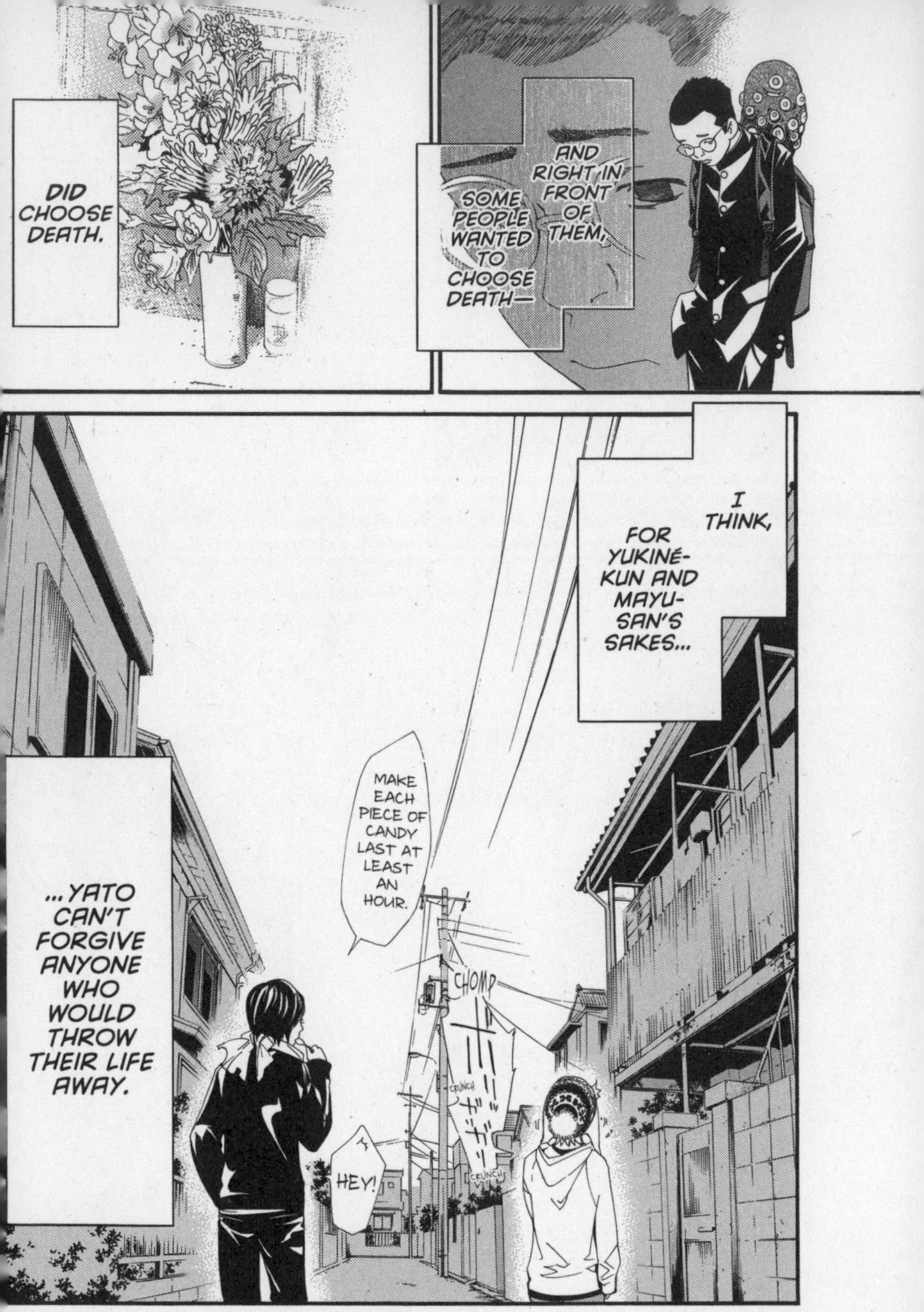
SOME PEOPLE WANTED TO CHOOSE DEATH—
AND RIGHT IN FRONT OF THEM,
DID CHOOSE DEATH.
I THINK, FOR YUKINÉ-KUN AND MAYU-SAN'S SAKES...
MAKE EACH PIECE OF CANDY LAST AT LEAST AN HOUR.
CHOMP
CRUNCH
CRUNCH
HEY!
...YATO CAN'T FORGIVE ANYONE WHO WOULD THROW THEIR LIFE AWAY.

CHAPTER 4 / END

野

兒

神

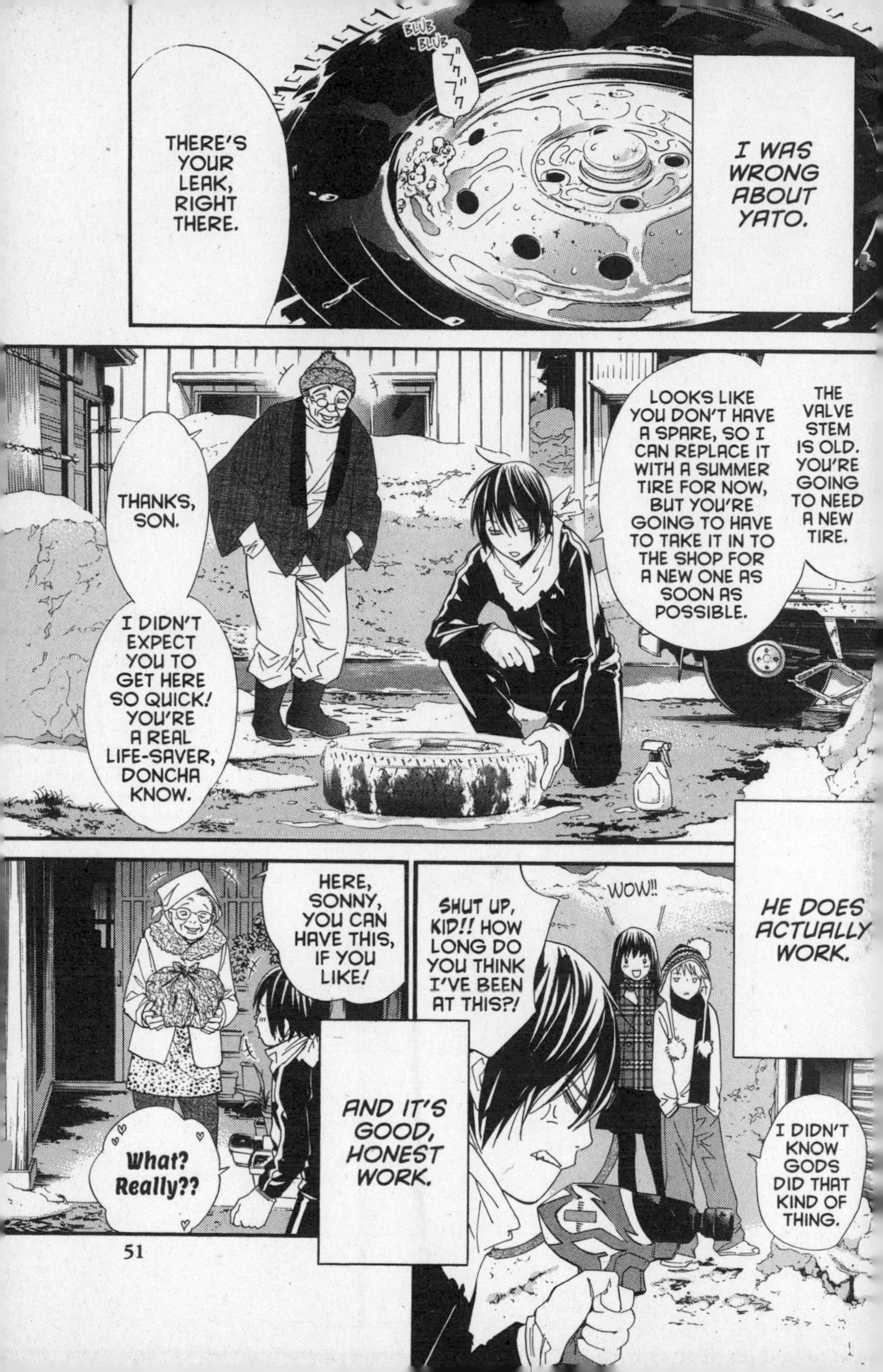
I WAS WRONG ABOUT YATO.
BLUB BLUB
ブクブク
THERE'S YOUR LEAK, RIGHT THERE.
THE VALVE STEM IS OLD. YOU'RE GOING TO NEED A NEW TIRE.
LOOKS LIKE YOU DON'T HAVE A SPARE, SO I CAN REPLACE IT WITH A SUMMER TIRE FOR NOW, BUT YOU'RE GOING TO HAVE TO TAKE IT IN TO THE SHOP FOR A NEW ONE AS SOON AS POSSIBLE.
THANKS, SON.
I DIDN'T EXPECT YOU TO GET HERE SO QUICK! YOU'RE A REAL LIFE-SAVER, DONCHA KNOW.
HE DOES ACTUALLY WORK.
WOW!!
I DIDN'T KNOW GODS DID THAT KIND OF THING.
SHUT UP, KID!! HOW LONG DO YOU THINK I'VE BEEN AT THIS?!
AND IT'S GOOD, HONEST WORK.
HERE, SONNY, YOU CAN HAVE THIS, IF YOU LIKE!
What? Really??

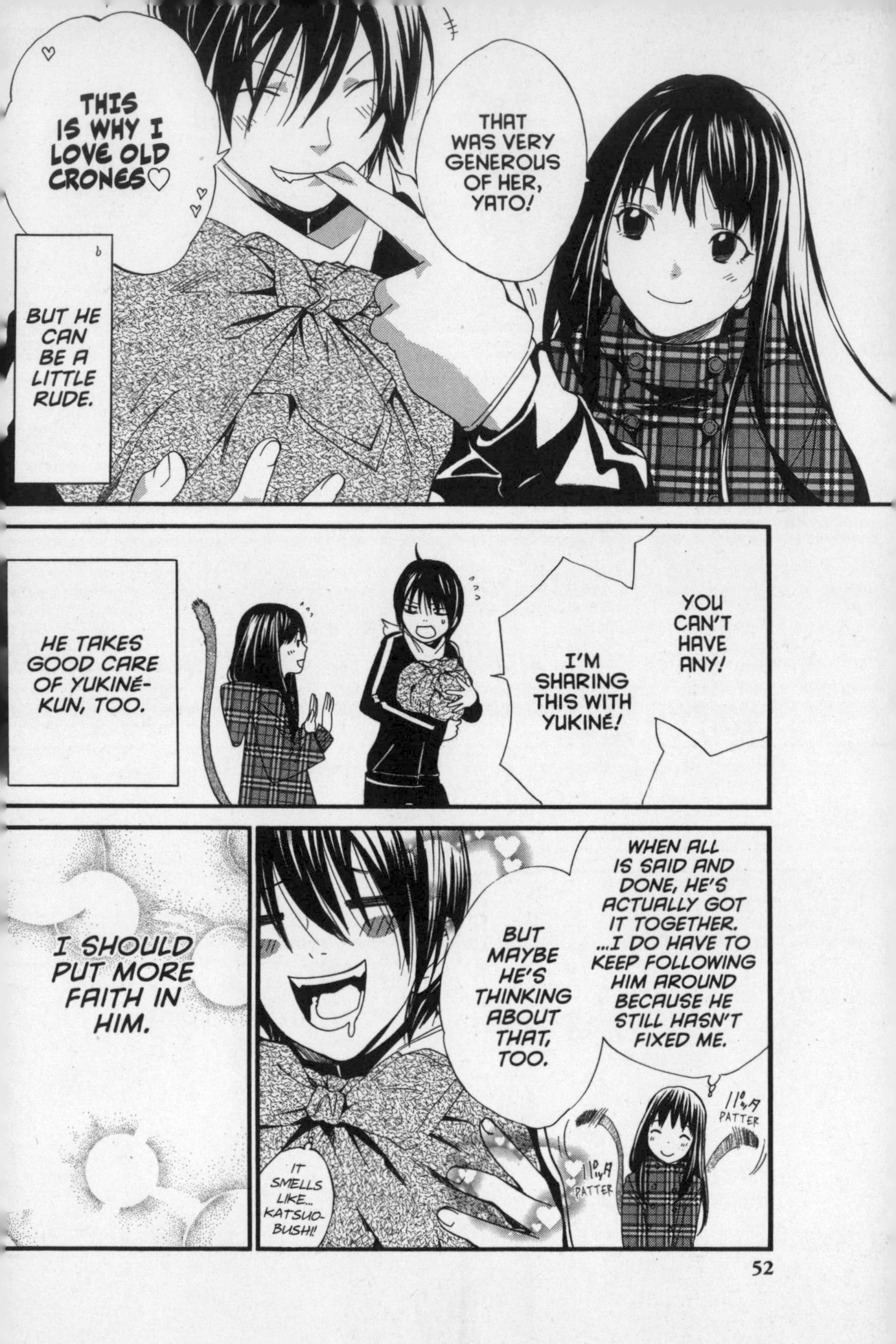
THAT WAS VERY GENEROUS OF HER, YATO!
THIS IS WHY I LOVE OLD CRONES♡
BUT HE CAN BE A LITTLE RUDE.
YOU CAN'T HAVE ANY!
I'M SHARING THIS WITH YUKINÉ!
HE TAKES GOOD CARE OF YUKINÉ-KUN, TOO.
WHEN ALL IS SAID AND DONE, HE'S ACTUALLY GOT IT TOGETHER. ...I DO HAVE TO KEEP FOLLOWING HIM AROUND BECAUSE HE STILL HASN'T FIXED ME.
BUT MAYBE HE'S THINKING ABOUT THAT, TOO.
PATTER
PATTER
IT SMELLS LIKE... KATSUO-BUSHI!
I SHOULD PUT MORE FAITH IN HIM.

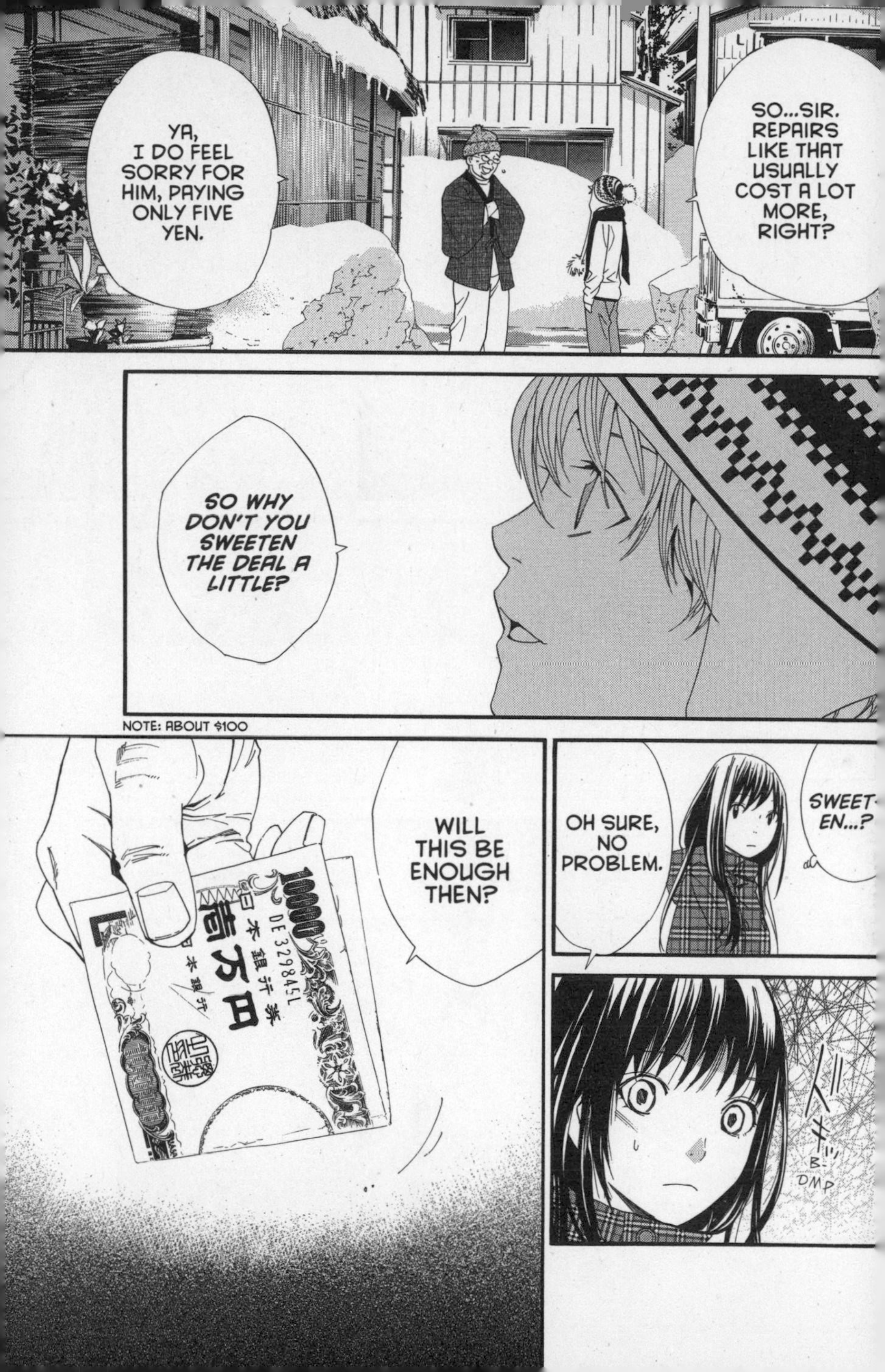
SO...SIR. REPAIRS LIKE THAT USUALLY COST A LOT MORE, RIGHT?
YA, I DO FEEL SORRY FOR HIM, PAYING ONLY FIVE YEN.
SO WHY DON'T YOU SWEETEN THE DEAL A LITTLE?
NOTE: ABOUT $100
SWEET-EN...?
OH SURE, NO PROBLEM.
B-DMP
WILL THIS BE ENOUGH THEN?

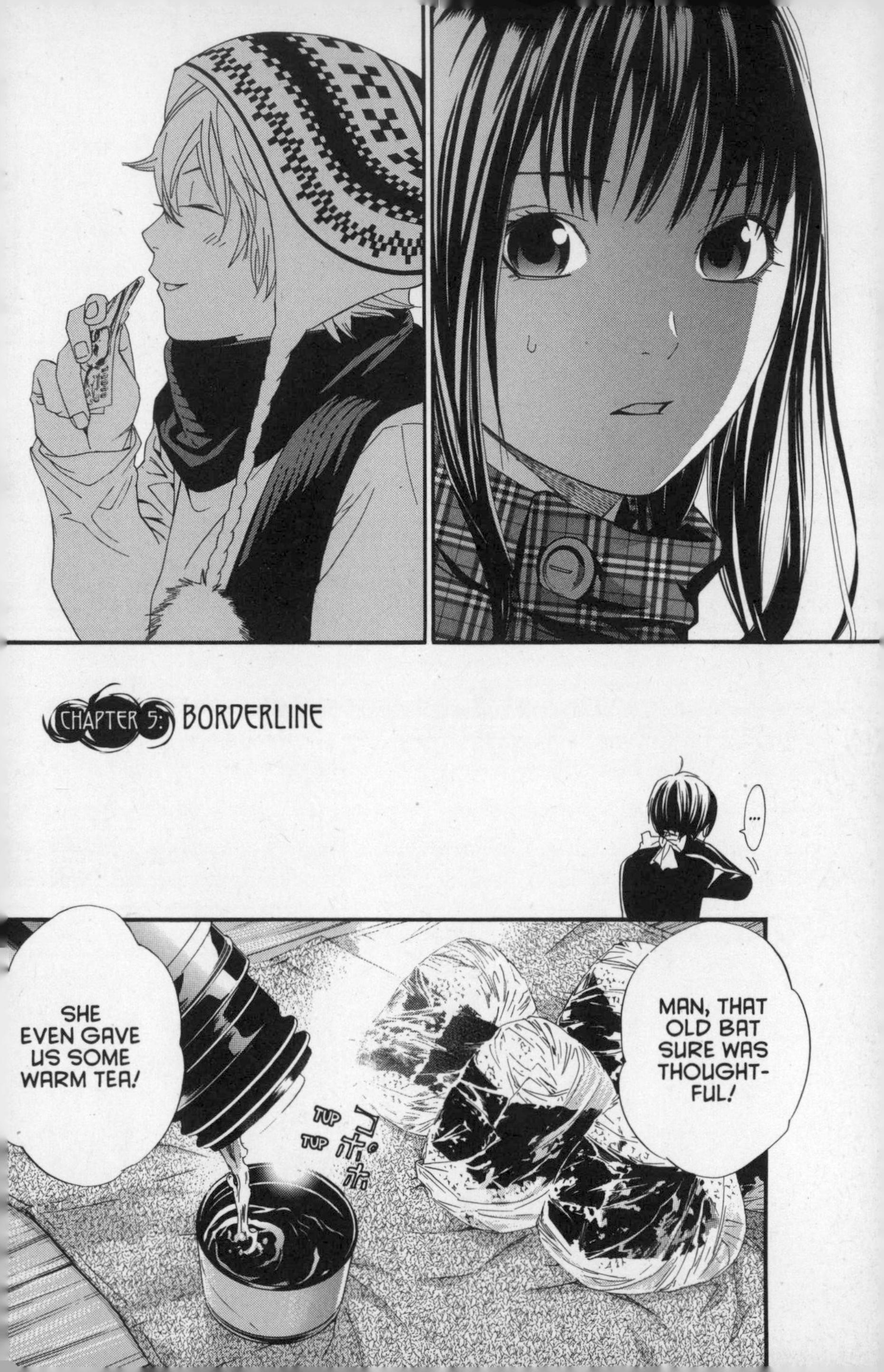
CHAPTER 5: BORDERLINE
...
MAN, THAT OLD BAT SURE WAS THOUGHT-FUL!
TUP TUP
SHE EVEN GAVE US SOME WARM TEA!

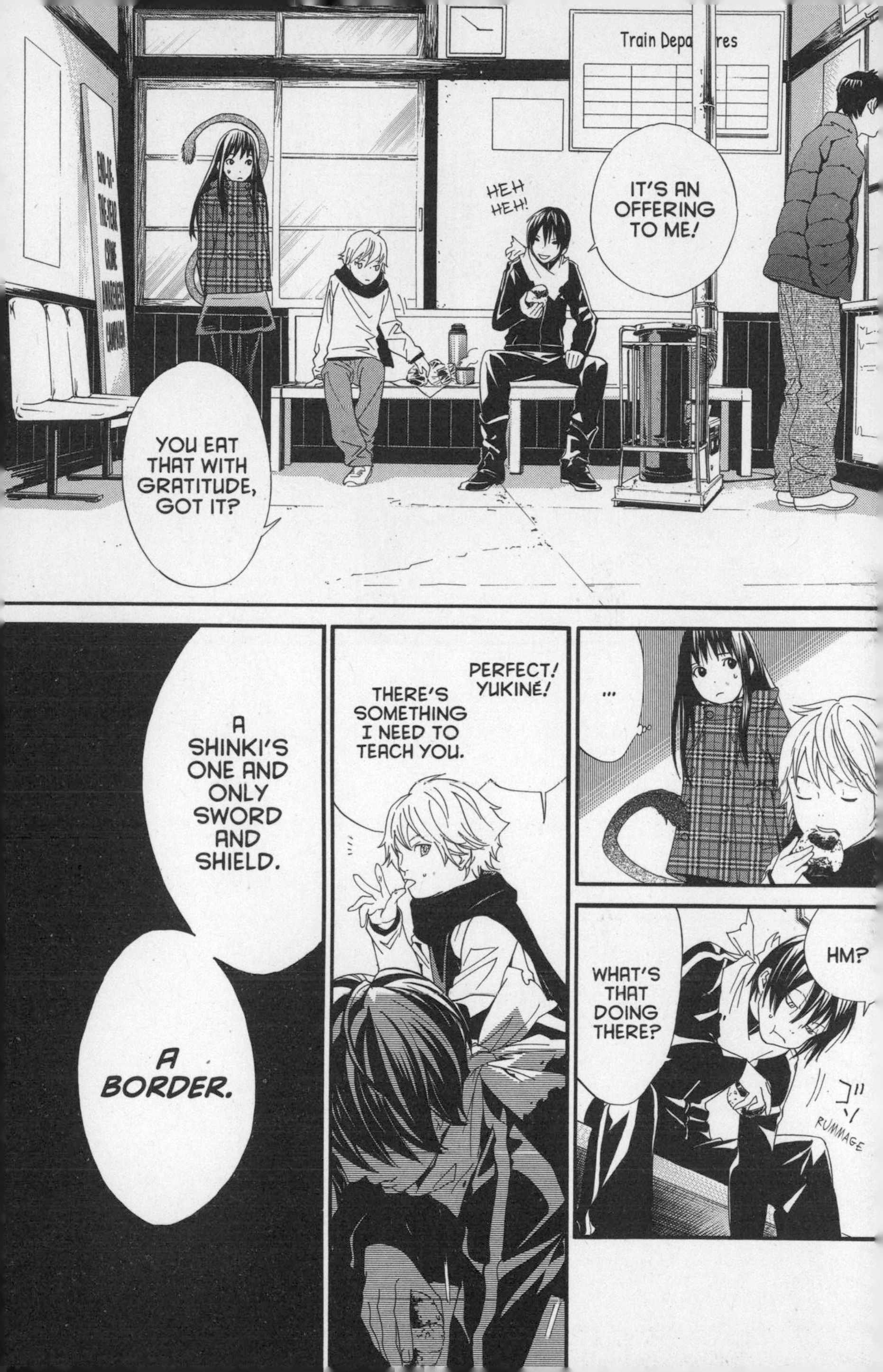
IT'S AN OFFERING TO ME!
HEH HEH!
YOU EAT THAT WITH GRATITUDE, GOT IT?
...
HM?
WHAT'S THAT DOING THERE?
RUMMAGE
PERFECT! YUKINÉ!
THERE'S SOMETHING I NEED TO TEACH YOU.
A SHINKI'S ONE AND ONLY SWORD AND SHIELD.
A BORDER.

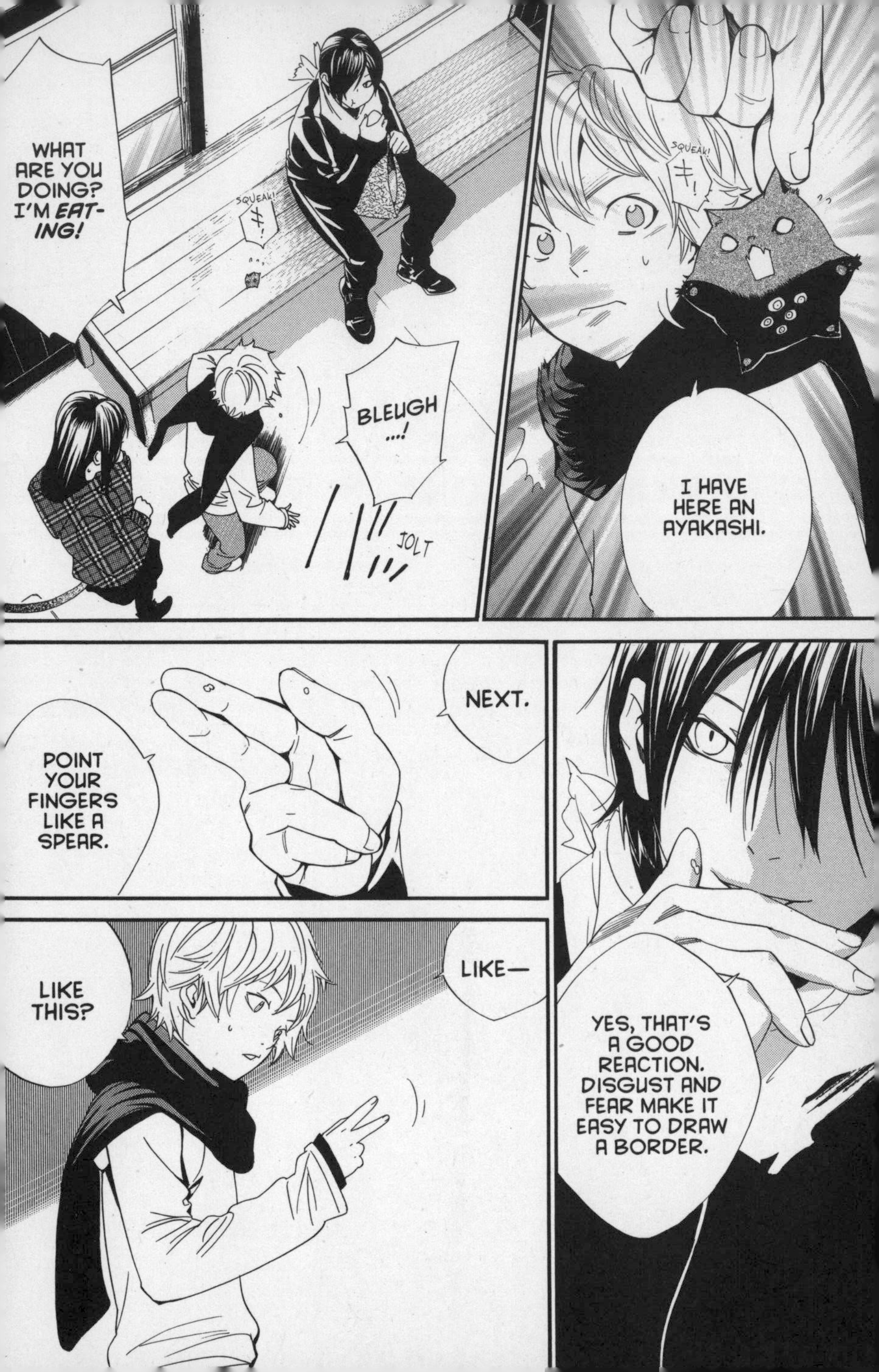
SQUEAK!
I HAVE HERE AN AYAKASHI.
WHAT ARE YOU DOING? I'M *EATING!*
SQUEAK!
BLEUGH ...!
JOLT
YES, THAT'S A GOOD REACTION. DISGUST AND FEAR MAKE IT EASY TO DRAW A BORDER.
NEXT.
POINT YOUR FINGERS LIKE A SPEAR.
LIKE—
LIKE THIS?

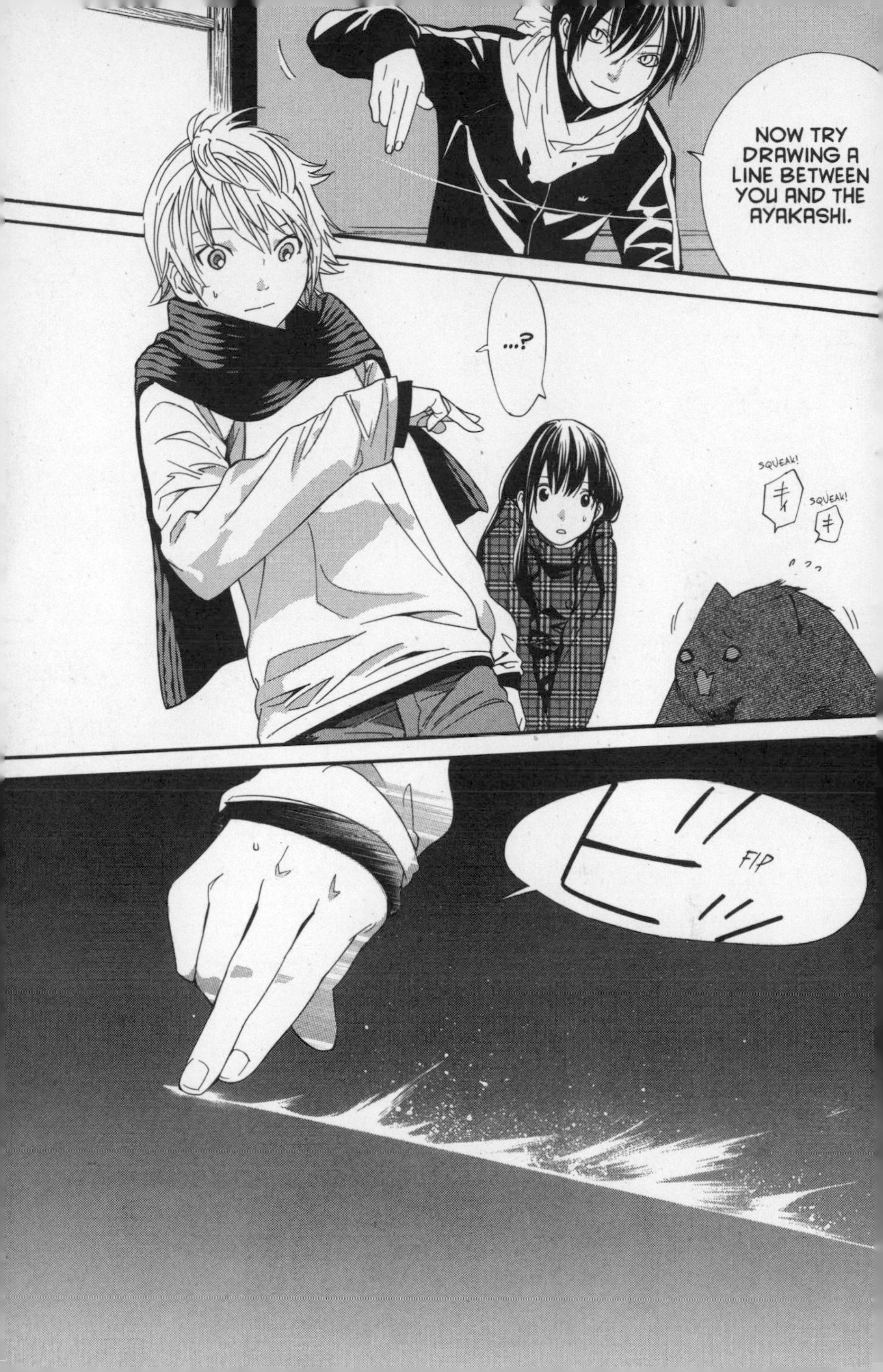
NOW TRY DRAWING A LINE BETWEEN YOU AND THE AYAKASHI.
...?
SQUEAK!
SQUEAK!
FIP

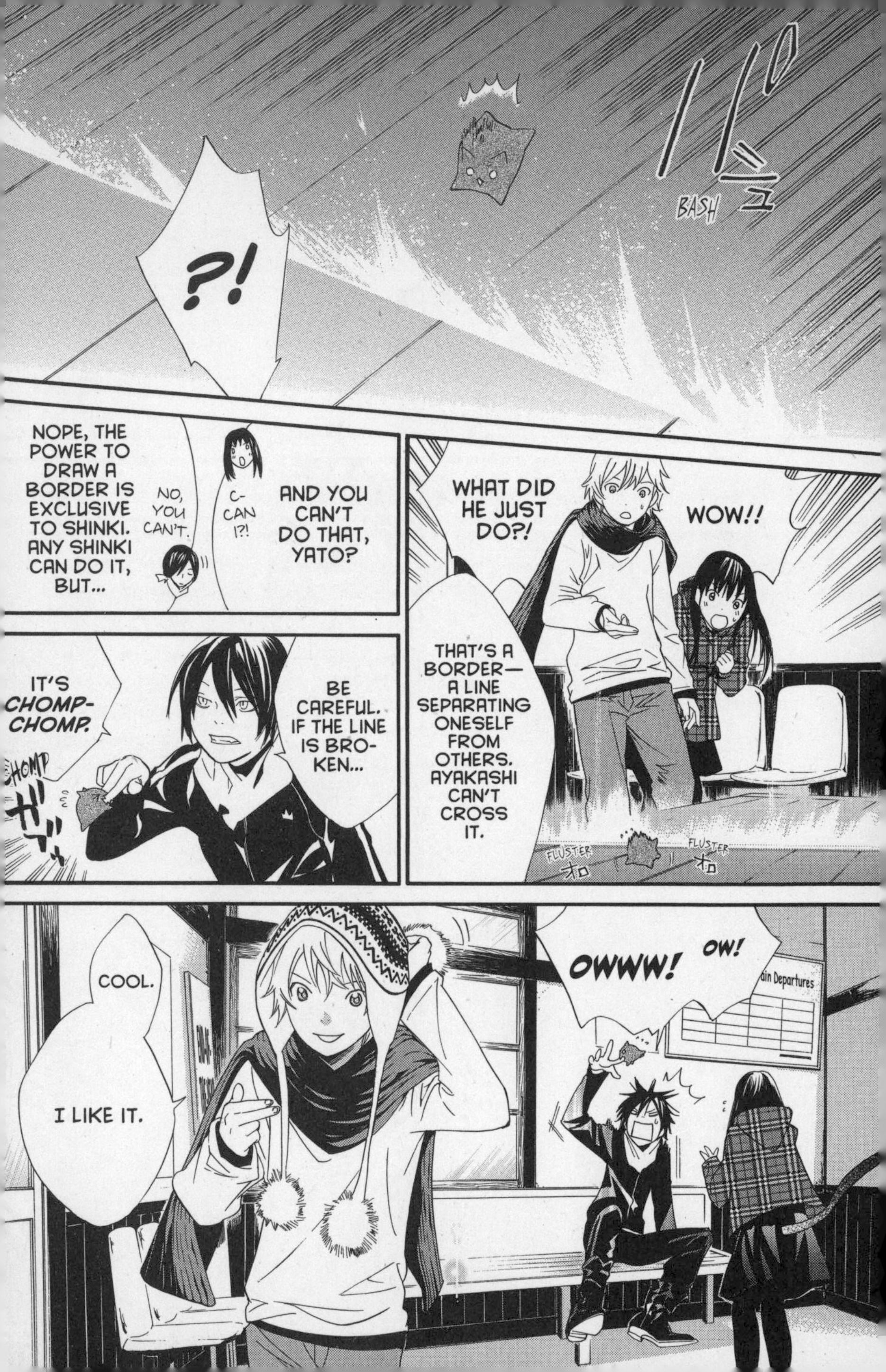
BASH
?!
WOW!!
WHAT DID HE JUST DO?!
THAT'S A BORDER—A LINE SEPARATING ONESELF FROM OTHERS. AYAKASHI CAN'T CROSS IT.
FLUSTER
FLUSTER
AND YOU CAN'T DO THAT, YATO?
C-CAN !?!
NO, YOU CAN'T.
NOPE, THE POWER TO DRAW A BORDER IS EXCLUSIVE TO SHINKI. ANY SHINKI CAN DO IT, BUT...
BE CAREFUL. IF THE LINE IS BRO-KEN...
IT'S *CHOMP-CHOMP.*
CHOMP
OW!
OWWW!
Train Departures
COOL.
I LIKE IT.

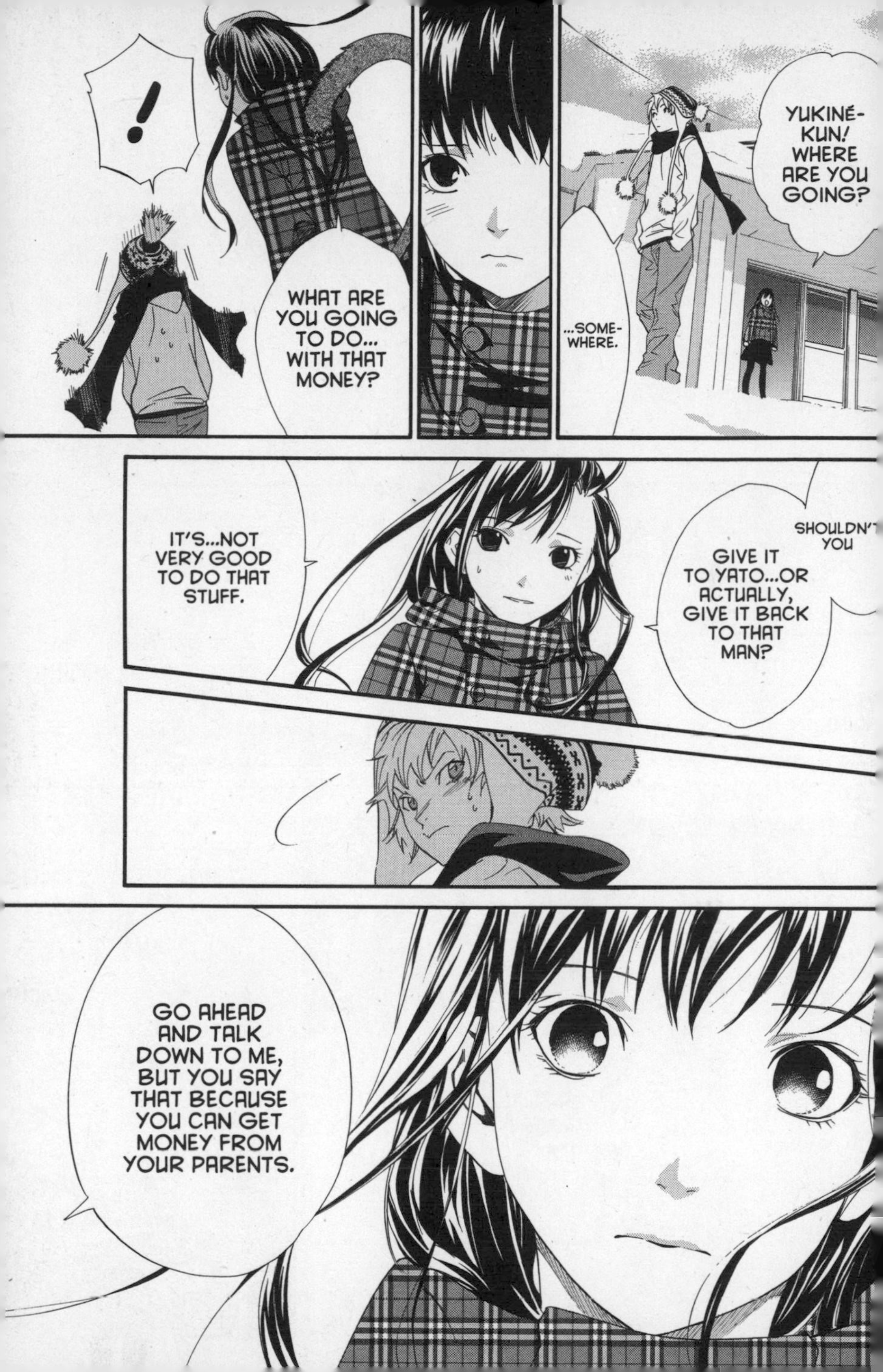
YUKINÉ-KUN! WHERE ARE YOU GOING?
...SOME-WHERE.
WHAT ARE YOU GOING TO DO... WITH THAT MONEY?
!
SHOULDN'T YOU GIVE IT TO YATO...OR ACTUALLY, GIVE IT BACK TO THAT MAN?
IT'S...NOT VERY GOOD TO DO THAT STUFF.
GO AHEAD AND TALK DOWN TO ME, BUT YOU SAY THAT BECAUSE YOU CAN GET MONEY FROM YOUR PARENTS.

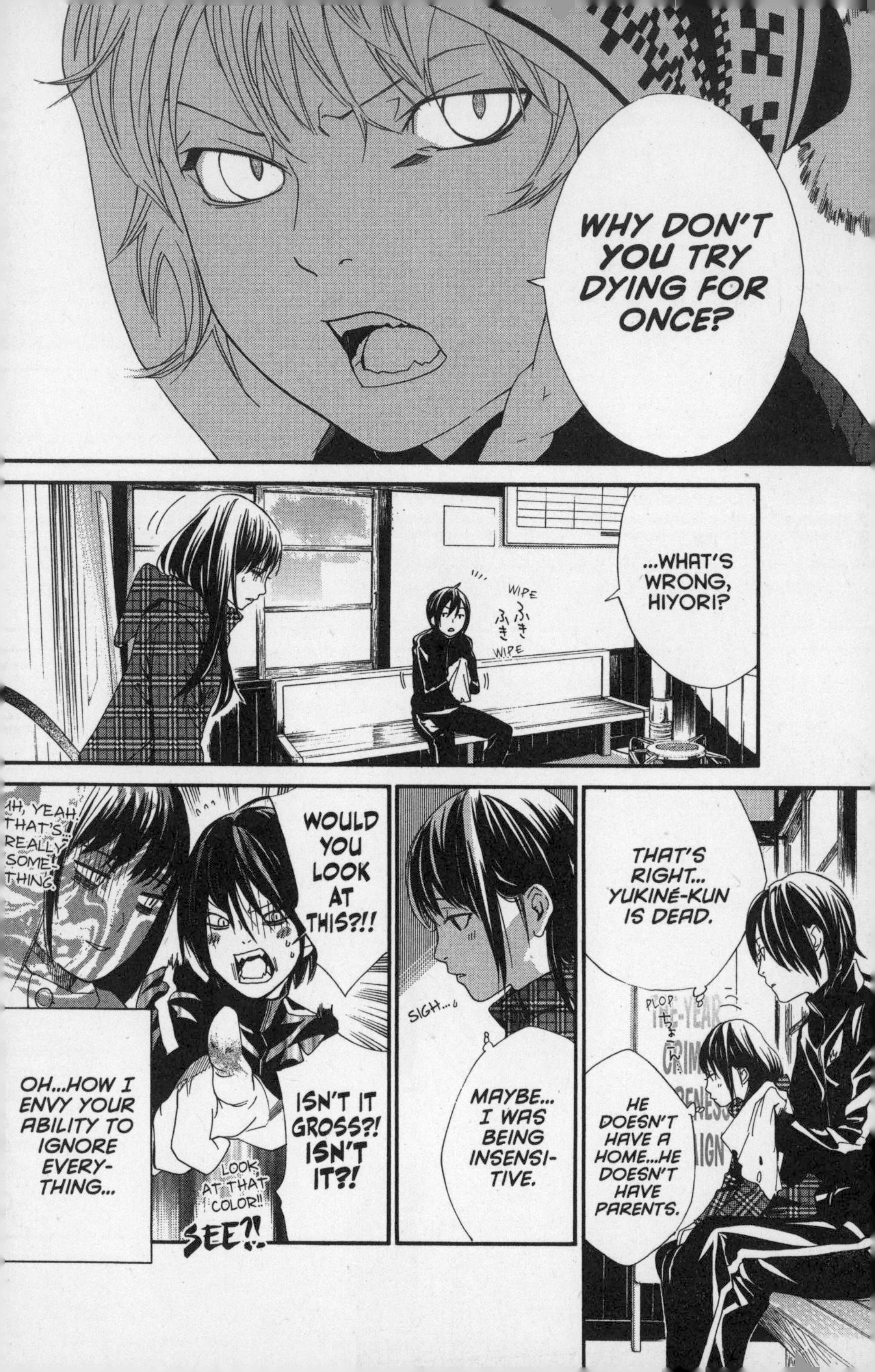
WHY DON'T YOU TRY DYING FOR ONCE?
...WHAT'S WRONG, HIYORI?
WIPE
ふき ふき
WIPE
THAT'S RIGHT... YUKINÉ-KUN IS DEAD.
PLOP
ちょこん
HE DOESN'T HAVE A HOME...HE DOESN'T HAVE PARENTS.
SIGH...
MAYBE... I WAS BEING INSENSI-TIVE.
WOULD YOU LOOK AT THIS?!!
ISN'T IT GROSS?! ISN'T IT?!
LOOK AT THAT COLOR!!
SEE?!
H, YEAH. THAT'S... REALLY SOME-THING.
OH...HOW I ENVY YOUR ABILITY TO IGNORE EVERY-THING...

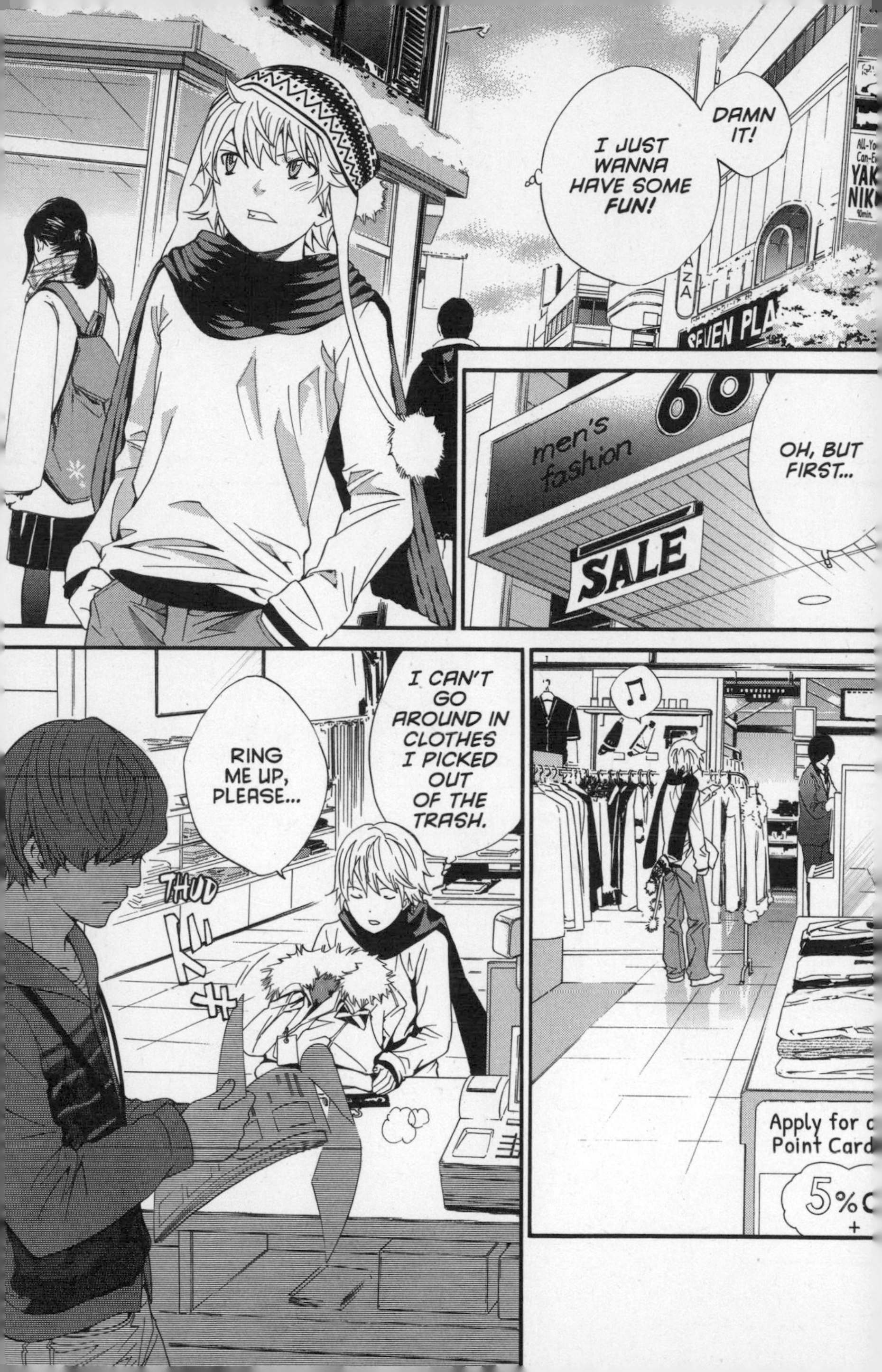
DAMN IT!
I JUST WANNA HAVE SOME FUN!
men's fashion
SALE
OH, BUT FIRST...
♪
Apply for a Point Card
5%
I CAN'T GO AROUND IN CLOTHES I PICKED OUT OF THE TRASH.
RING ME UP, PLEASE...
THUD

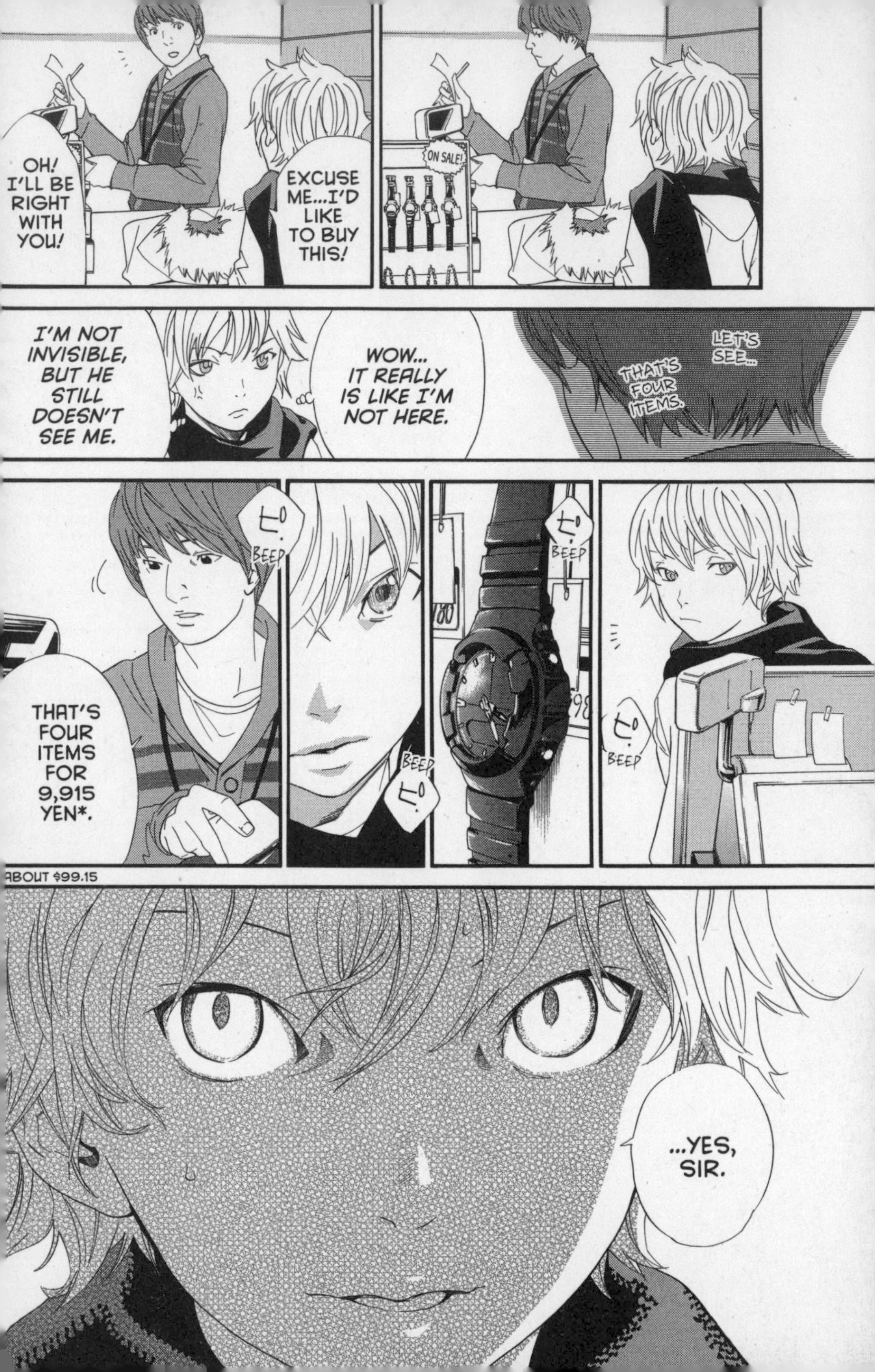
ON SALE!
EXCUSE ME...I'D LIKE TO BUY THIS!
OH! I'LL BE RIGHT WITH YOU!
LET'S SEE...
THAT'S FOUR ITEMS.
WOW... IT REALLY IS LIKE I'M NOT HERE.
I'M NOT INVISIBLE, BUT HE STILL DOESN'T SEE ME.
ピ
BEEP
ピ
BEEP
ピ
BEEP
ピ
BEEP
THAT'S FOUR ITEMS FOR 9,915 YEN*.
ABOUT $99.15
...YES, SIR.

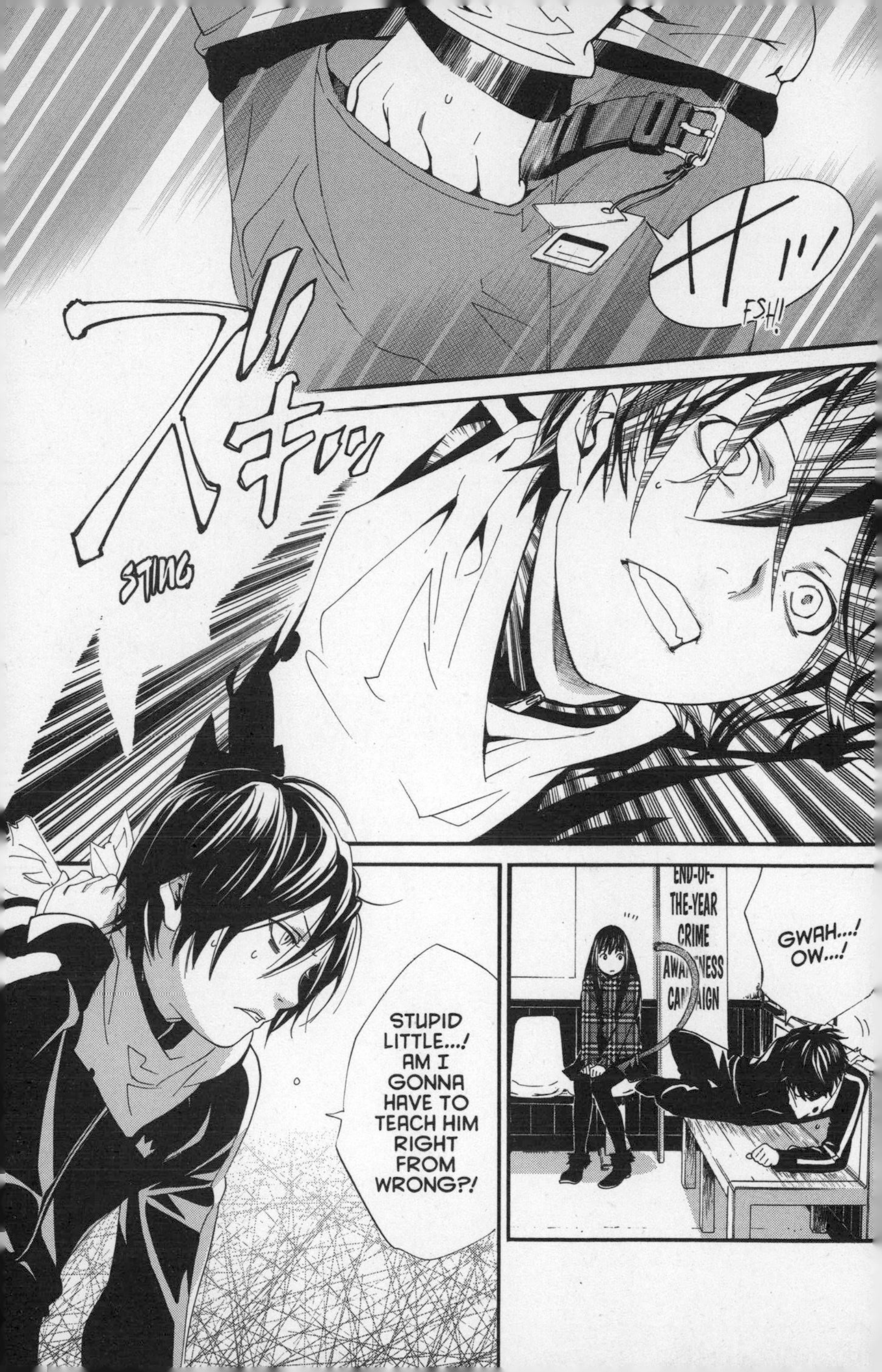
FSH!
STING
GWAH...! OW...!
END-OF-THE-YEAR CRIME AWARENESS CAMPAIGN
STUPID LITTLE...! AM I GONNA HAVE TO TEACH HIM RIGHT FROM WRONG?!

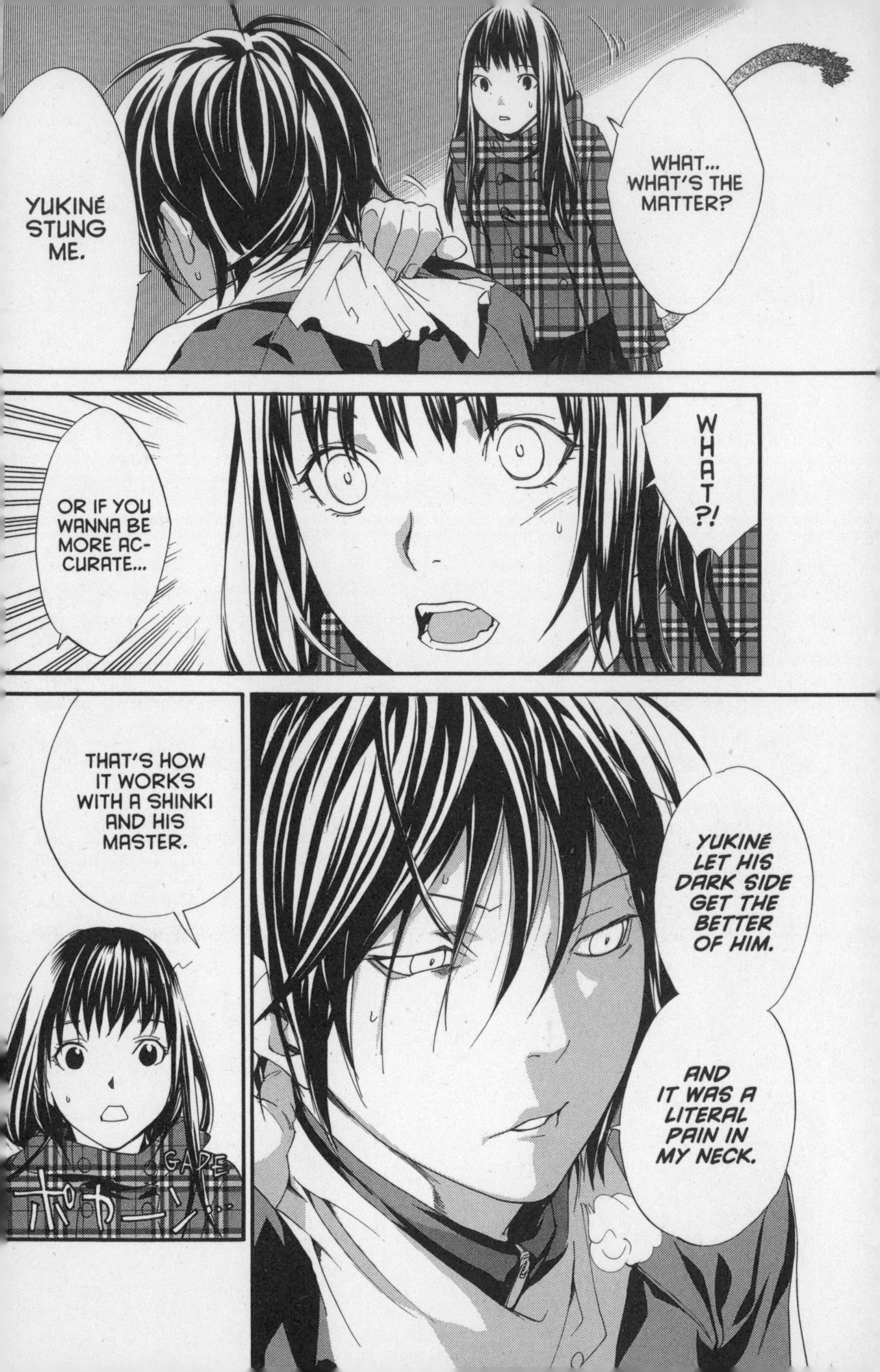
WHAT... WHAT'S THE MATTER?
YUKINÉ STUNG ME.
WHAT?!
OR IF YOU WANNA BE MORE AC-CURATE...
YUKINÉ LET HIS DARK SIDE GET THE BETTER OF HIM.
AND IT WAS A LITERAL PAIN IN MY NECK.
THAT'S HOW IT WORKS WITH A SHINKI AND HIS MASTER.
GAPE

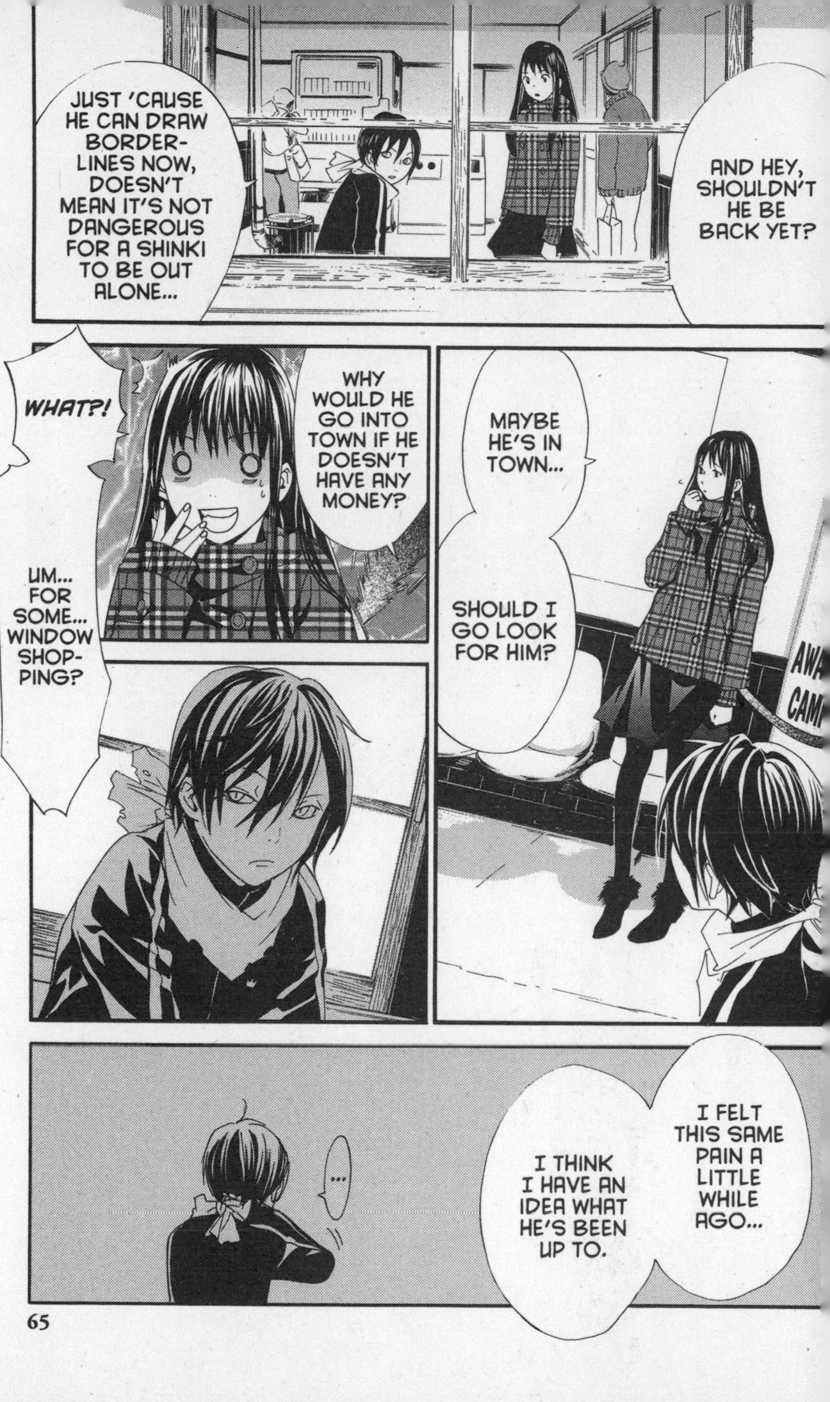
AND HEY, SHOULDN'T HE BE BACK YET?
JUST 'CAUSE HE CAN DRAW BORDER-LINES NOW, DOESN'T MEAN IT'S NOT DANGEROUS FOR A SHINKI TO BE OUT ALONE...
MAYBE HE'S IN TOWN...
SHOULD I GO LOOK FOR HIM?
WHY WOULD HE GO INTO TOWN IF HE DOESN'T HAVE ANY MONEY?
WHAT?!
UM... FOR SOME... WINDOW SHOP-PING?
I FELT THIS SAME PAIN A LITTLE WHILE AGO...
I THINK I HAVE AN IDEA WHAT HE'S BEEN UP TO.
...

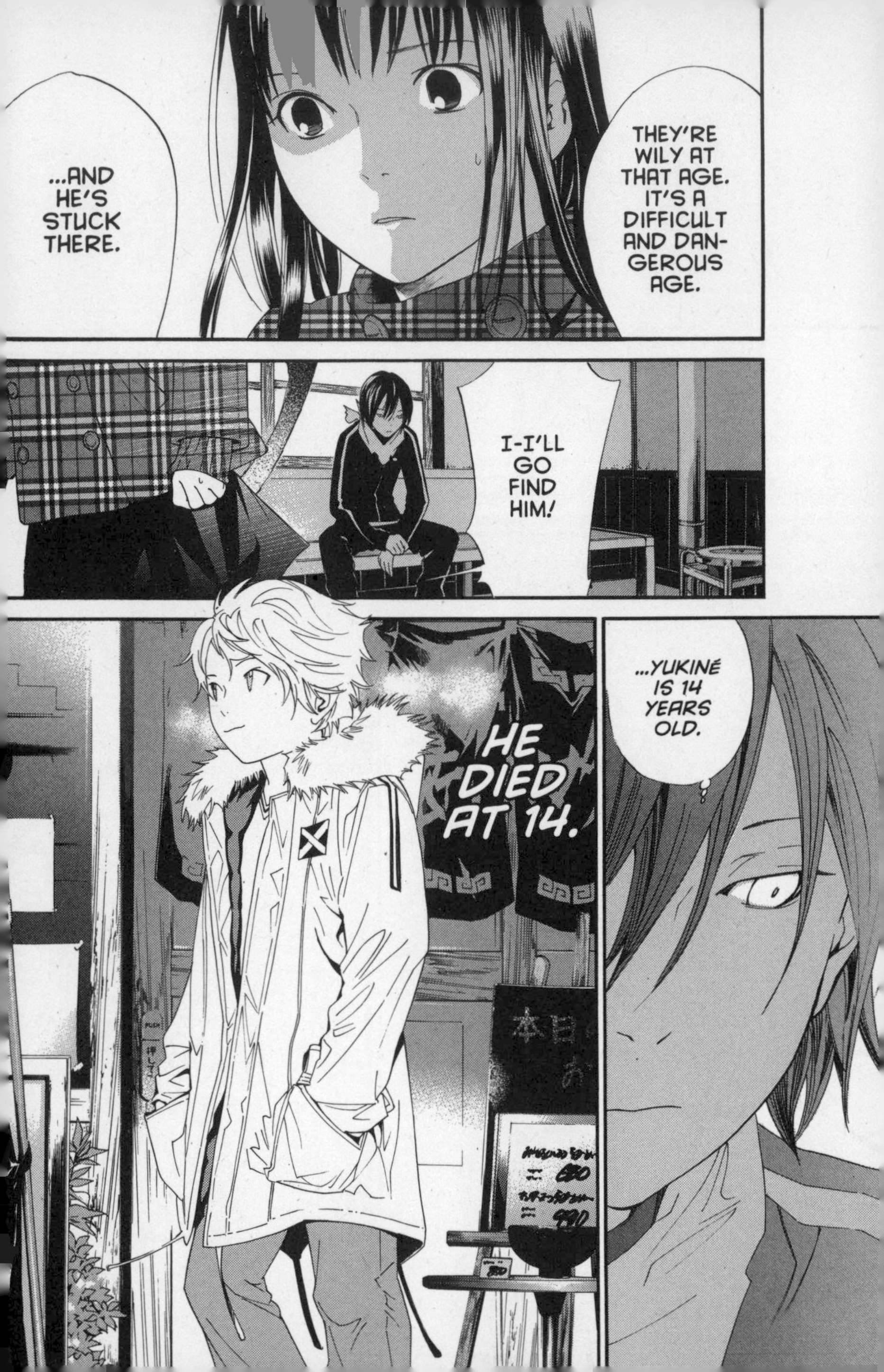
THEY'RE WILY AT THAT AGE. IT'S A DIFFICULT AND DANGEROUS AGE.
...AND HE'S STUCK THERE.
I-I'LL GO FIND HIM!
...YUKINE IS 14 YEARS OLD.
HE DIED AT 14.

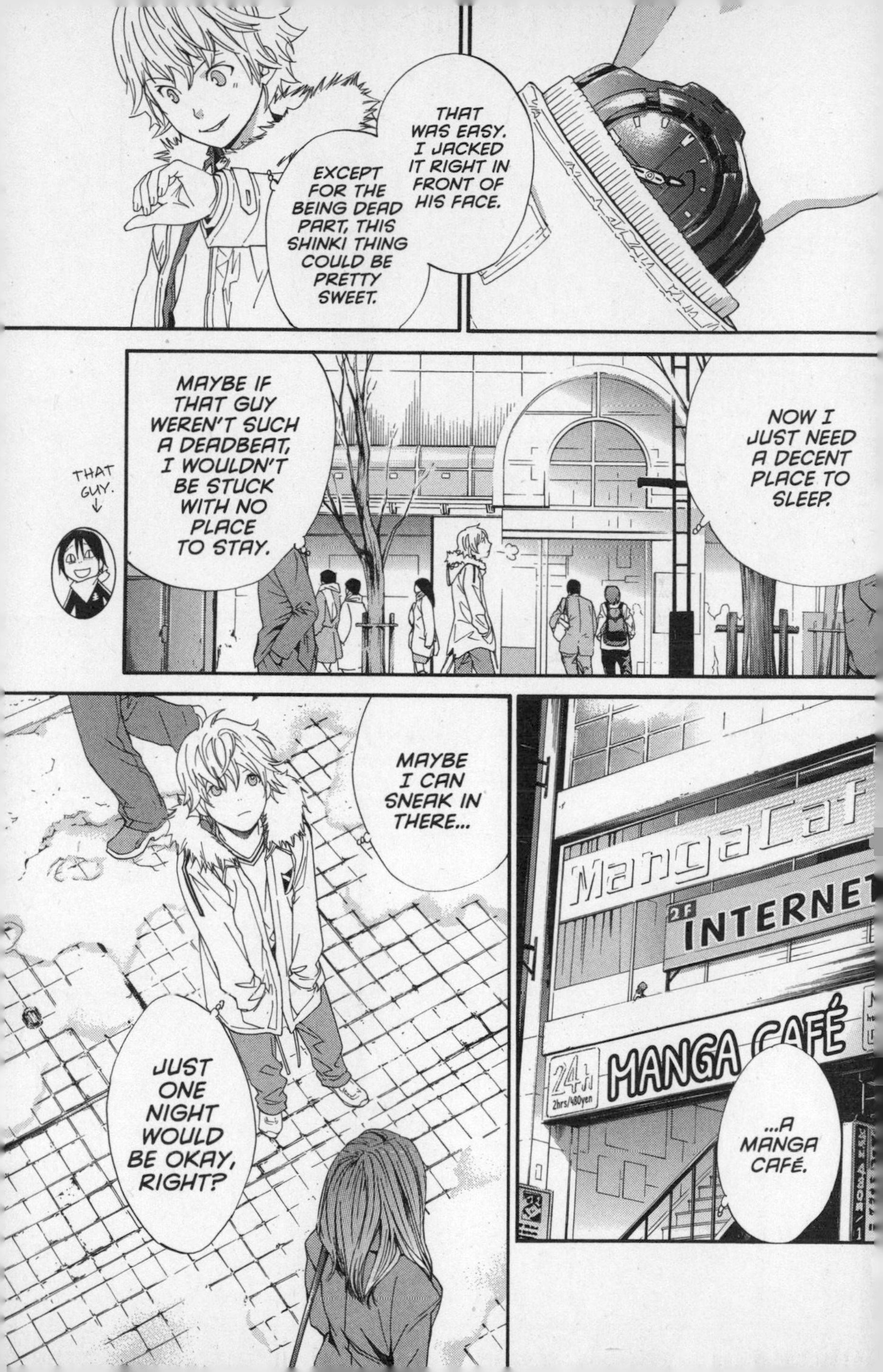
THAT WAS EASY. I JACKED IT RIGHT IN FRONT OF HIS FACE.
EXCEPT FOR THE BEING DEAD PART, THIS SHINKI THING COULD BE PRETTY SWEET.
NOW I JUST NEED A DECENT PLACE TO SLEEP.
MAYBE IF THAT GUY WEREN'T SUCH A DEADBEAT, I WOULDN'T BE STUCK WITH NO PLACE TO STAY.
THAT GUY.
MangaCaf
2F INTERNET
24
2hrs/480yen
MANGA CAFÉ
...A MANGA CAFÉ.
MAYBE I CAN SNEAK IN THERE...
JUST ONE NIGHT WOULD BE OKAY, RIGHT?

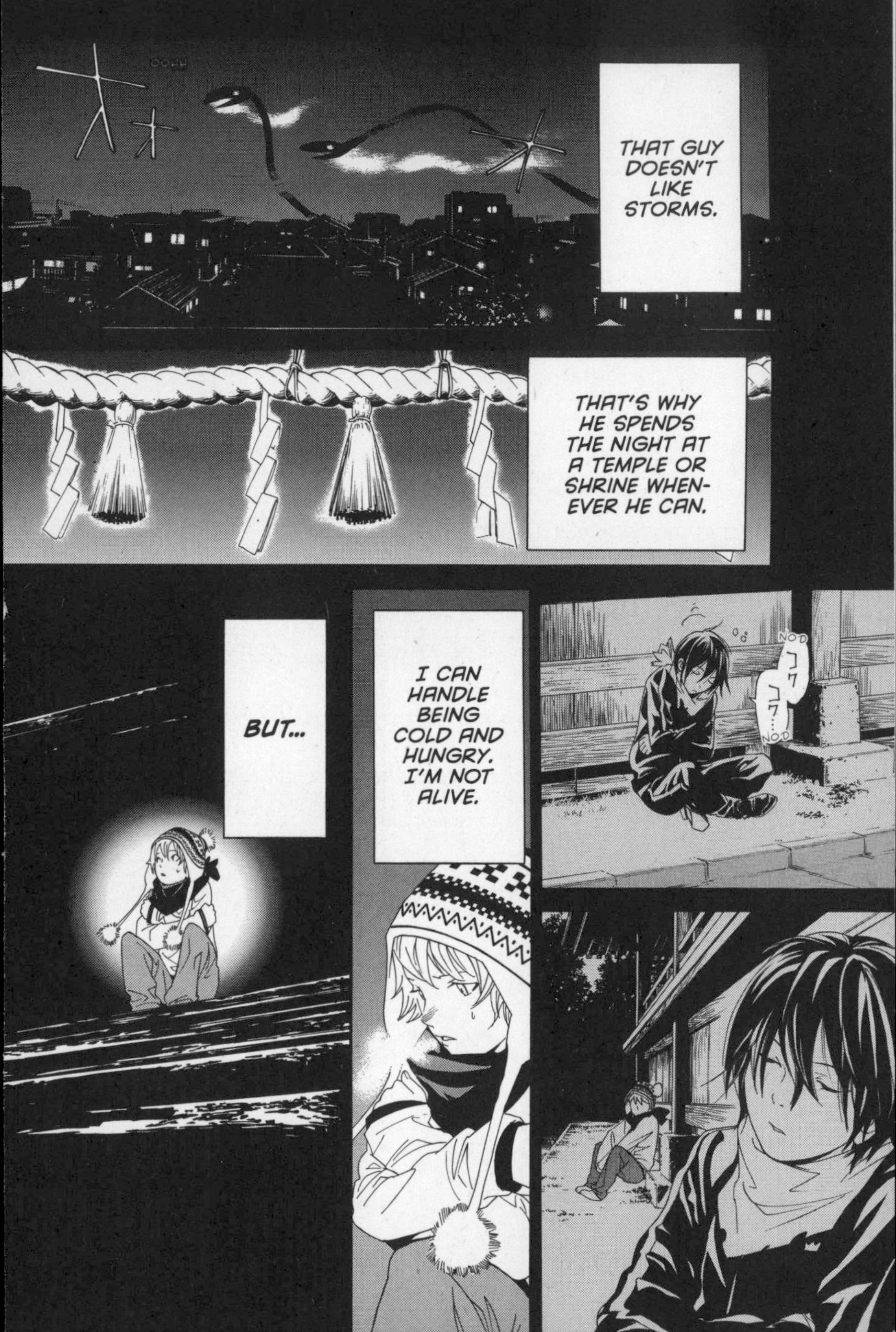
THAT GUY DOESN'T LIKE STORMS.
THAT'S WHY HE SPENDS THE NIGHT AT A TEMPLE OR SHRINE WHEN-EVER HE CAN.
NOD
NOD
I CAN HANDLE BEING COLD AND HUNGRY. I'M NOT ALIVE.
BUT...

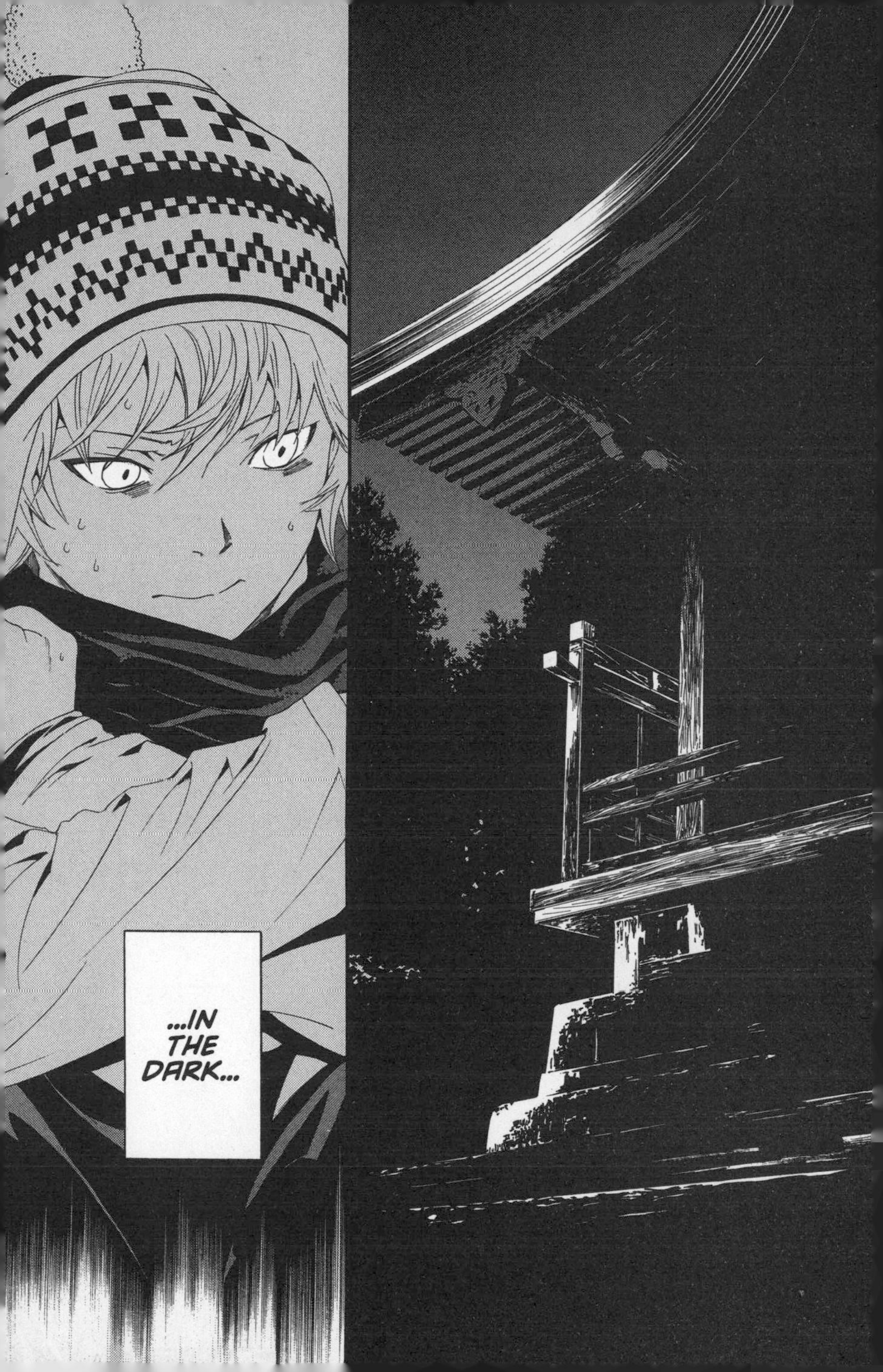
...IN THE DARK...

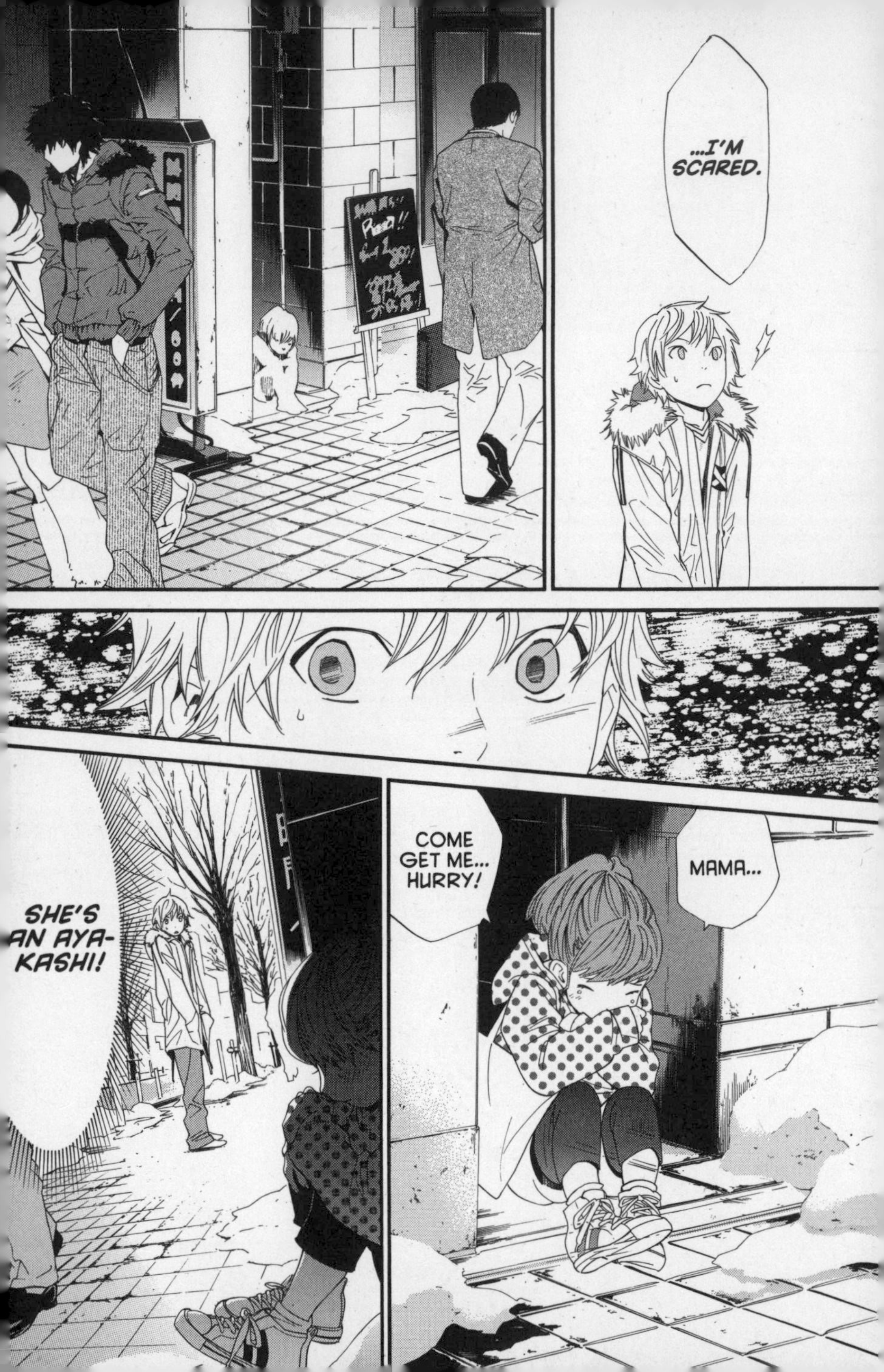
...I'M SCARED.
MAMA...
COME GET ME... HURRY!
SHE'S AN AYA-KASHI!

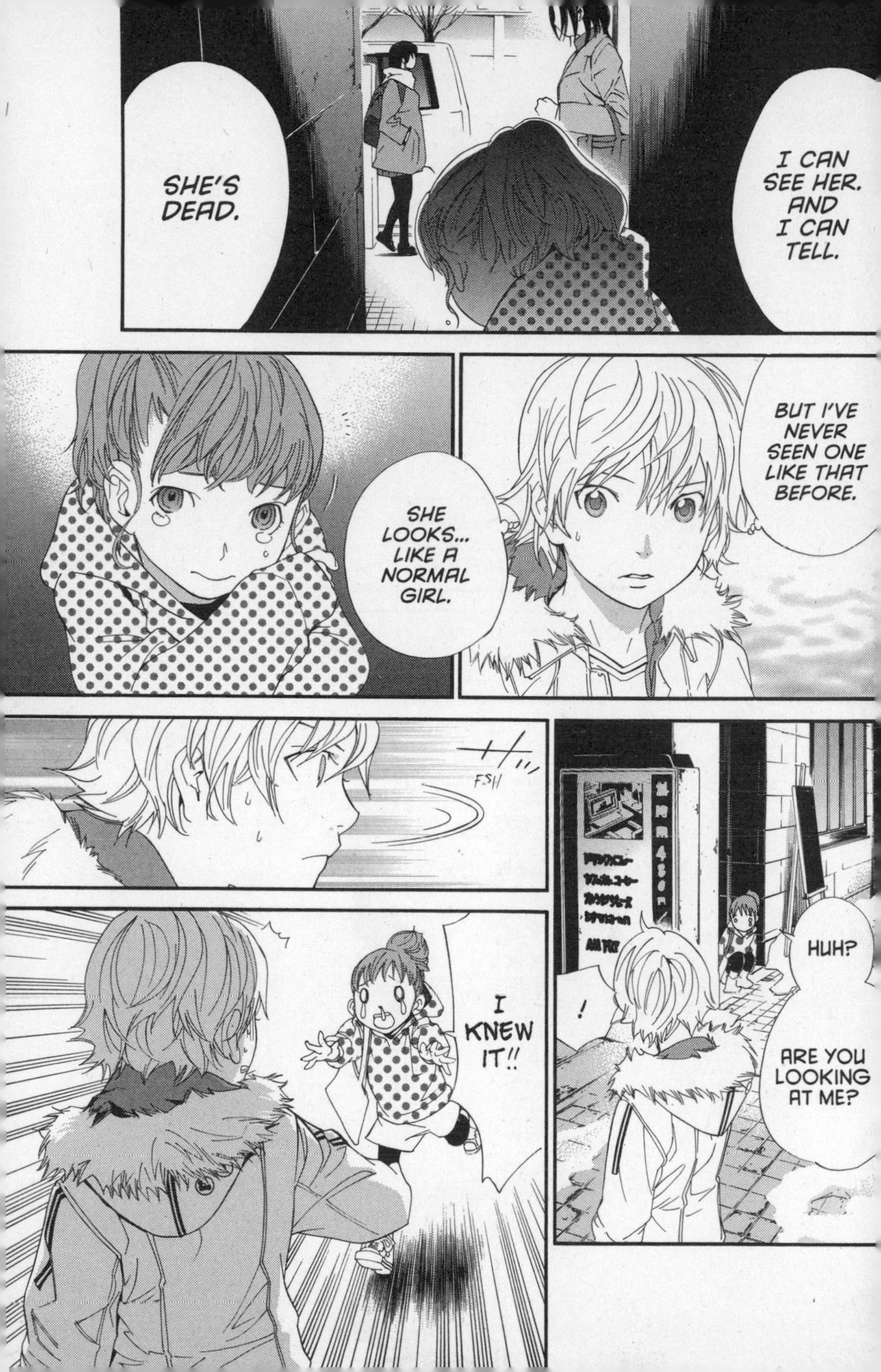
I CAN SEE HER. AND I CAN TELL.
SHE'S DEAD.
BUT I'VE NEVER SEEN ONE LIKE THAT BEFORE.
SHE LOOKS... LIKE A NORMAL GIRL.
HUH?
ARE YOU LOOKING AT ME?
FSH
I KNEW IT!!

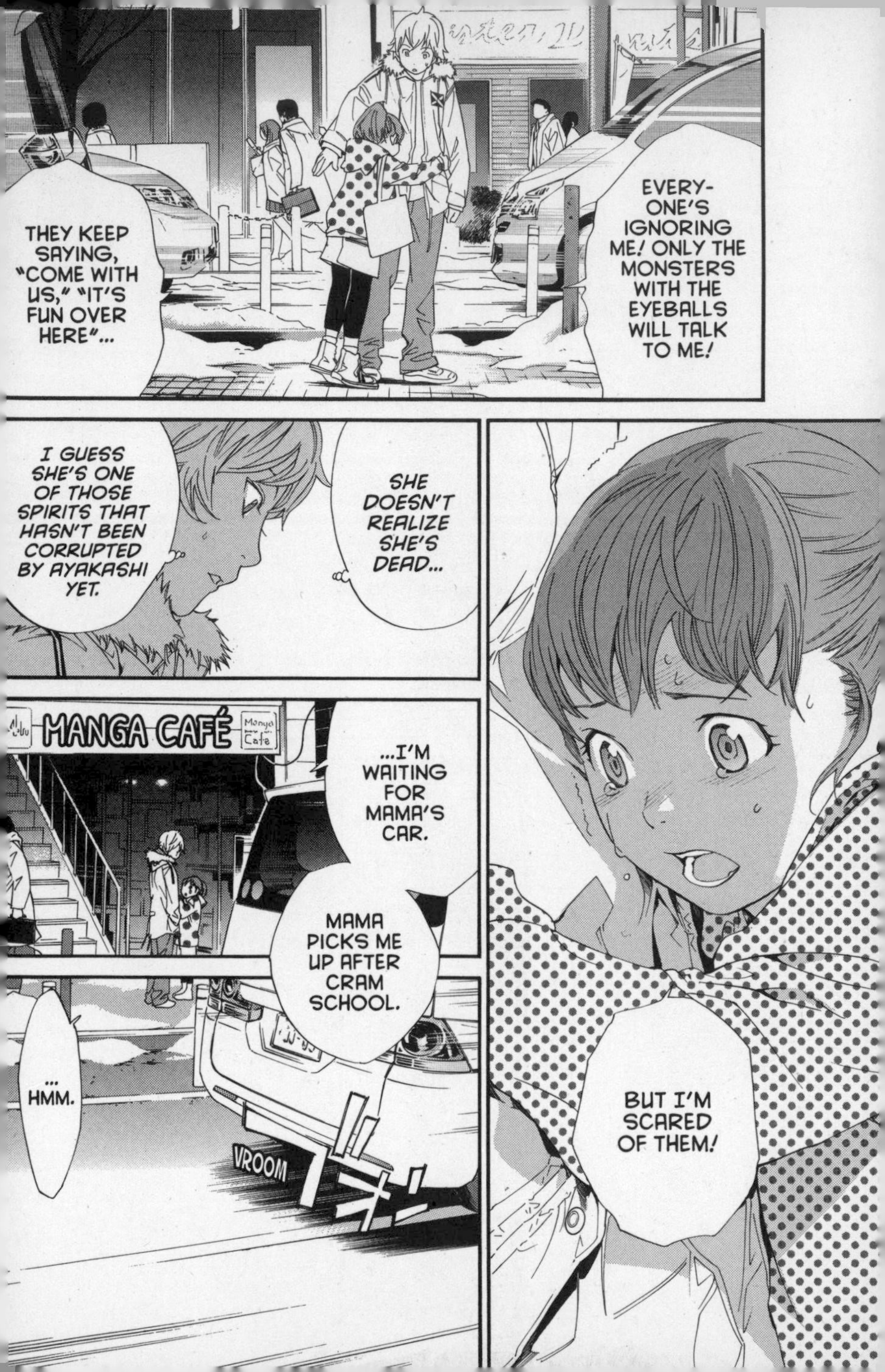
EVERY-ONE'S IGNORING ME! ONLY THE MONSTERS WITH THE EYEBALLS WILL TALK TO ME!
THEY KEEP SAYING, "COME WITH US," "IT'S FUN OVER HERE"...
BUT I'M SCARED OF THEM!
SHE DOESN'T REALIZE SHE'S DEAD...
I GUESS SHE'S ONE OF THOSE SPIRITS THAT HASN'T BEEN CORRUPTED BY AYAKASHI YET.
MANGA CAFÉ
Manga Café
...I'M WAITING FOR MAMA'S CAR.
MAMA PICKS ME UP AFTER CRAM SCHOOL.
VROOM
... HMM.

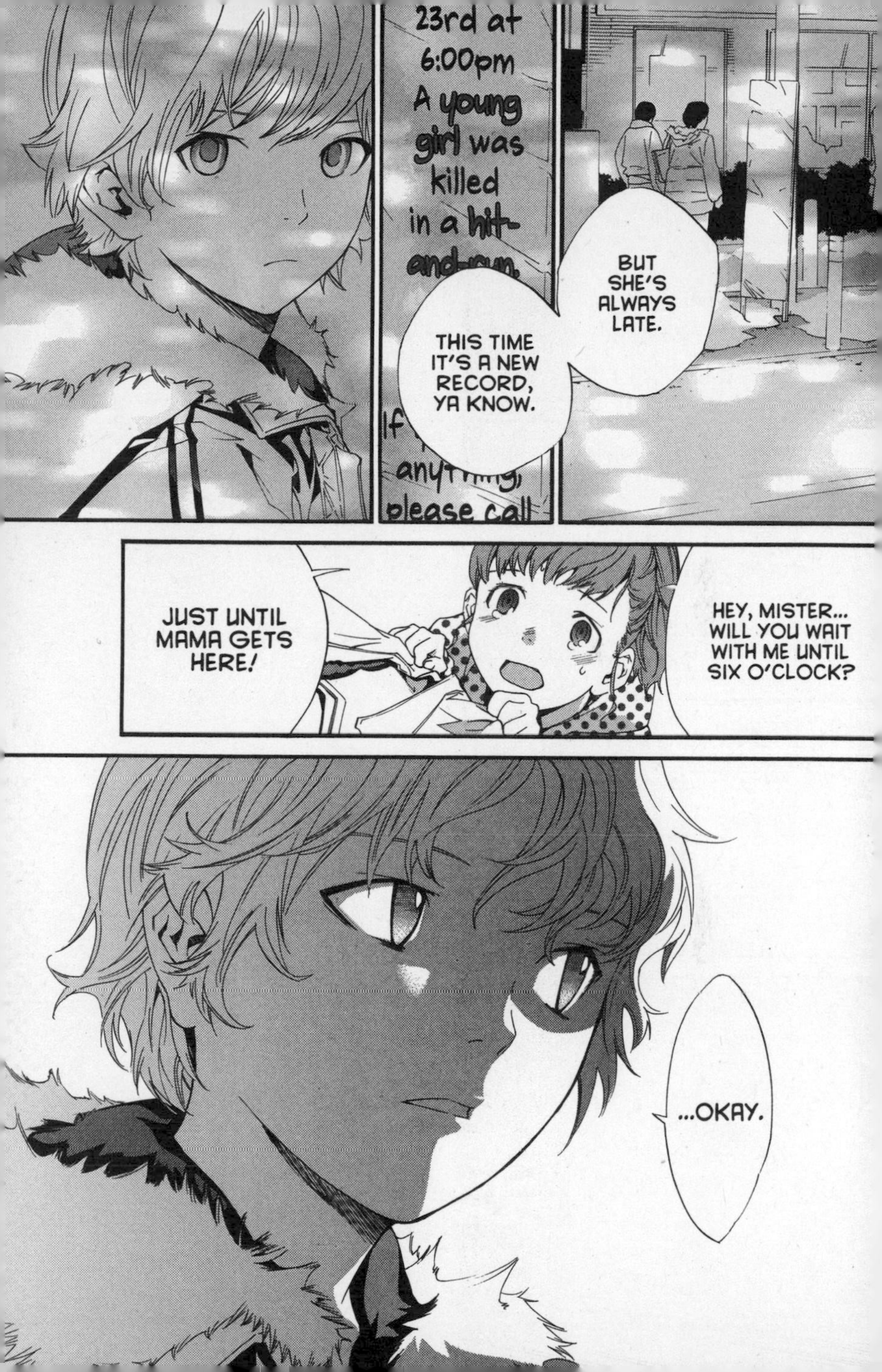
BUT SHE'S ALWAYS LATE.
THIS TIME IT'S A NEW RECORD, YA KNOW.
23rd at 6:00pm A young girl was killed in a hit-and-run.
please call
HEY, MISTER... WILL YOU WAIT WITH ME UNTIL SIX O'CLOCK?
JUST UNTIL MAMA GETS HERE!
...OKAY.

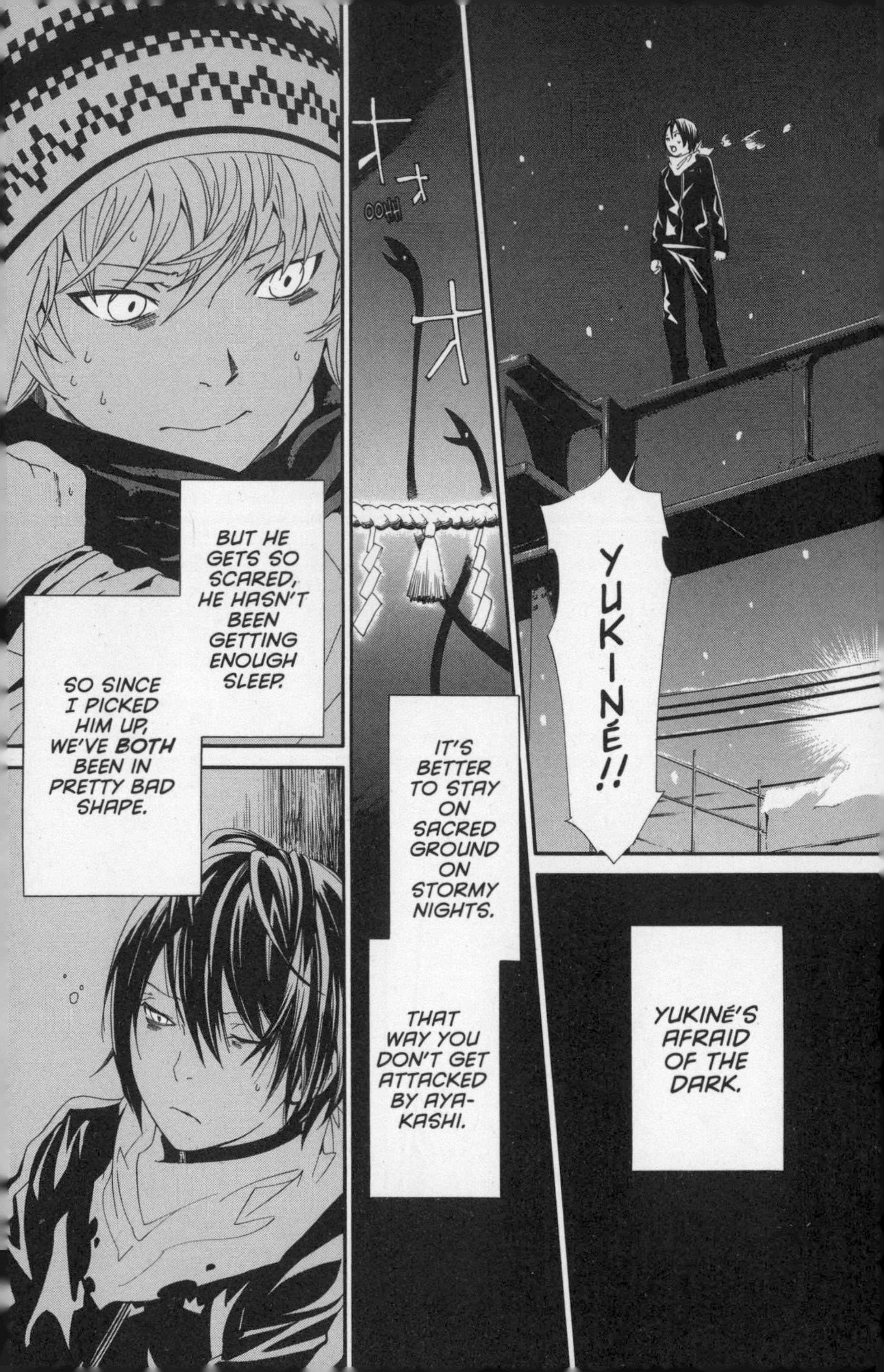
YUKINÉ!!
YUKINÉ'S AFRAID OF THE DARK.
OOH!!
IT'S BETTER TO STAY ON SACRED GROUND ON STORMY NIGHTS.
THAT WAY YOU DON'T GET ATTACKED BY AYA-KASHI.
BUT HE GETS SO SCARED, HE HASN'T BEEN GETTING ENOUGH SLEEP.
SO SINCE I PICKED HIM UP, WE'VE BOTH BEEN IN PRETTY BAD SHAPE.

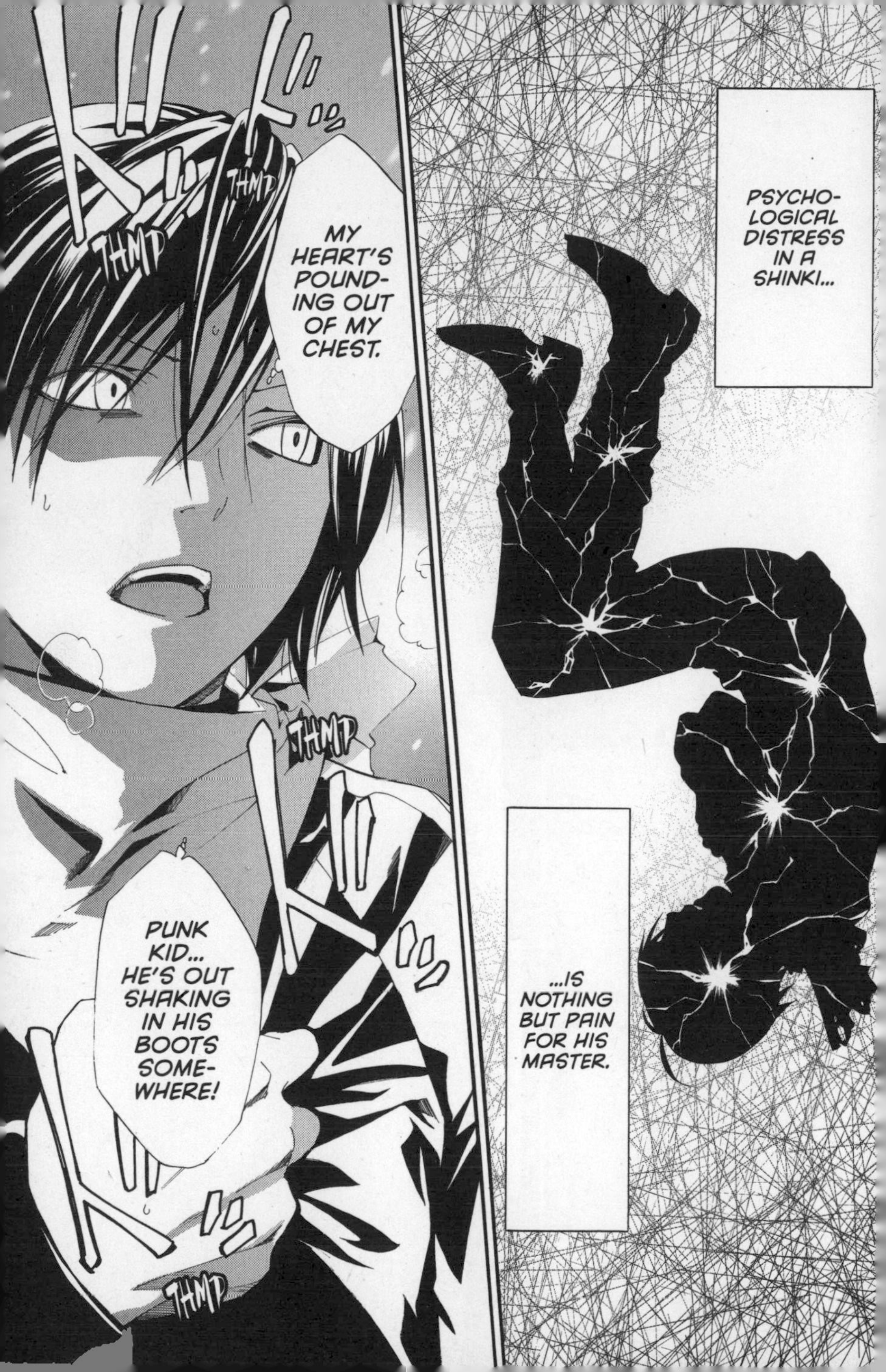
PSYCHO-LOGICAL DISTRESS IN A SHINKI...
...IS NOTHING BUT PAIN FOR HIS MASTER.
THMP
THMP
MY HEART'S POUND-ING OUT OF MY CHEST.
THMP
PUNK KID... HE'S OUT SHAKING IN HIS BOOTS SOME-WHERE!
THMP

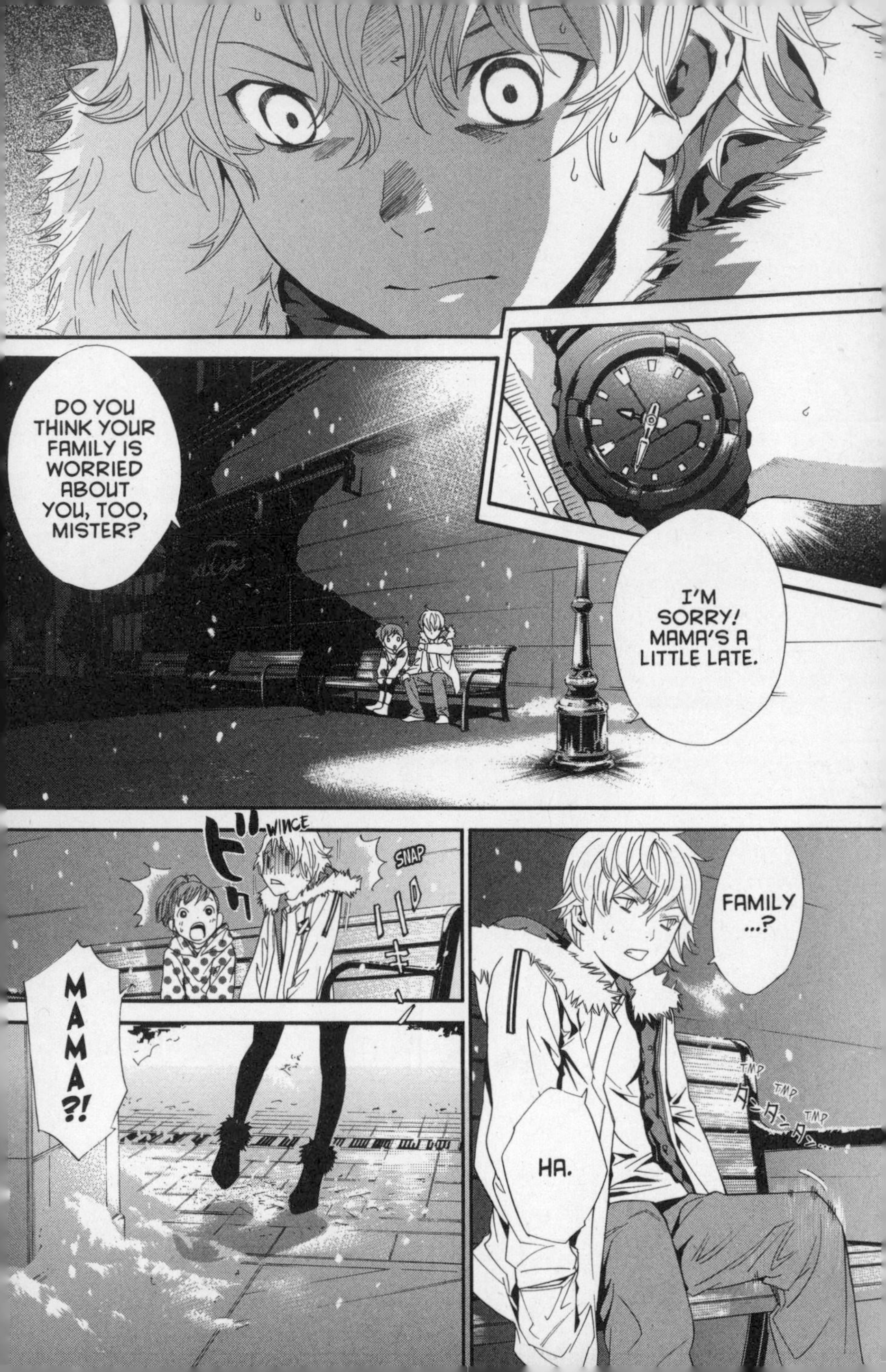
I'M SORRY! MAMA'S A LITTLE LATE.
DO YOU THINK YOUR FAMILY IS WORRIED ABOUT YOU, TOO, MISTER?
FAMILY ...?
HA.
TMP TMP TMP
WINCE
SNAP
MAMA?!

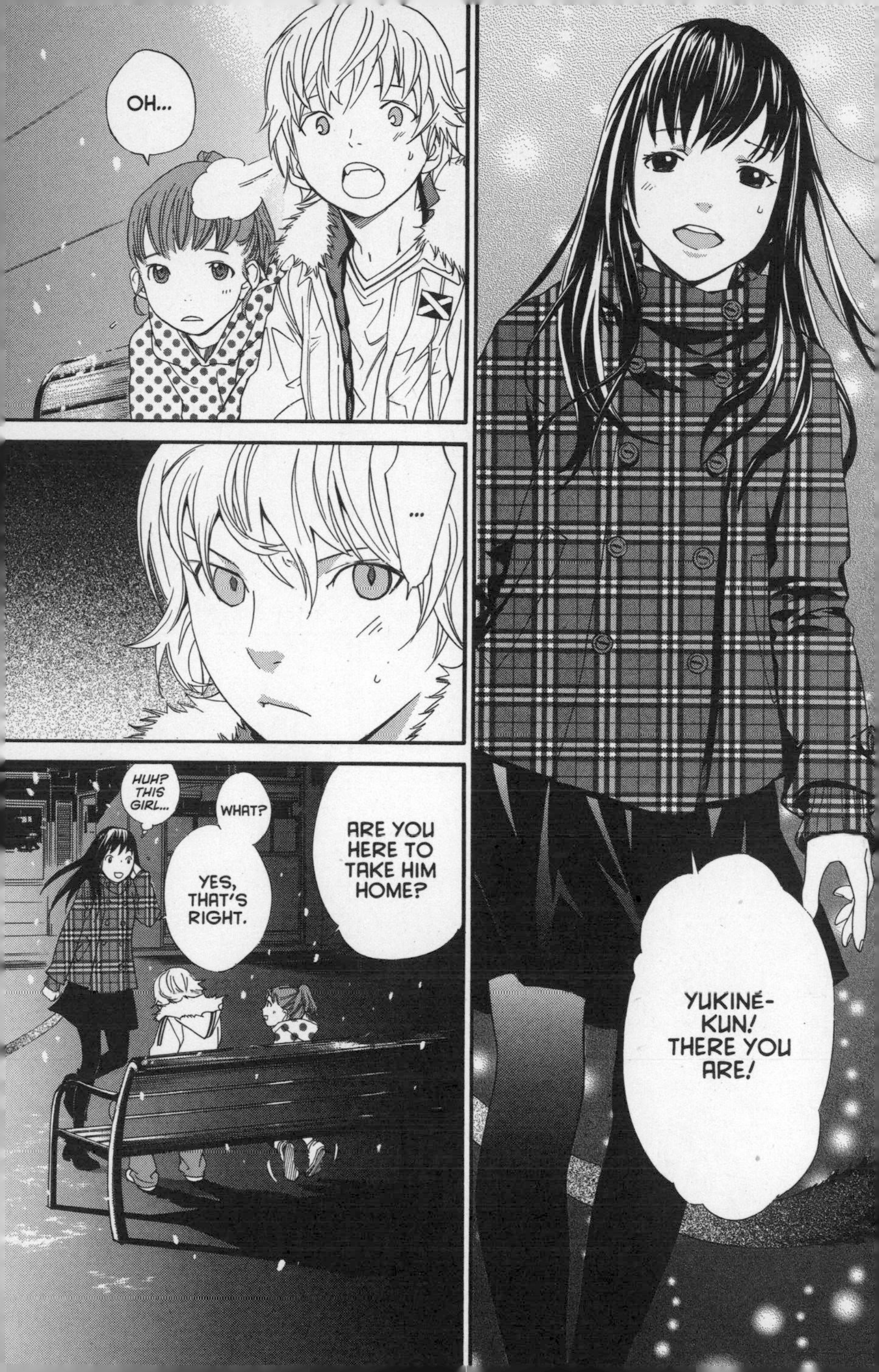
YUKINÉ-KUN! THERE YOU ARE!
OH...
...
ARE YOU HERE TO TAKE HIM HOME?
WHAT?
HUH? THIS GIRL...
YES, THAT'S RIGHT.

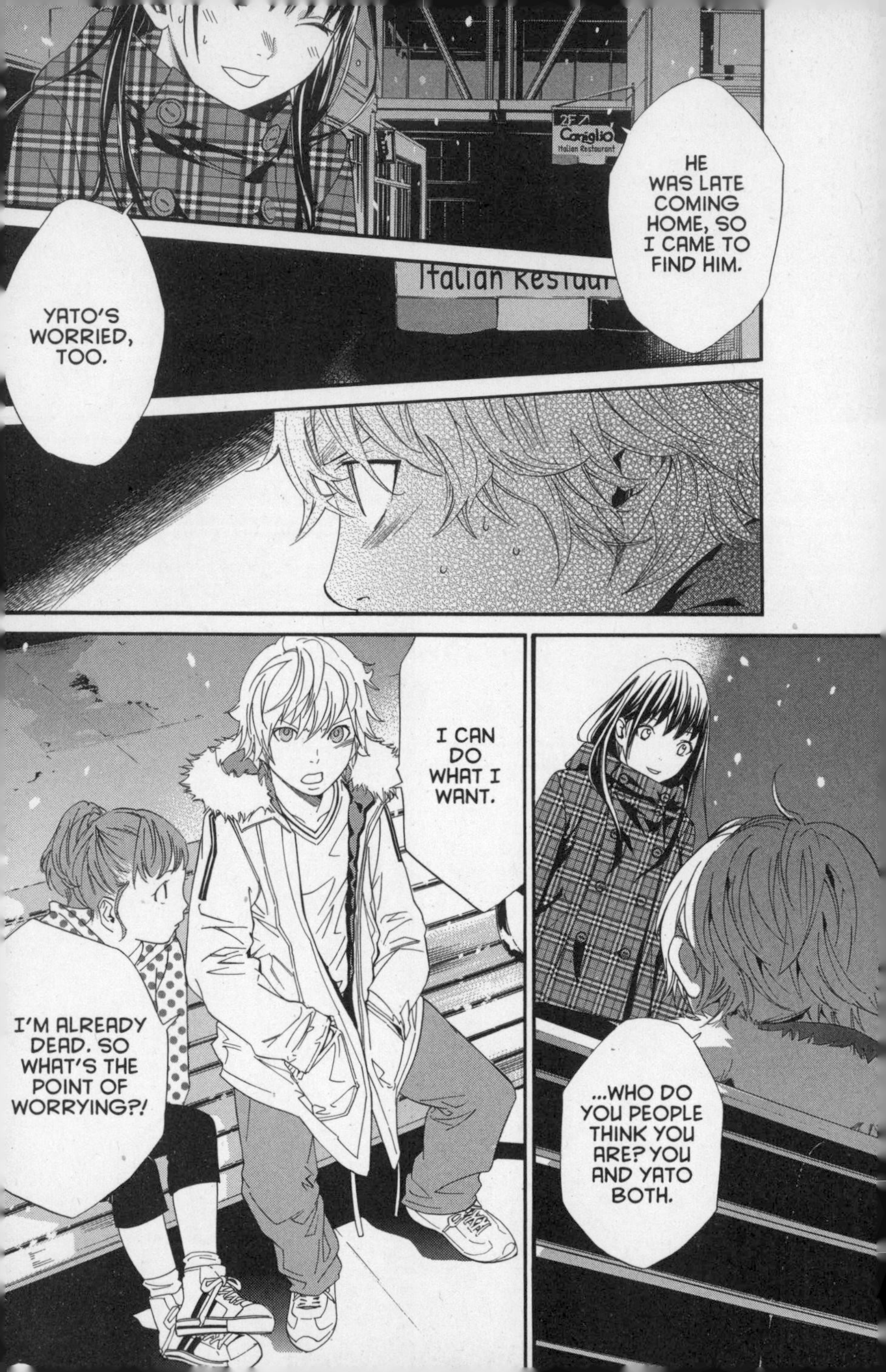
2F
Coniglio
Italian Restaurant
HE WAS LATE COMING HOME, SO I CAME TO FIND HIM.
Italian Restaur
YATO'S WORRIED, TOO.
...WHO DO YOU PEOPLE THINK YOU ARE? YOU AND YATO BOTH.
I CAN DO WHAT I WANT.
I'M ALREADY DEAD. SO WHAT'S THE POINT OF WORRYING?!

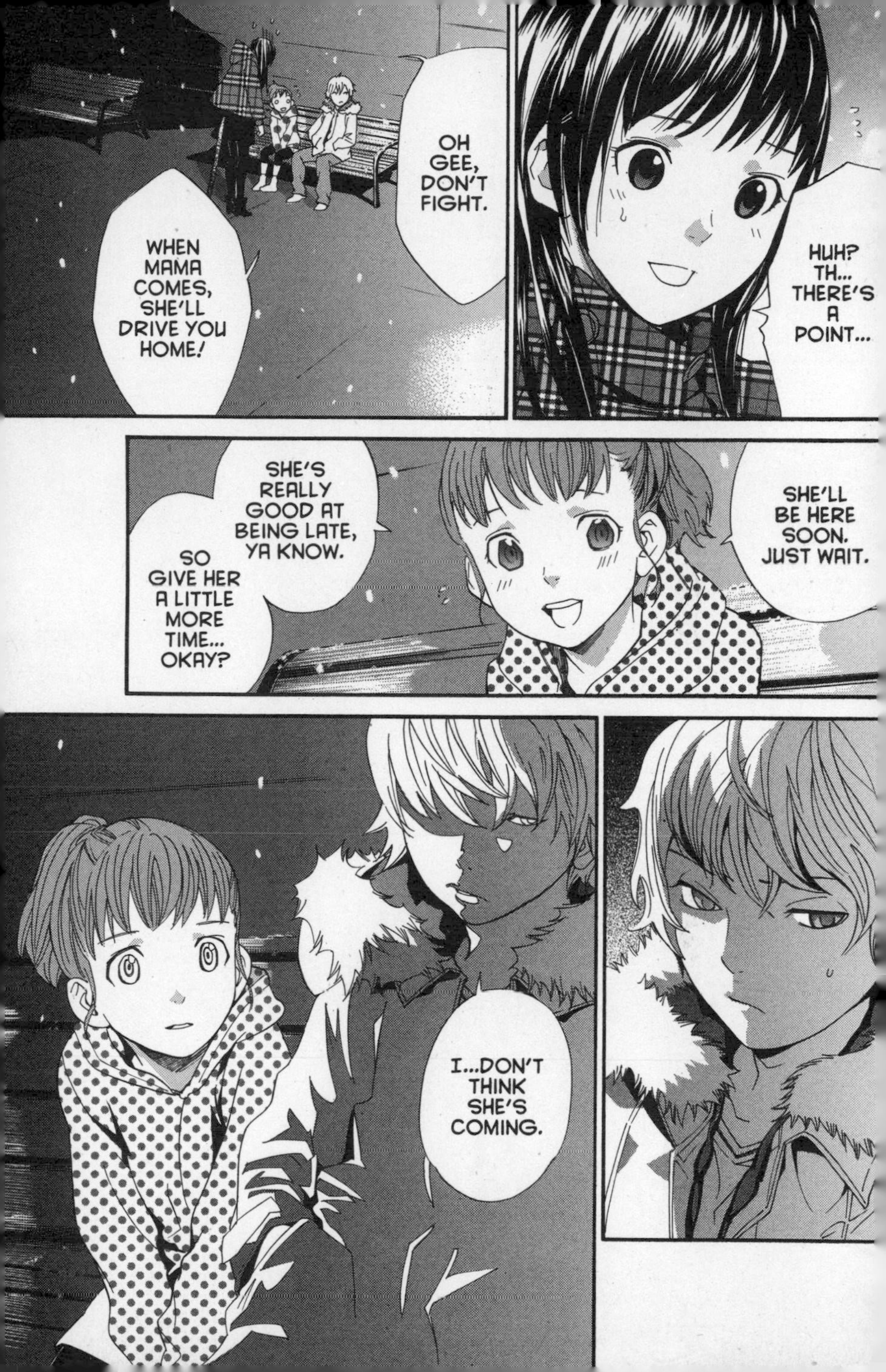
HUH? TH... THERE'S A POINT...
OH GEE, DON'T FIGHT.
WHEN MAMA COMES, SHE'LL DRIVE YOU HOME!
SHE'LL BE HERE SOON. JUST WAIT.
SHE'S REALLY GOOD AT BEING LATE, YA KNOW.
SO GIVE HER A LITTLE MORE TIME... OKAY?
I...DON'T THINK SHE'S COMING.

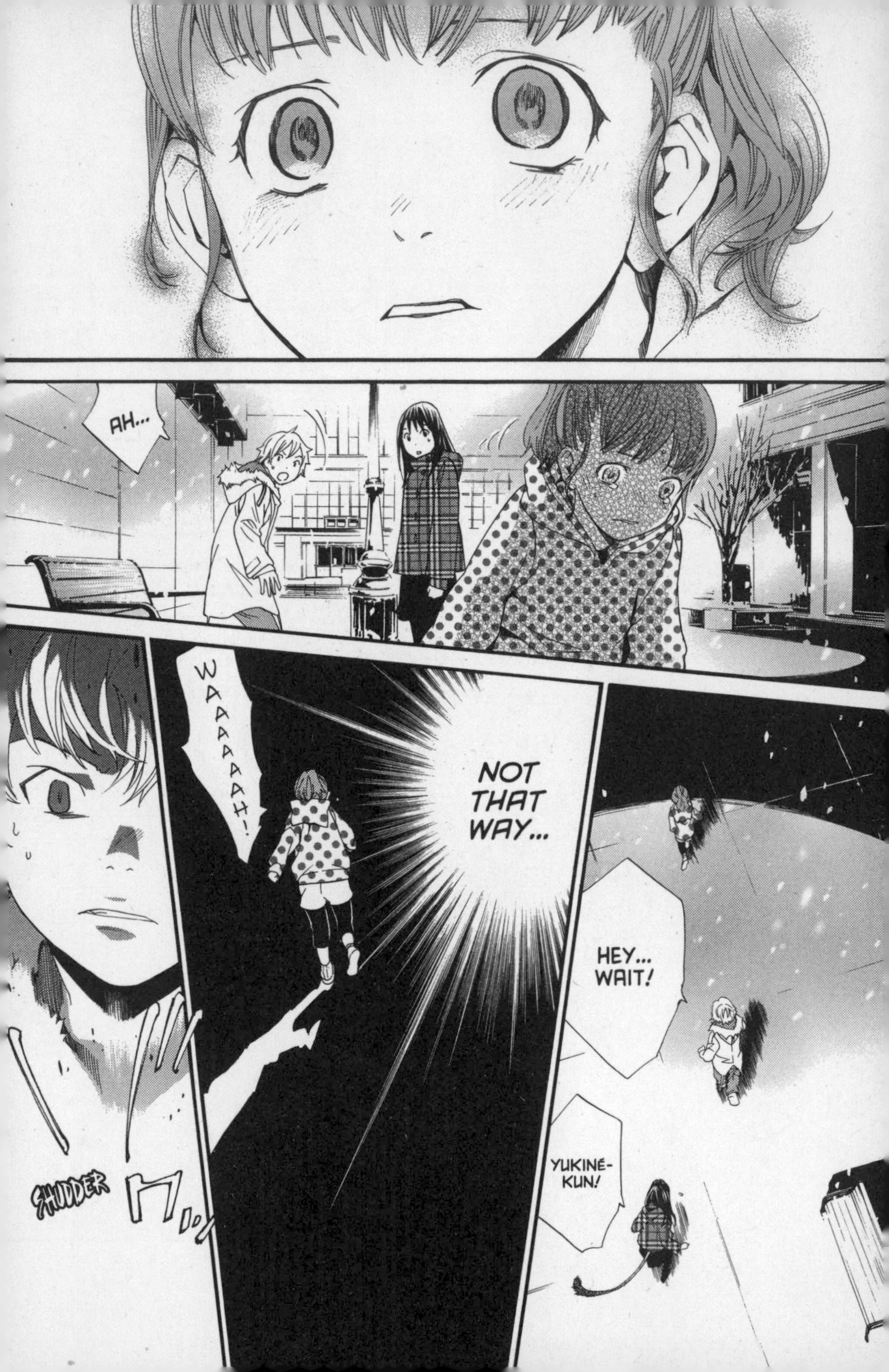
AH...
HEY... WAIT!
YUKINÉ-KUN!
NOT THAT WAY...
WAAAAAAAH!
SHUDDER

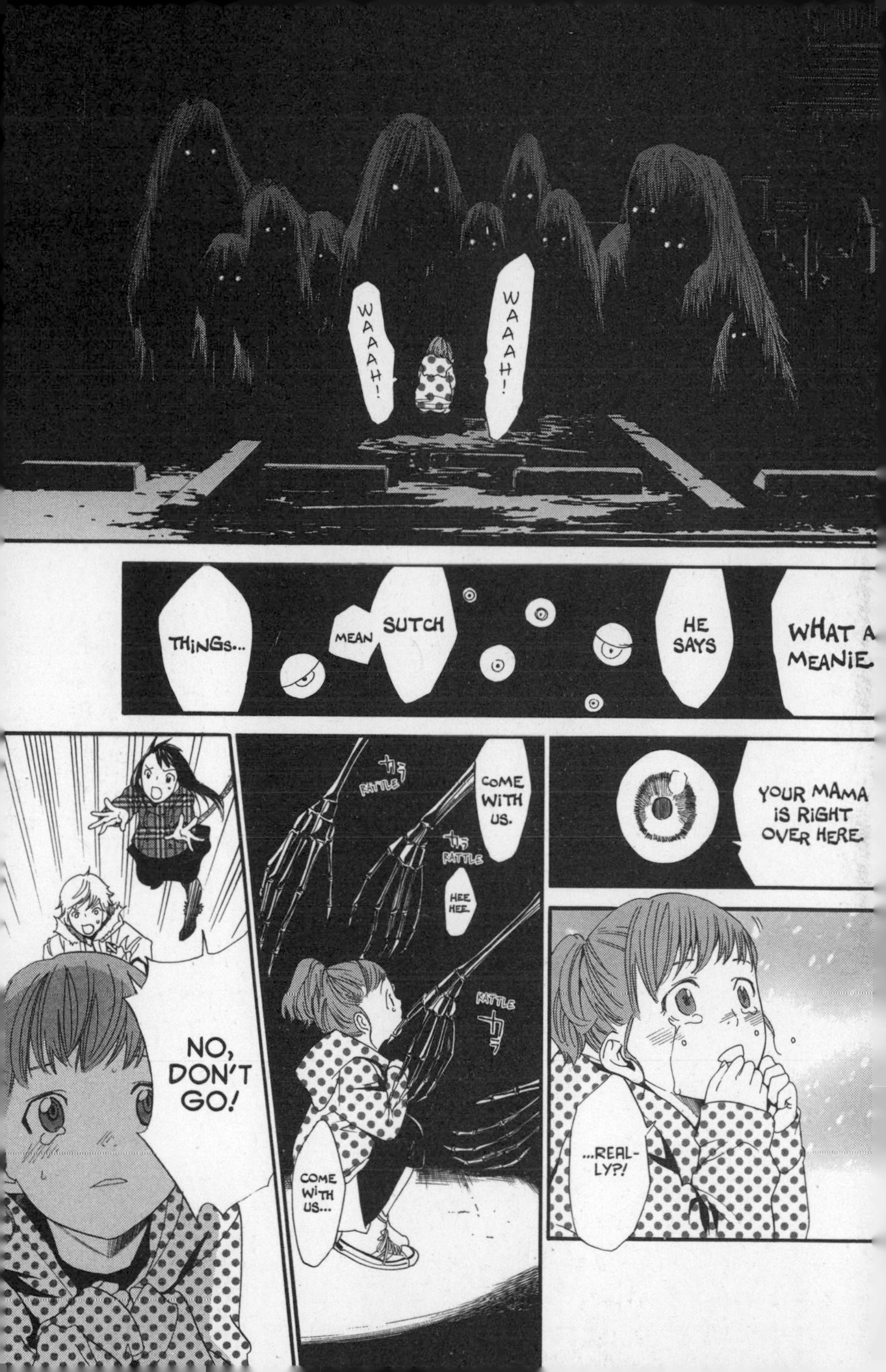

WAAAAH!
WAAAH!
WHAT A MEANIE.
HE SAYS
SUTCH
MEAN
THINGS...
YOUR MAMA IS RIGHT OVER HERE.
...REAL-LY?!
COME WITH US.
RATTLE
RATTLE
HEE HEE
RATTLE
COME WITH US...
NO, DON'T GO!

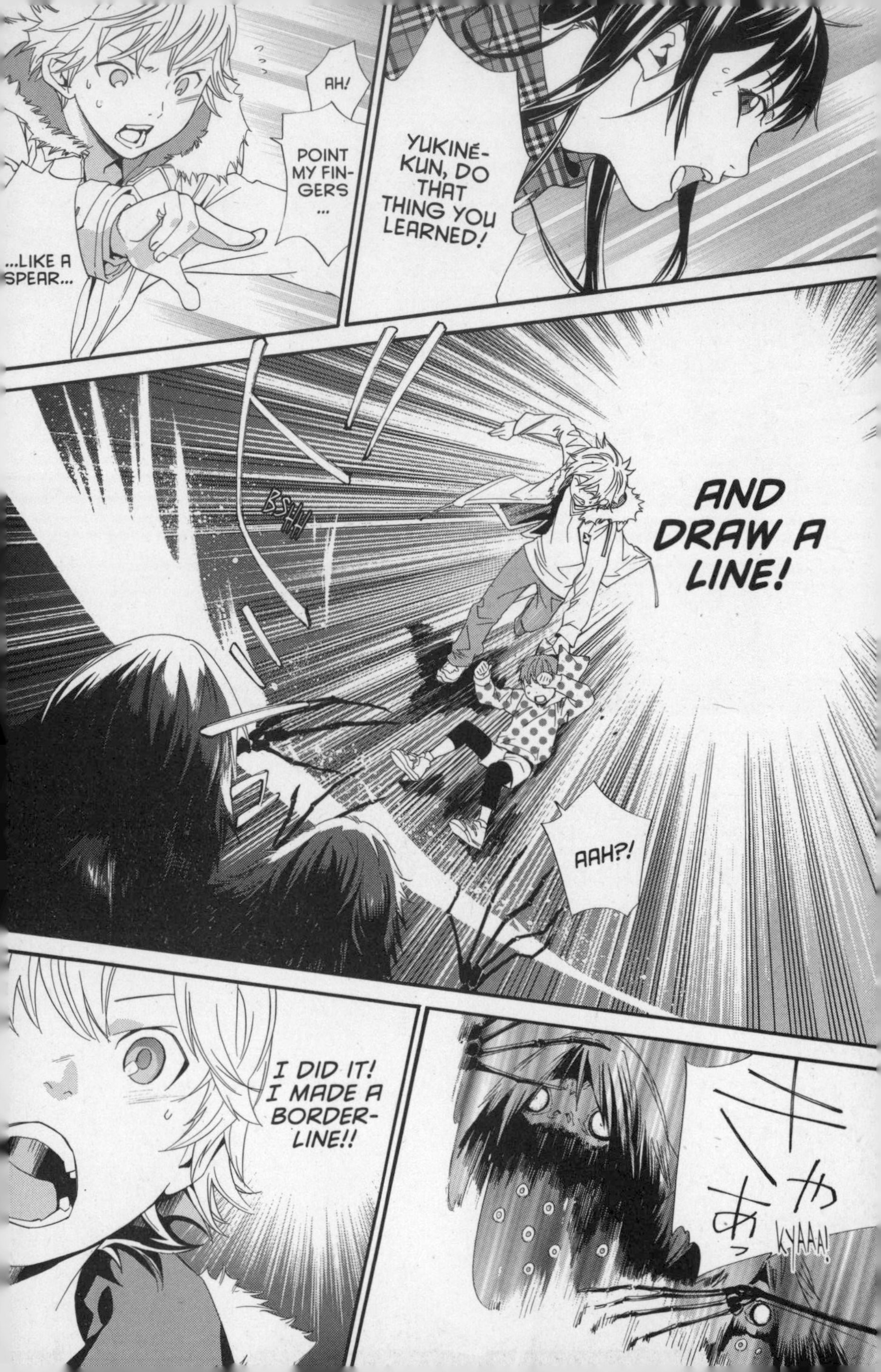
YUKINÉ-KUN, DO THAT THING YOU LEARNED!
AH!
POINT MY FINGERS ...
...LIKE A SPEAR...
AND DRAW A LINE!
B-SHH
AAH?!
KYAAA!
I DID IT! I MADE A BORDER-LINE!!

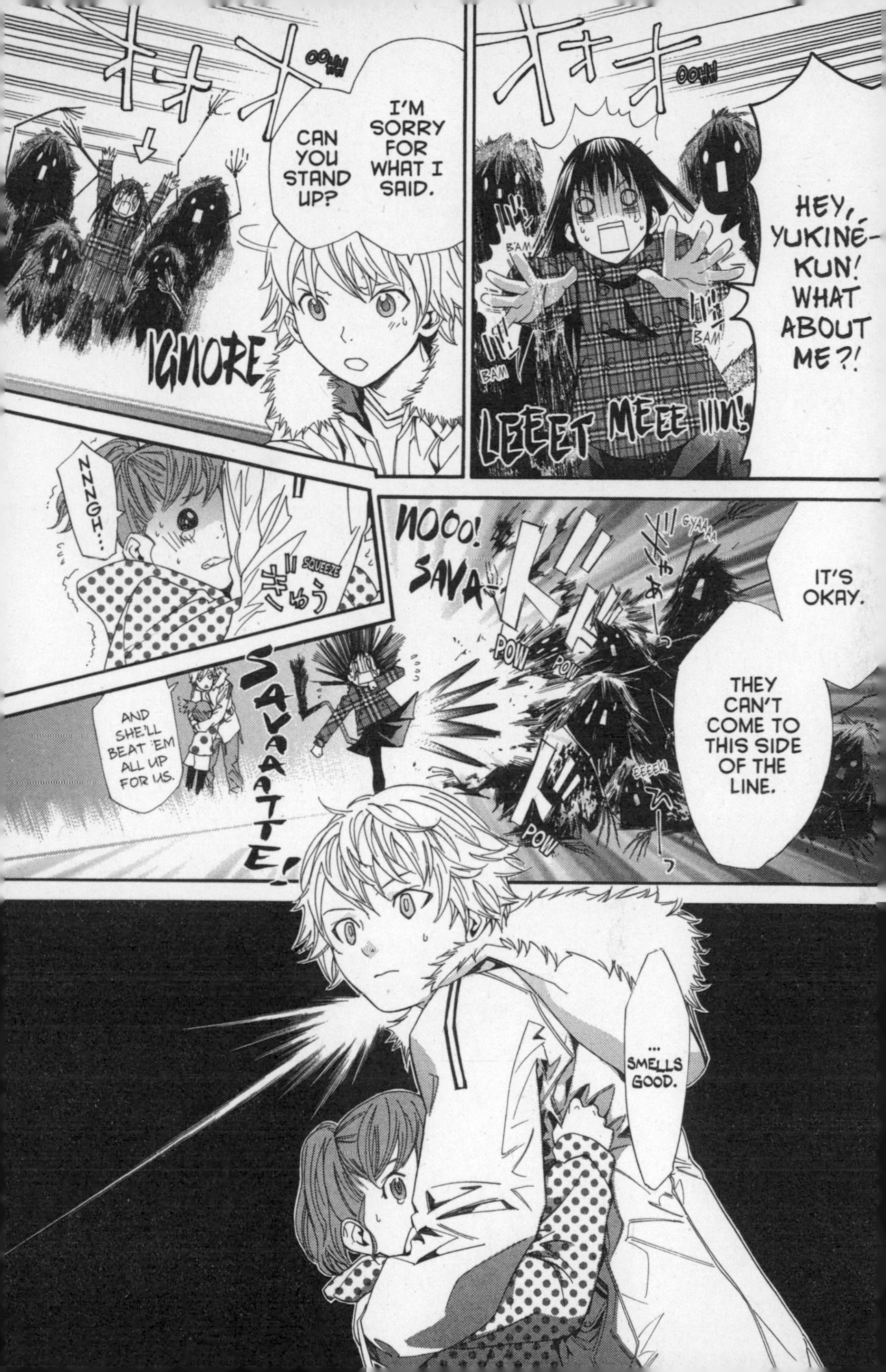
OOHH
HEY, YUKINÉ-KUN! WHAT ABOUT ME?!
BAM
BAM
BAM
LEEEET MEEE IIIN!
OOHH
I'M SORRY FOR WHAT I SAID.
CAN YOU STAND UP?
IGNORE
NOOO! SAVA-
GYAAA
POW
POW
POW
IT'S OKAY.
THEY CAN'T COME TO THIS SIDE OF THE LINE.
EEEEK!
NNNGH...
SQUEEZE
きゅう
SAVAAATTE!
AND SHE'LL BEAT 'EM ALL UP FOR US.
... SMELLS GOOD.

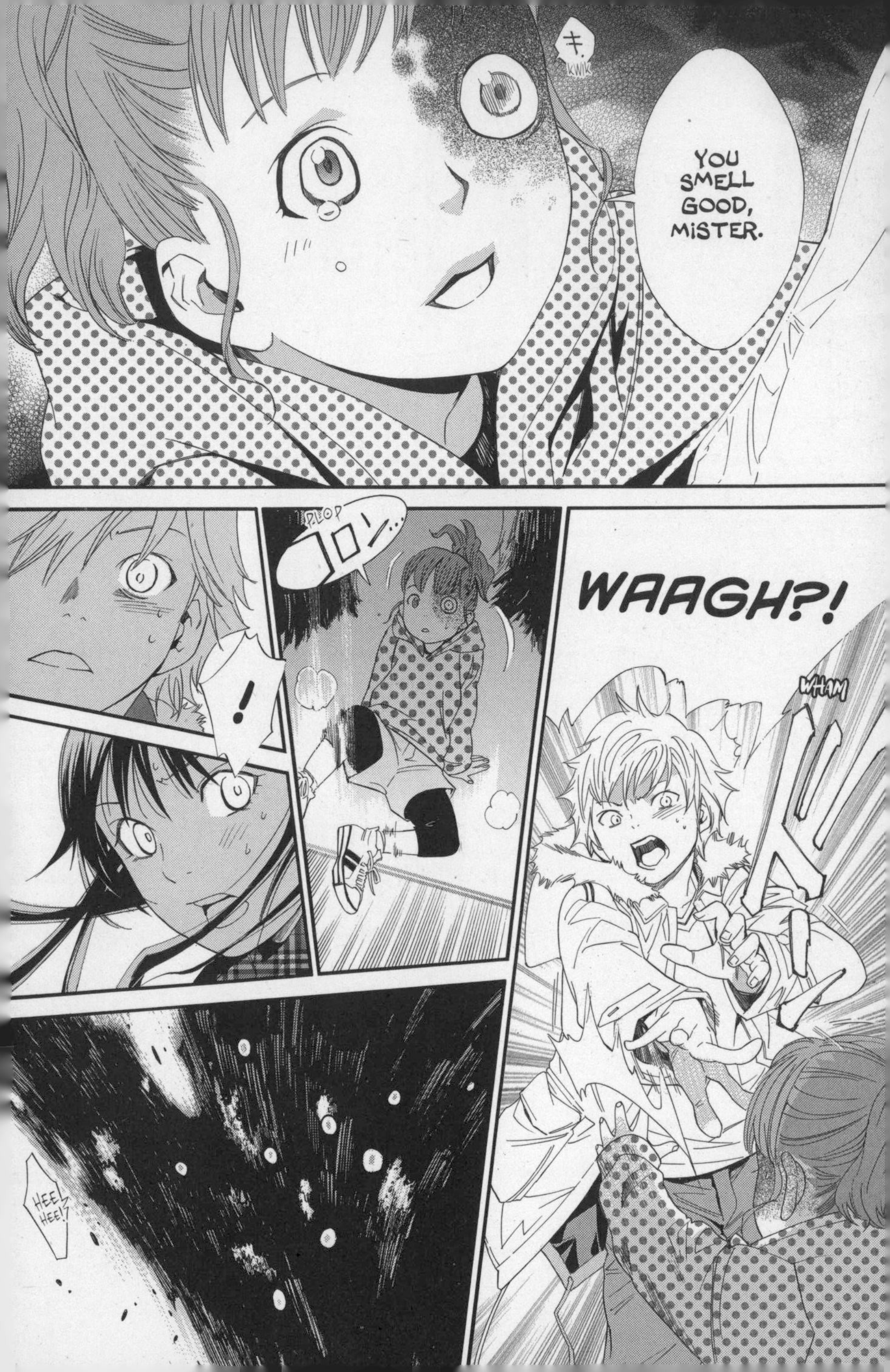
KWIK
YOU SMELL GOOD, MISTER.
WAAGH?!
WHAM
PLOP
!
HEE! HEE!

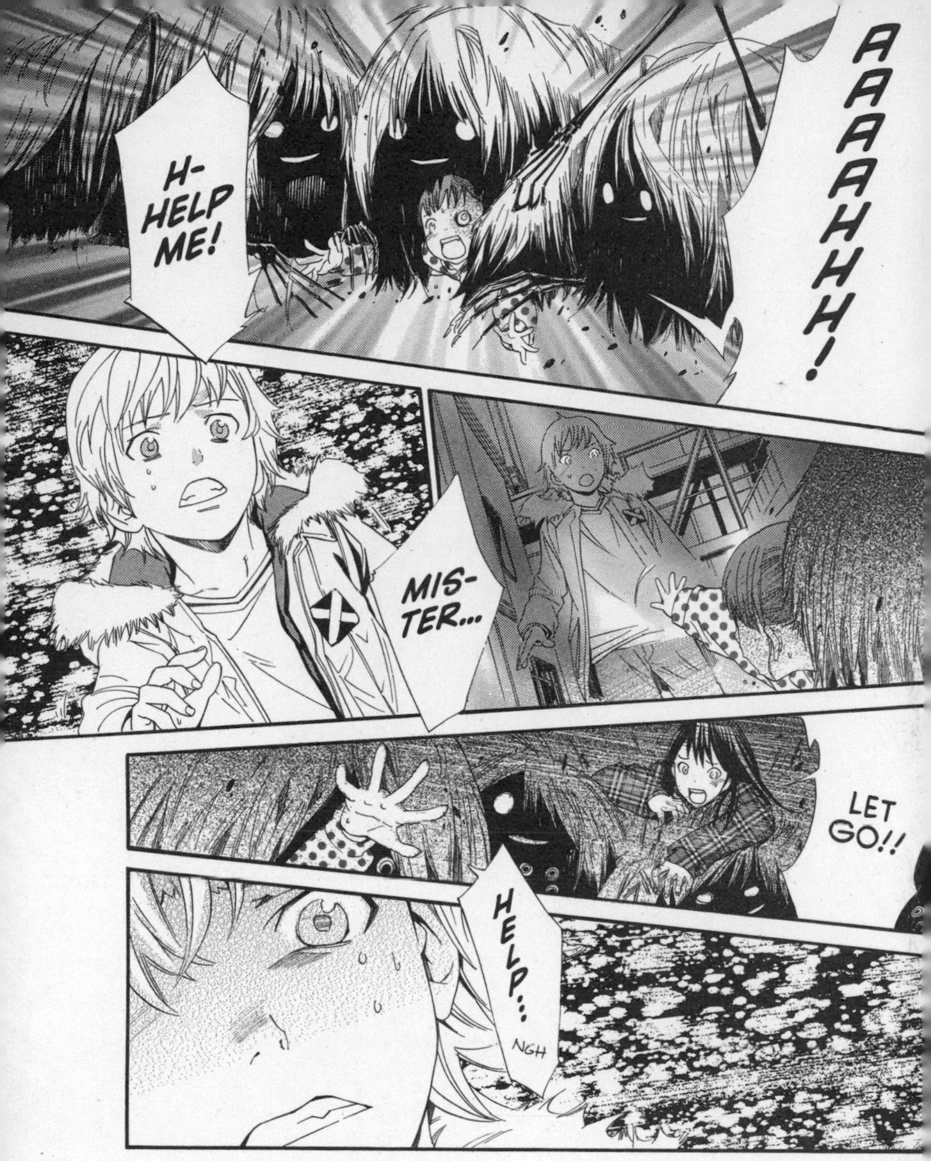
AAAAHHHH!
H-HELP ME!
MIS-TER...
LET GO!!
HELP...
NGH
SNAP

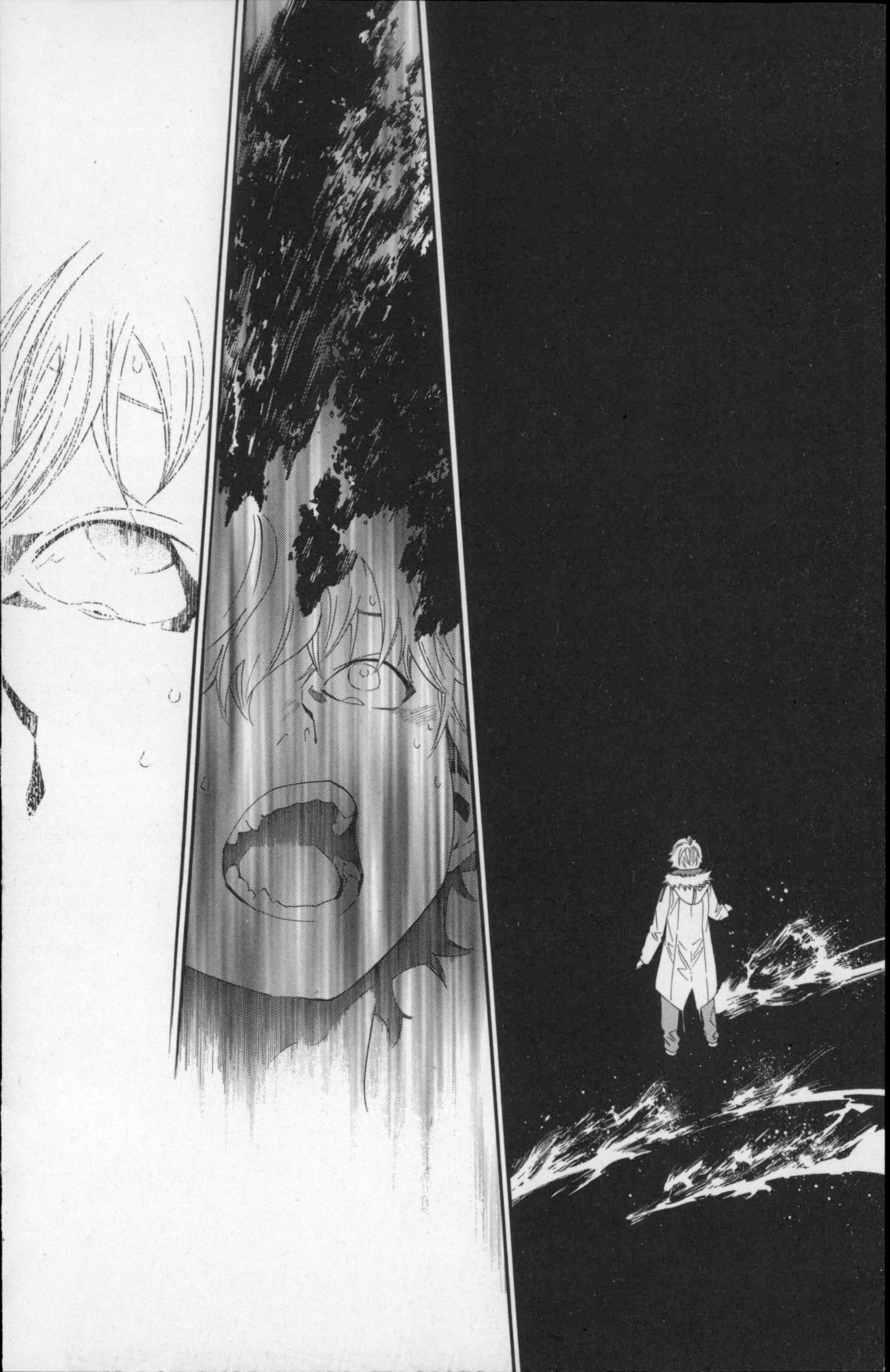

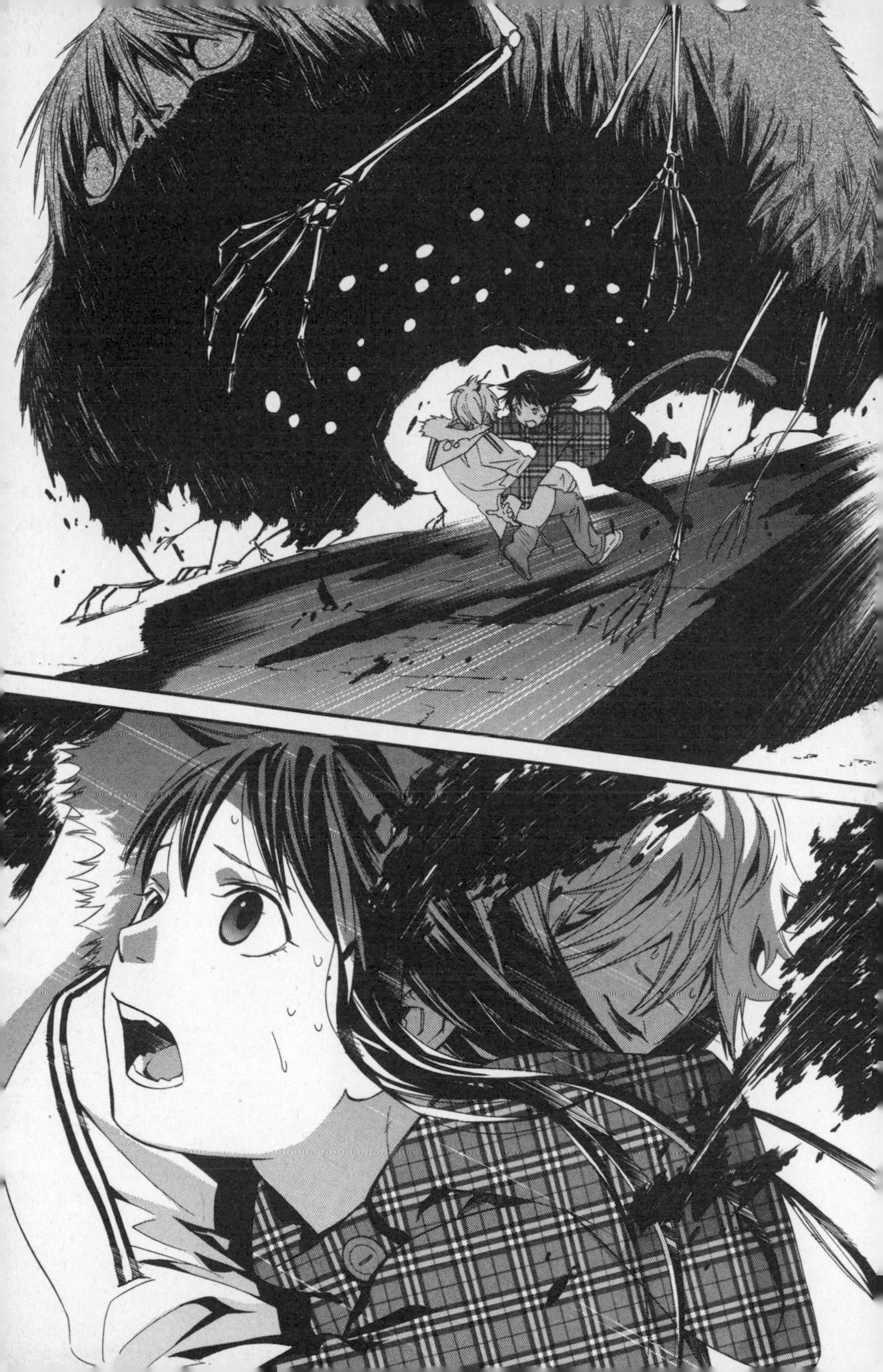

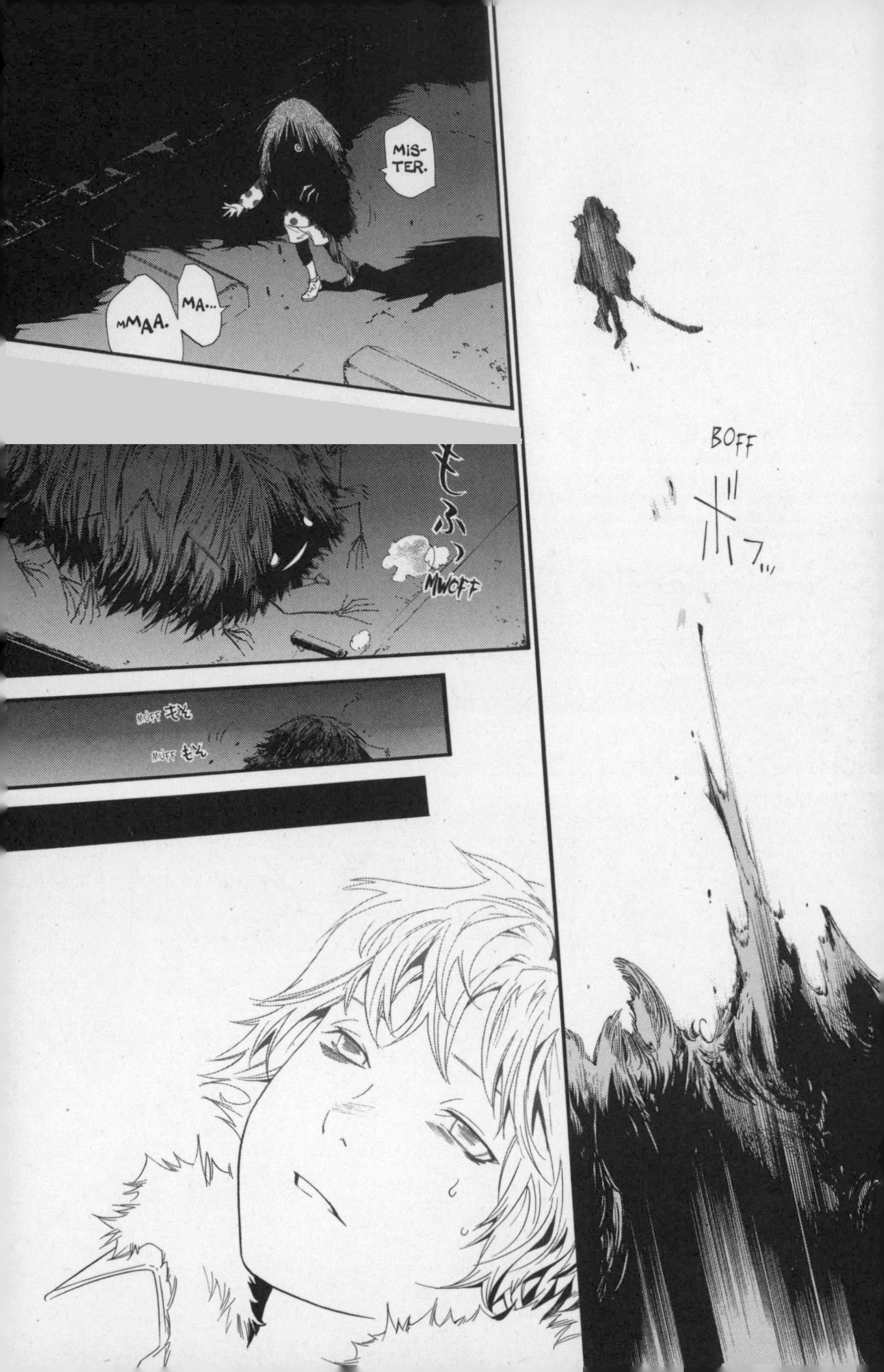
BOFF
ボフッ
MIS-TER.
MA...
MMAA.
もふっ
MWOFF
MUFF もそ
MUFF もそ

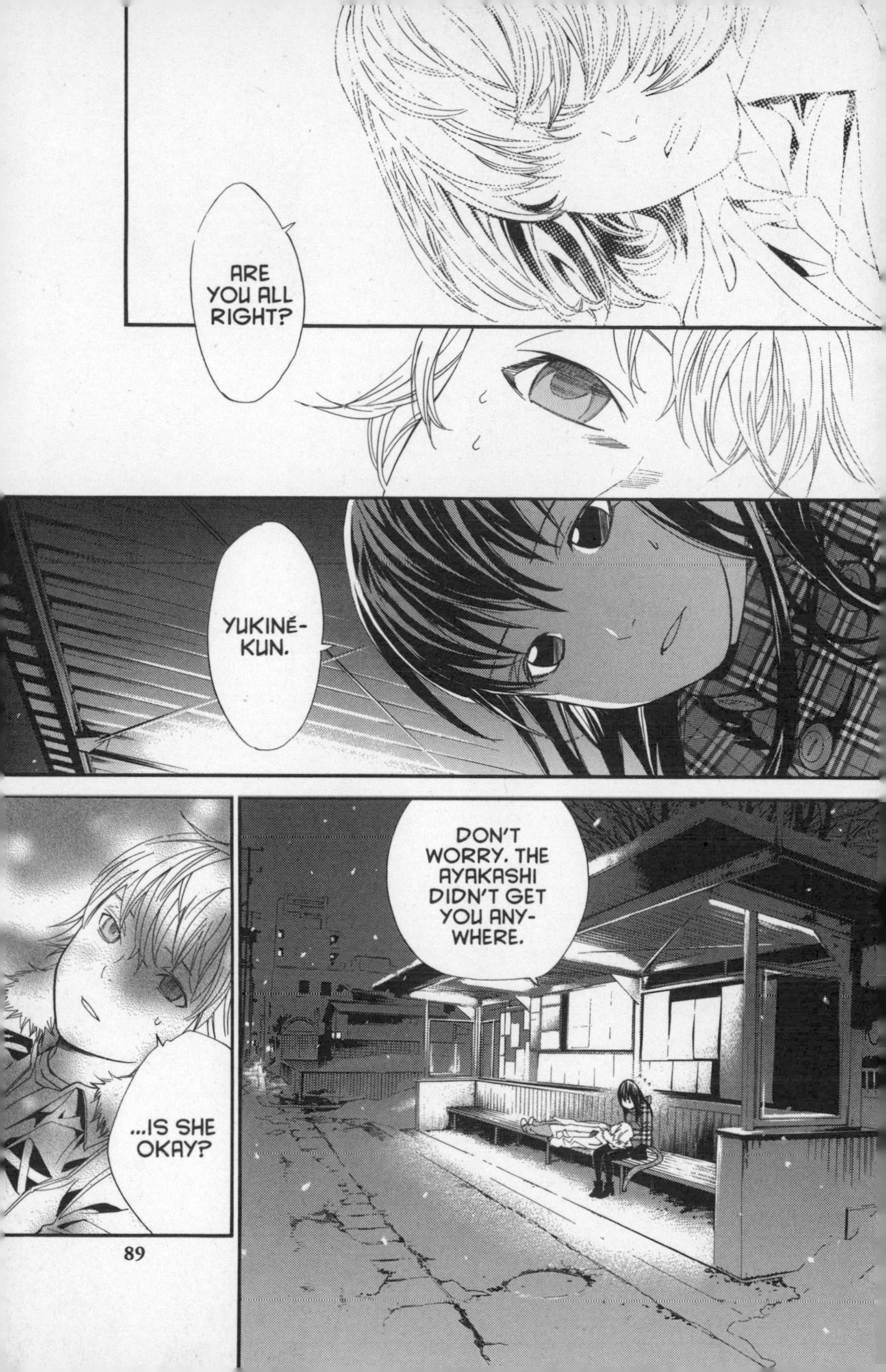
ARE YOU ALL RIGHT?
YUKINÉ-KUN.
DON'T WORRY. THE AYAKASHI DIDN'T GET YOU ANY-WHERE.
...IS SHE OKAY?

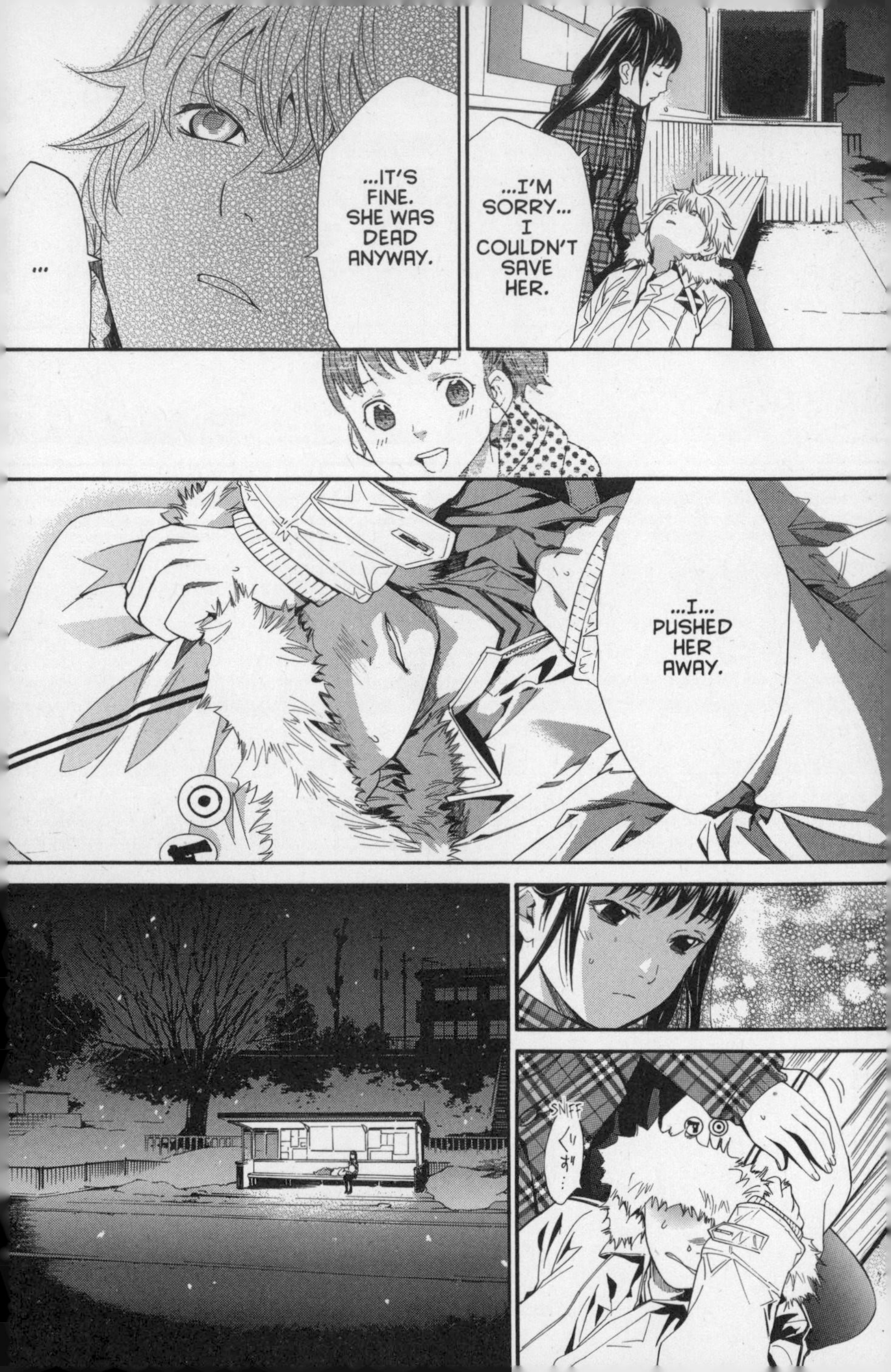
...I'M SORRY... I COULDN'T SAVE HER.
...IT'S FINE. SHE WAS DEAD ANYWAY.
...
...I... PUSHED HER AWAY.
SNIFF
ぐりず...

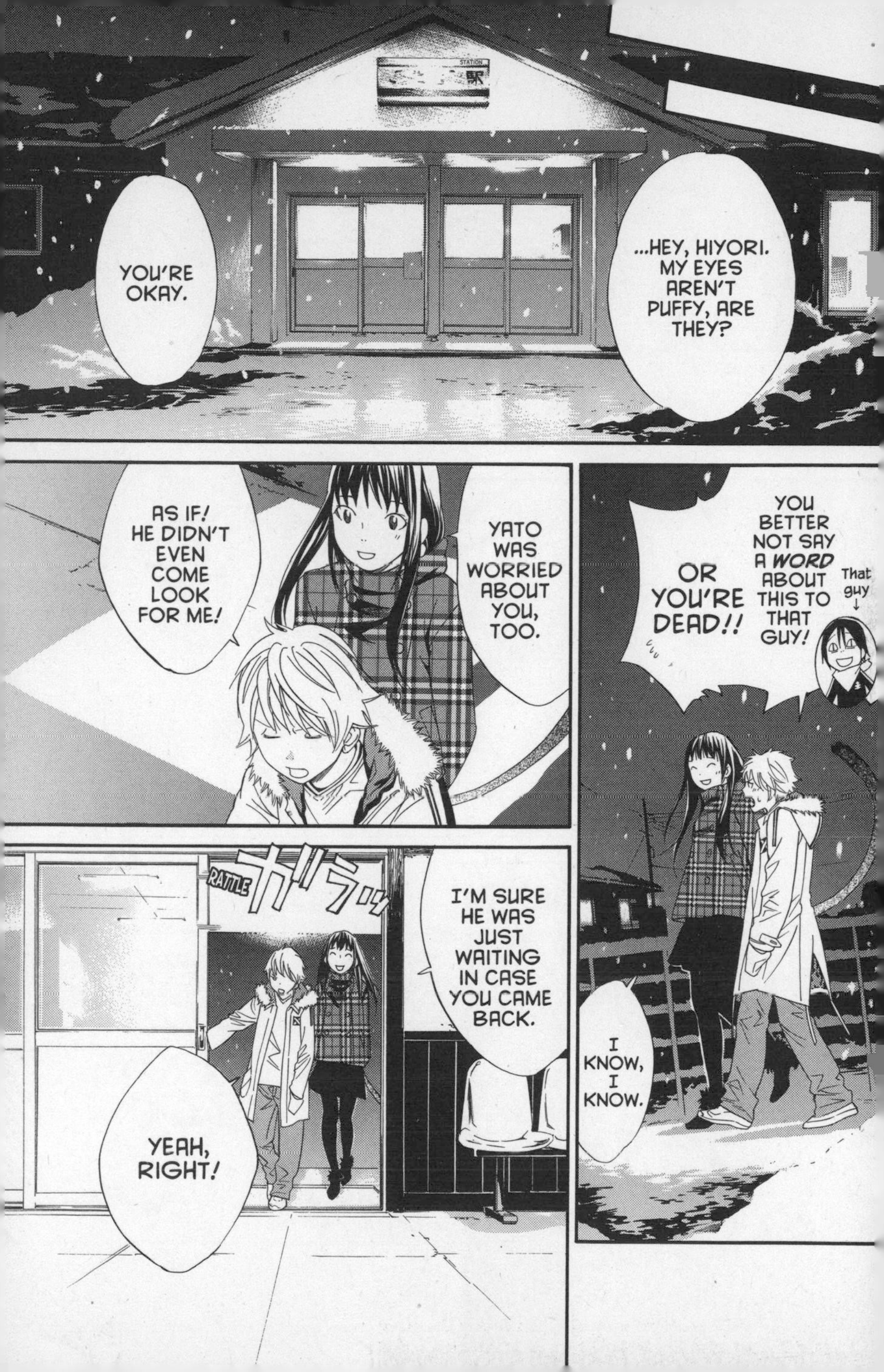
...HEY, HIYORI. MY EYES AREN'T PUFFY, ARE THEY?
YOU'RE OKAY.
YOU BETTER NOT SAY A *WORD* ABOUT THIS TO THAT GUY!
OR YOU'RE DEAD!!
That guy ↓
I KNOW, I KNOW.
YATO WAS WORRIED ABOUT YOU, TOO.
AS IF! HE DIDN'T EVEN COME LOOK FOR ME!
RATTLE
I'M SURE HE WAS JUST WAITING IN CASE YOU CAME BACK.
YEAH, RIGHT!

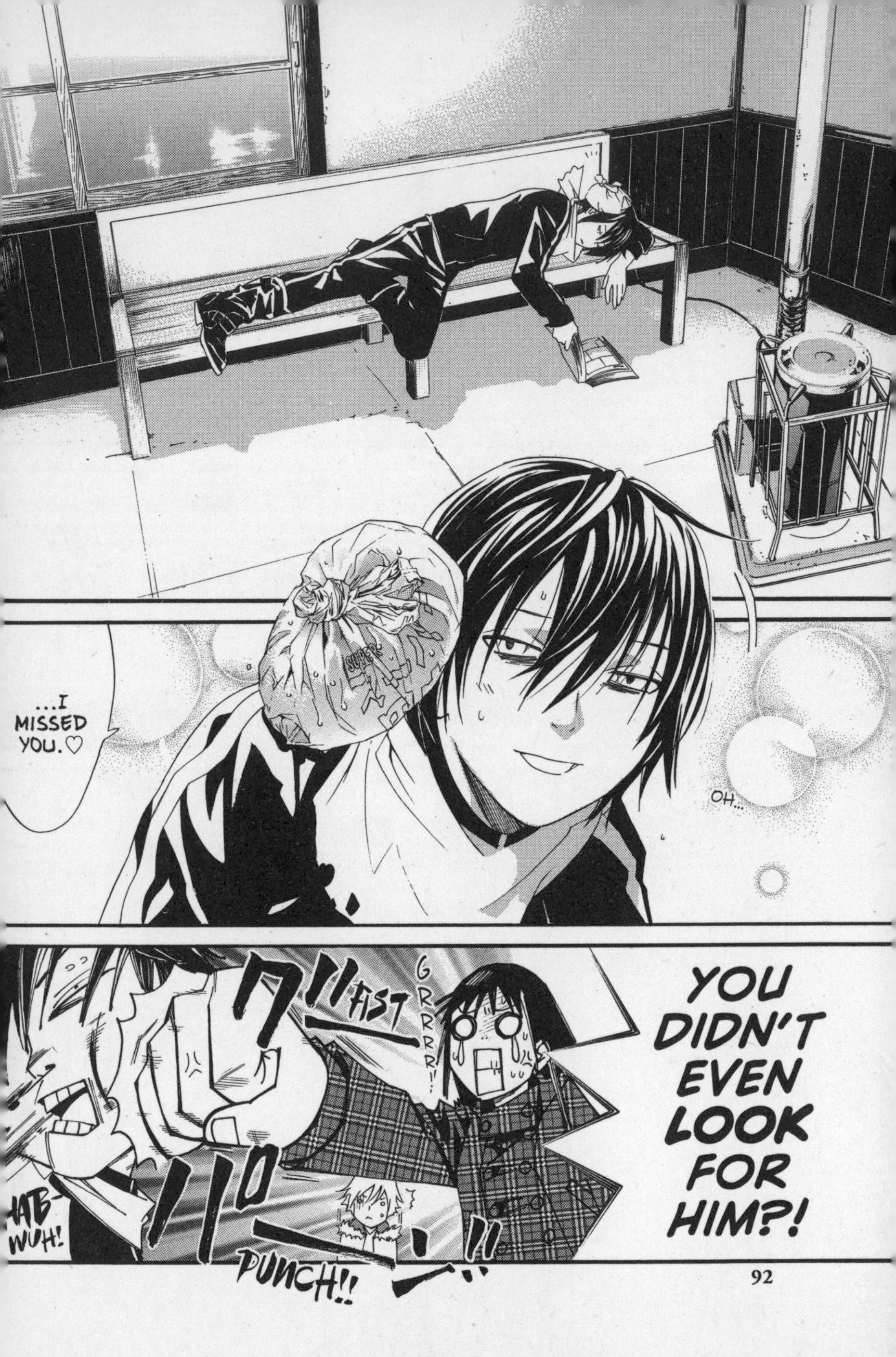
OH...
...I MISSED YOU.♡
YOU DIDN'T EVEN LOOK FOR HIM?!
GRRRR!!
FIST
PUNCH!!
HATB-WUH!

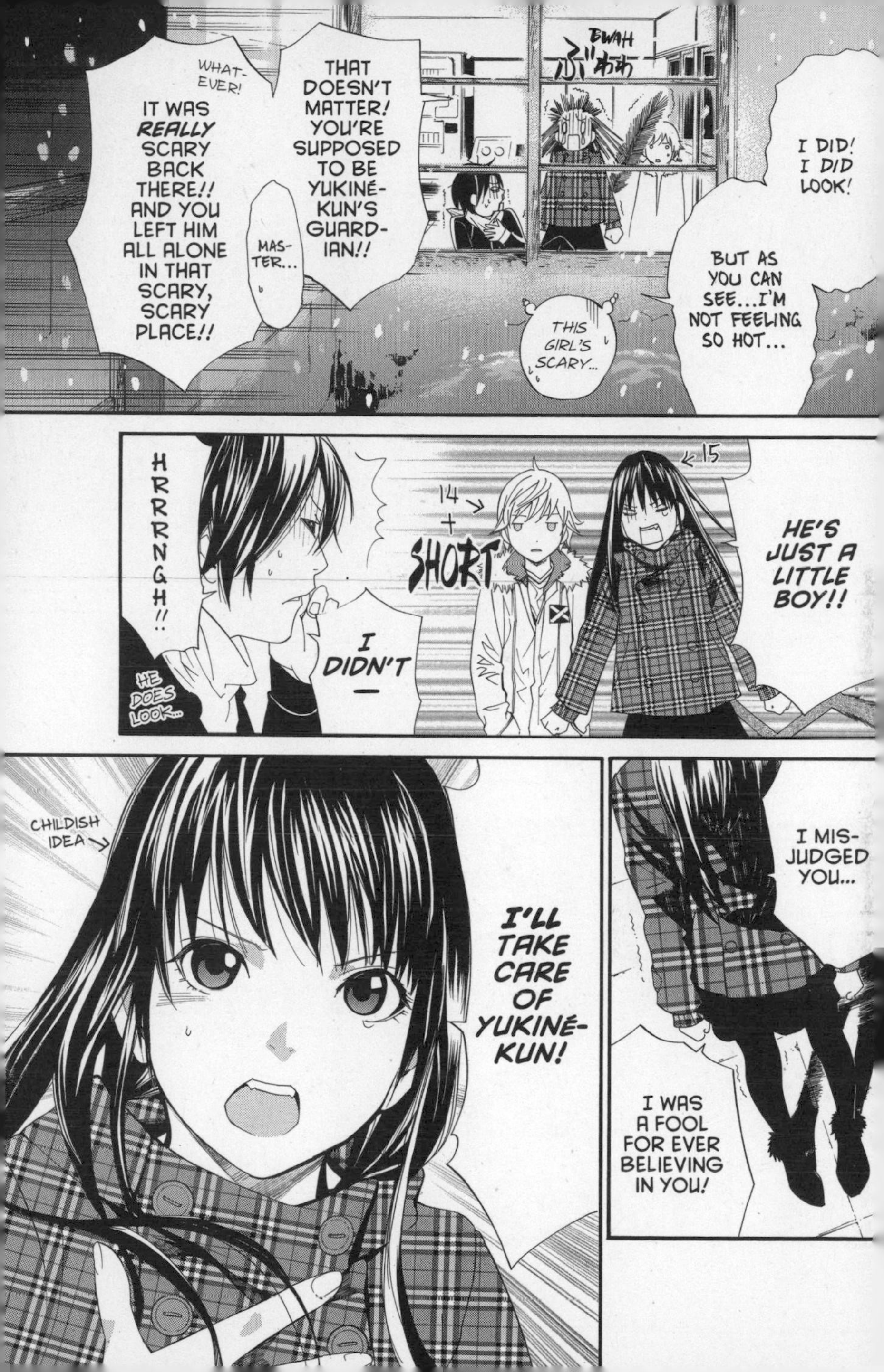
I DID! I DID LOOK!
BUT AS YOU CAN SEE...I'M NOT FEELING SO HOT...
THIS GIRL'S SCARY...
BWAH
ぶわあ
THAT DOESN'T MATTER! YOU'RE SUPPOSED TO BE YUKINÉ-KUN'S GUARDIAN!!
MASTER...
WHATEVER!
IT WAS REALLY SCARY BACK THERE!! AND YOU LEFT HIM ALL ALONE IN THAT SCARY, SCARY PLACE!!
HE'S JUST A LITTLE BOY!!
←15
14→
SHORT
I DIDN'T—
HRRRNGH!!
HE DOES LOOK...
I MISJUDGED YOU...
I WAS A FOOL FOR EVER BELIEVING IN YOU!
I'LL TAKE CARE OF YUKINÉ-KUN!
CHILDISH IDEA→

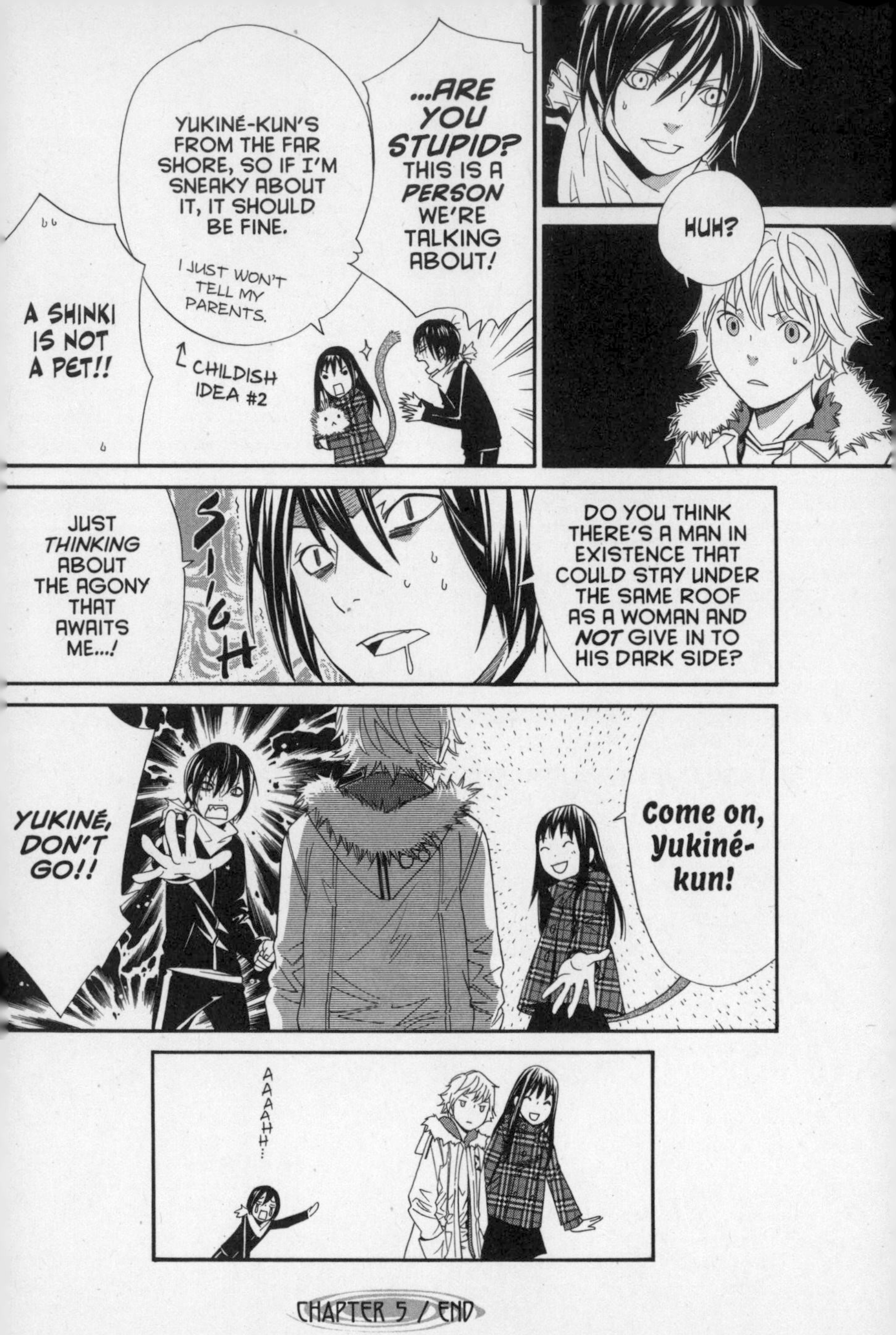
HUH?
...ARE YOU STUPID? THIS IS A PERSON WE'RE TALKING ABOUT!
YUKINÉ-KUN'S FROM THE FAR SHORE, SO IF I'M SNEAKY ABOUT IT, IT SHOULD BE FINE.
I JUST WON'T TELL MY PARENTS.
CHILDISH IDEA #2
A SHINKI IS NOT A PET!!
DO YOU THINK THERE'S A MAN IN EXISTENCE THAT COULD STAY UNDER THE SAME ROOF AS A WOMAN AND NOT GIVE IN TO HIS DARK SIDE?
SIGH
JUST THINKING ABOUT THE AGONY THAT AWAITS ME...!
Come on, Yukiné-kun!
YUKINÉ, DON'T GO!!
AAAAHH...

CHAPTER 5 / END

野

思

神

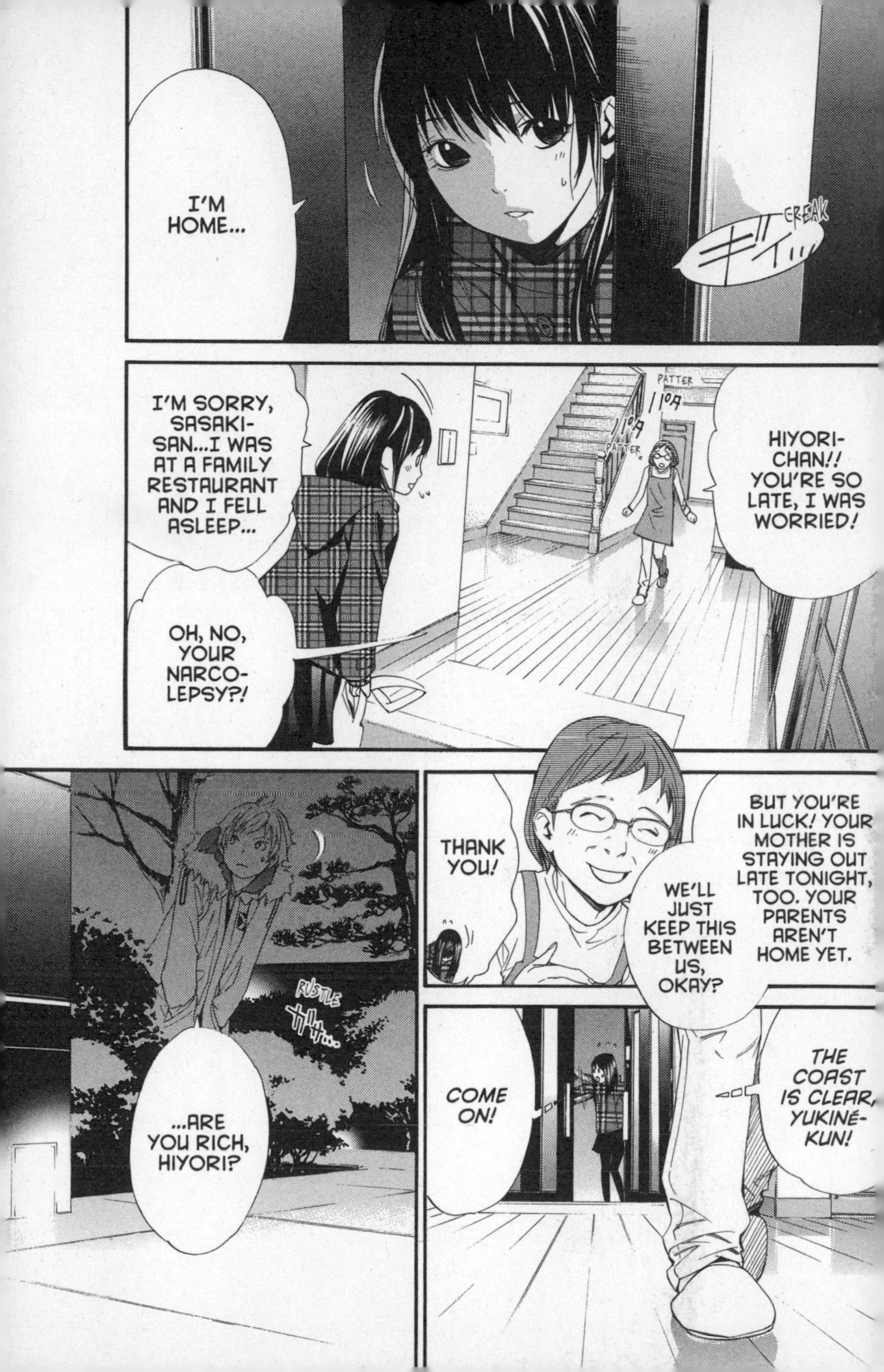
I'M HOME...
CREAK
PATTER
PATTER
HIYORI-CHAN!! YOU'RE SO LATE, I WAS WORRIED!
I'M SORRY, SASAKI-SAN...I WAS AT A FAMILY RESTAURANT AND I FELL ASLEEP...
OH, NO, YOUR NARCOLEPSY?!
BUT YOU'RE IN LUCK! YOUR MOTHER IS STAYING OUT LATE TONIGHT, TOO. YOUR PARENTS AREN'T HOME YET.
WE'LL JUST KEEP THIS BETWEEN US, OKAY?
THANK YOU!
THE COAST IS CLEAR, YUKINÉ-KUN!
COME ON!
RUSTLE
...ARE YOU RICH, HIYORI?

CHAPTER 6: BE AFRAID

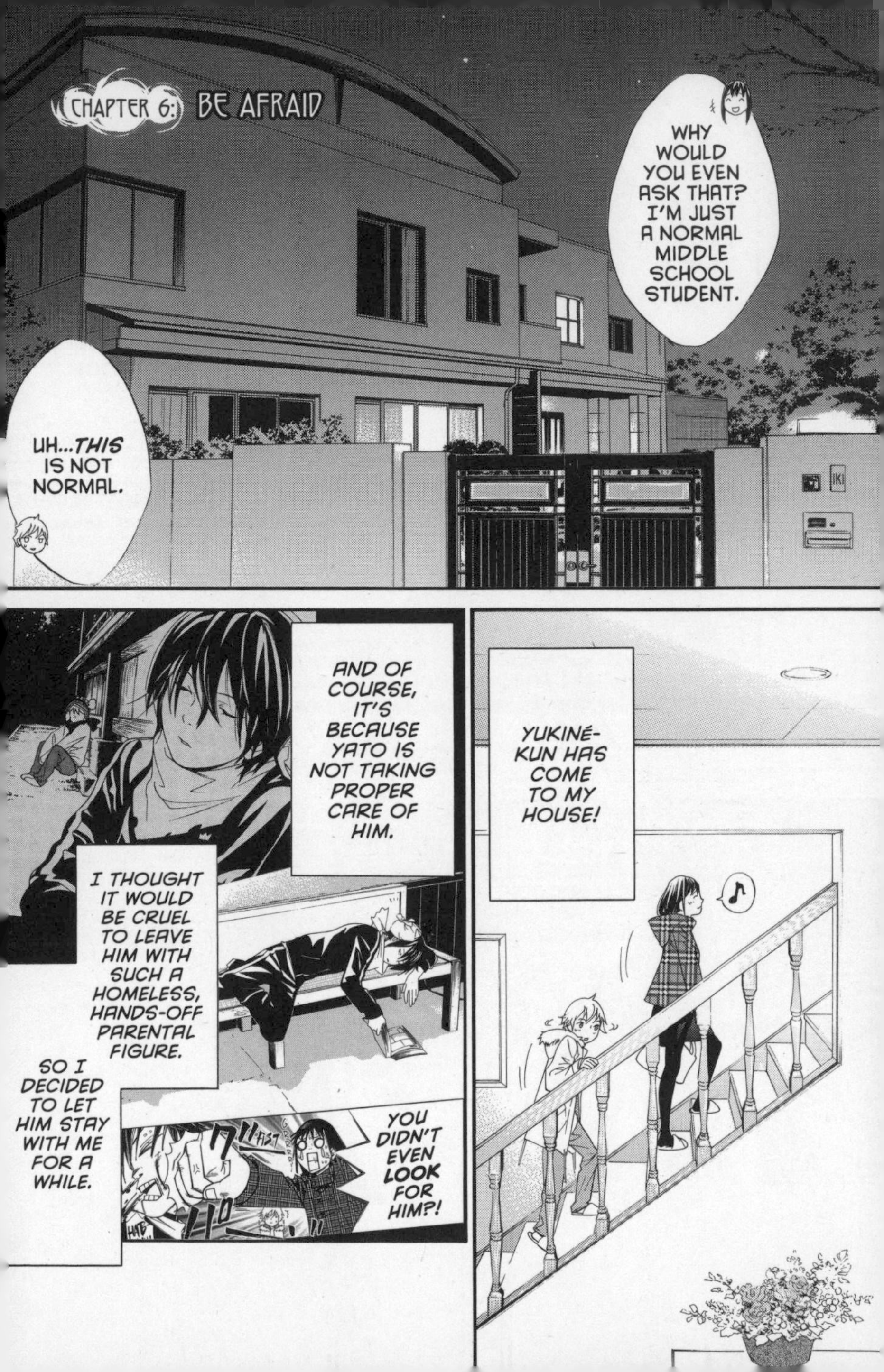
WHY WOULD YOU EVEN ASK THAT? I'M JUST A NORMAL MIDDLE SCHOOL STUDENT.
UH...*THIS* IS NOT NORMAL.
IKI
YUKINÉ-KUN HAS COME TO MY HOUSE!
AND OF COURSE, IT'S BECAUSE YATO IS NOT TAKING PROPER CARE OF HIM.
I THOUGHT IT WOULD BE CRUEL TO LEAVE HIM WITH SUCH A HOMELESS, HANDS-OFF PARENTAL FIGURE.
SO I DECIDED TO LET HIM STAY WITH ME FOR A WHILE.
YOU DIDN'T EVEN **LOOK** FOR HIM?!
FIST
HATE

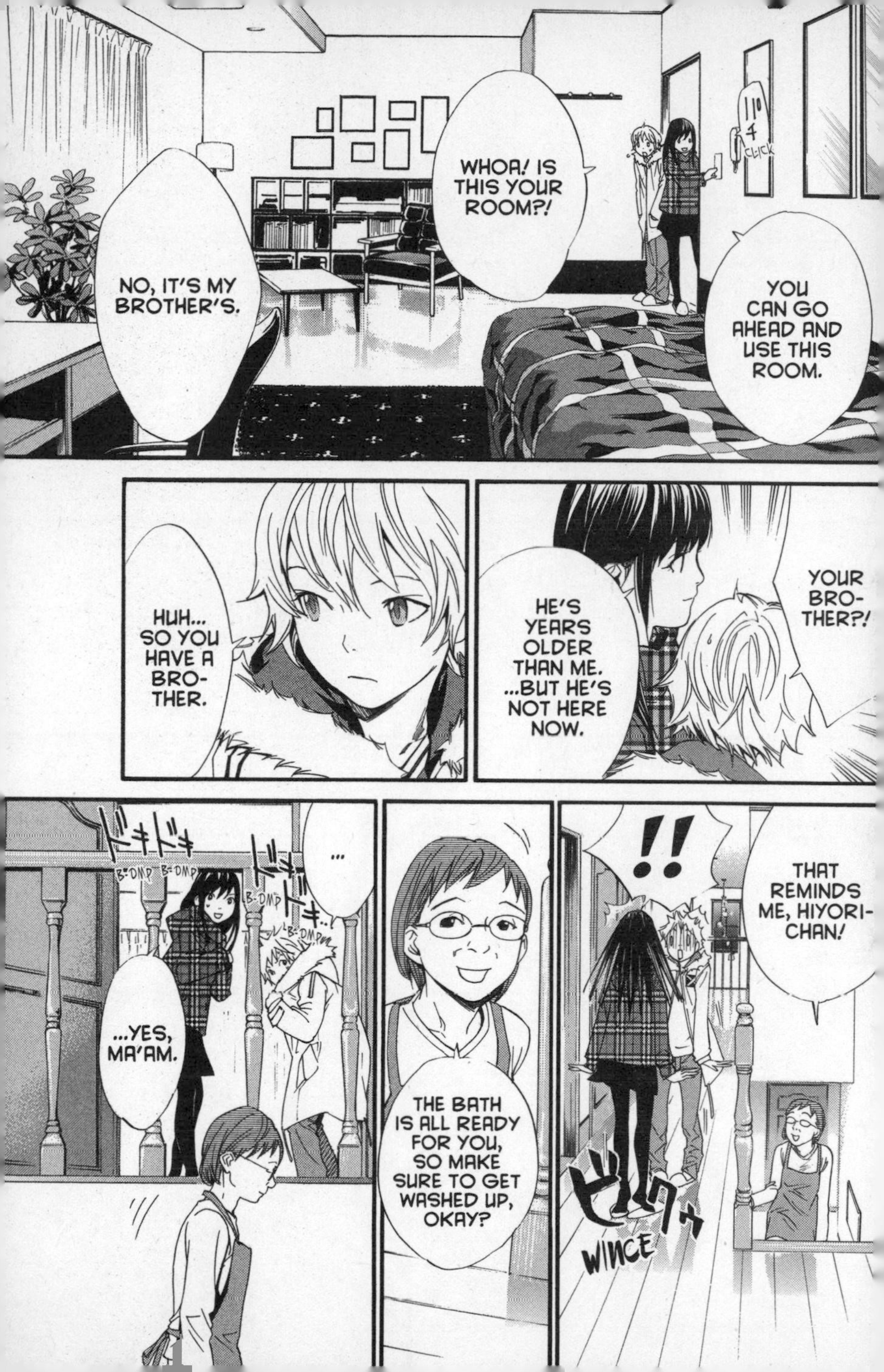
パチ CLICK
WHOA! IS THIS YOUR ROOM?!
YOU CAN GO AHEAD AND USE THIS ROOM.
NO, IT'S MY BROTHER'S.
YOUR BRO-THER?!
HE'S YEARS OLDER THAN ME. ...BUT HE'S NOT HERE NOW.
HUH... SO YOU HAVE A BROTHER.
THAT REMINDS ME, HIYORI-CHAN!
!!
ビクッ WINCE
THE BATH IS ALL READY FOR YOU, SO MAKE SURE TO GET WASHED UP, OKAY?
...
ドキドキ B-DMP B-DMP
ドキドキ B-DMP B-DMP
...YES, MA'AM.

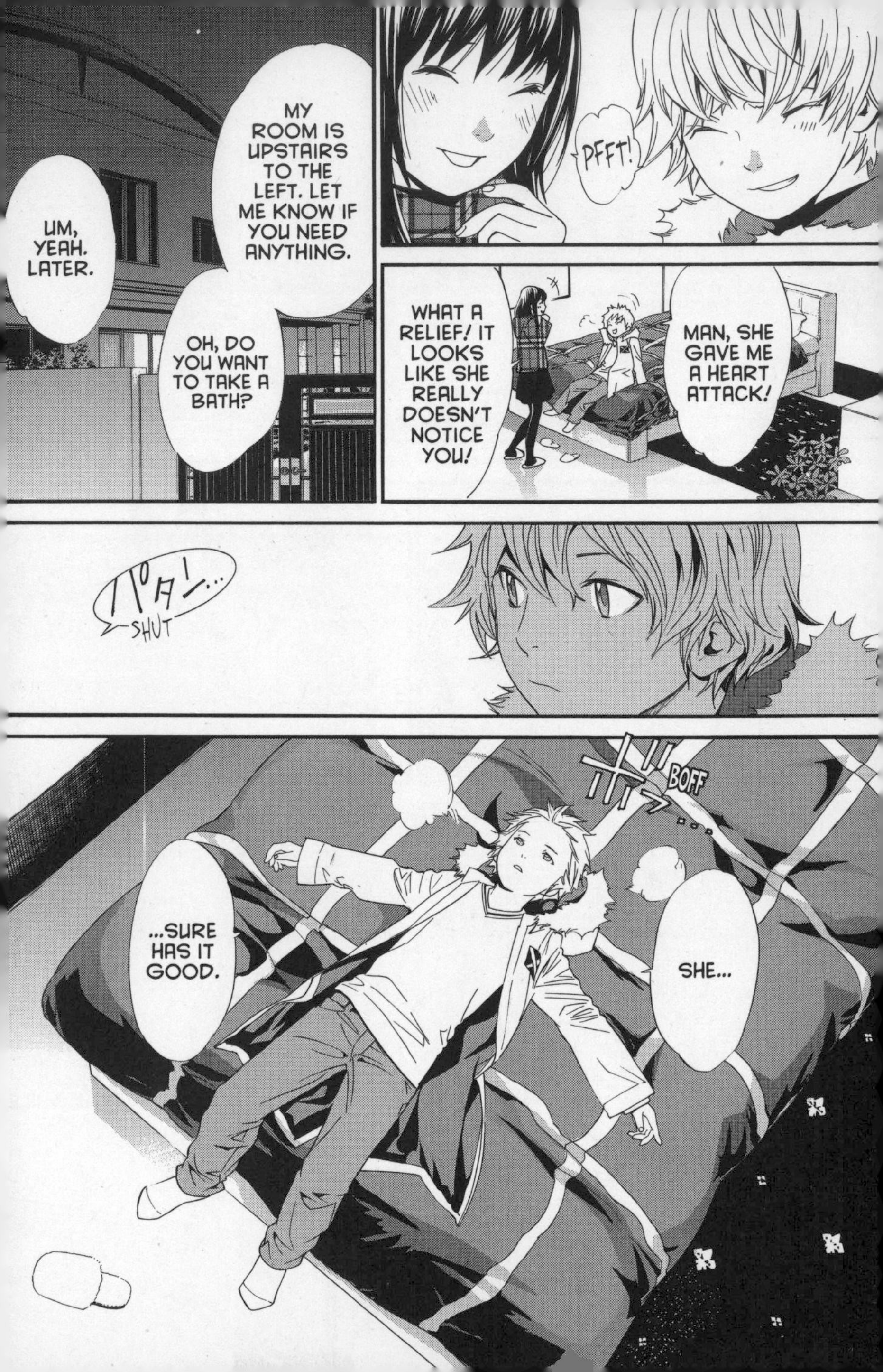
PFFT!
MAN, SHE GAVE ME A HEART ATTACK!
WHAT A RELIEF! IT LOOKS LIKE SHE REALLY DOESN'T NOTICE YOU!
MY ROOM IS UPSTAIRS TO THE LEFT. LET ME KNOW IF YOU NEED ANYTHING.
OH, DO YOU WANT TO TAKE A BATH?
UM, YEAH. LATER.
パタン…
SHUT
ボフッ
BOFF
SHE...
...SURE HAS IT GOOD.

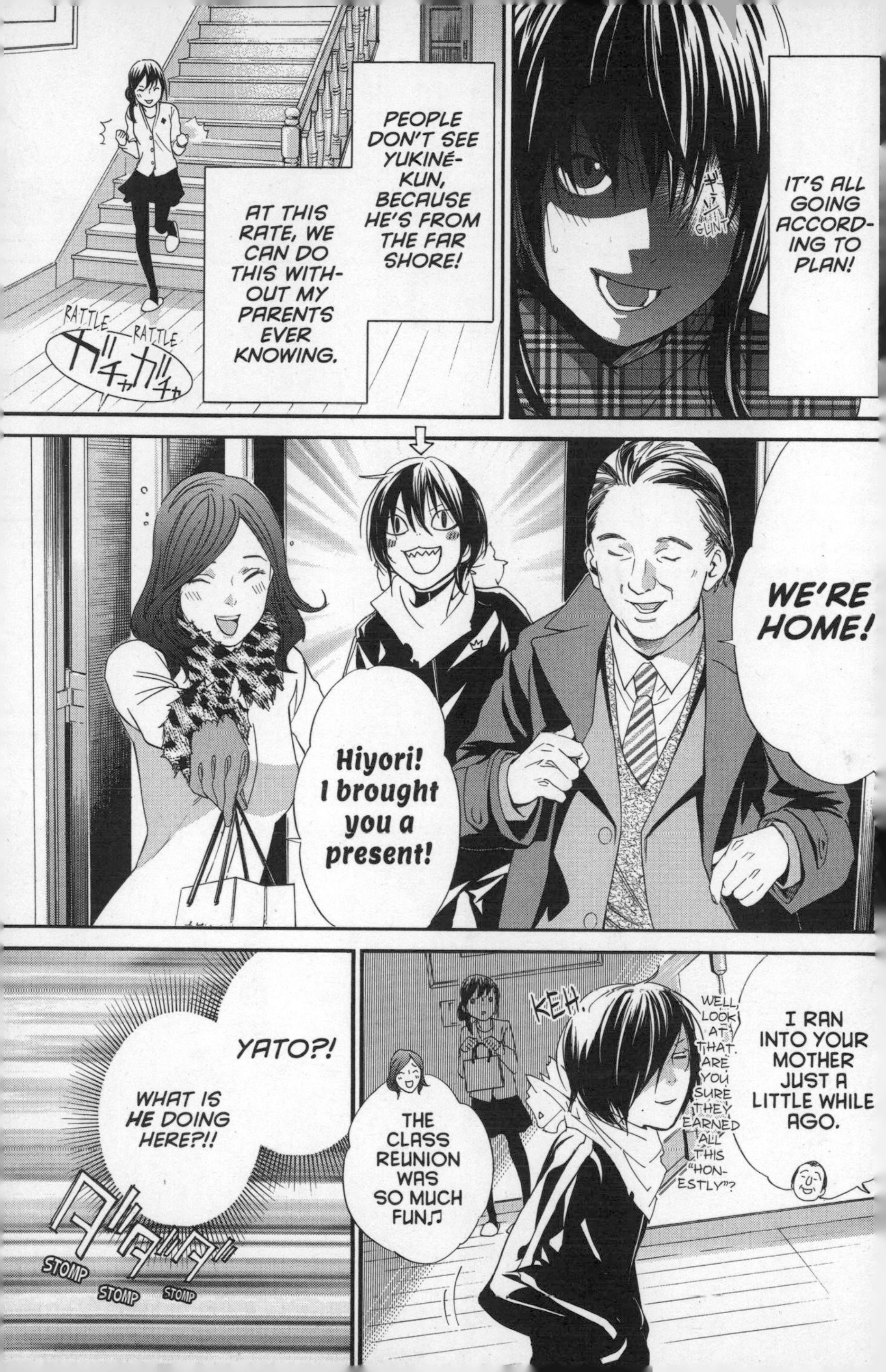

IT'S ALL GOING ACCORDING TO PLAN!
GLINT
PEOPLE DON'T SEE YUKINÉ-KUN, BECAUSE HE'S FROM THE FAR SHORE!
AT THIS RATE, WE CAN DO THIS WITHOUT MY PARENTS EVER KNOWING.
RATTLE RATTLE
WE'RE HOME!
Hiyori! I brought you a present!
I RAN INTO YOUR MOTHER JUST A LITTLE WHILE AGO.
WELL, LOOK AT THAT. ARE YOU SURE THEY EARNED ALL THIS "HONESTLY"?
KEH.
THE CLASS REUNION WAS SO MUCH FUN♫
YATO?!
WHAT IS HE DOING HERE?!!
STOMP STOMP STOMP

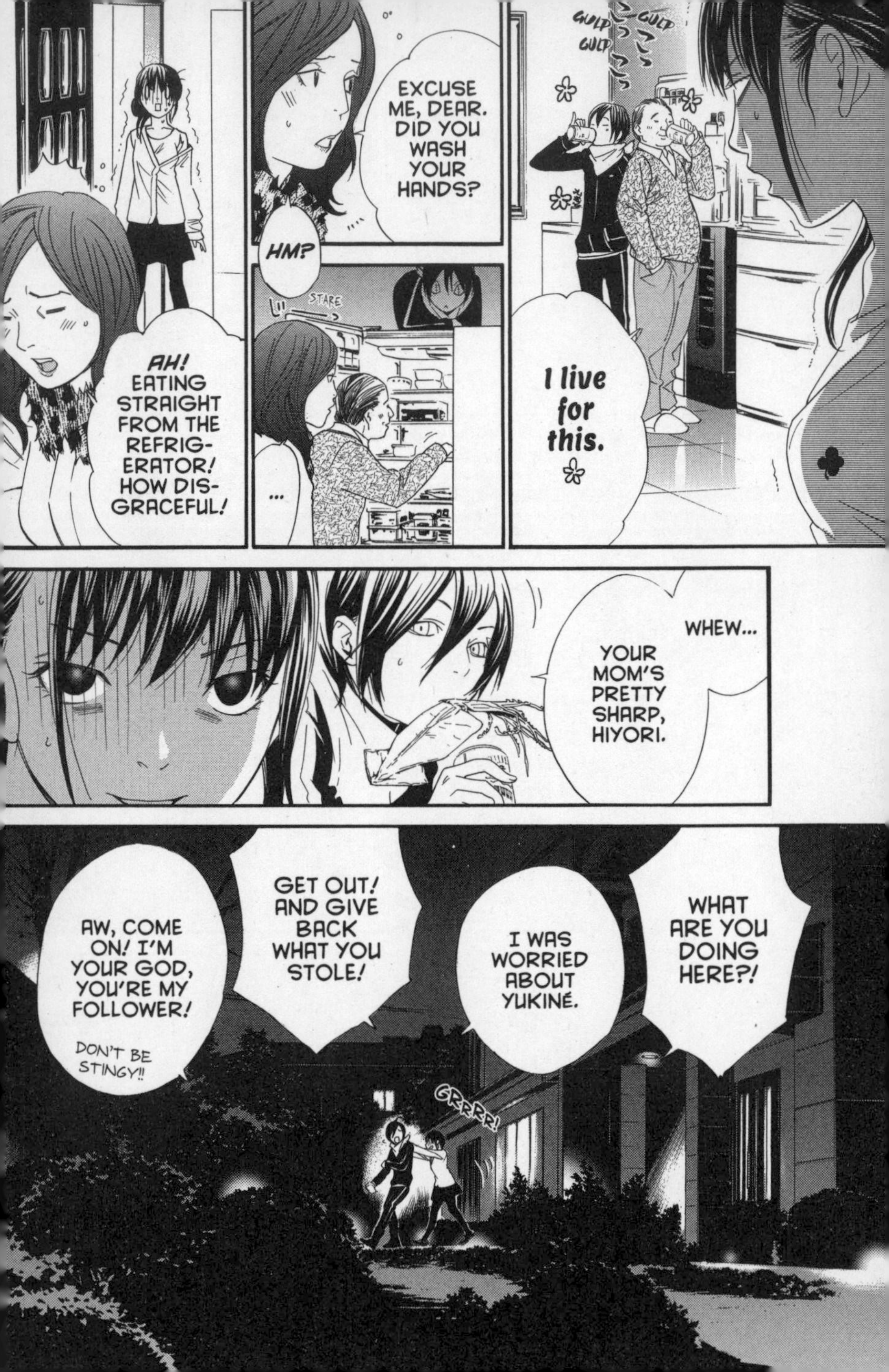
GULP
GULP
GULP
GULP
I live for this.
EXCUSE ME, DEAR. DID YOU WASH YOUR HANDS?
HM?
STARE
...
AH! EATING STRAIGHT FROM THE REFRIG-ERATOR! HOW DIS-GRACEFUL!
WHEW...
YOUR MOM'S PRETTY SHARP, HIYORI.
WHAT ARE YOU DOING HERE?!
I WAS WORRIED ABOUT YUKINÉ.
GET OUT! AND GIVE BACK WHAT YOU STOLE!
AW, COME ON! I'M YOUR GOD, YOU'RE MY FOLLOWER!
DON'T BE STINGY!!
GRRRR!

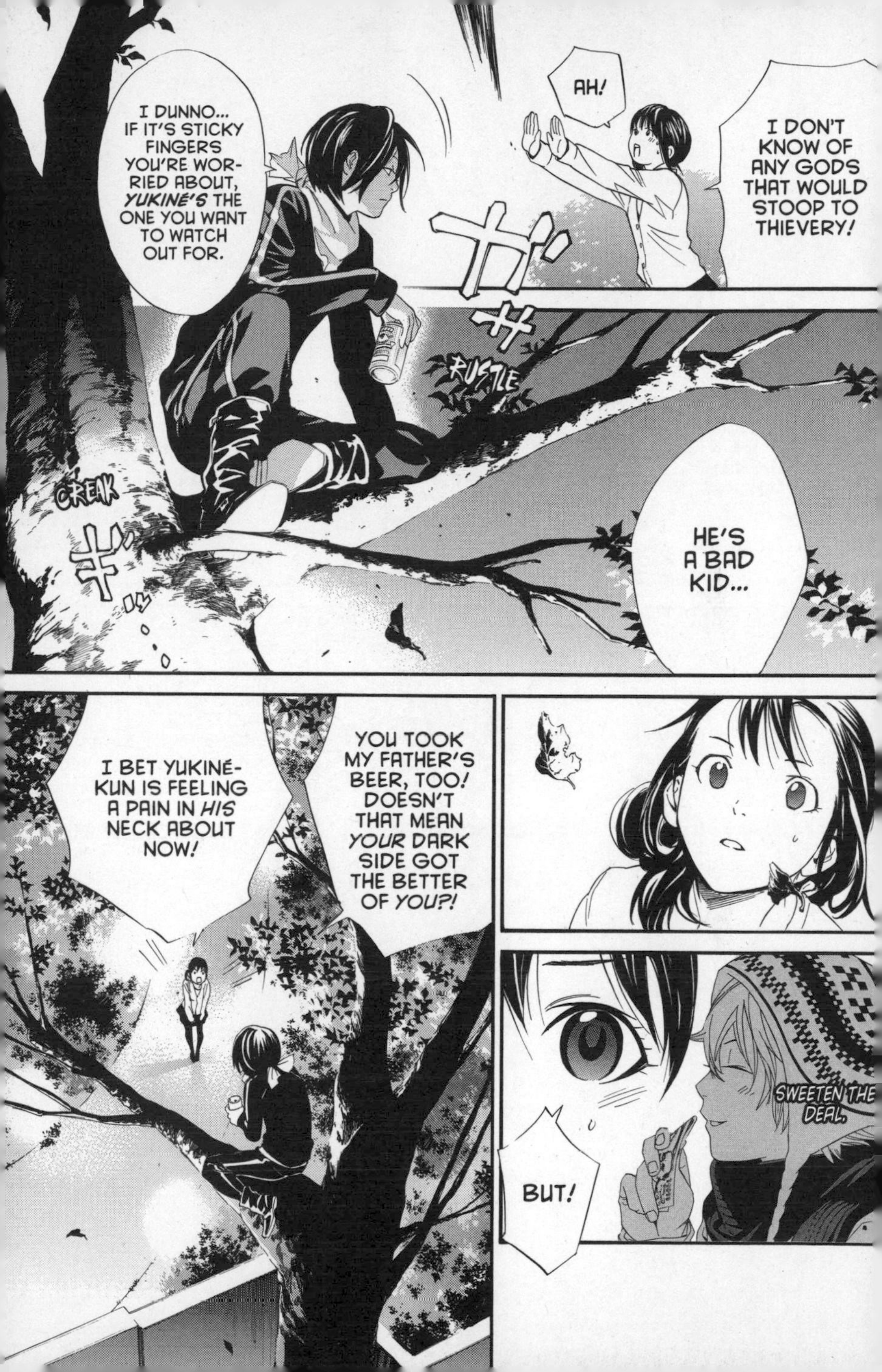
I DON'T KNOW OF ANY GODS THAT WOULD STOOP TO THIEVERY!
AH!
I DUNNO... IF IT'S STICKY FINGERS YOU'RE WORRIED ABOUT, *YUKINÉ'S* THE ONE YOU WANT TO WATCH OUT FOR.
ガサ
RUSTLE
HE'S A BAD KID...
CREAK
ギッ
SWEETEN THE DEAL.
BUT!
YOU TOOK MY FATHER'S BEER, TOO! DOESN'T THAT MEAN *YOUR* DARK SIDE GOT THE BETTER OF *YOU*?!
I BET YUKINÉ-KUN IS FEELING A PAIN IN *HIS* NECK ABOUT NOW!

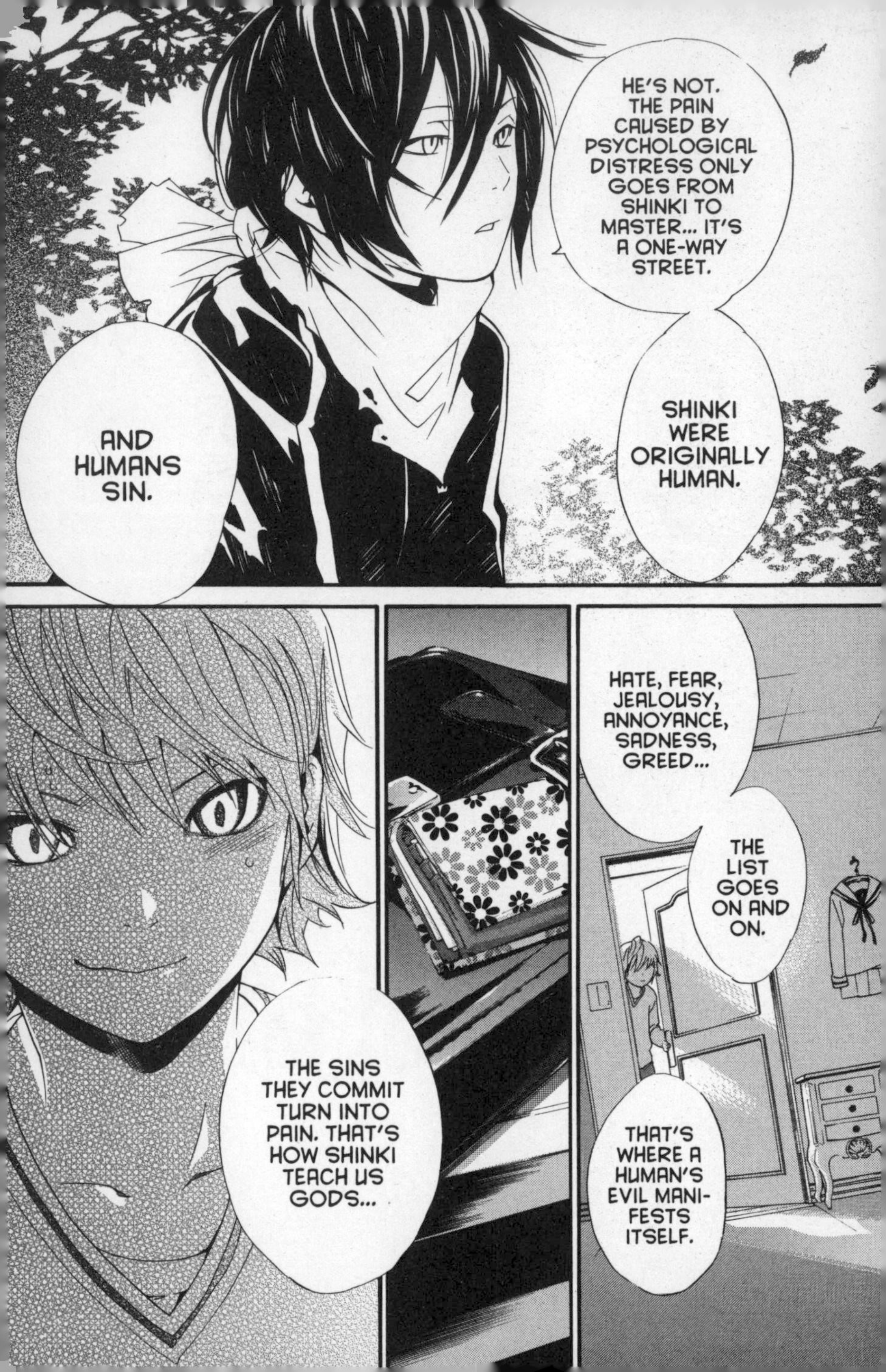
HE'S NOT. THE PAIN CAUSED BY PSYCHOLOGICAL DISTRESS ONLY GOES FROM SHINKI TO MASTER... IT'S A ONE-WAY STREET.
SHINKI WERE ORIGINALLY HUMAN.
AND HUMANS SIN.
HATE, FEAR, JEALOUSY, ANNOYANCE, SADNESS, GREED...
THE LIST GOES ON AND ON.
THAT'S WHERE A HUMAN'S EVIL MANI-FESTS ITSELF.
THE SINS THEY COMMIT TURN INTO PAIN. THAT'S HOW SHINKI TEACH US GODS...

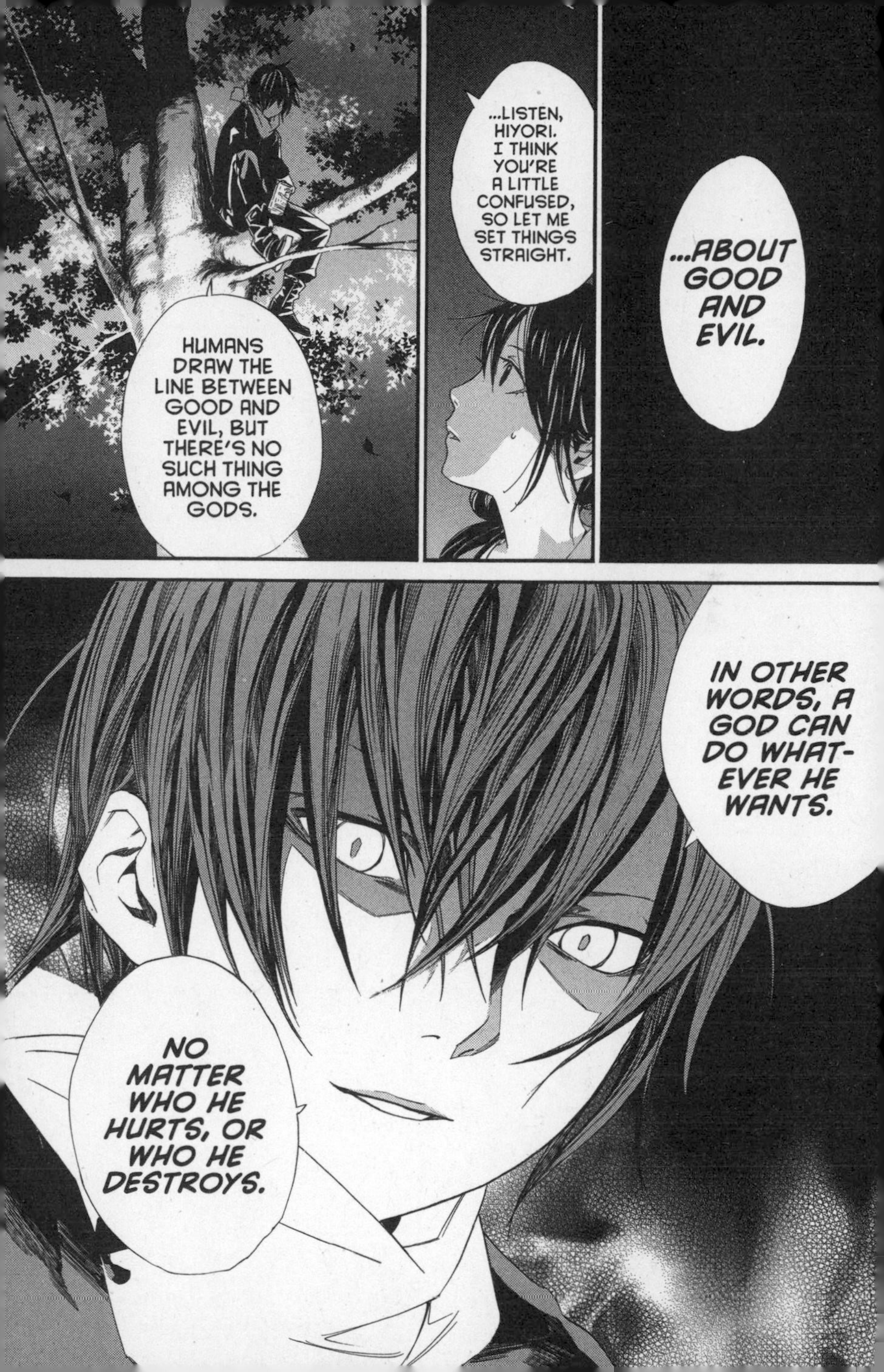
HUMANS DRAW THE LINE BETWEEN GOOD AND EVIL, BUT THERE'S NO SUCH THING AMONG THE GODS.
...LISTEN, HIYORI. I THINK YOU'RE A LITTLE CONFUSED, SO LET ME SET THINGS STRAIGHT.
...ABOUT GOOD AND EVIL.
IN OTHER WORDS, A GOD CAN DO WHAT-EVER HE WANTS.
NO MATTER WHO HE HURTS, OR WHO HE DESTROYS.

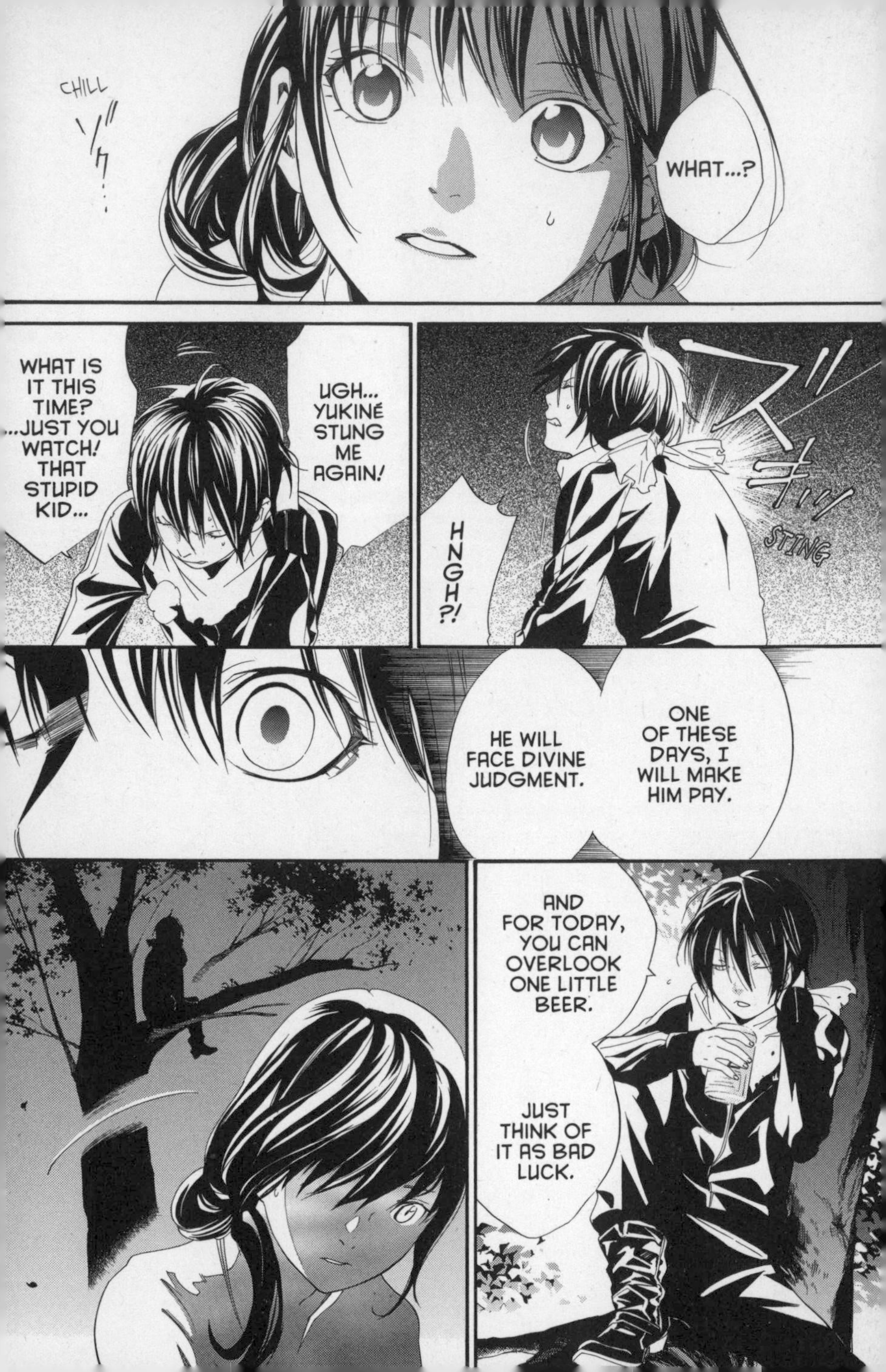
CHILL
WHAT...?
STING
HNGH?!
UGH... YUKINÉ STUNG ME AGAIN!
WHAT IS IT THIS TIME? ...JUST YOU WATCH! THAT STUPID KID...
ONE OF THESE DAYS, I WILL MAKE HIM PAY.
HE WILL FACE DIVINE JUDGMENT.
AND FOR TODAY, YOU CAN OVERLOOK ONE LITTLE BEER.
JUST THINK OF IT AS BAD LUCK.

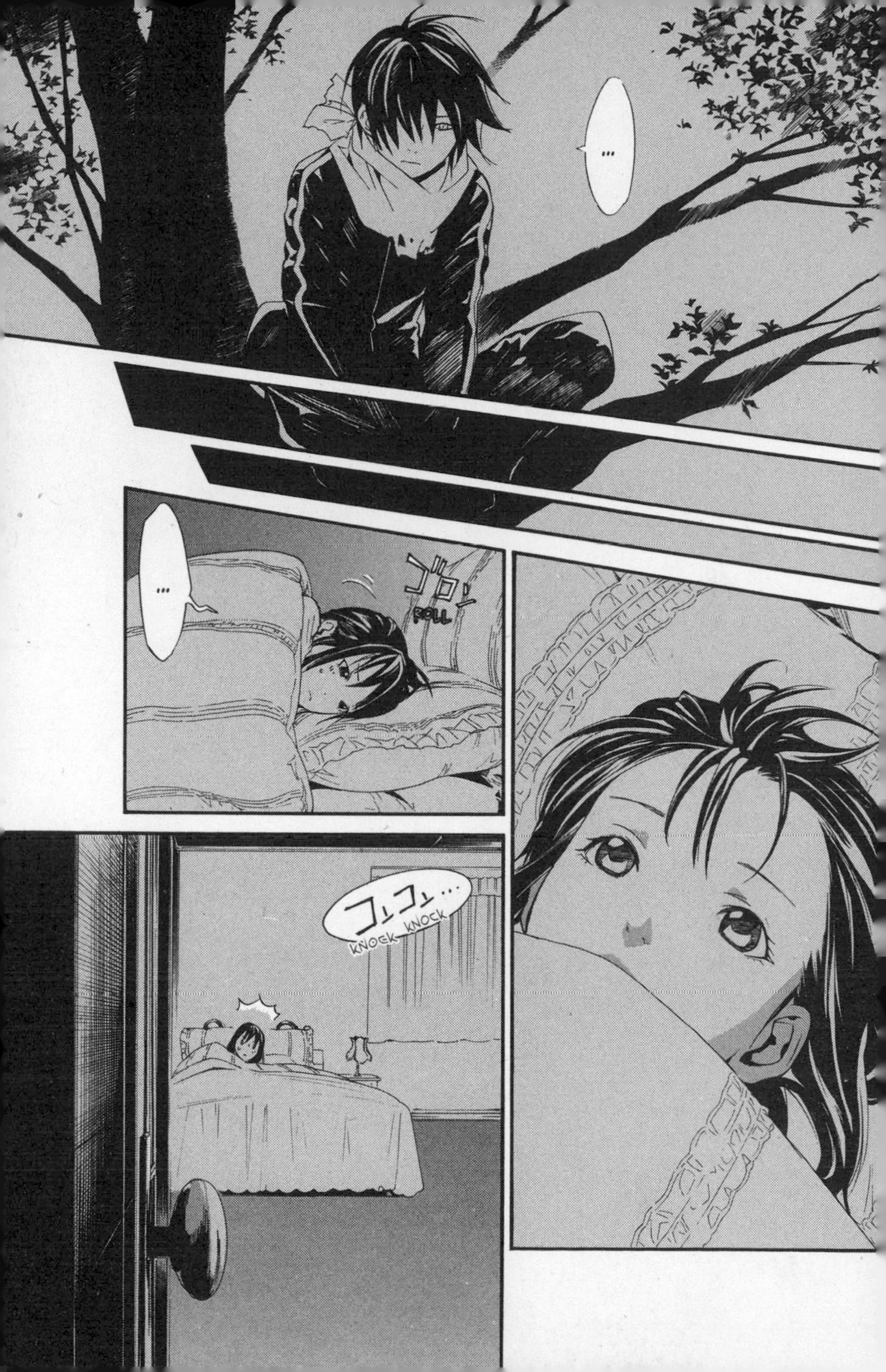
...
...
ゴロッ
ROLL
コッコッ…
KNOCK KNOCK

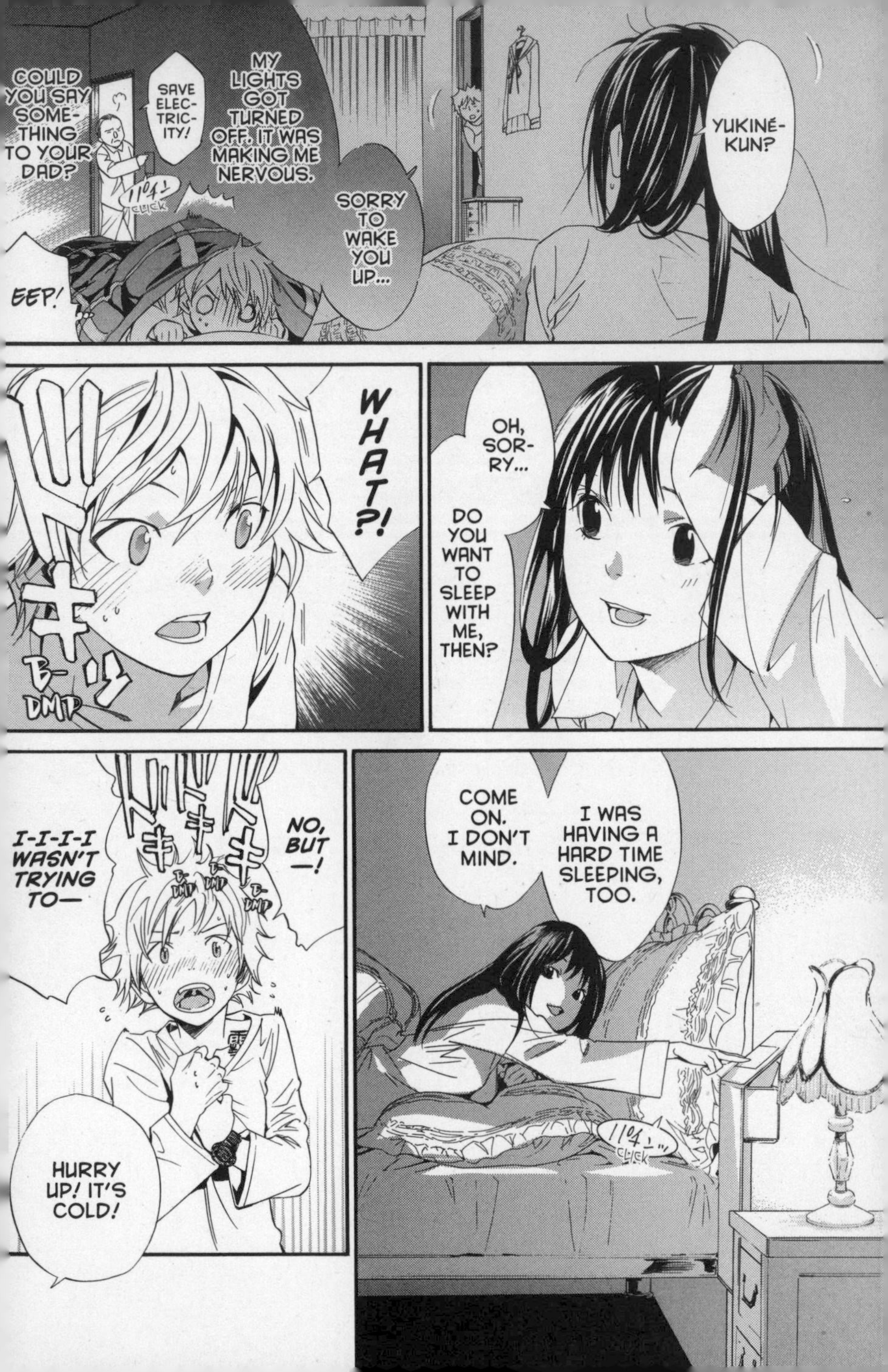
YUKINÉ-KUN?
SORRY TO WAKE YOU UP...
MY LIGHTS GOT TURNED OFF. IT WAS MAKING ME NERVOUS.
SAVE ELECTRICITY!
COULD YOU SAY SOMETHING TO YOUR DAD?
CLICK
EEP!
OH, SORRY...
DO YOU WANT TO SLEEP WITH ME, THEN?
WHAT?!
B-DMP
I WAS HAVING A HARD TIME SLEEPING, TOO.
COME ON. I DON'T MIND.
CLICK
NO, BUT—!
I-I-I-I WASN'T TRYING TO—
B-DMP
B-DMP
B-DMP
HURRY UP! IT'S COLD!

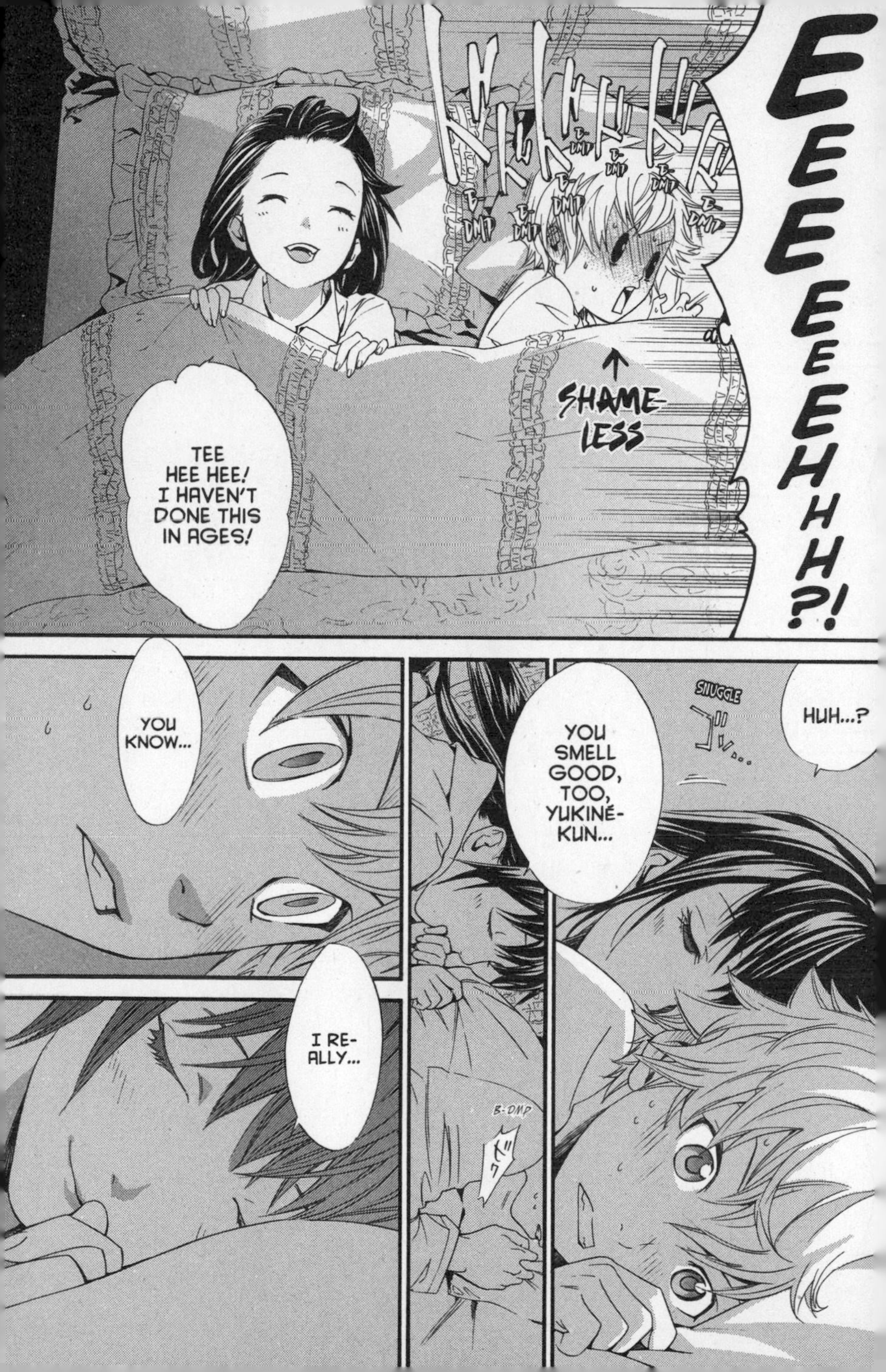
EEEEEEHHH?!
B-DMP B-DMP B-DMP B-DMP B-DMP B-DMP B-DMP B-DMP
SHAME-LESS
TEE HEE HEE! I HAVEN'T DONE THIS IN AGES!
HUH...?
SNUGGLE
YOU SMELL GOOD, TOO, YUKINE-KUN...
YOU KNOW...
B-DMP
I RE-ALLY...

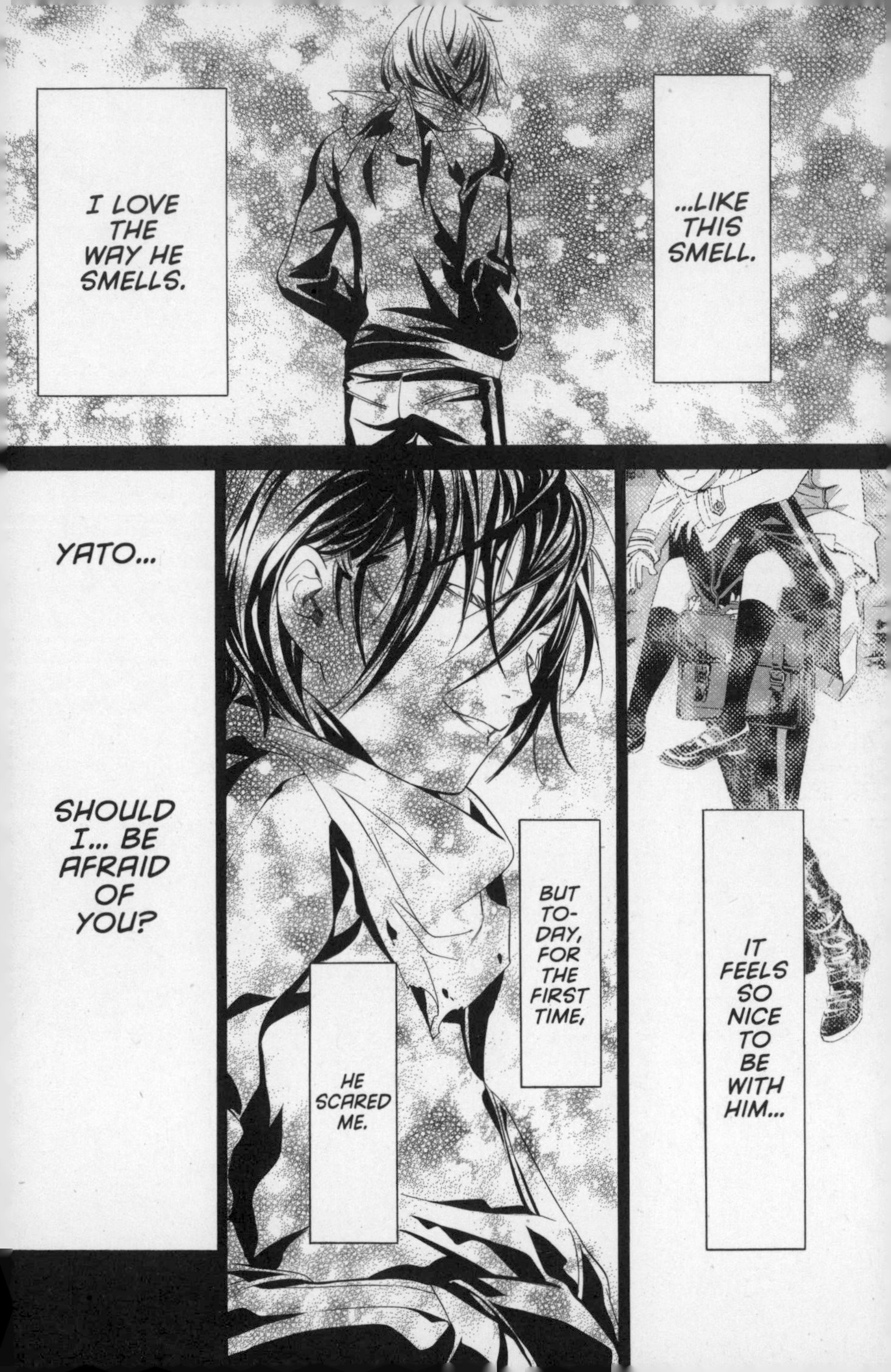
...LIKE THIS SMELL.
I LOVE THE WAY HE SMELLS.
IT FEELS SO NICE TO BE WITH HIM...
BUT TO-DAY, FOR THE FIRST TIME,
HE SCARED ME.
YATO...
SHOULD I... BE AFRAID OF YOU?

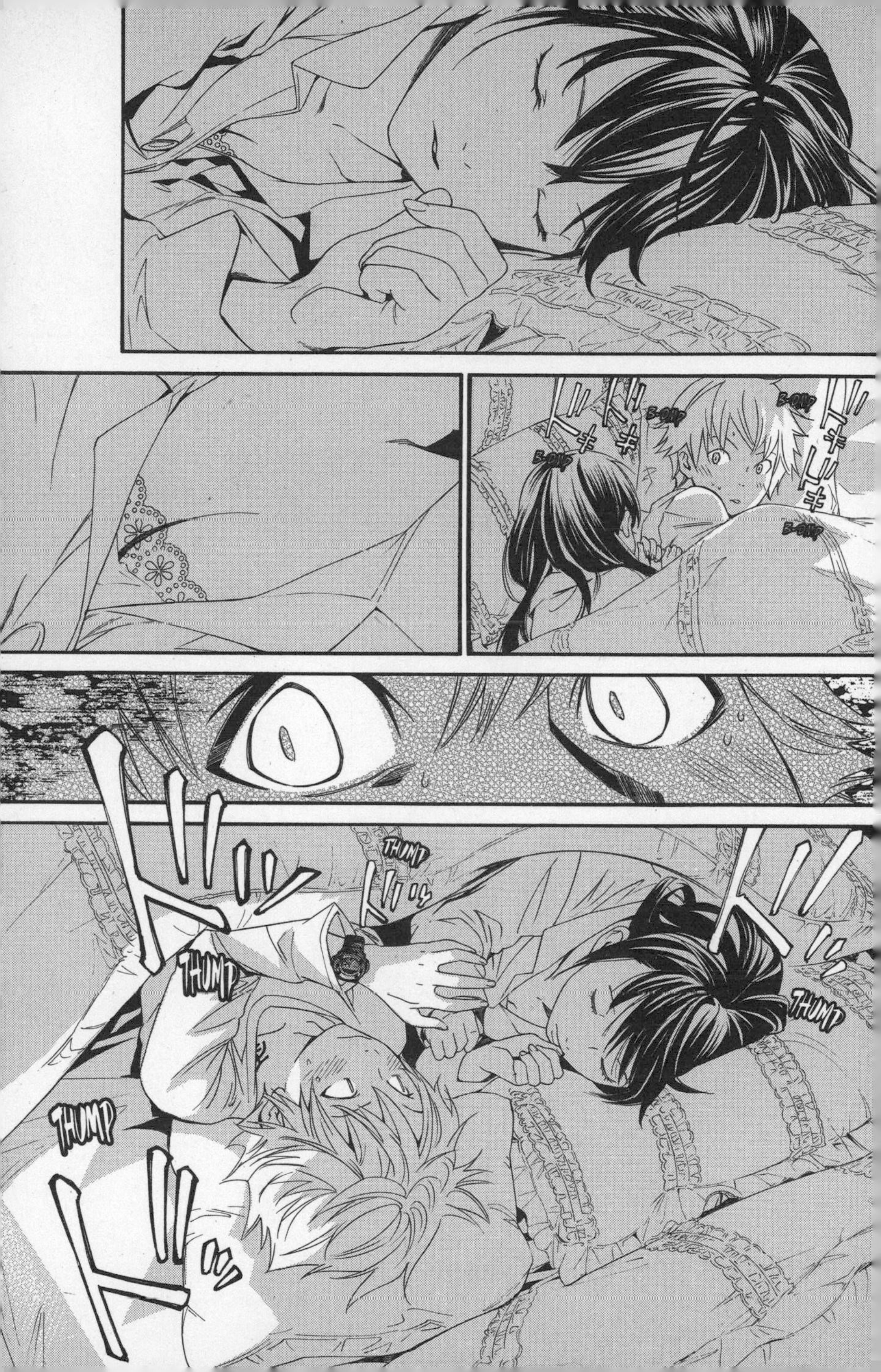
B-OMP
B-OMP
B-OMP
B-OMP
THUMP
THUMP
THUMP
THUMP

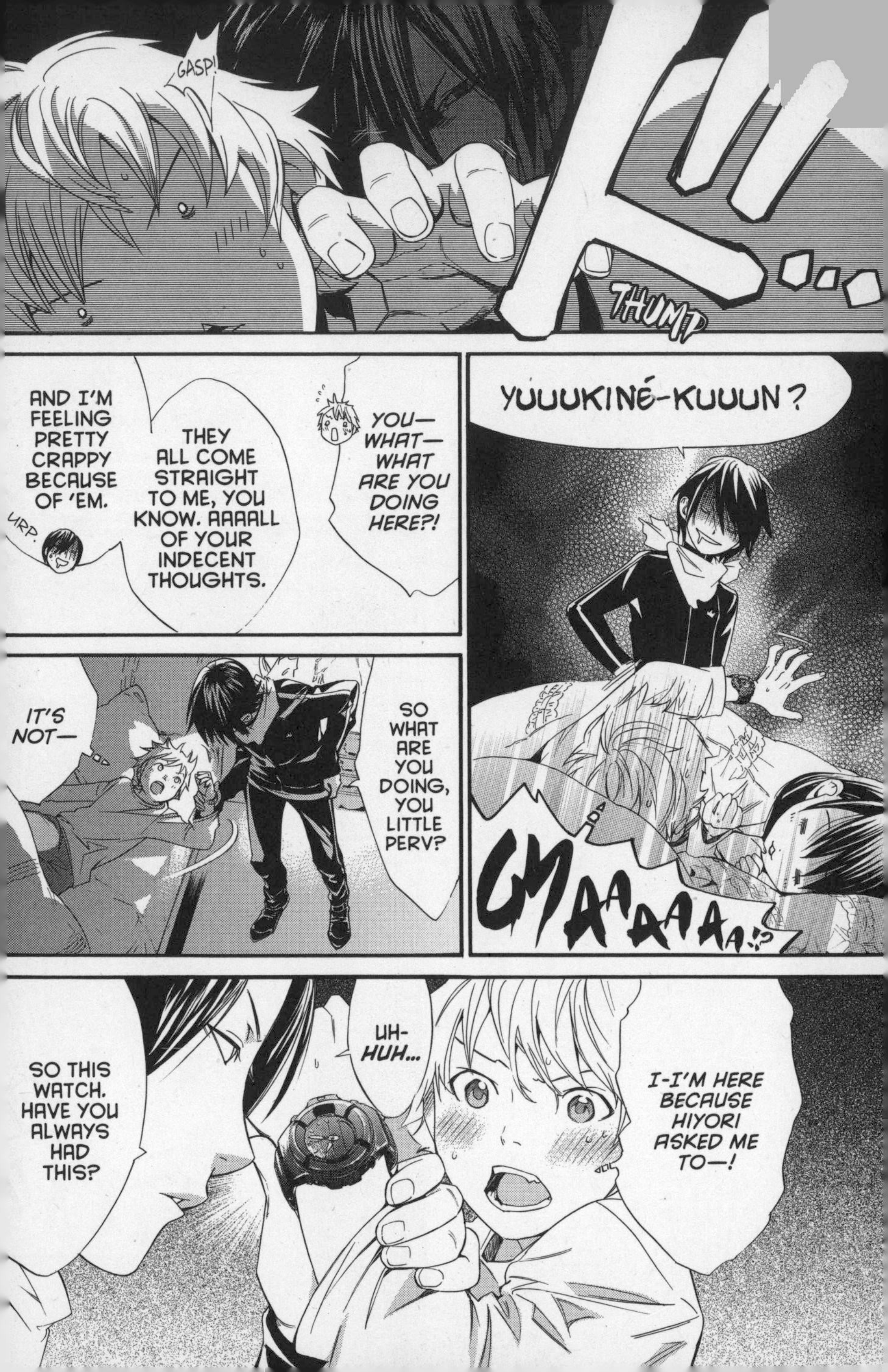
THUMP
GASP!
YUUUKINÉ-KUUUN?
GYAAAAAA!?
YOU—WHAT—WHAT ARE YOU DOING HERE?!
THEY ALL COME STRAIGHT TO ME, YOU KNOW. AAAALL OF YOUR INDECENT THOUGHTS.
AND I'M FEELING PRETTY CRAPPY BECAUSE OF 'EM.
URP.
SO WHAT ARE YOU DOING, YOU LITTLE PERV?
IT'S NOT—
I-I'M HERE BECAUSE HIYORI ASKED ME TO—!
UH-HUH...
SO THIS WATCH. HAVE YOU ALWAYS HAD THIS?

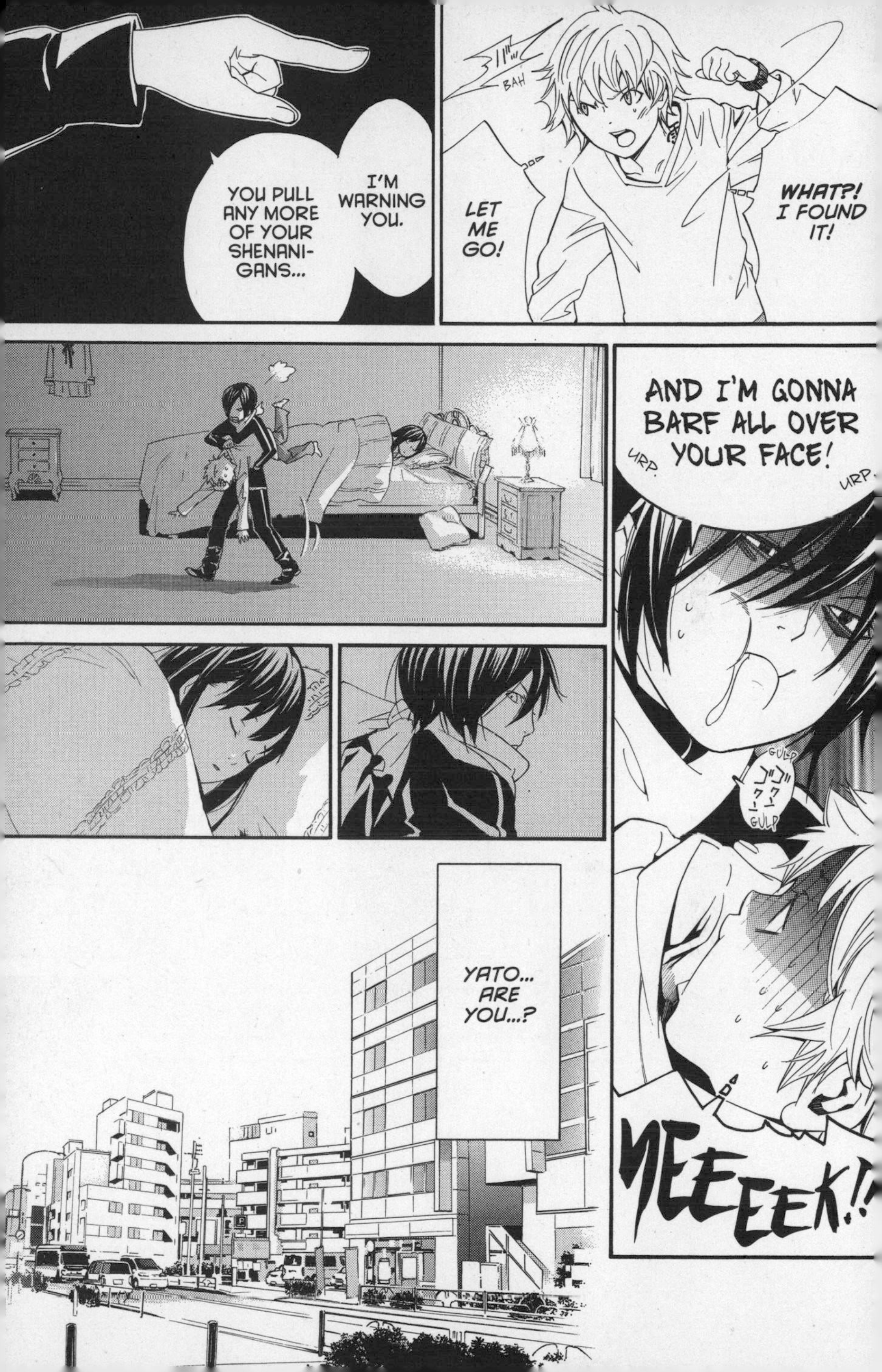
BAH
WHAT?! I FOUND IT!
LET ME GO!
I'M WARNING YOU.
YOU PULL ANY MORE OF YOUR SHENANI-GANS...
AND I'M GONNA BARF ALL OVER YOUR FACE!
URP.
URP.
GULP
GULP
YEEEEK!!
YATO... ARE YOU...?

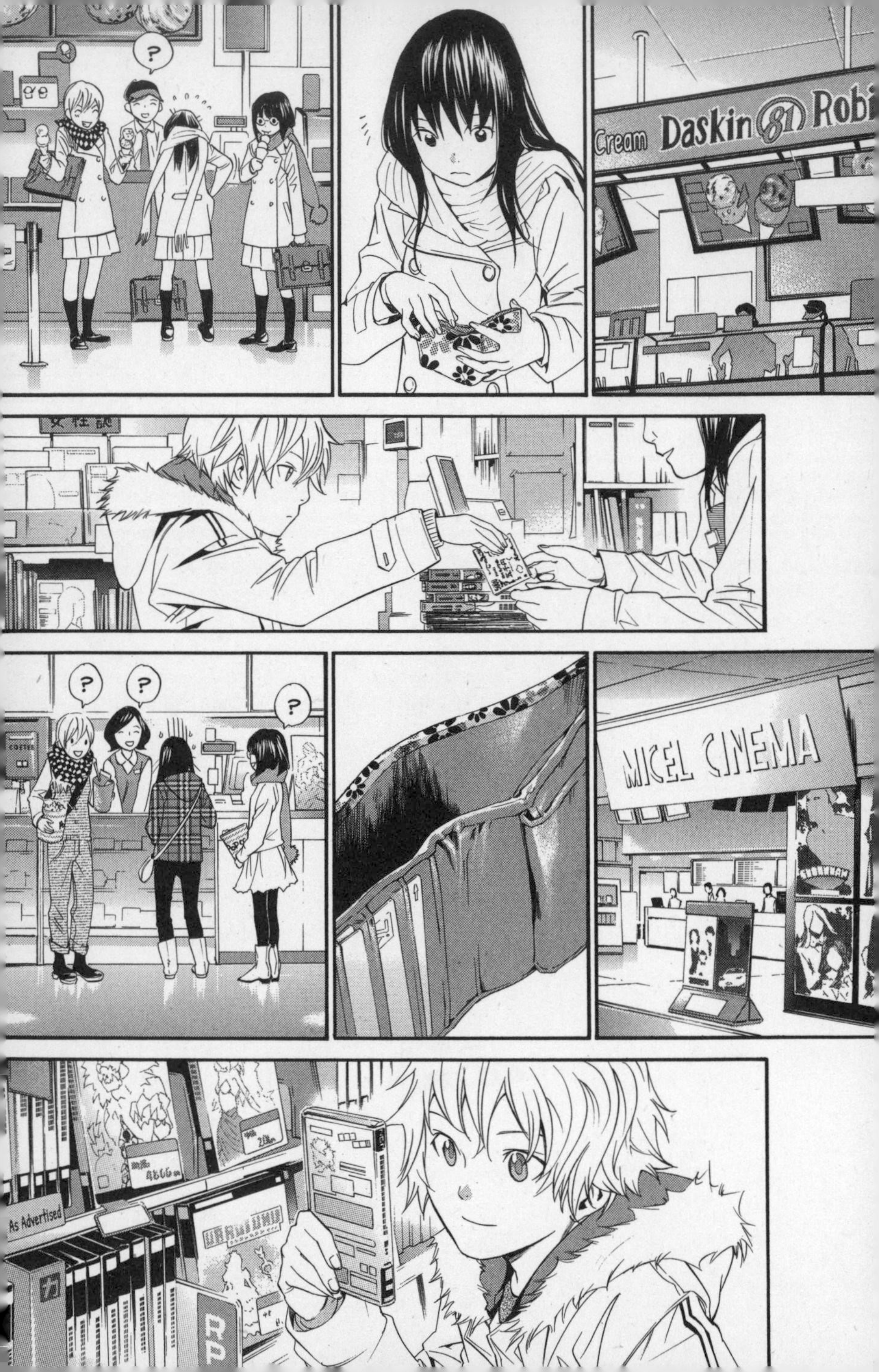
Cream Daskin 81 Robi
?
MICEL CINEMA
?
?
?
As Advertised

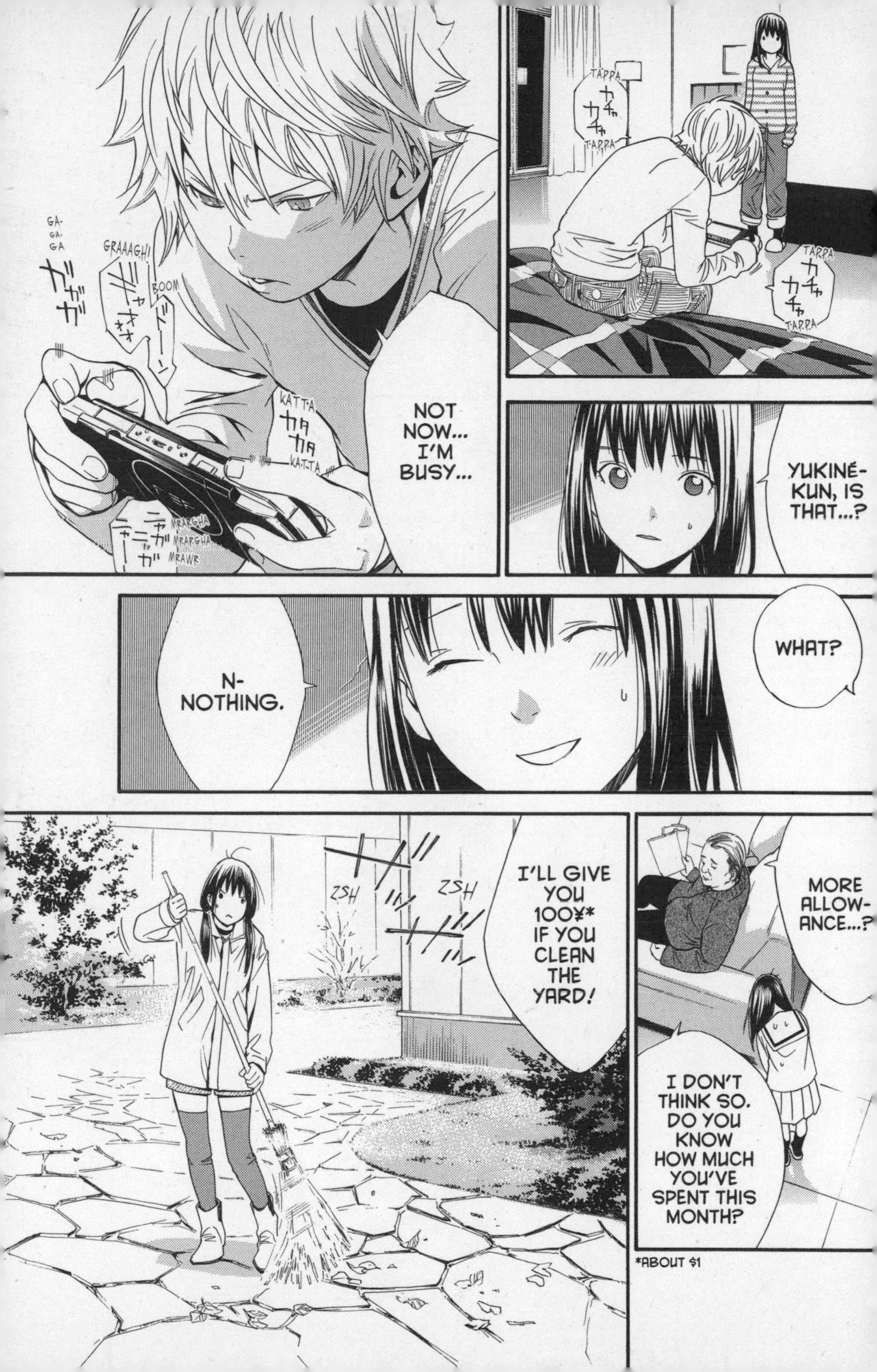
TAPPA
カチャカチャ
TAPPA
TAPPA
カチャカチャ
TAPPA
YUKINÉ-KUN, IS THAT...?
GA-GA-GA
ガガガ
GRAAAGH!
ギャオオ
BOOM
ドーン
KATTA
カタカタ
KATTA
NOT NOW... I'M BUSY...
MRARGHA
MRARGHA
MRAWR
WHAT?
N-NOTHING.
MORE ALLOWANCE...?
I DON'T THINK SO. DO YOU KNOW HOW MUCH YOU'VE SPENT THIS MONTH?
I'LL GIVE YOU 100¥* IF YOU CLEAN THE YARD!
ZSH
ZSH

*ABOUT $1

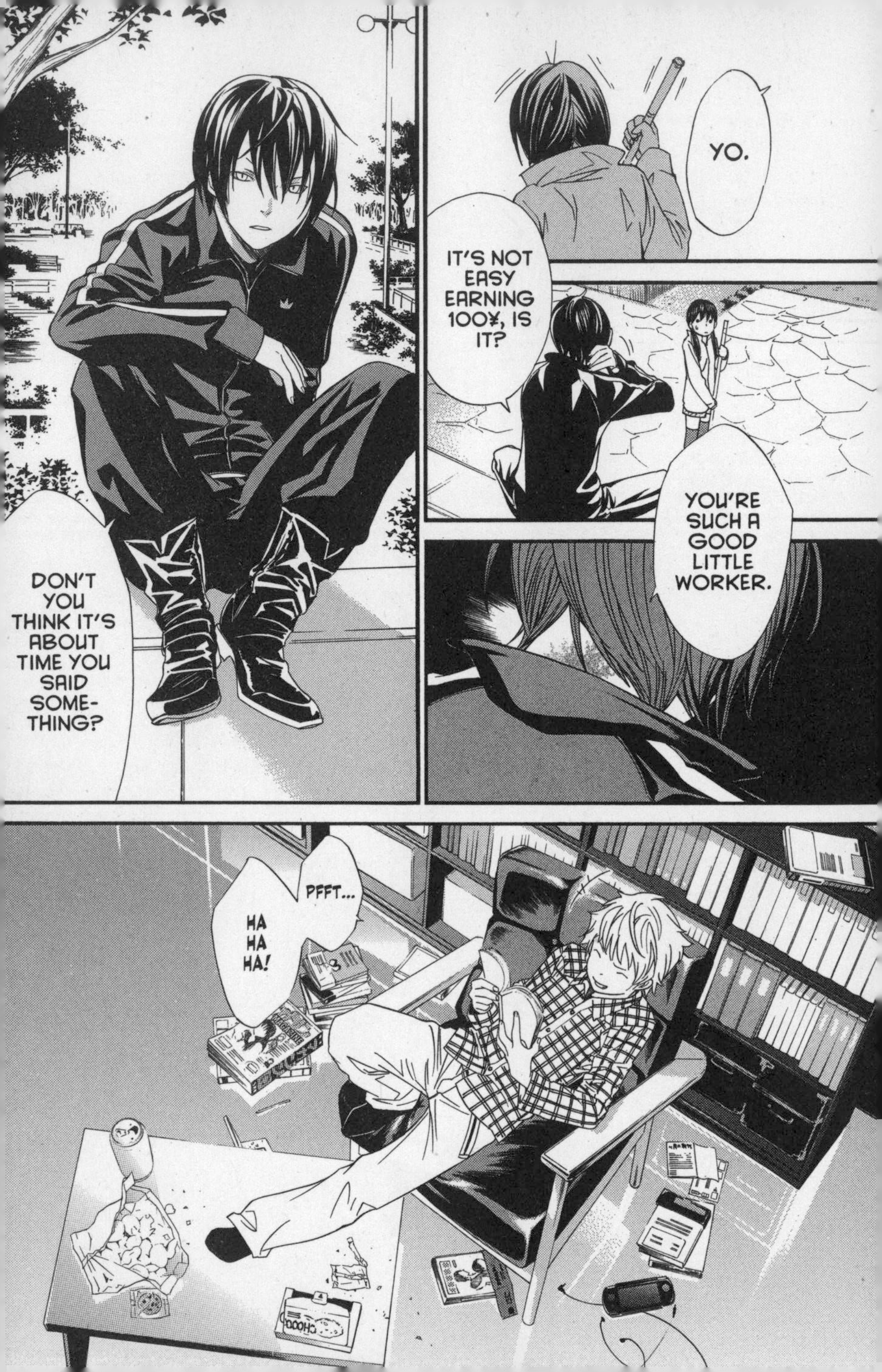
YO.
IT'S NOT EASY EARNING 100¥, IS IT?
YOU'RE SUCH A GOOD LITTLE WORKER.
DON'T YOU THINK IT'S ABOUT TIME YOU SAID SOME-THING?
PFFT...
HA HA HA!

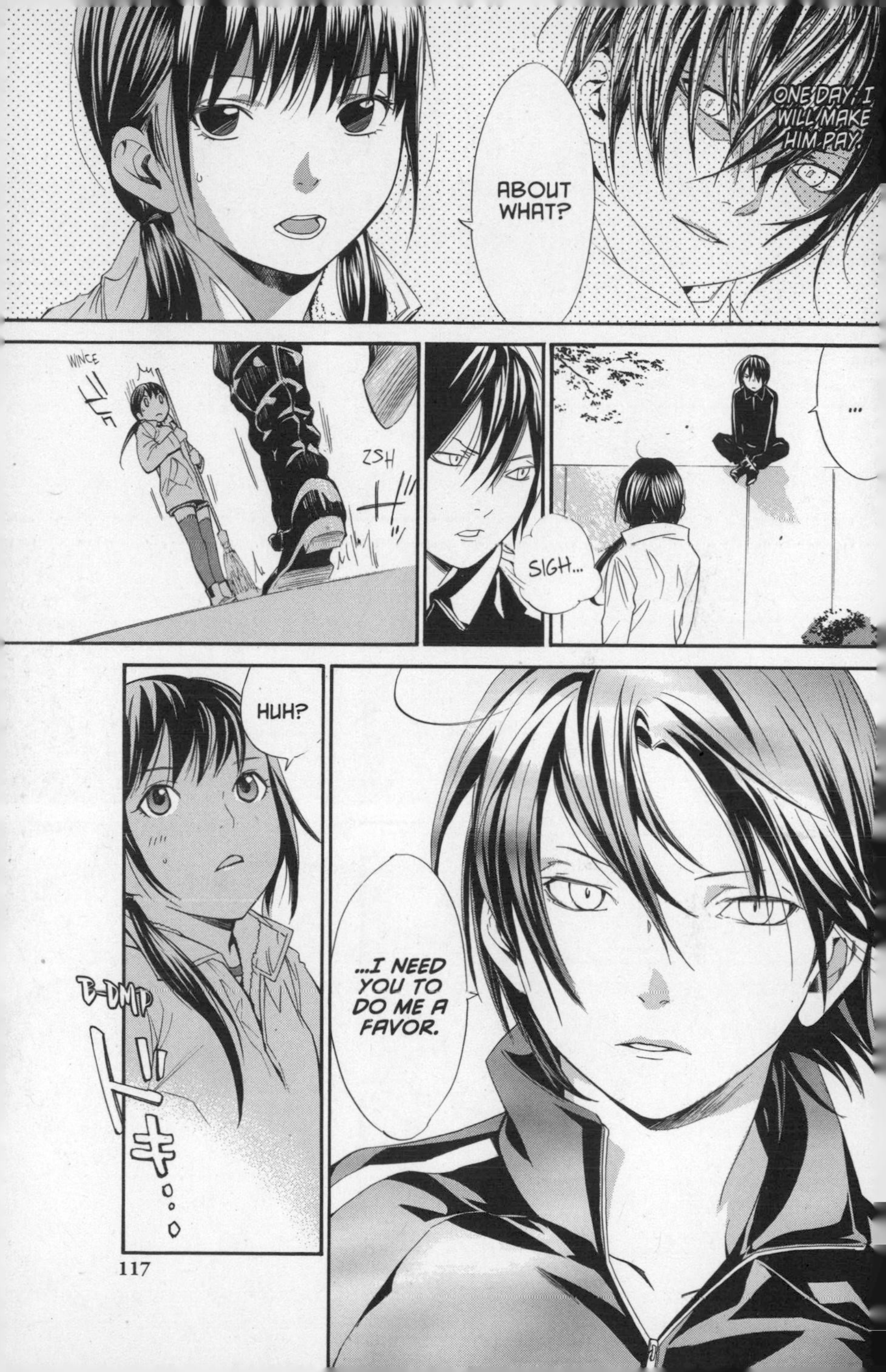
ONE DAY, I WILL MAKE HIM PAY.
ABOUT WHAT?
...
SIGH...
ZSH
WINCE
...I NEED YOU TO DO ME A FAVOR.
HUH?
B-DMP

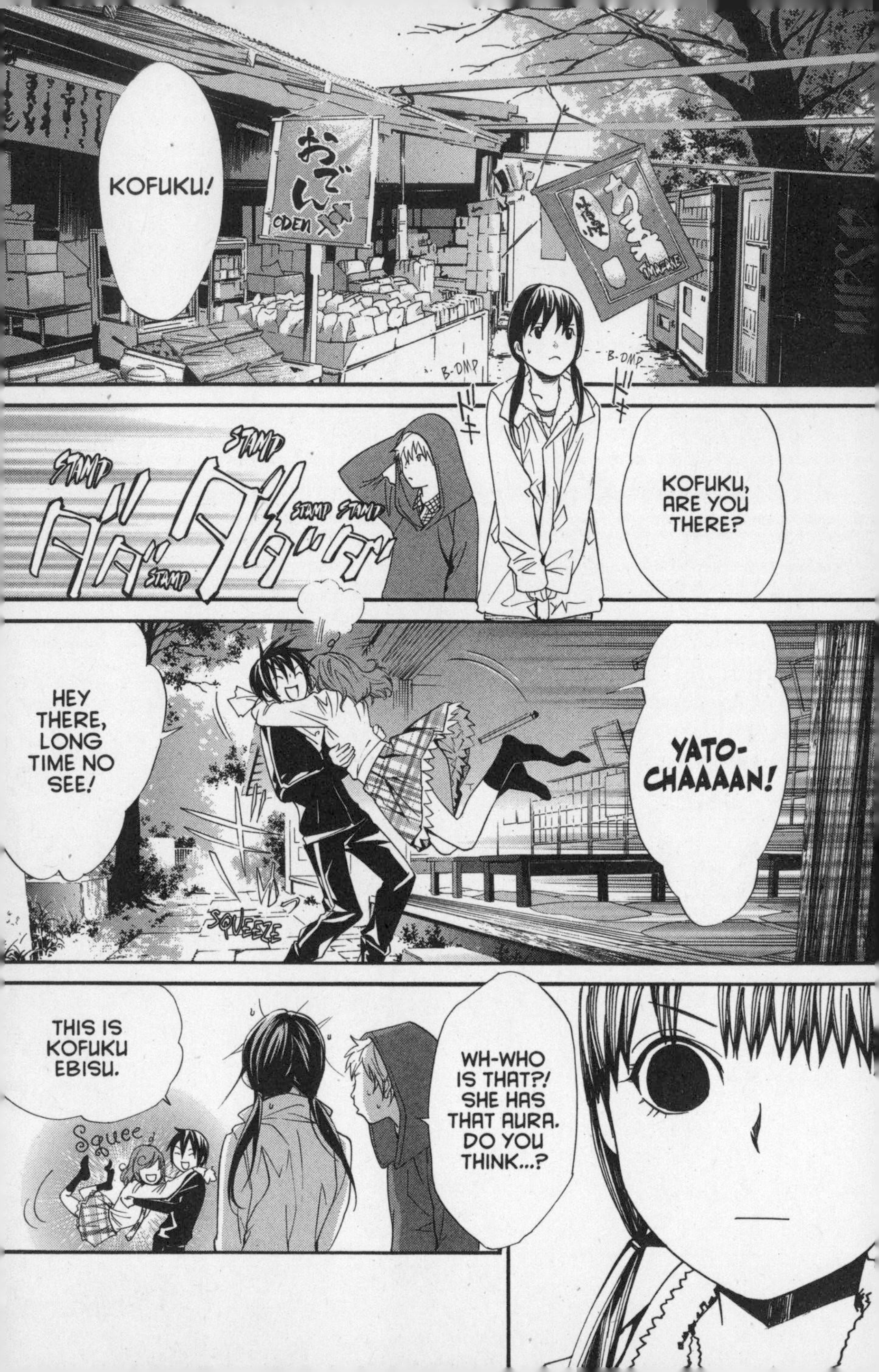
KOFUKU!
ODEN
B-DMP
B-DMP
KOFUKU, ARE YOU THERE?
STAMP
STAMP
STAMP STAMP
STAMP
YATO-CHAAAAN!
HEY THERE, LONG TIME NO SEE!
SQUEEZE
WH-WHO IS THAT?! SHE HAS THAT AURA. DO YOU THINK...?
THIS IS KOFUKU EBISU.
Squee

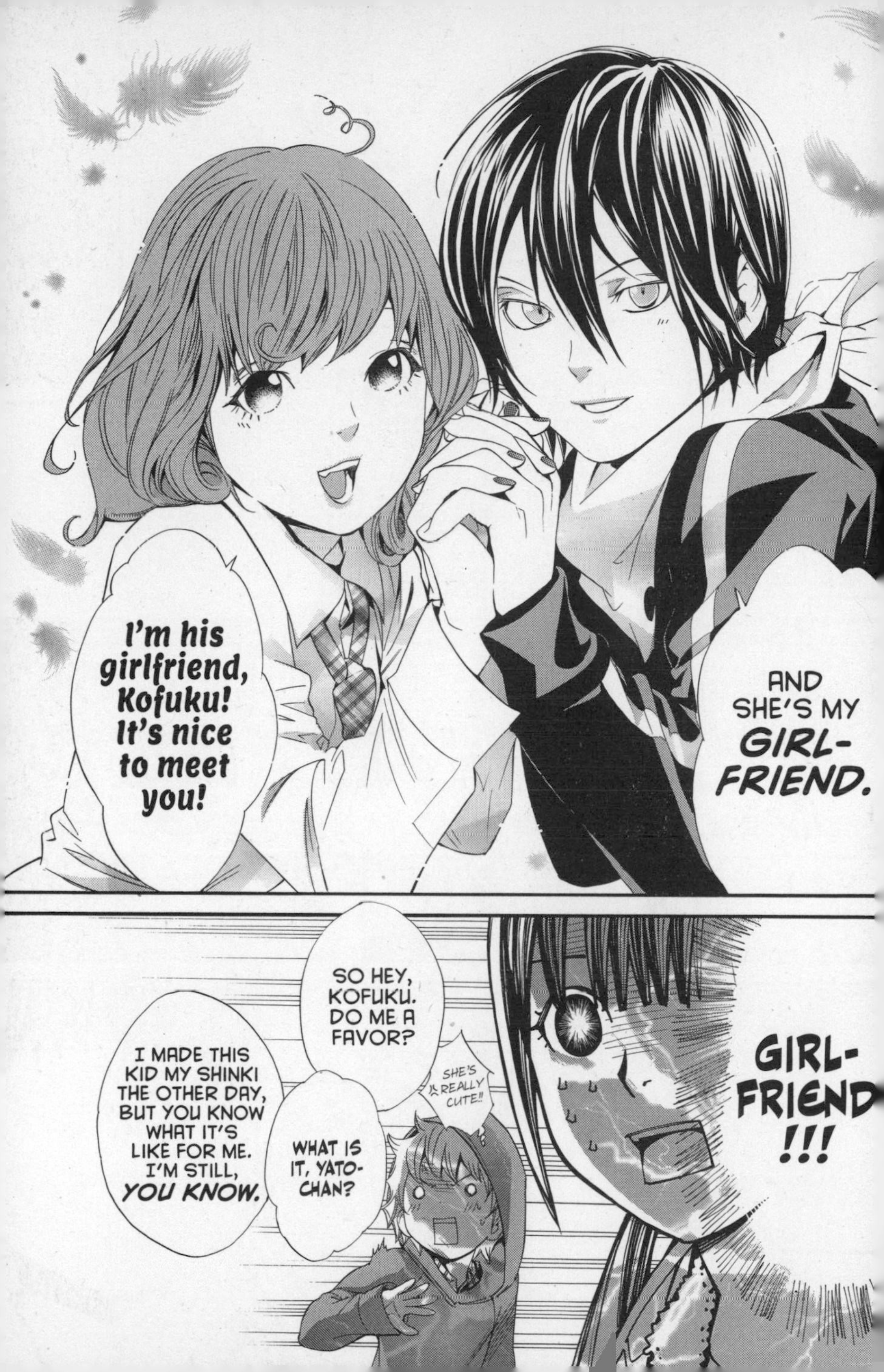
I'm his girlfriend, Kofuku! It's nice to meet you!
AND SHE'S MY GIRL-FRIEND.
GIRL-FRIEND!!!
SHE'S REALLY CUTE!!
SO HEY, KOFUKU. DO ME A FAVOR?
WHAT IS IT, YATO-CHAN?
I MADE THIS KID MY SHINKI THE OTHER DAY, BUT YOU KNOW WHAT IT'S LIKE FOR ME. I'M STILL, YOU KNOW.

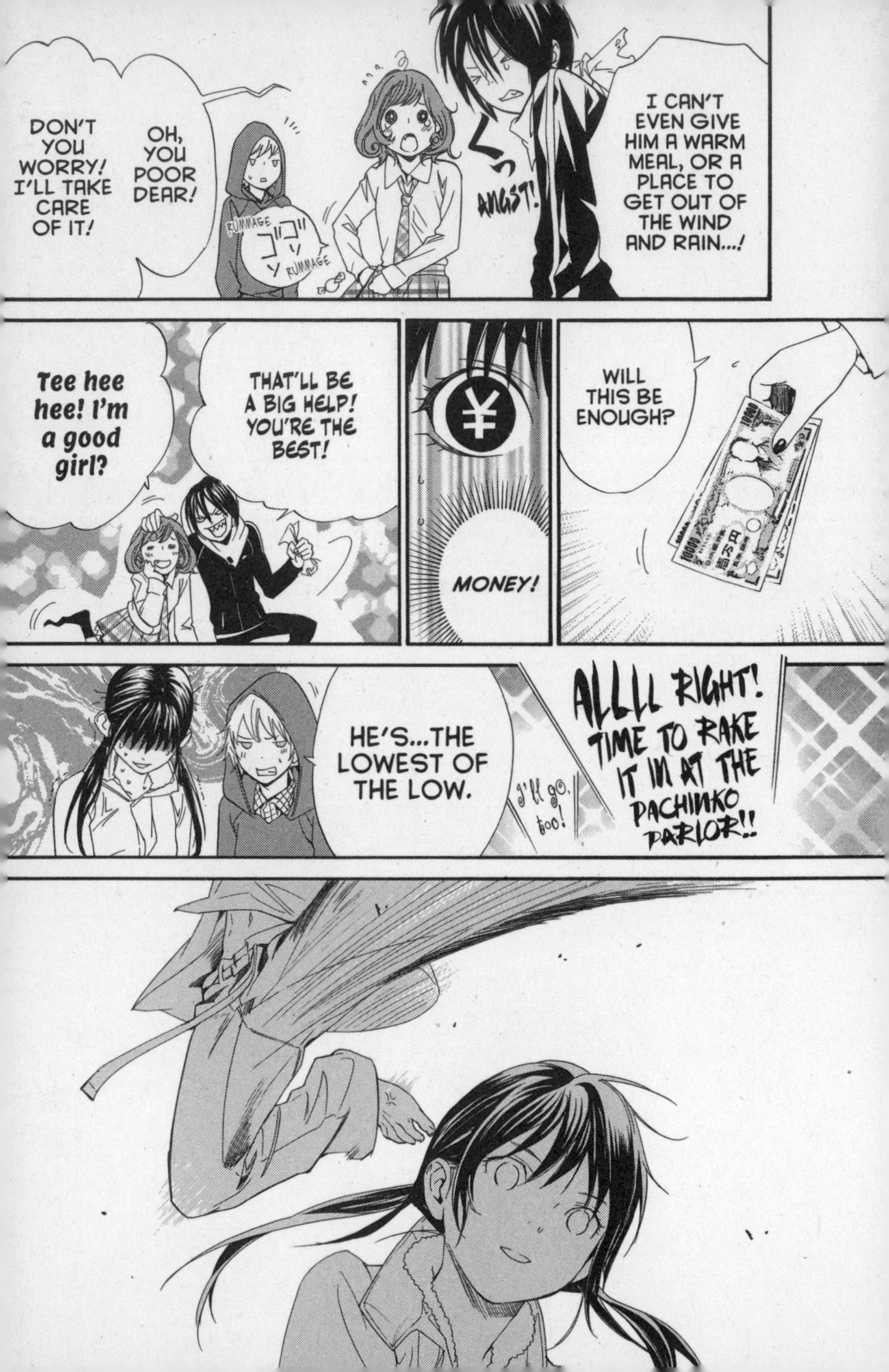
I CAN'T EVEN GIVE HIM A WARM MEAL, OR A PLACE TO GET OUT OF THE WIND AND RAIN...!
ANGST!
OH, YOU POOR DEAR!
DON'T YOU WORRY! I'LL TAKE CARE OF IT!
RUMMAGE RUMMAGE
WILL THIS BE ENOUGH?
MONEY!
THAT'LL BE A BIG HELP! YOU'RE THE BEST!
Tee hee hee! I'm a good girl?
ALLLL RIGHT! TIME TO RAKE IT IN AT THE PACHINKO PARLOR!!
I'll go, too!
HE'S...THE LOWEST OF THE LOW.

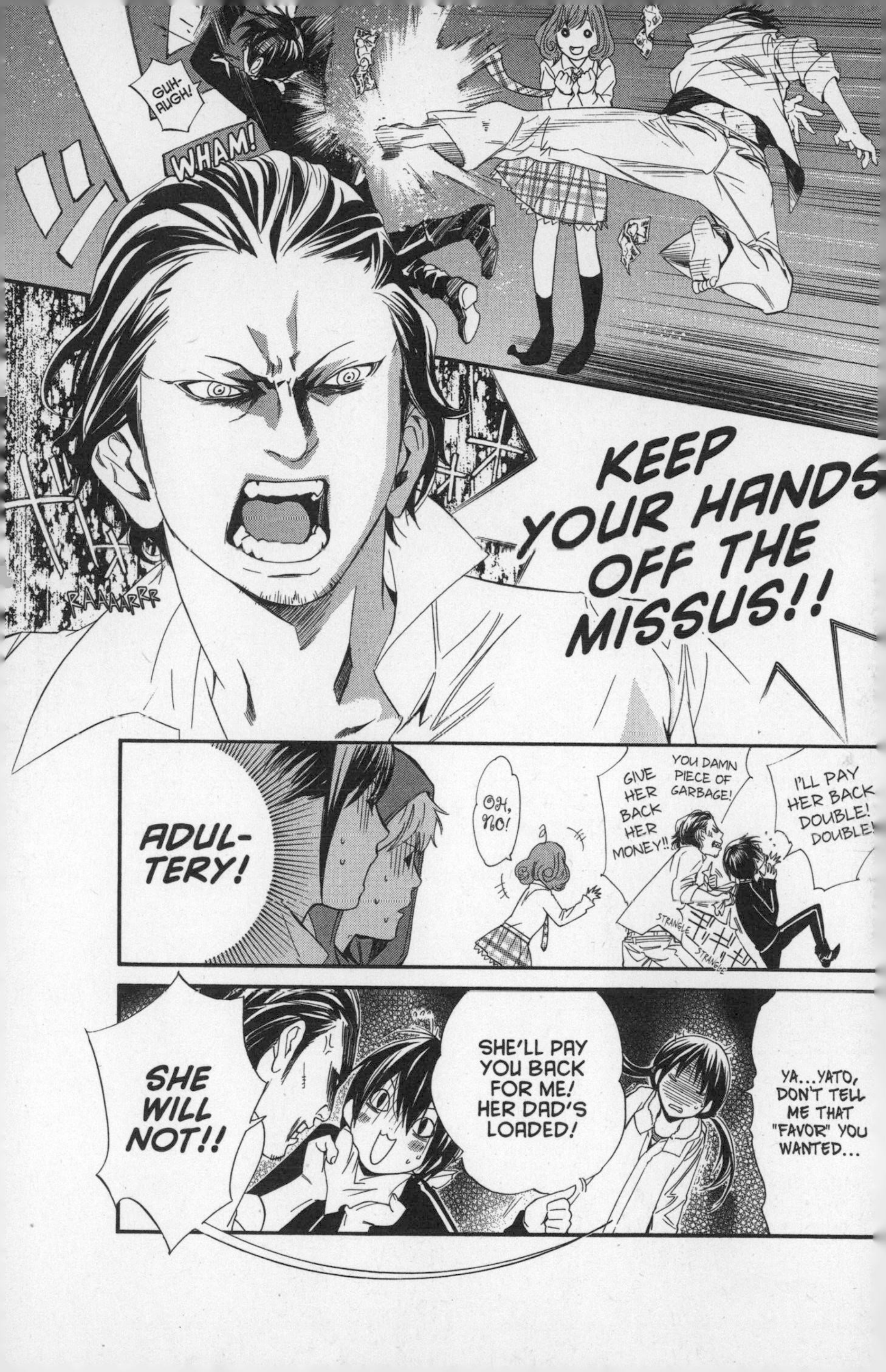
GUH-AUGH!
WHAM!
KEEP YOUR HANDS OFF THE MISSUS!!
RAAAARRR
I'LL PAY HER BACK DOUBLE! DOUBLE!
YOU DAMN PIECE OF GARBAGE!
GIVE HER BACK HER MONEY!!
OH, NO!
STRANGLE
STRANGLE
ADULTERY!
YA...YATO, DON'T TELL ME THAT "FAVOR" YOU WANTED...
SHE'LL PAY YOU BACK FOR ME! HER DAD'S LOADED!
SHE WILL NOT!!

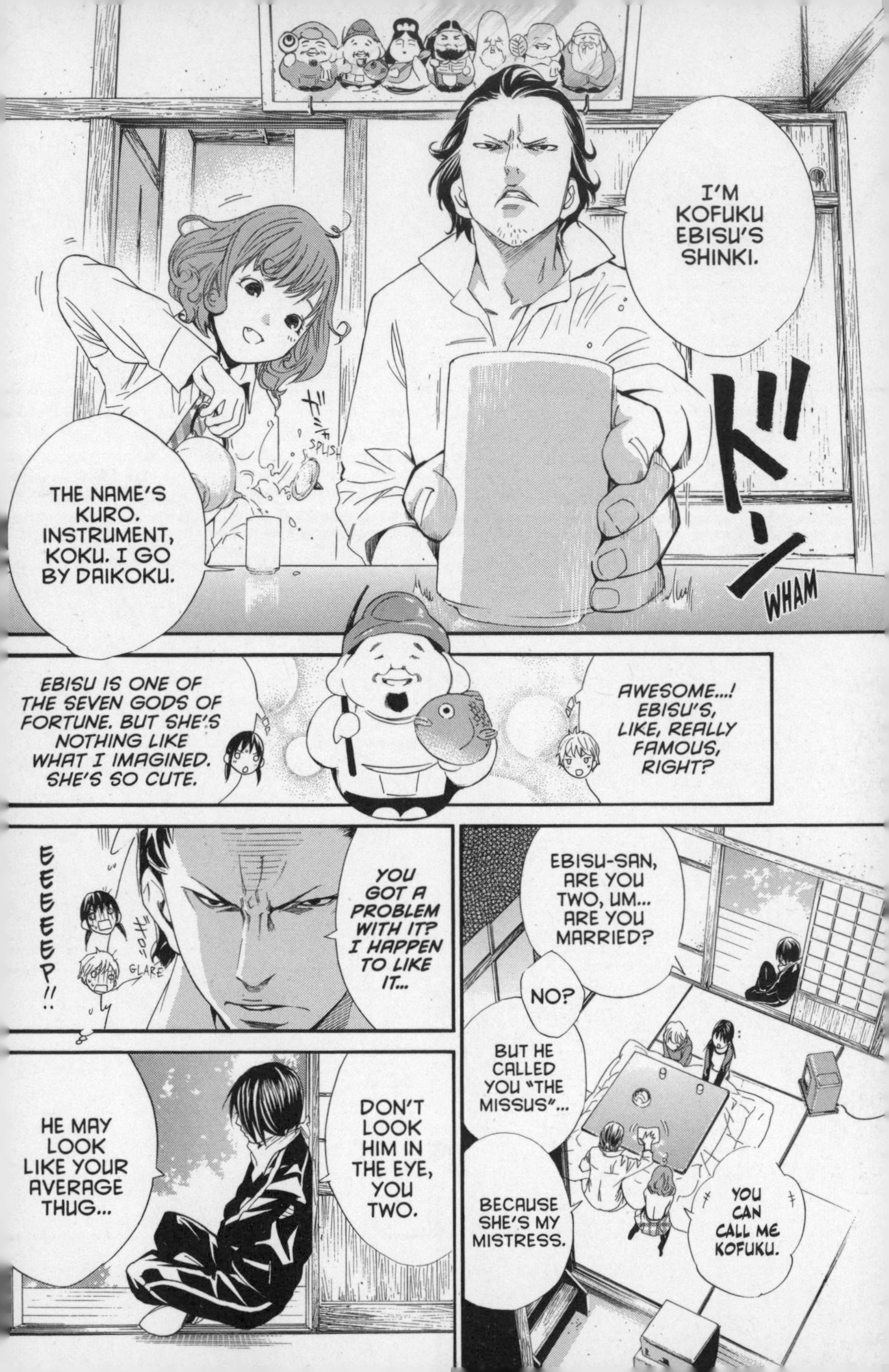
I'M KOFUKU EBISU'S SHINKI.
WHAM
SPLISH
THE NAME'S KURO. INSTRUMENT, KOKU. I GO BY DAIKOKU.
AWESOME...! EBISU'S, LIKE, REALLY FAMOUS, RIGHT?
EBISU IS ONE OF THE SEVEN GODS OF FORTUNE. BUT SHE'S NOTHING LIKE WHAT I IMAGINED. SHE'S SO CUTE.
EBISU-SAN, ARE YOU TWO, UM... ARE YOU MARRIED?
NO?
BUT HE CALLED YOU "THE MISSUS"...
YOU CAN CALL ME KOFUKU.
BECAUSE SHE'S MY MISTRESS.
YOU GOT A PROBLEM WITH IT? I HAPPEN TO LIKE IT...
GLARE
EEEEEEP!!
DON'T LOOK HIM IN THE EYE, YOU TWO.
HE MAY LOOK LIKE YOUR AVERAGE THUG...

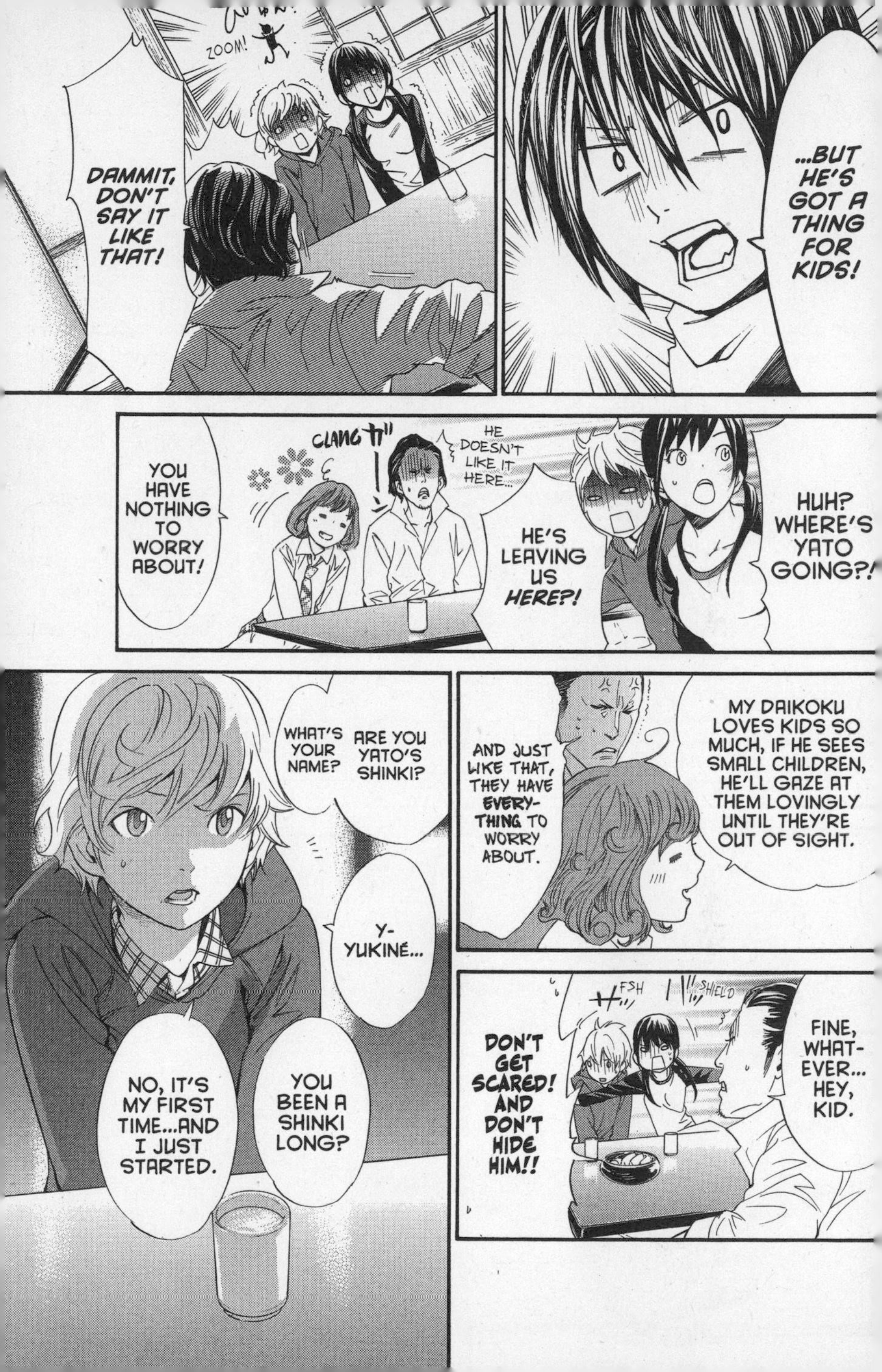
...BUT HE'S GOT A THING FOR KIDS!
ZOOM!
DAMMIT, DON'T SAY IT LIKE THAT!
HUH? WHERE'S YATO GOING?!
HE'S LEAVING US HERE?!
HE DOESN'T LIKE IT HERE...
CLANG
YOU HAVE NOTHING TO WORRY ABOUT!
MY DAIKOKU LOVES KIDS SO MUCH, IF HE SEES SMALL CHILDREN, HE'LL GAZE AT THEM LOVINGLY UNTIL THEY'RE OUT OF SIGHT.
AND JUST LIKE THAT, THEY HAVE EVERYTHING TO WORRY ABOUT.
FINE, WHATEVER... HEY, KID.
SHIELD
FSH
DON'T GET SCARED! AND DON'T HIDE HIM!!
ARE YOU YATO'S SHINKI?
WHAT'S YOUR NAME?
Y-YUKINÉ...
YOU BEEN A SHINKI LONG?
NO, IT'S MY FIRST TIME...AND I JUST STARTED.

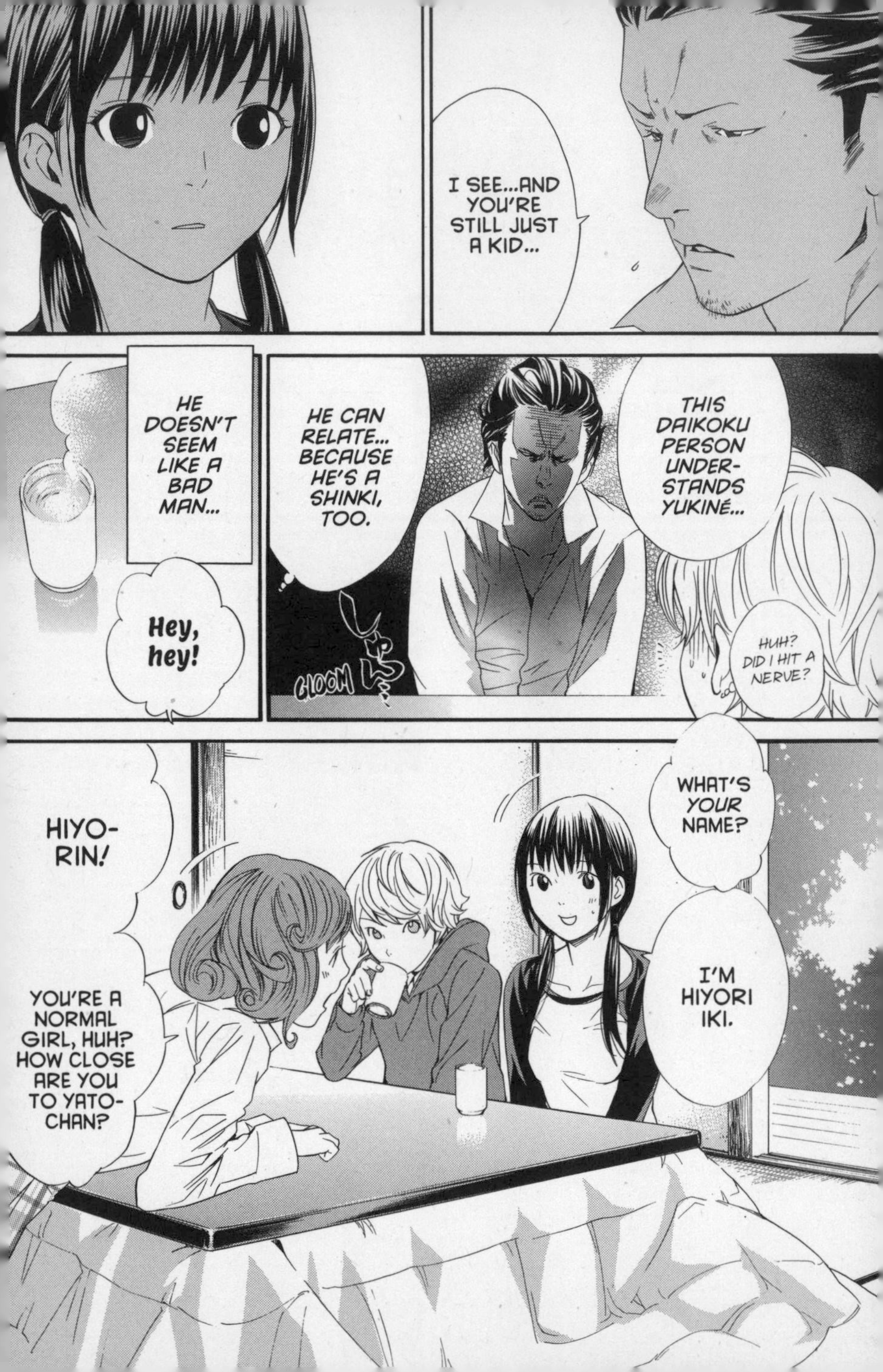
I SEE...AND YOU'RE STILL JUST A KID...
THIS DAIKOKU PERSON UNDER-STANDS YUKINÉ...
HUH? DID I HIT A NERVE?
HE CAN RELATE... BECAUSE HE'S A SHINKI, TOO.
GLOOM
HE DOESN'T SEEM LIKE A BAD MAN...
Hey, hey!
WHAT'S YOUR NAME?
I'M HIYORI IKI.
HIYO-RIN!
YOU'RE A NORMAL GIRL, HUH? HOW CLOSE ARE YOU TO YATO-CHAN?

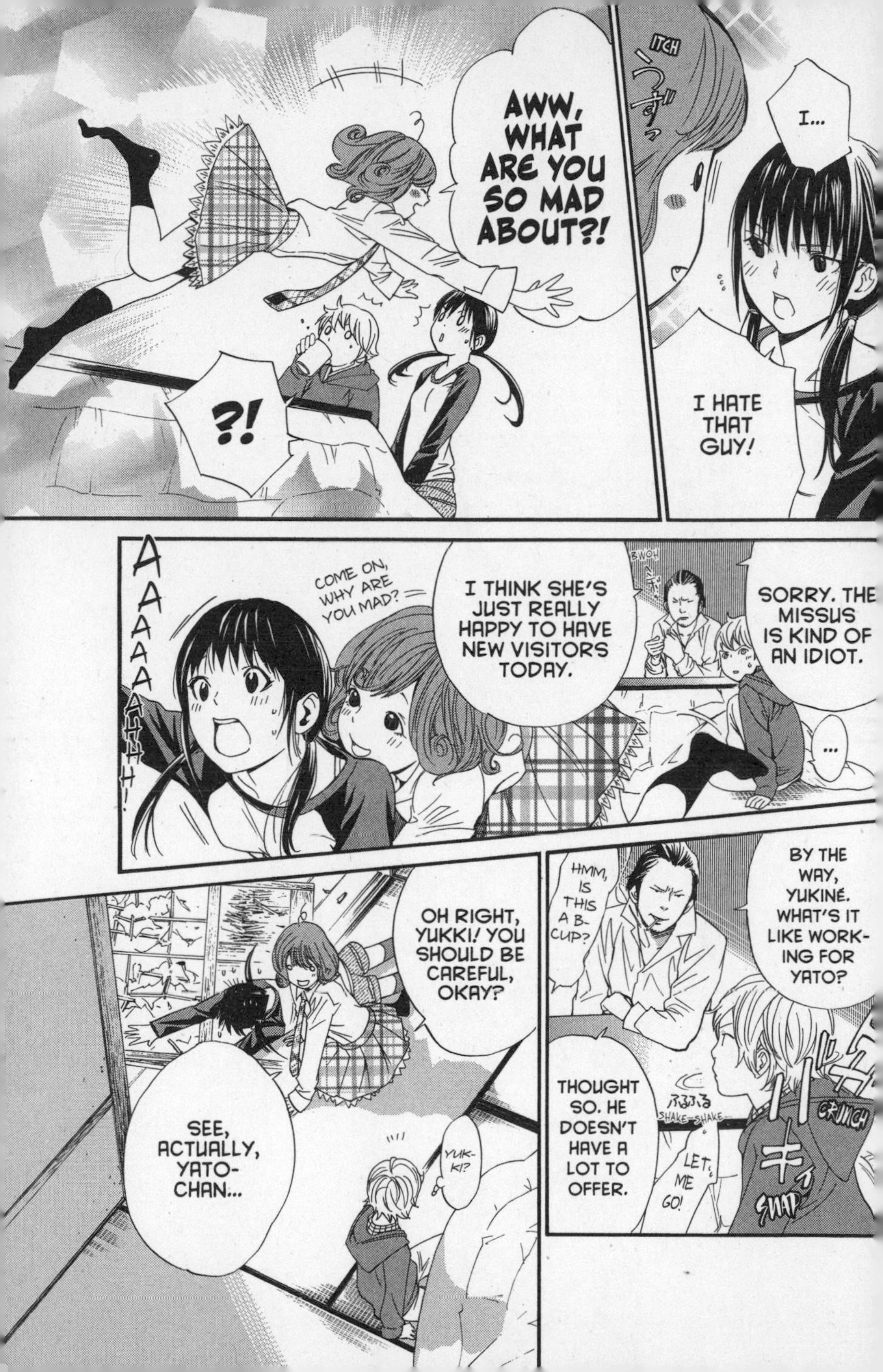
ITCH
I...
I HATE THAT GUY!
AWW, WHAT ARE YOU SO MAD ABOUT?!
?!
SORRY. THE MISSUS IS KIND OF AN IDIOT.
BWOH
...
I THINK SHE'S JUST REALLY HAPPY TO HAVE NEW VISITORS TODAY.
COME ON, WHY ARE YOU MAD?
AAAAAAAAHHH!
BY THE WAY, YUKINÉ. WHAT'S IT LIKE WORKING FOR YATO?
HMM, IS THIS A B-CUP?
CRUNCH
SNAP
THOUGHT SO. HE DOESN'T HAVE A LOT TO OFFER.
SHAKE SHAKE
LET ME GO!
OH RIGHT, YUKKI! YOU SHOULD BE CAREFUL, OKAY?
SEE, ACTUALLY, YATO-CHAN...
YUKKI?

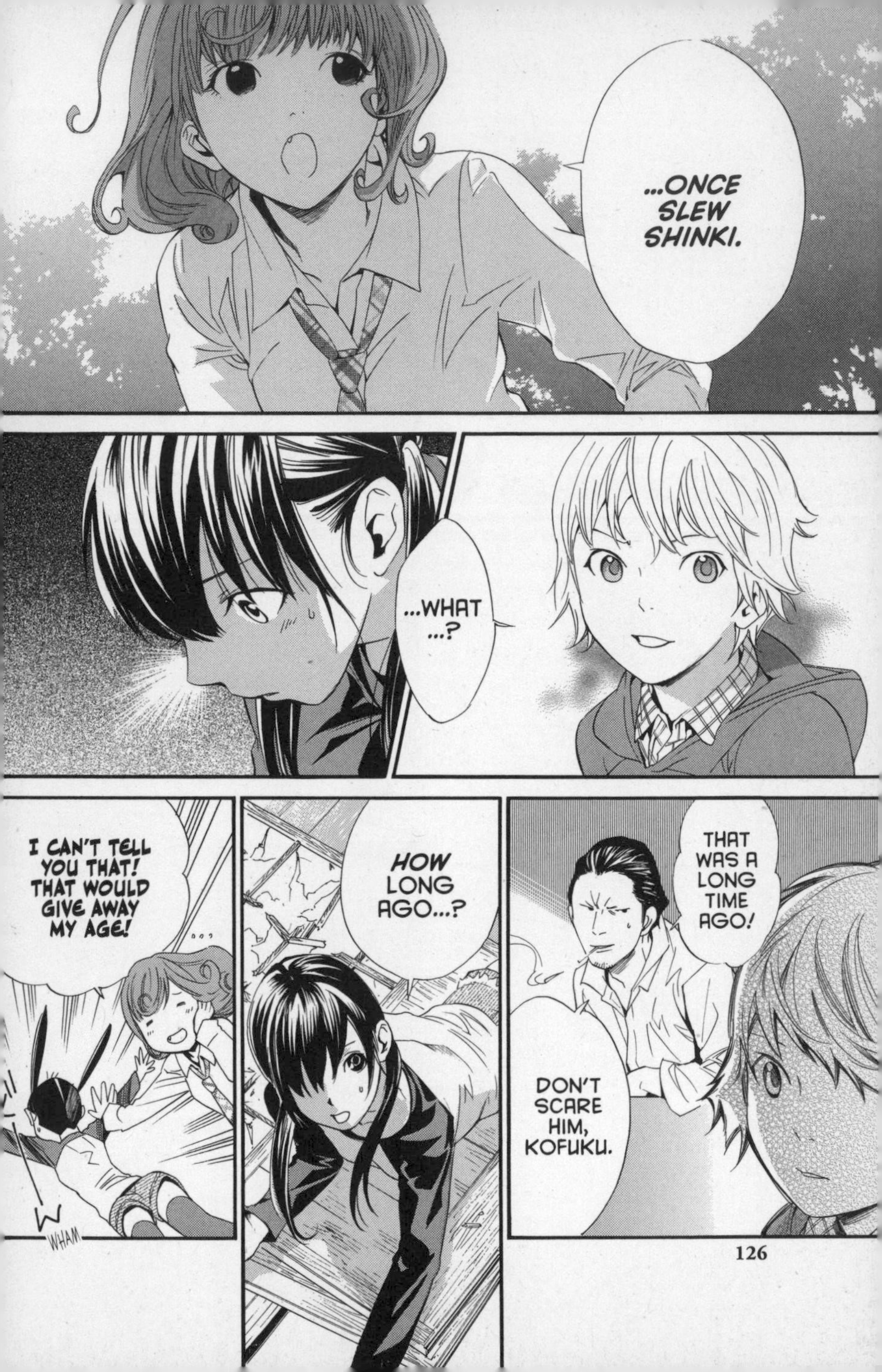
...ONCE SLEW SHINKI.
...WHAT ...?
THAT WAS A LONG TIME AGO!
DON'T SCARE HIM, KOFUKU.
HOW LONG AGO...?
I CAN'T TELL YOU THAT! THAT WOULD GIVE AWAY MY AGE!
WHAM

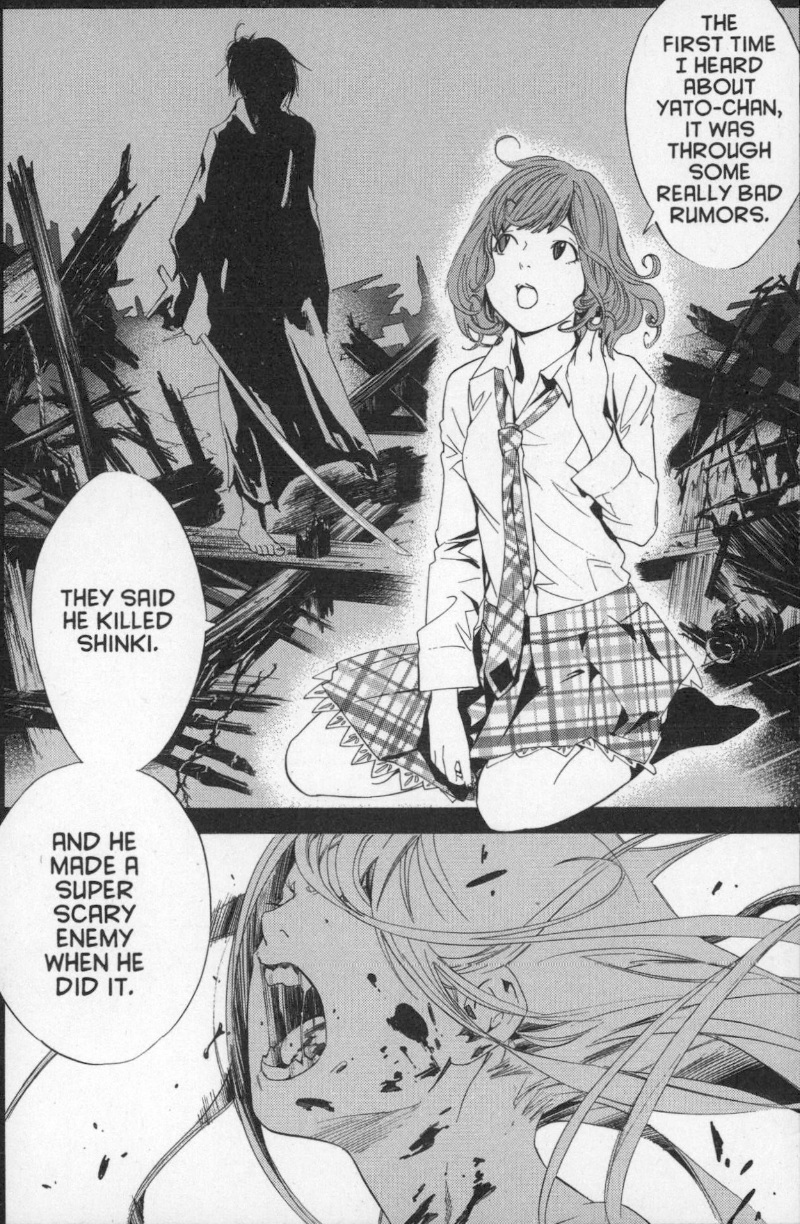
THE FIRST TIME I HEARD ABOUT YATO-CHAN, IT WAS THROUGH SOME REALLY BAD RUMORS.
THEY SAID HE KILLED SHINKI.
AND HE MADE A SUPER SCARY ENEMY WHEN HE DID IT.

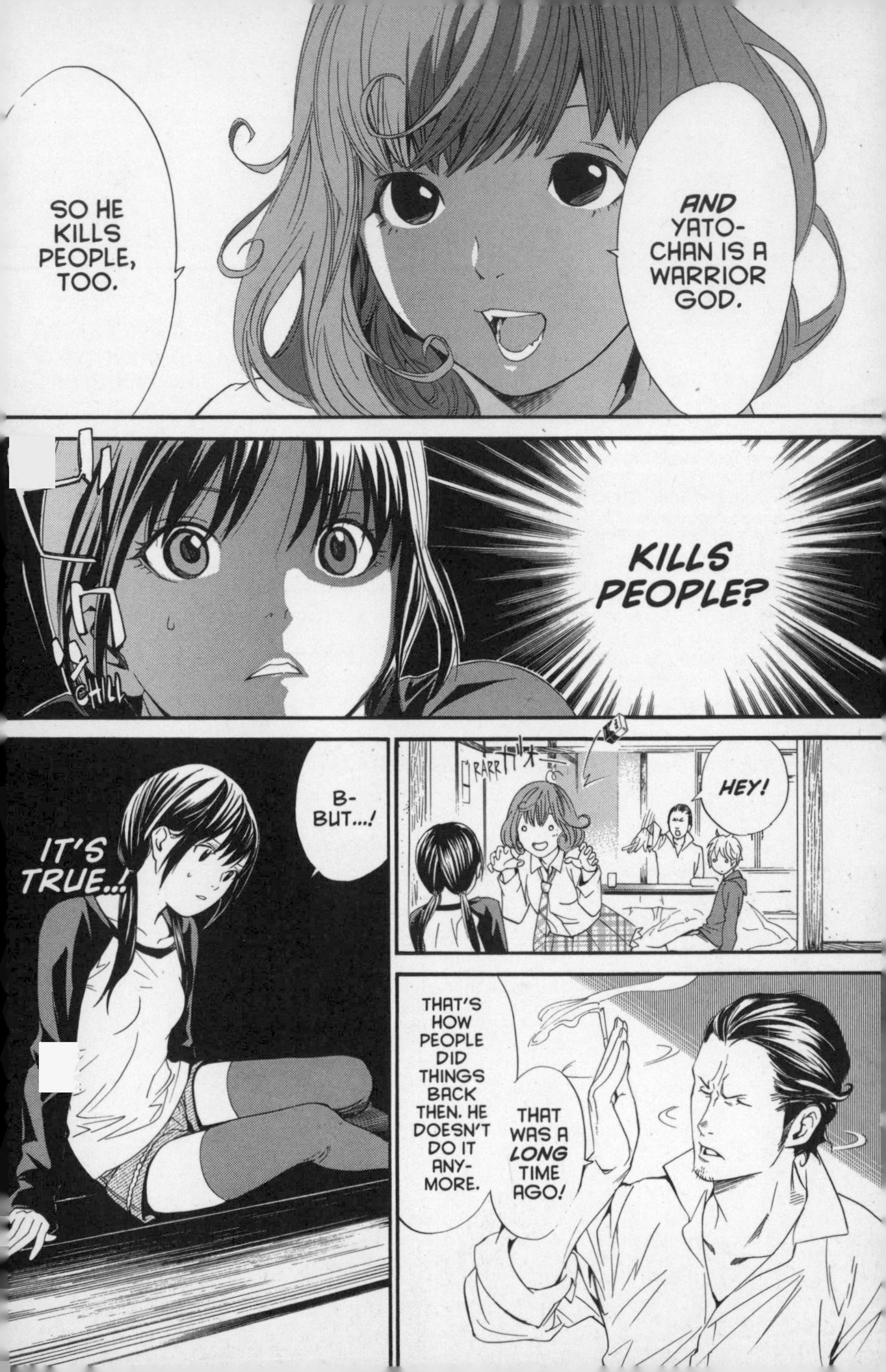
AND YATO-CHAN IS A WARRIOR GOD.
SO HE KILLS PEOPLE, TOO.
KILLS PEOPLE?
CHILL
RARR
HEY!
THAT WAS A LONG TIME AGO!
THAT'S HOW PEOPLE DID THINGS BACK THEN. HE DOESN'T DO IT ANY-MORE.
B-BUT...!
IT'S TRUE...!

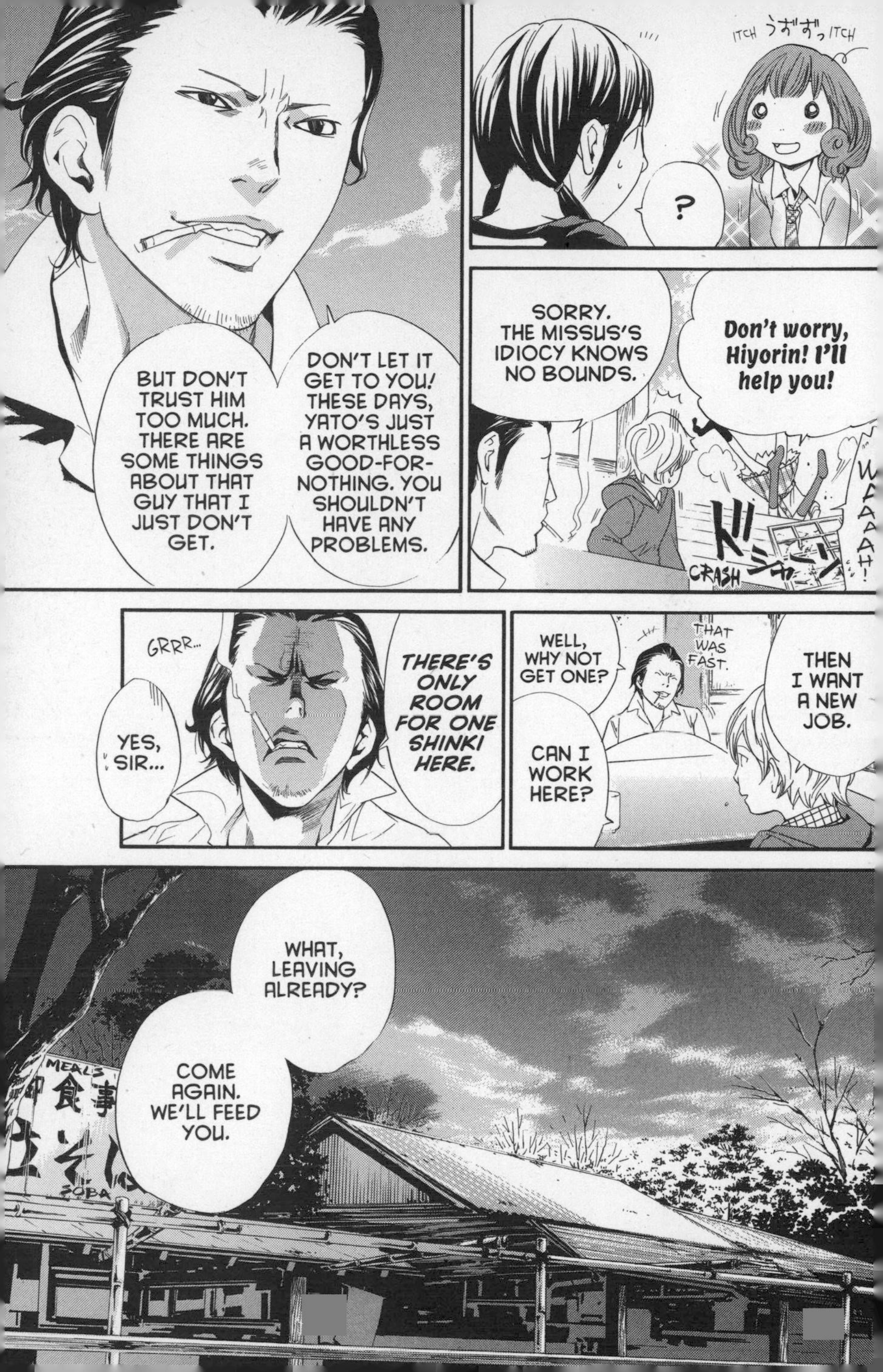
ITCH うずずっ ITCH
?
Don't worry, Hiyorin! I'll help you!
WAAAAH!
SORRY. THE MISSUS'S IDIOCY KNOWS NO BOUNDS.
CRASH
DON'T LET IT GET TO YOU! THESE DAYS, YATO'S JUST A WORTHLESS GOOD-FOR-NOTHING. YOU SHOULDN'T HAVE ANY PROBLEMS.
BUT DON'T TRUST HIM TOO MUCH. THERE ARE SOME THINGS ABOUT THAT GUY THAT I JUST DON'T GET.
THEN I WANT A NEW JOB.
THAT WAS FAST.
WELL, WHY NOT GET ONE?
CAN I WORK HERE?
THERE'S ONLY ROOM FOR ONE SHINKI HERE.
GRRR...
YES, SIR...
WHAT, LEAVING ALREADY?
COME AGAIN. WE'LL FEED YOU.
MEALS
食事
SOBA

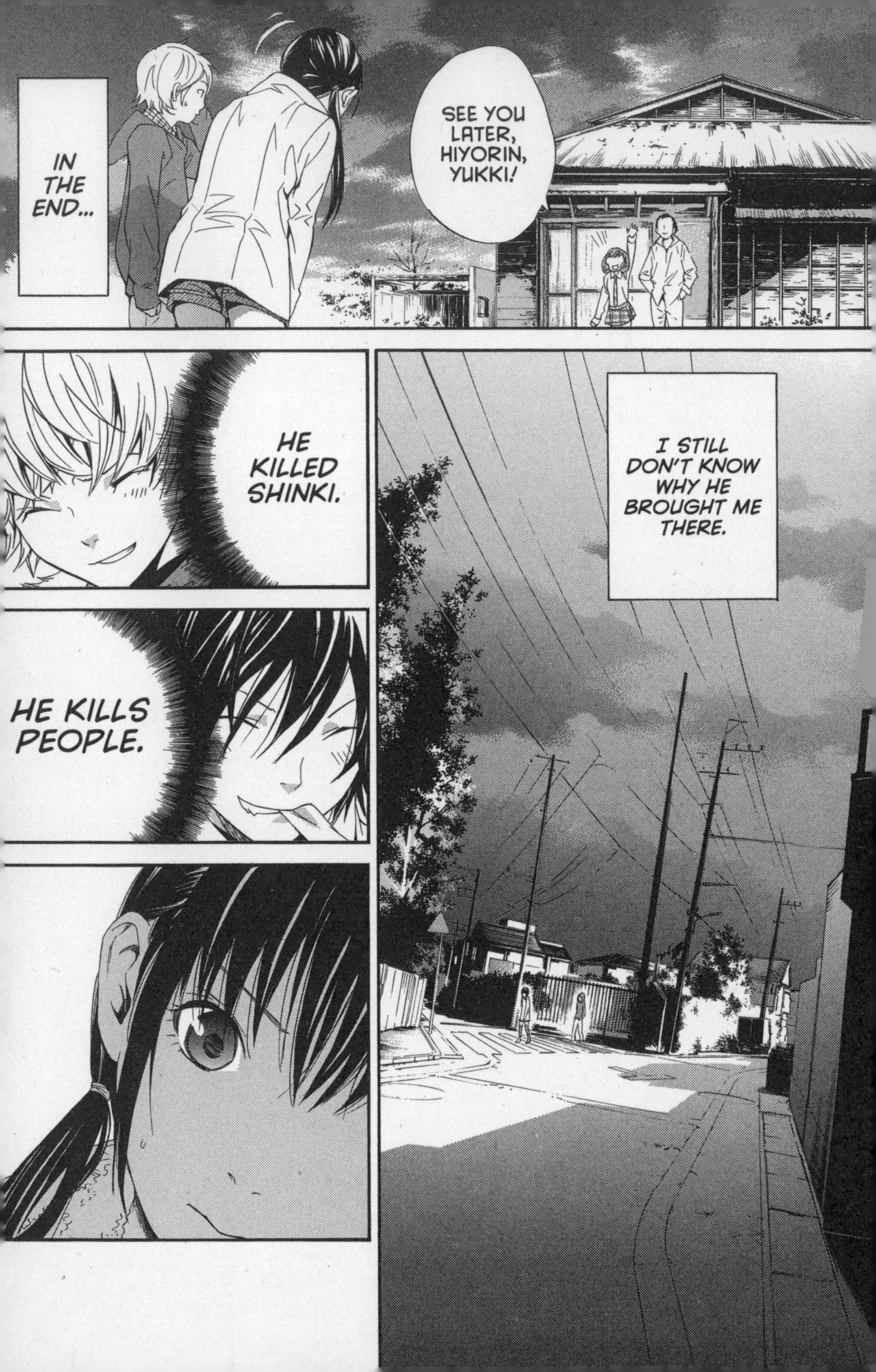
SEE YOU LATER, HIYORIN, YUKKI!
IN THE END...
I STILL DON'T KNOW WHY HE BROUGHT ME THERE.
HE KILLED SHINKI.
HE KILLS PEOPLE.

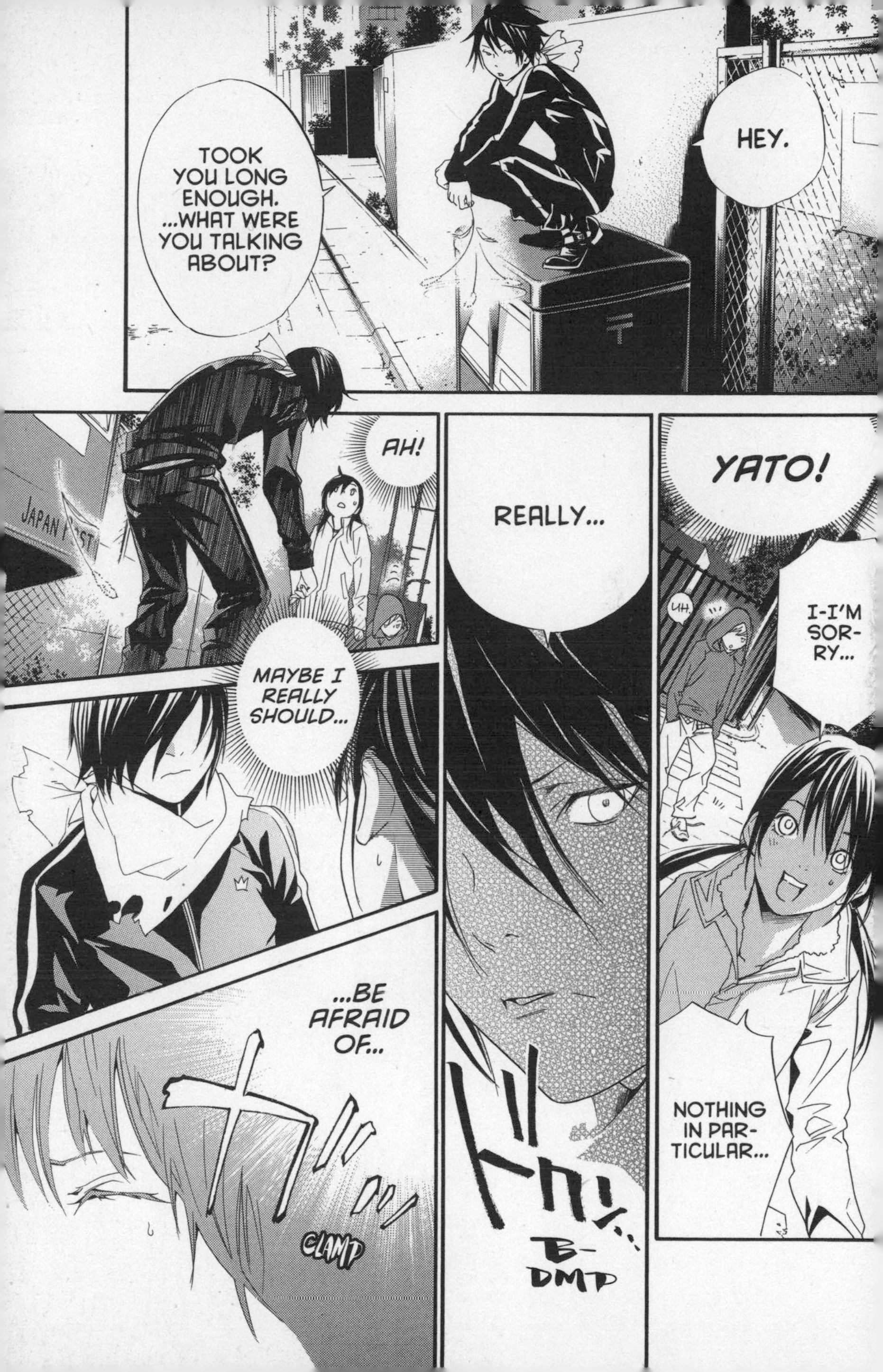
HEY.
TOOK YOU LONG ENOUGH. ...WHAT WERE YOU TALKING ABOUT?
YATO!
UH.
I-I'M SOR-RY...
NOTHING IN PAR-TICULAR...
REALLY...
B-DMP
AH!
MAYBE I REALLY SHOULD...
...BE AFRAID OF...
CLAMP

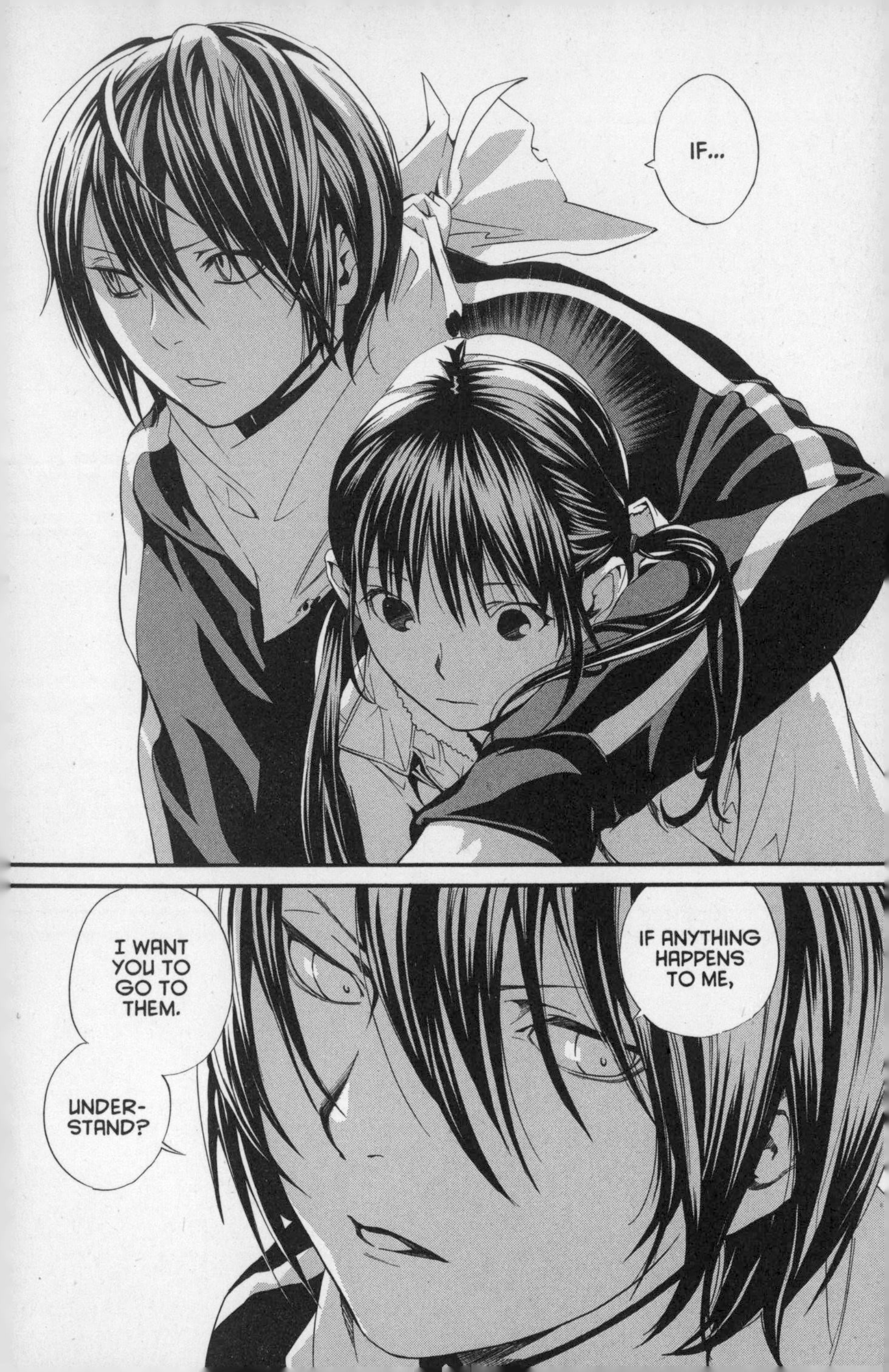
IF...
IF ANYTHING HAPPENS TO ME,
I WANT YOU TO GO TO THEM.
UNDER-STAND?

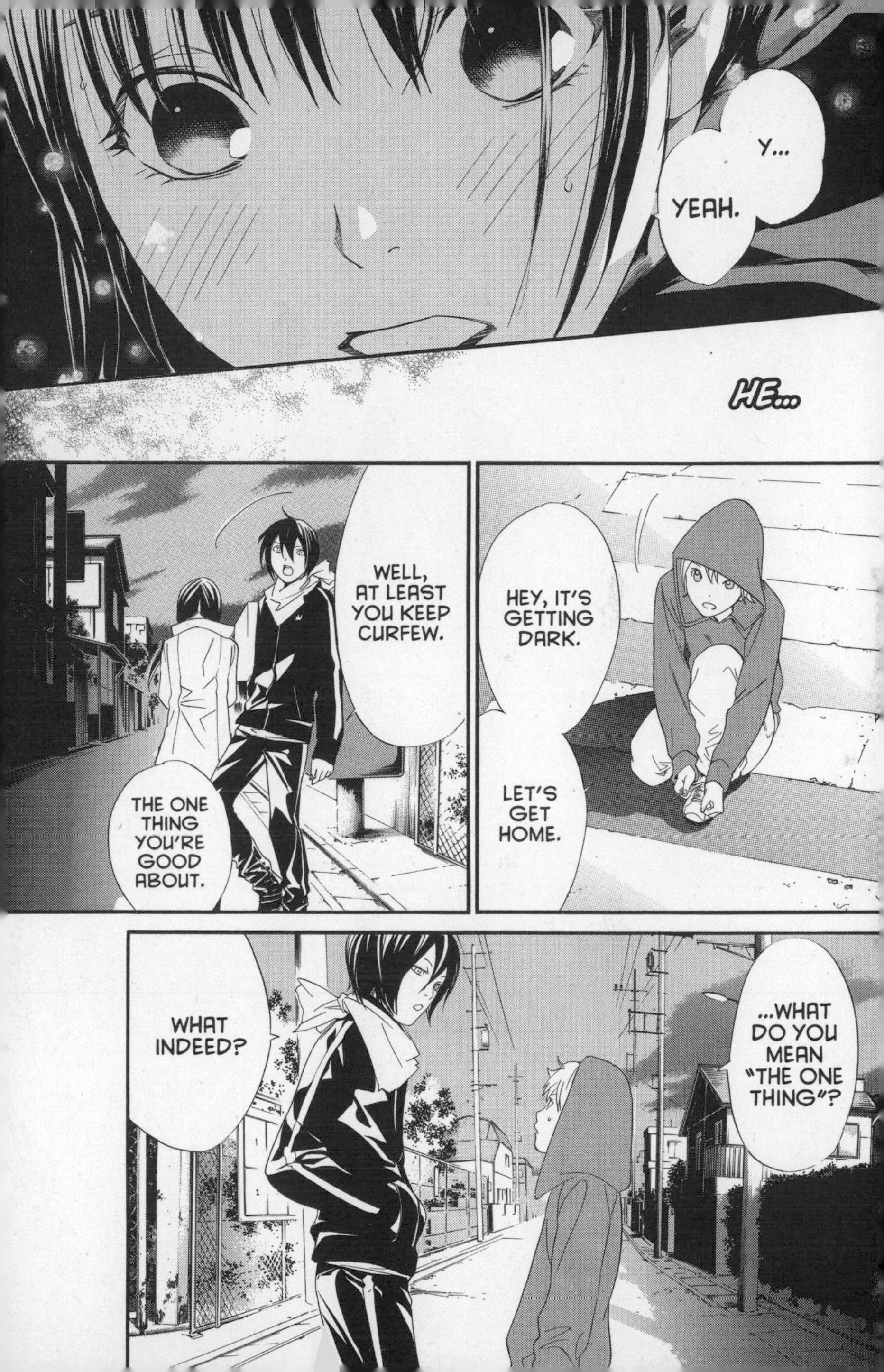
Y...
YEAH.
HE...
HEY, IT'S GETTING DARK.
LET'S GET HOME.
WELL, AT LEAST YOU KEEP CURFEW.
THE ONE THING YOU'RE GOOD ABOUT.
...WHAT DO YOU MEAN "THE ONE THING"?
WHAT INDEED?

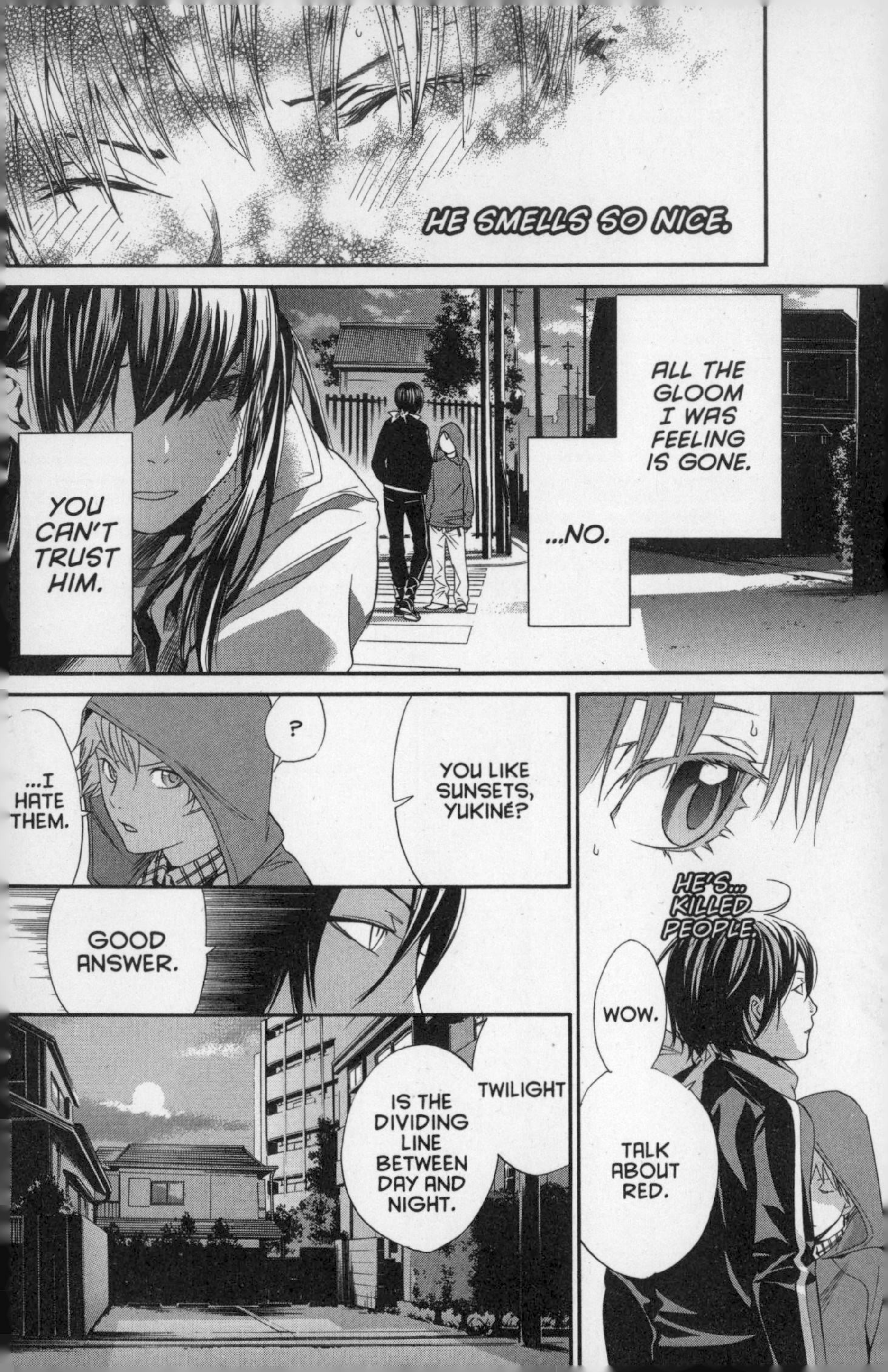
HE SMELLS SO NICE.
ALL THE GLOOM I WAS FEELING IS GONE.
...NO.
YOU CAN'T TRUST HIM.
HE'S... KILLED PEOPLE.
WOW.
TALK ABOUT RED.
YOU LIKE SUNSETS, YUKINÉ?
?
...I HATE THEM.
GOOD ANSWER.
TWILIGHT
IS THE DIVIDING LINE BETWEEN DAY AND NIGHT.

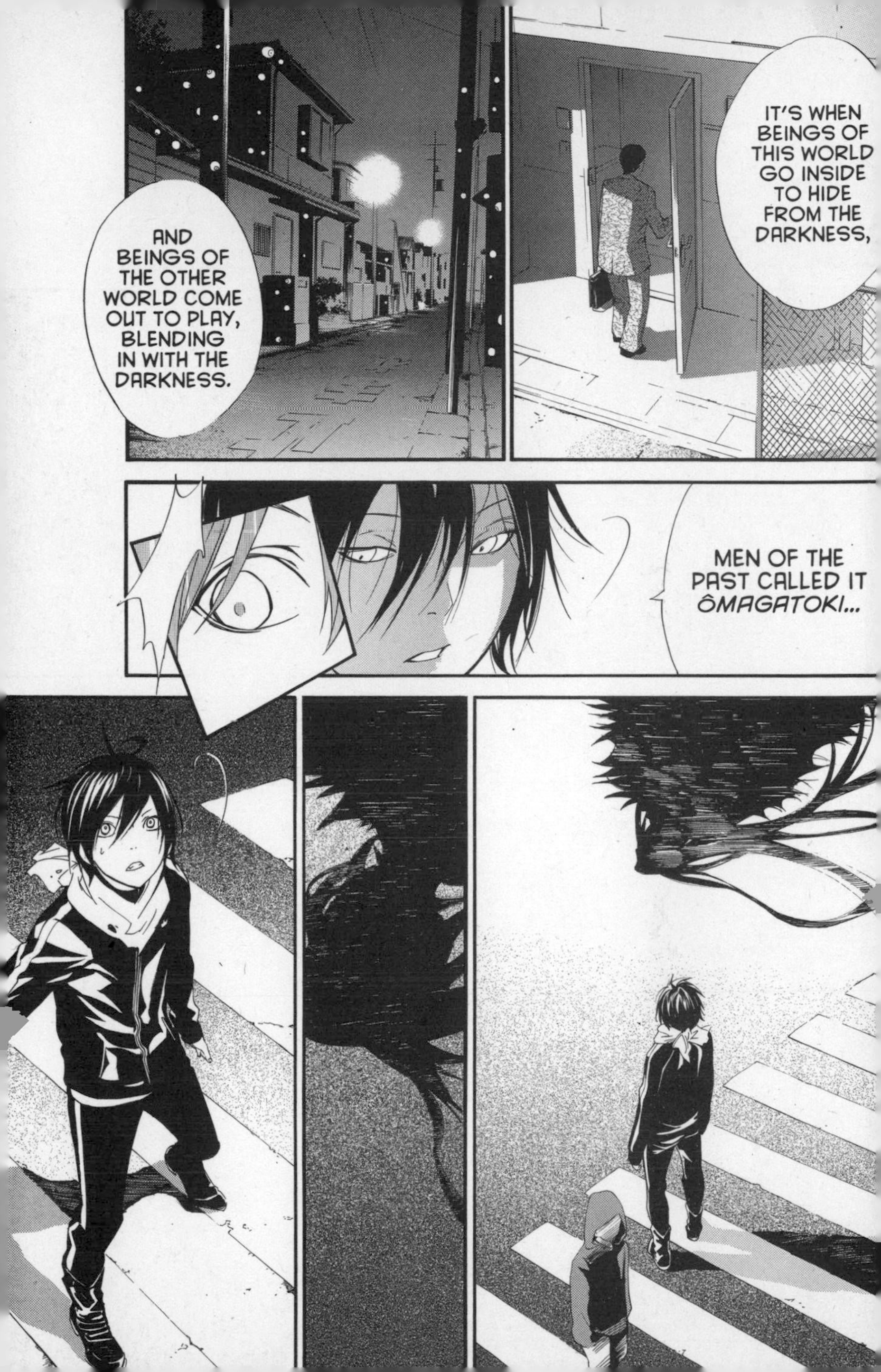
IT'S WHEN BEINGS OF THIS WORLD GO INSIDE TO HIDE FROM THE DARKNESS,
AND BEINGS OF THE OTHER WORLD COME OUT TO PLAY, BLENDING IN WITH THE DARKNESS.
MEN OF THE PAST CALLED IT ÔMAGATOKI...

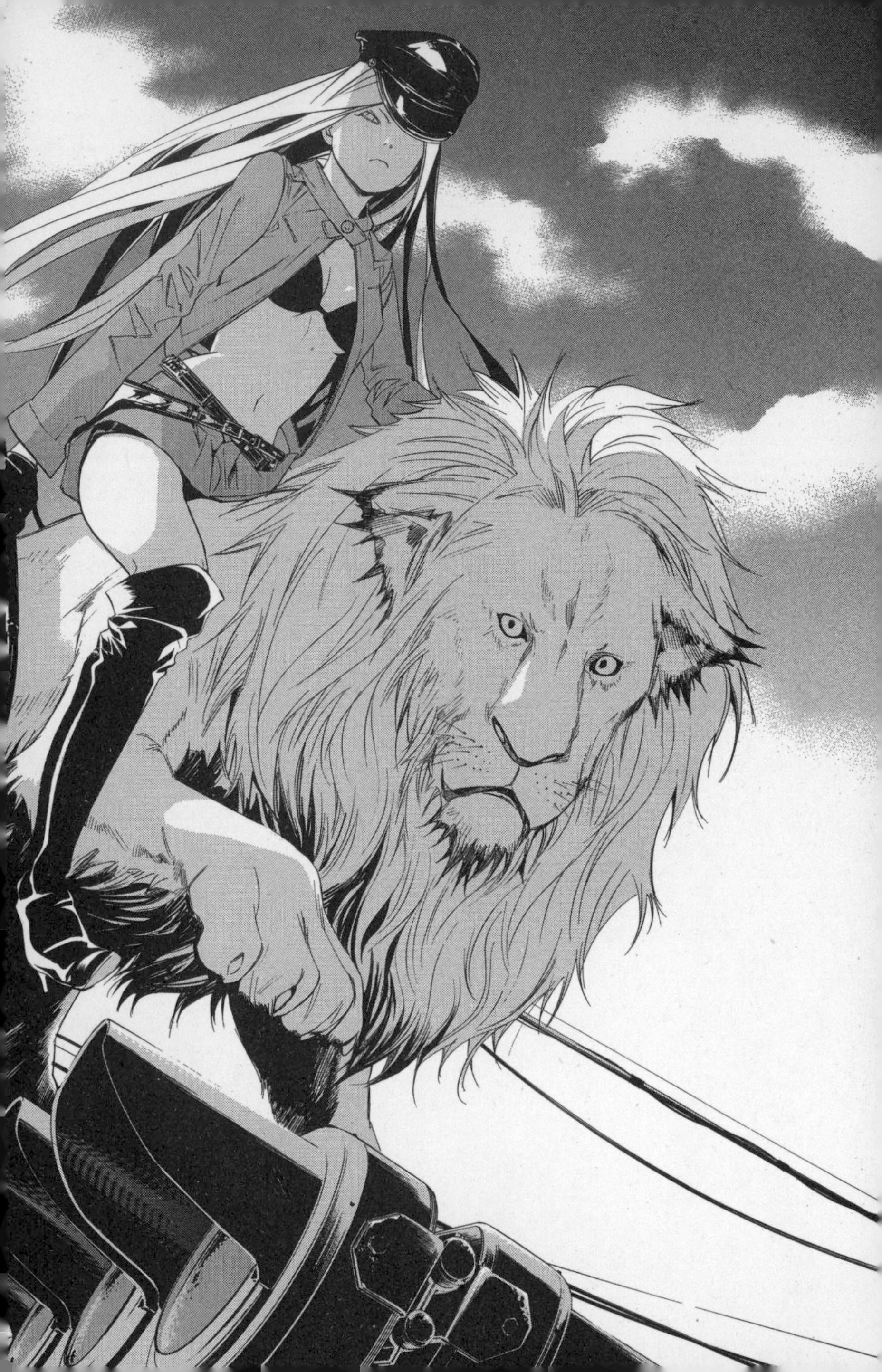

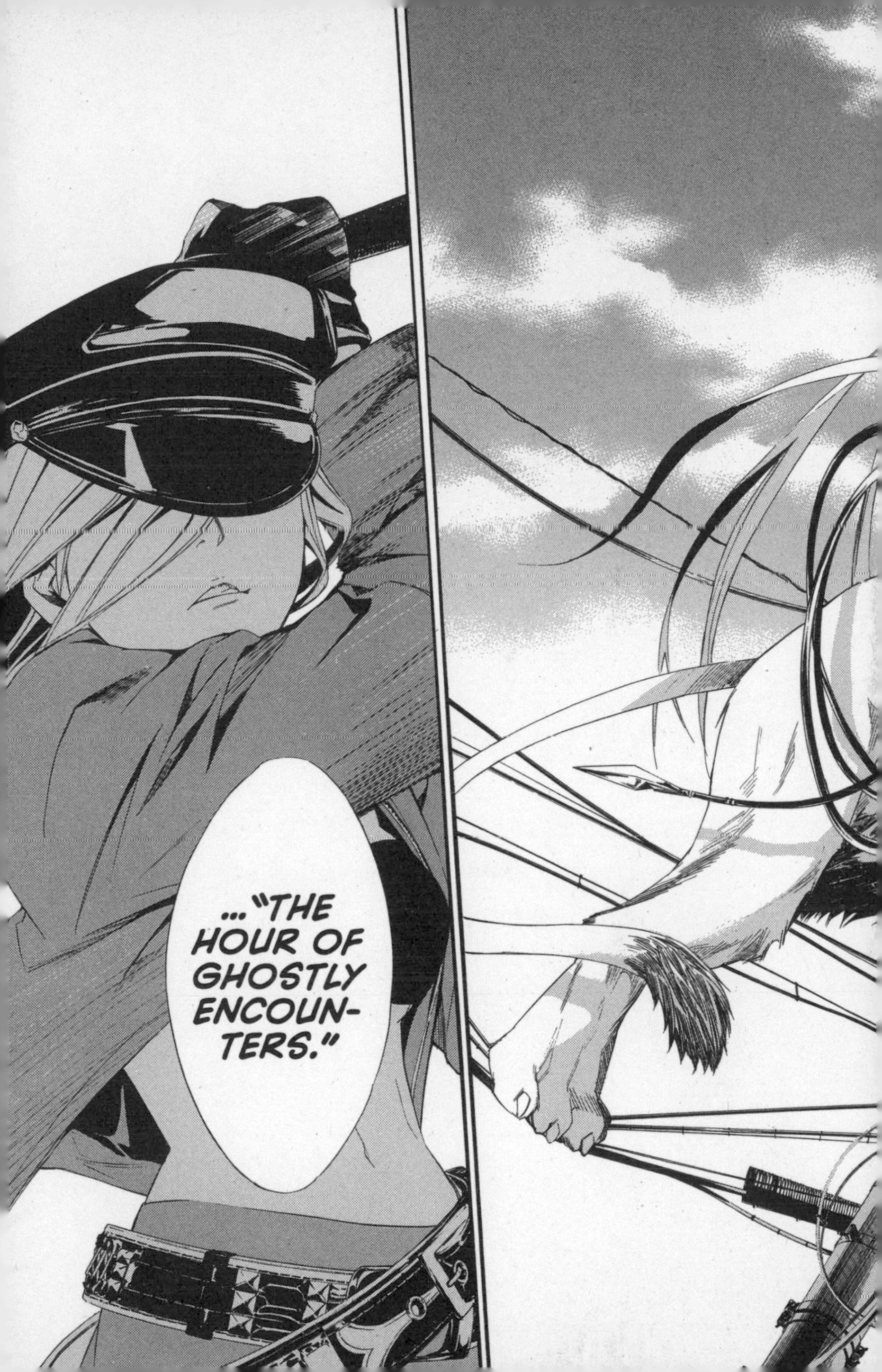
..."THE HOUR OF GHOSTLY ENCOUN- TERS."

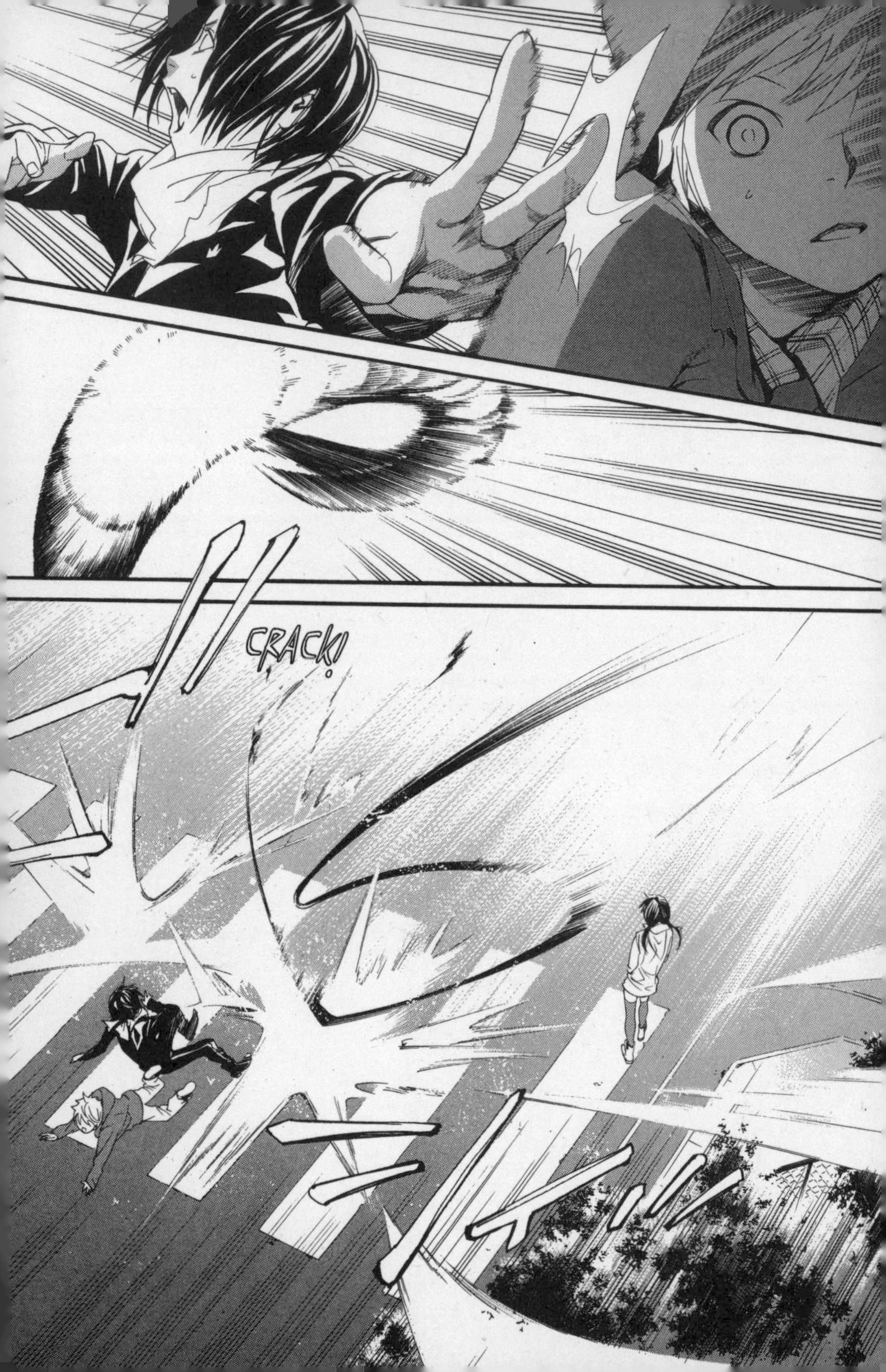
CRACK!

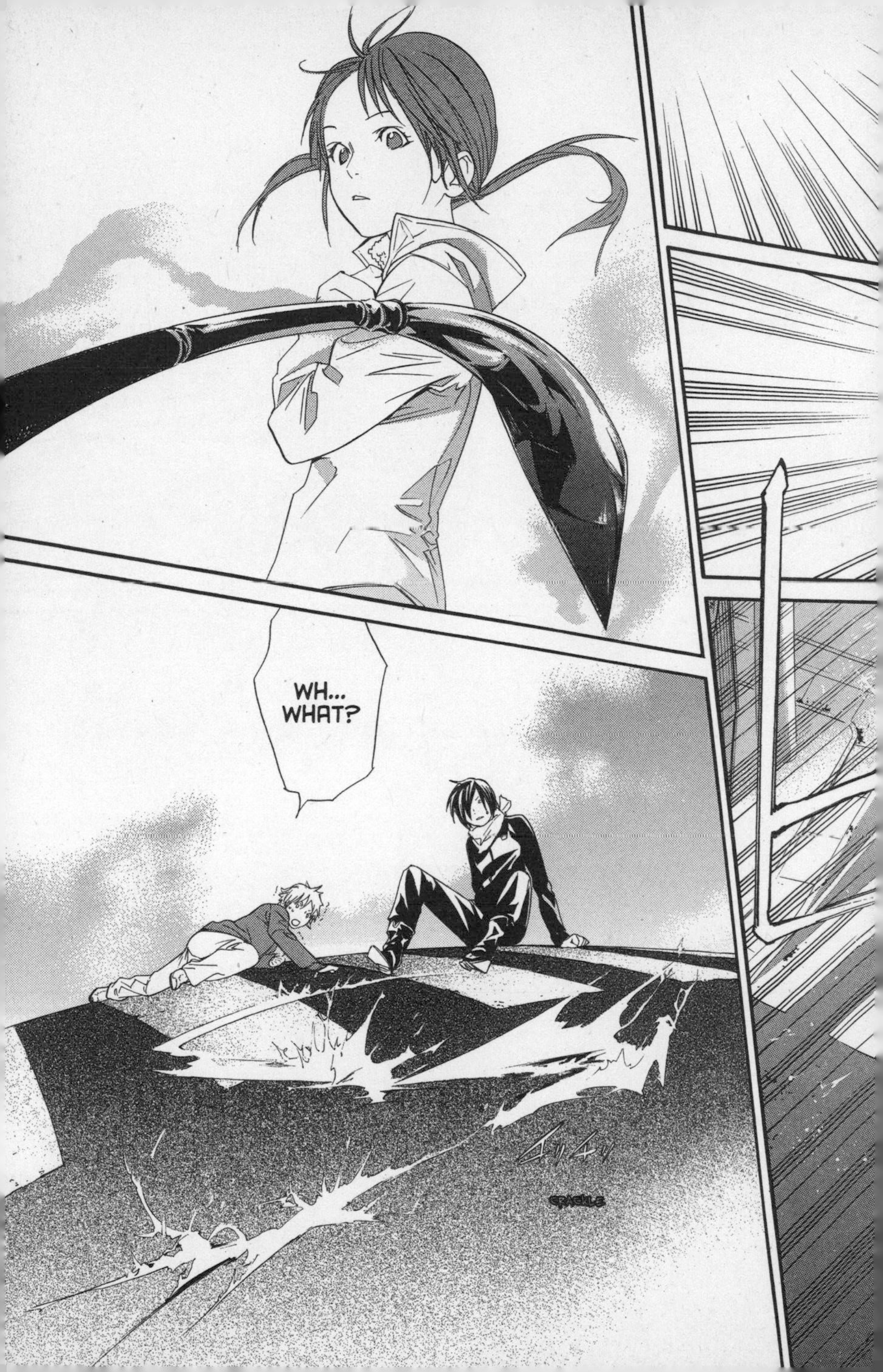
WH... WHAT?
CRACKLE

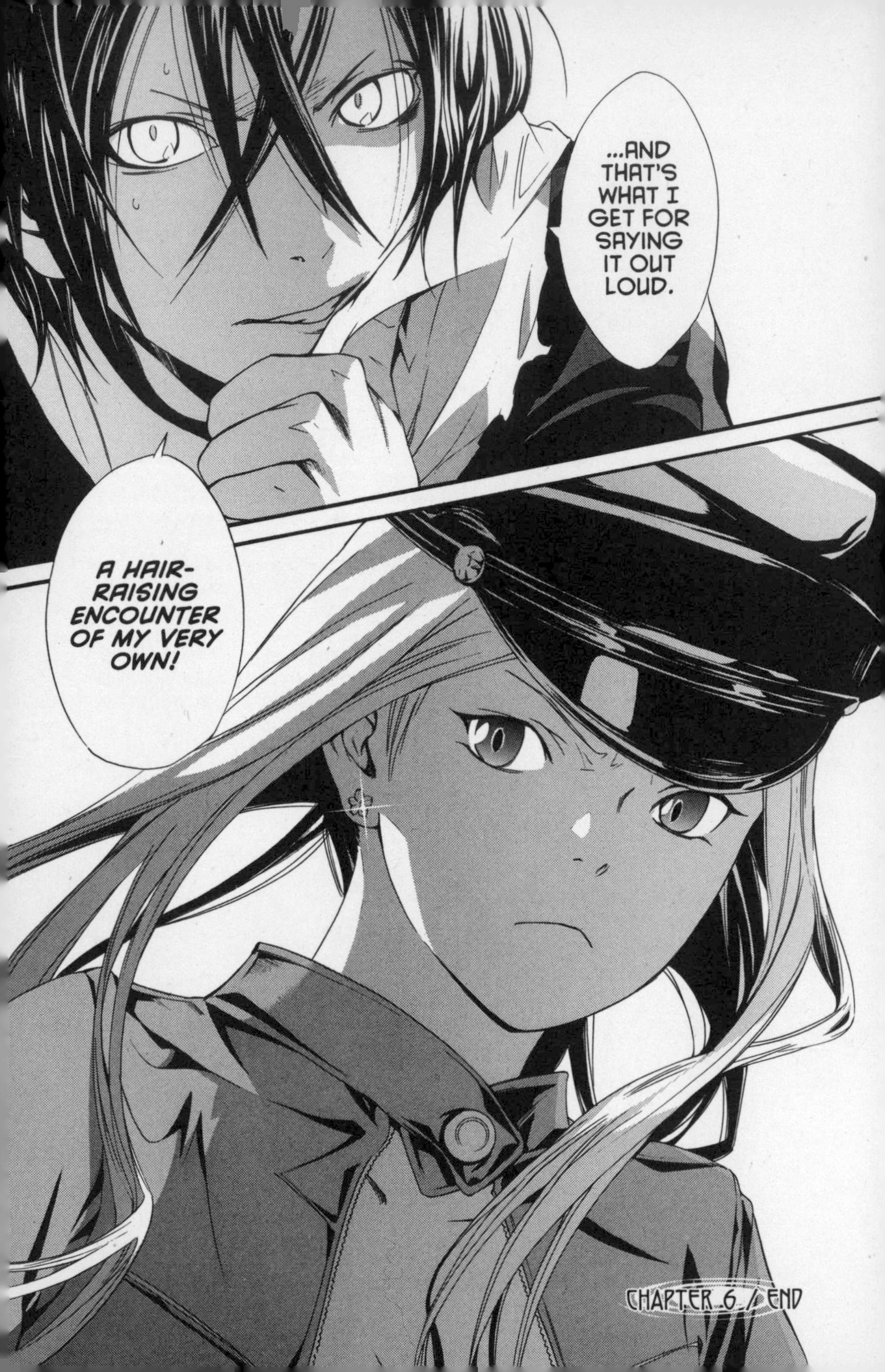
...AND THAT'S WHAT I GET FOR SAYING IT OUT LOUD.
A HAIR-RAISING ENCOUNTER OF MY VERY OWN!
CHAPTER 6 / END

野

罘

禅

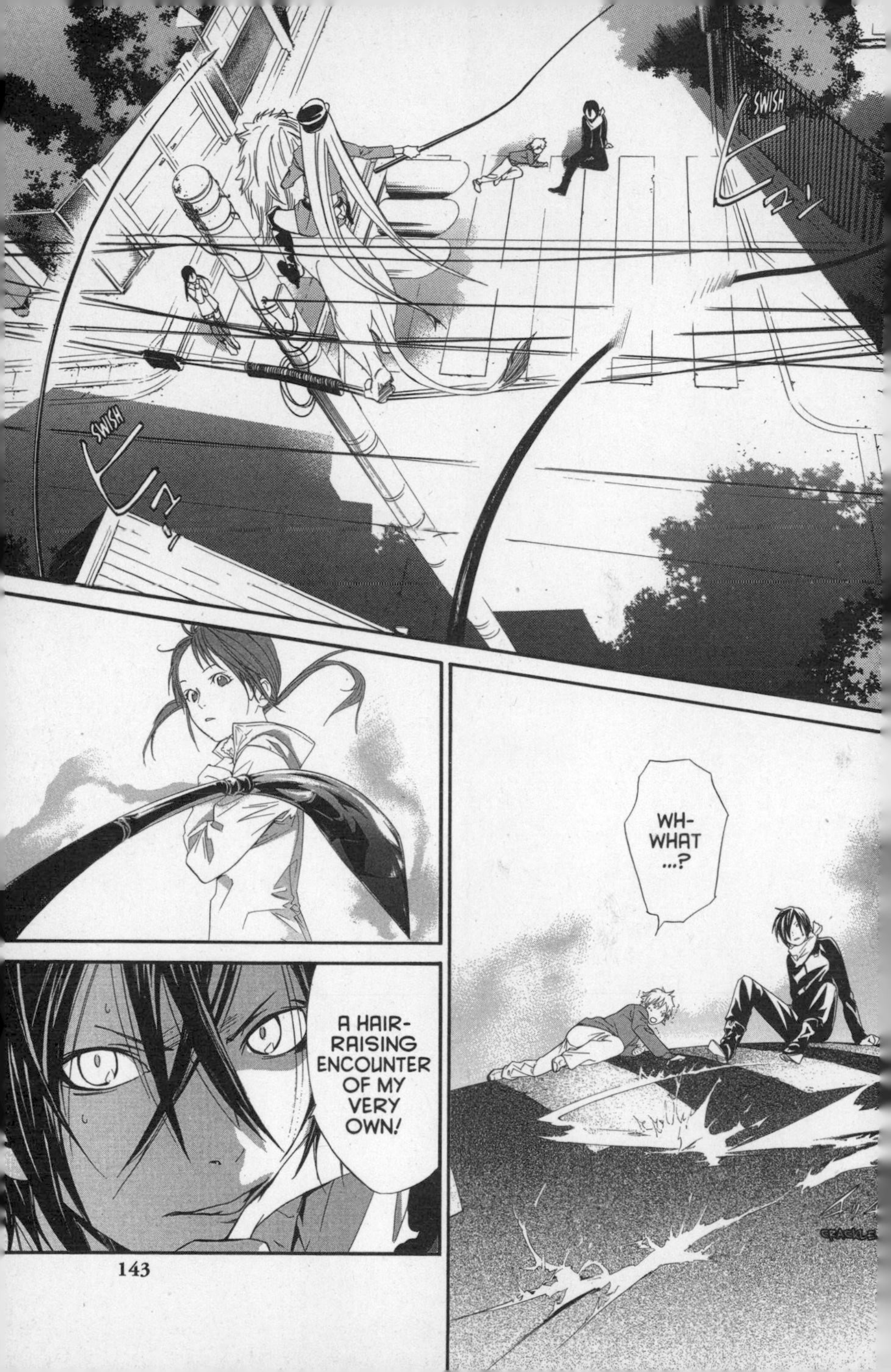
SWISH
SWISH
WH-WHAT ...?
CRACKLE
A HAIR-RAISING ENCOUNTER OF MY VERY OWN!

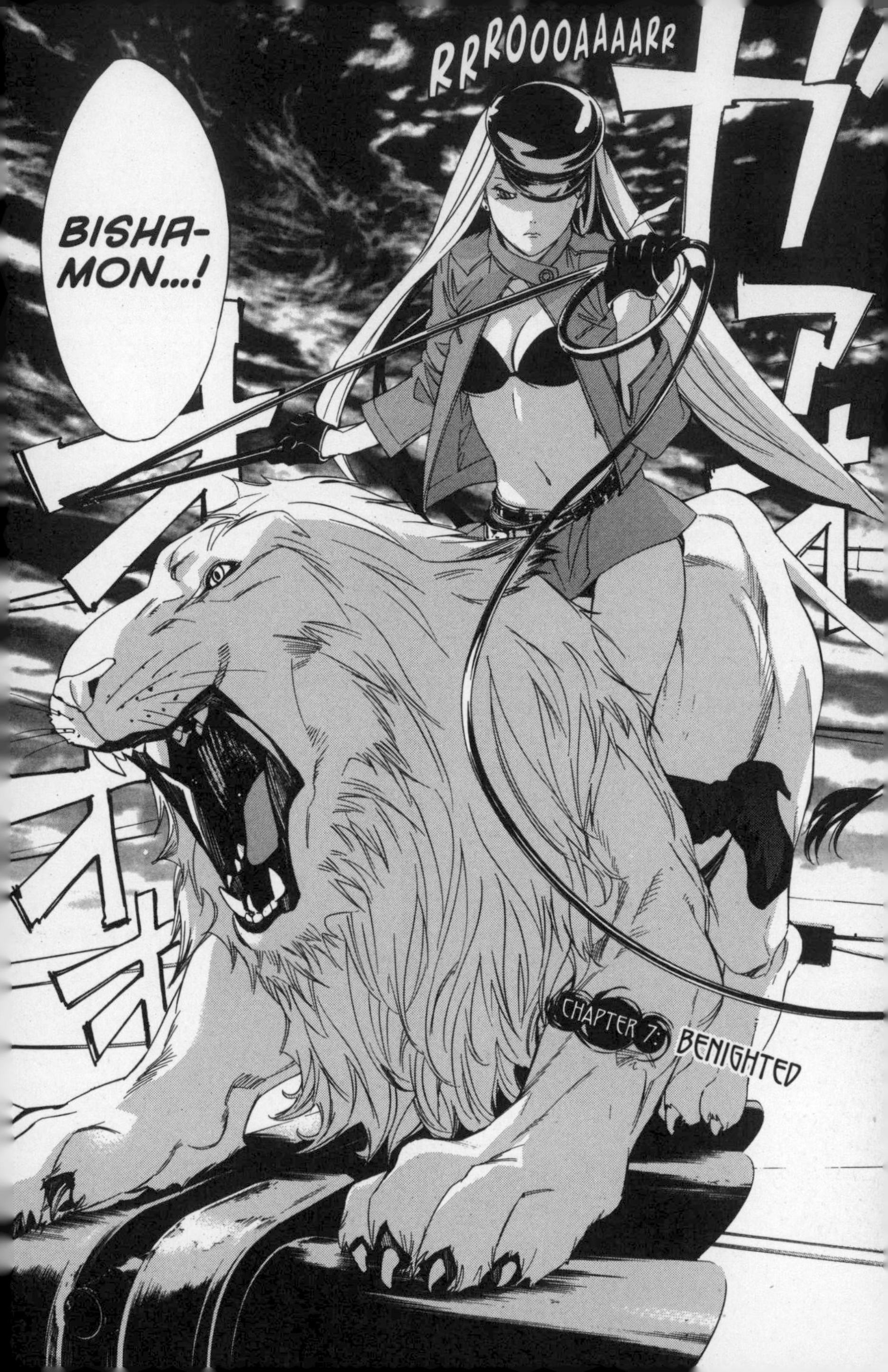
RRROOOAAAARR
BISHA-
MON...!
CHAPTER 7: BENIGHTED

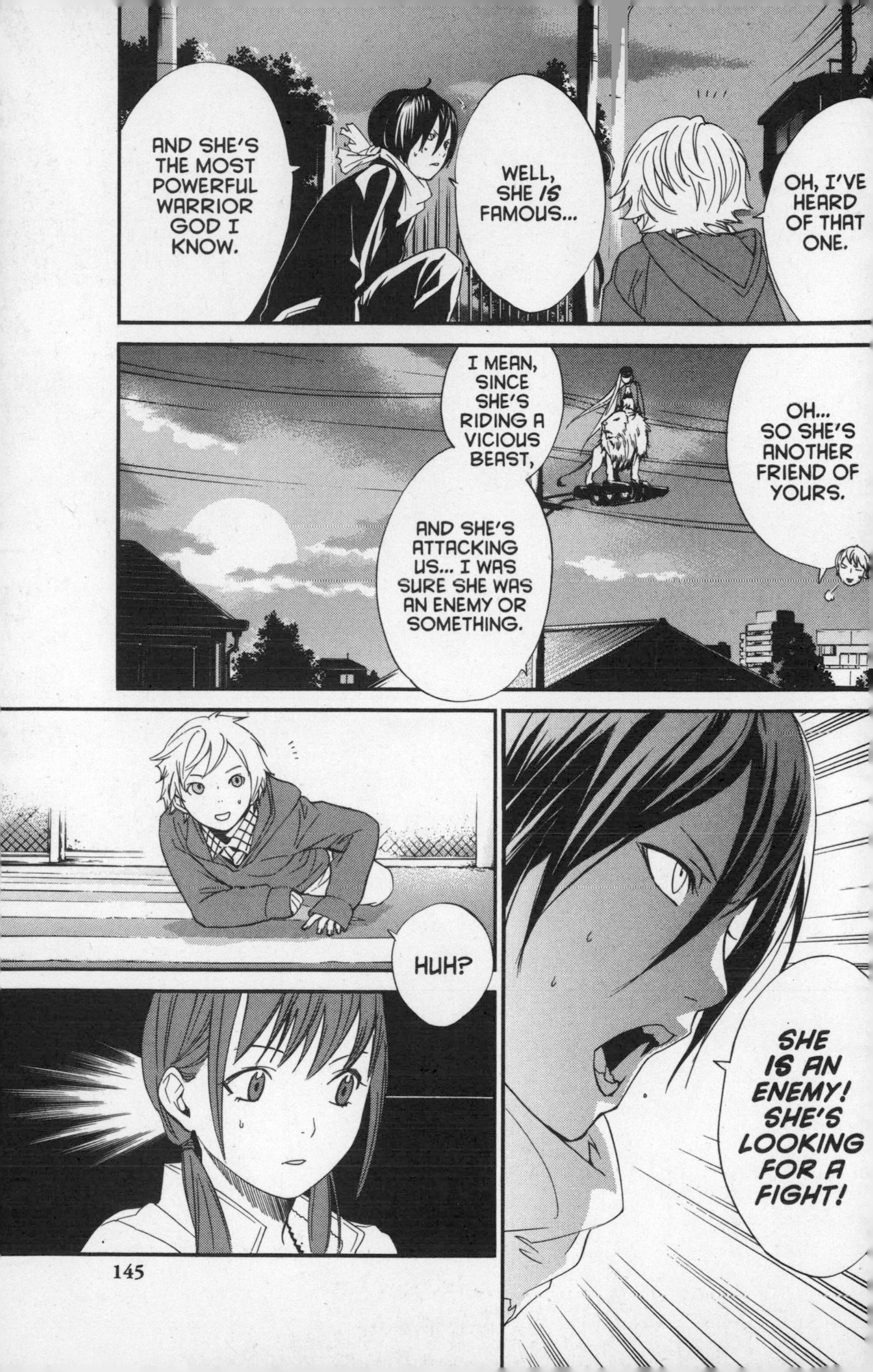
OH, I'VE HEARD OF THAT ONE.
WELL, SHE *IS* FAMOUS...
AND SHE'S THE MOST POWERFUL WARRIOR GOD I KNOW.
OH... SO SHE'S ANOTHER FRIEND OF YOURS.
I MEAN, SINCE SHE'S RIDING A VICIOUS BEAST,
AND SHE'S ATTACKING US... I WAS SURE SHE WAS AN ENEMY OR SOMETHING.
SHE IS AN ENEMY! SHE'S LOOKING FOR A FIGHT!
HUH?

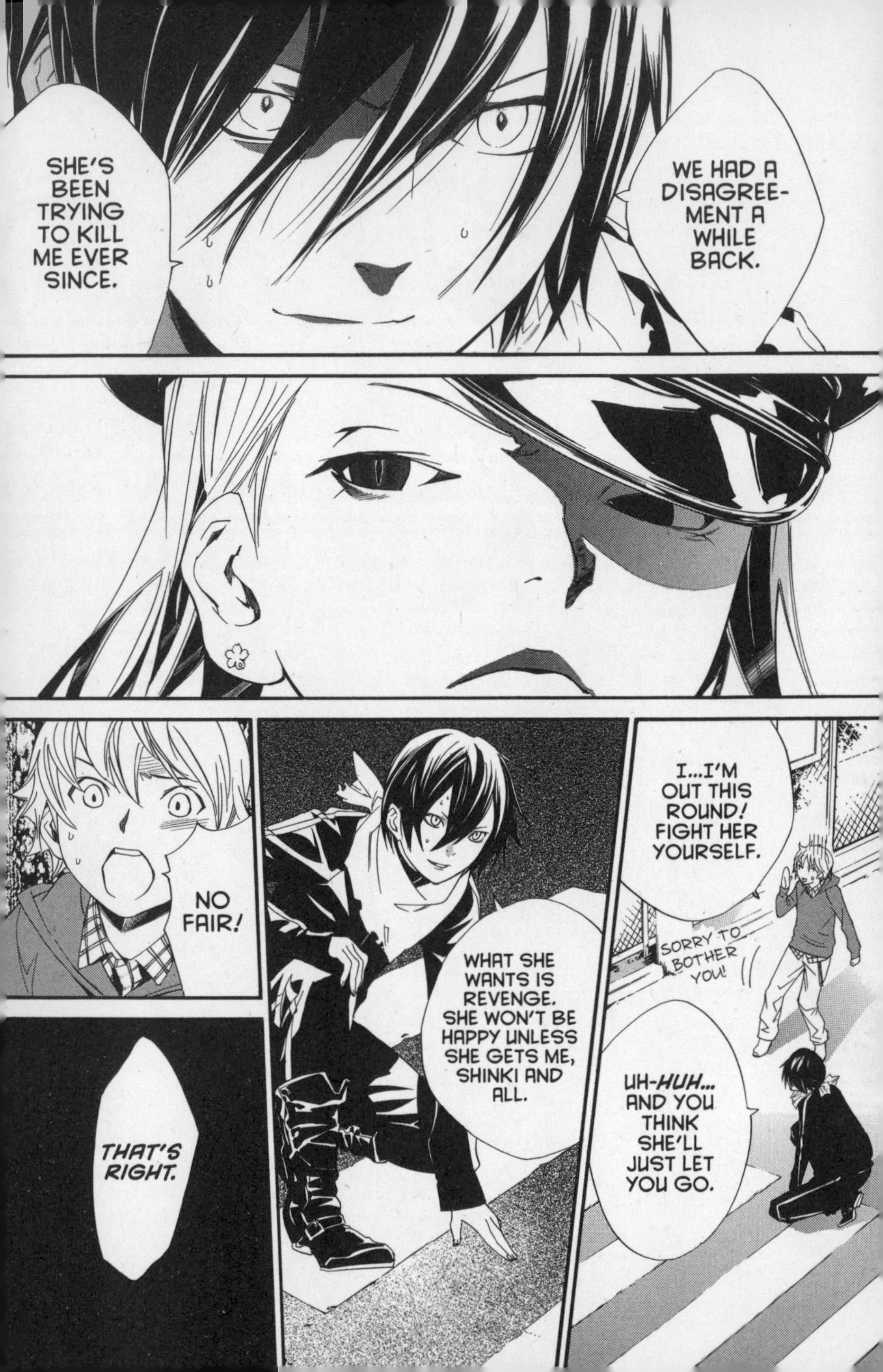
WE HAD A DISAGREE-MENT A WHILE BACK.
SHE'S BEEN TRYING TO KILL ME EVER SINCE.
I...I'M OUT THIS ROUND! FIGHT HER YOURSELF.
SORRY TO BOTHER YOU!
UH-*HUH*... AND YOU THINK SHE'LL JUST LET YOU GO.
WHAT SHE WANTS IS REVENGE. SHE WON'T BE HAPPY UNLESS SHE GETS ME, SHINKI AND ALL.
NO FAIR!
THAT'S RIGHT.

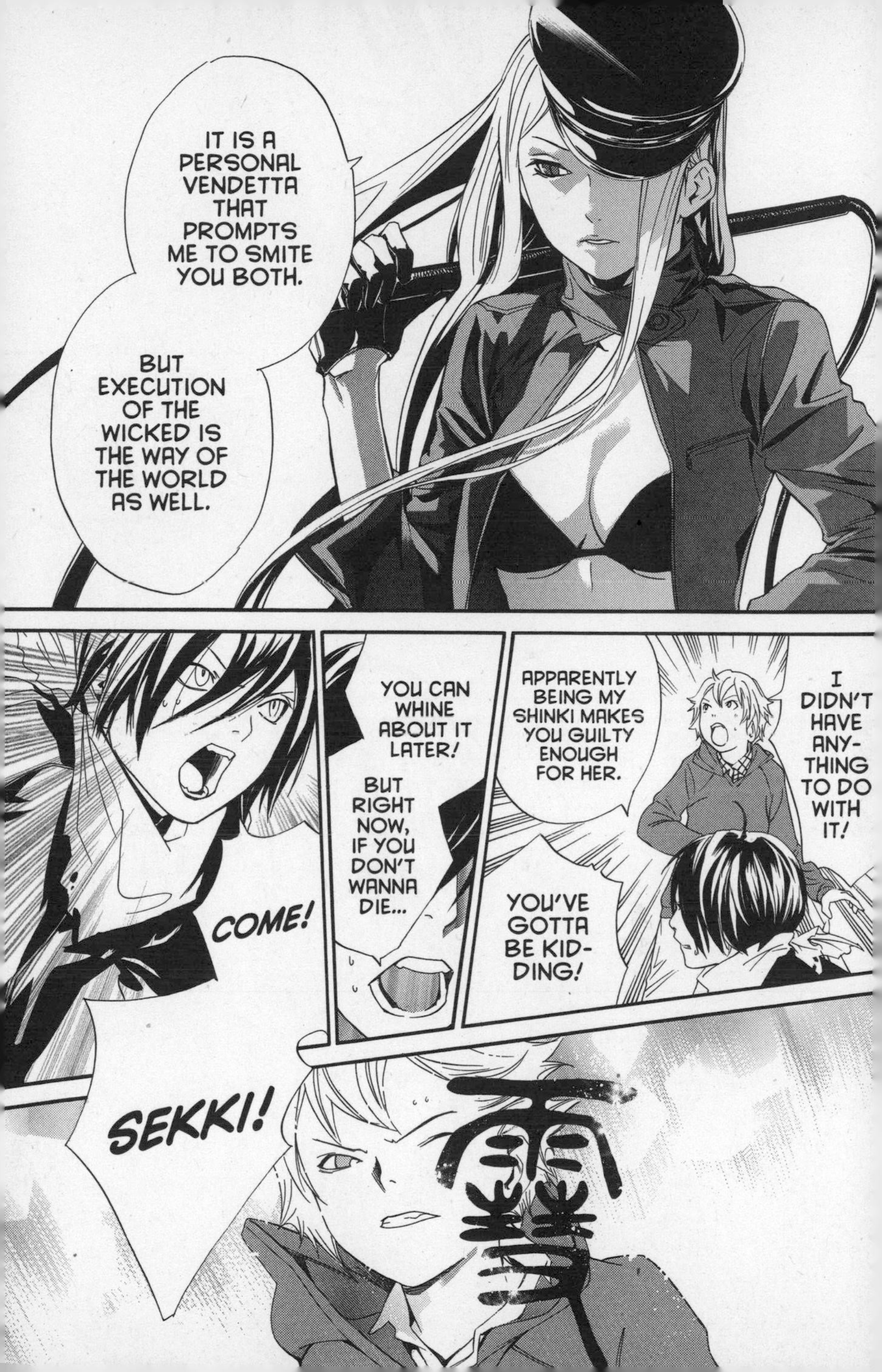
IT IS A PERSONAL VENDETTA THAT PROMPTS ME TO SMITE YOU BOTH.
BUT EXECUTION OF THE WICKED IS THE WAY OF THE WORLD AS WELL.
I DIDN'T HAVE ANY-THING TO DO WITH IT!
APPARENTLY BEING MY SHINKI MAKES YOU GUILTY ENOUGH FOR HER.
YOU'VE GOTTA BE KID-DING!
YOU CAN WHINE ABOUT IT LATER!
BUT RIGHT NOW, IF YOU DON'T WANNA DIE...
COME!
SEKKI!

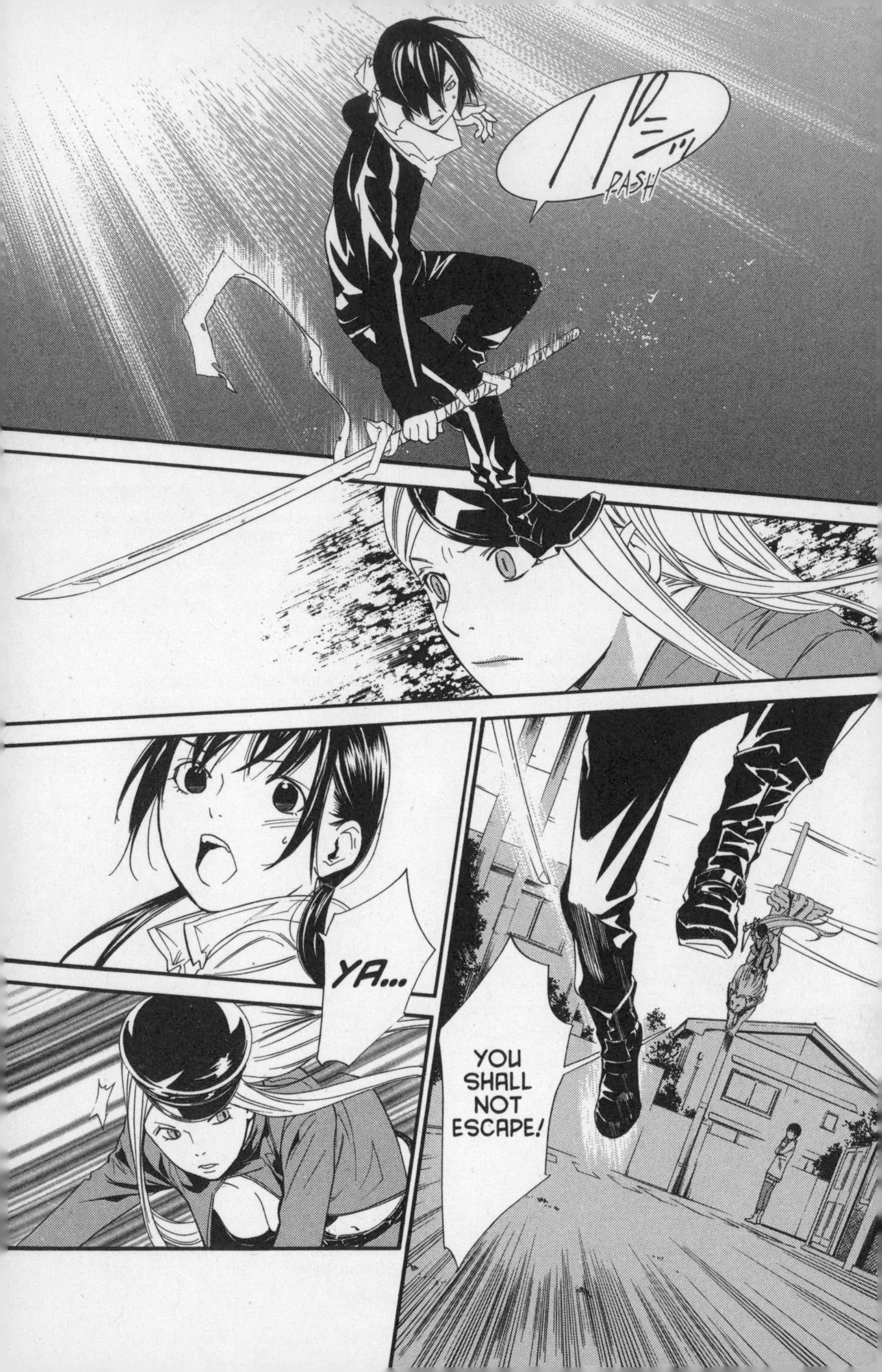
DASH
YA...
YOU SHALL NOT ESCAPE!

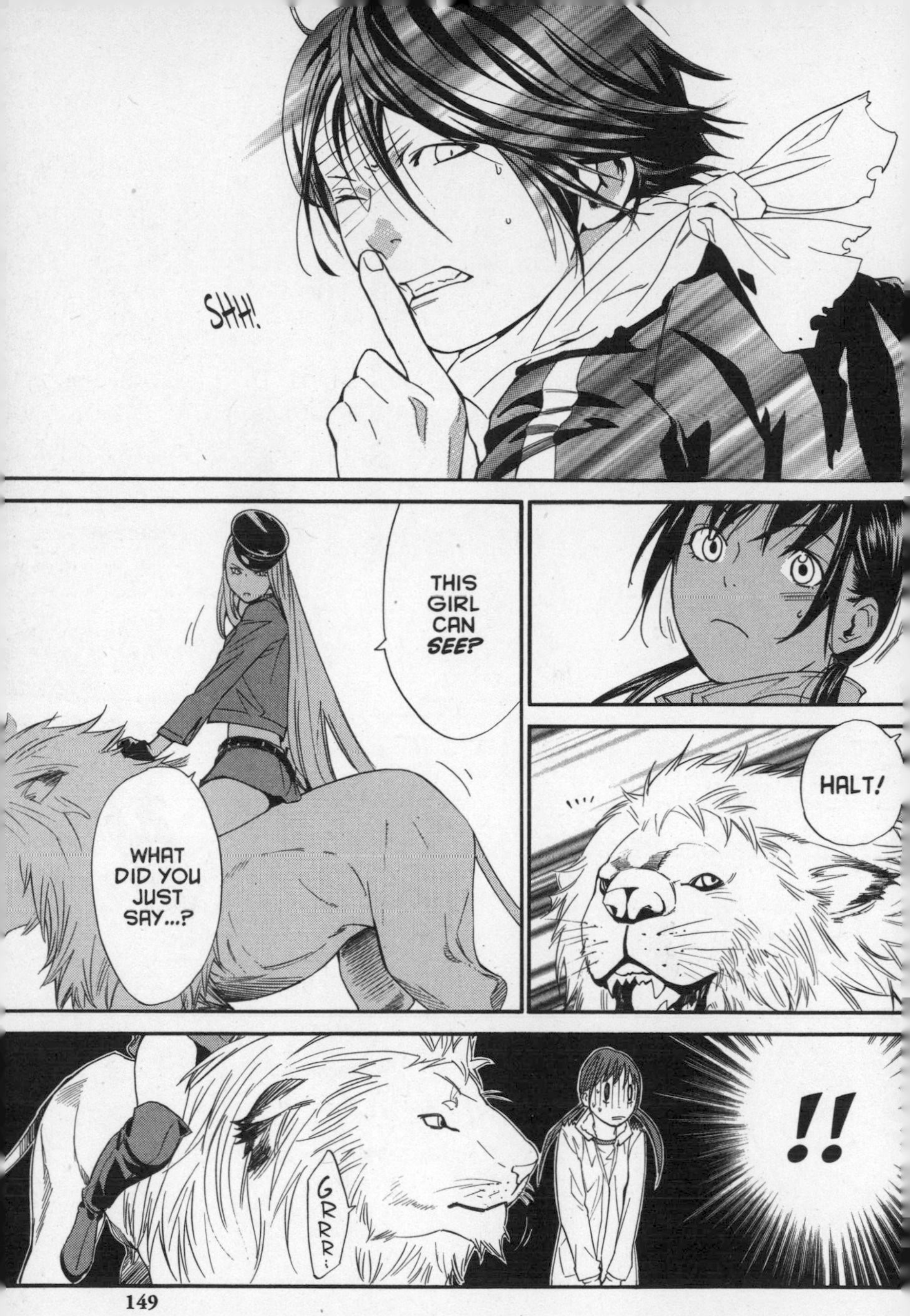
SHH!
HALT!
THIS GIRL CAN SEE?
WHAT DID YOU JUST SAY...?
!!
GRRR...

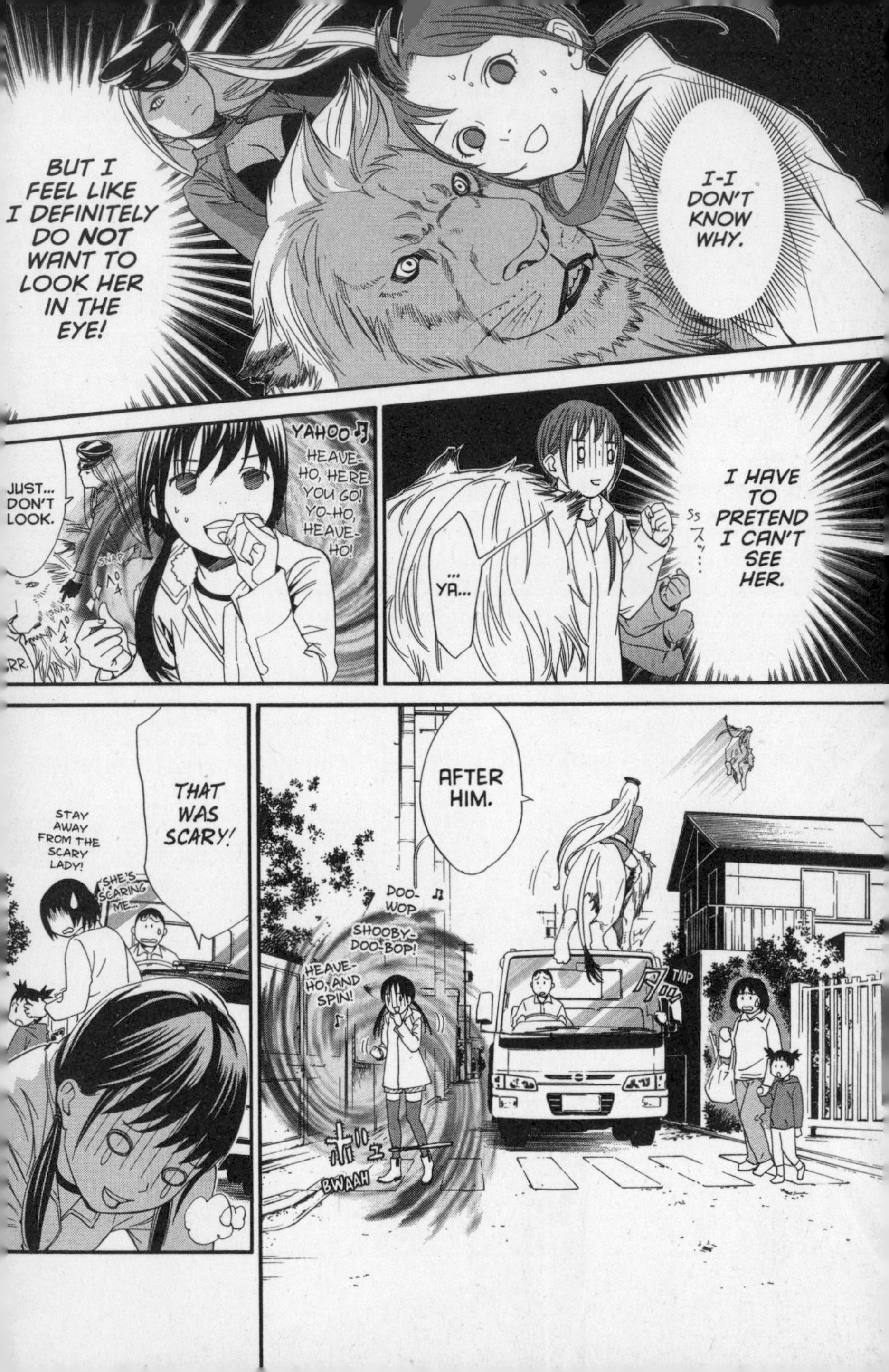
I-I DON'T KNOW WHY.
BUT I FEEL LIKE I DEFINITELY DO NOT WANT TO LOOK HER IN THE EYE!
I HAVE TO PRETEND I CAN'T SEE HER.
SS
... YA...
YAHOO
HEAVE-HO, HERE YOU GO! YO-HO, HEAVE-HO!
JUST... DON'T LOOK.
SNAP
SNAP
RR.
AFTER HIM.
TMP
DOO-WOP
SHOOBY-DOO-BOP!
HEAVE-HO, AND SPIN!
BWAAH
THAT WAS SCARY!
STAY AWAY FROM THE SCARY LADY!
SHE'S SCARING ME...

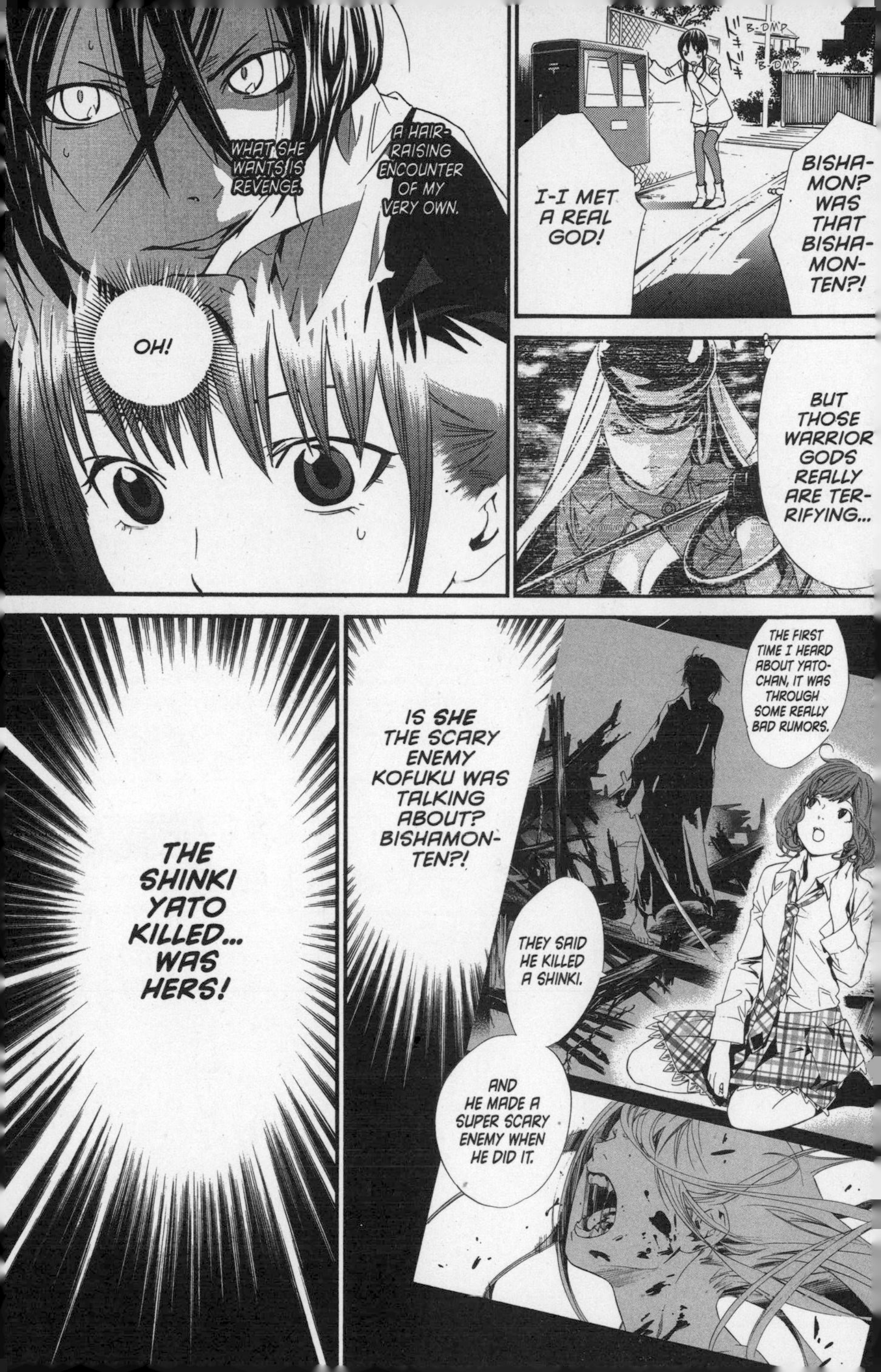
B-DMP
B-DMP
BISHA-MON? WAS THAT BISHA-MON-TEN?!
I-I MET A REAL GOD!
BUT THOSE WARRIOR GODS REALLY ARE TER-RIFYING...
A HAIR-RAISING ENCOUNTER OF MY VERY OWN.
WHAT SHE WANTS IS REVENGE.
OH!
THE FIRST TIME I HEARD ABOUT YATO-CHAN, IT WAS THROUGH SOME REALLY BAD RUMORS.
THEY SAID HE KILLED A SHINKI.
AND HE MADE A SUPER SCARY ENEMY WHEN HE DID IT.
IS SHE THE SCARY ENEMY KOFUKU WAS TALKING ABOUT? BISHAMON-TEN?!
THE SHINKI YATO KILLED... WAS HERS!

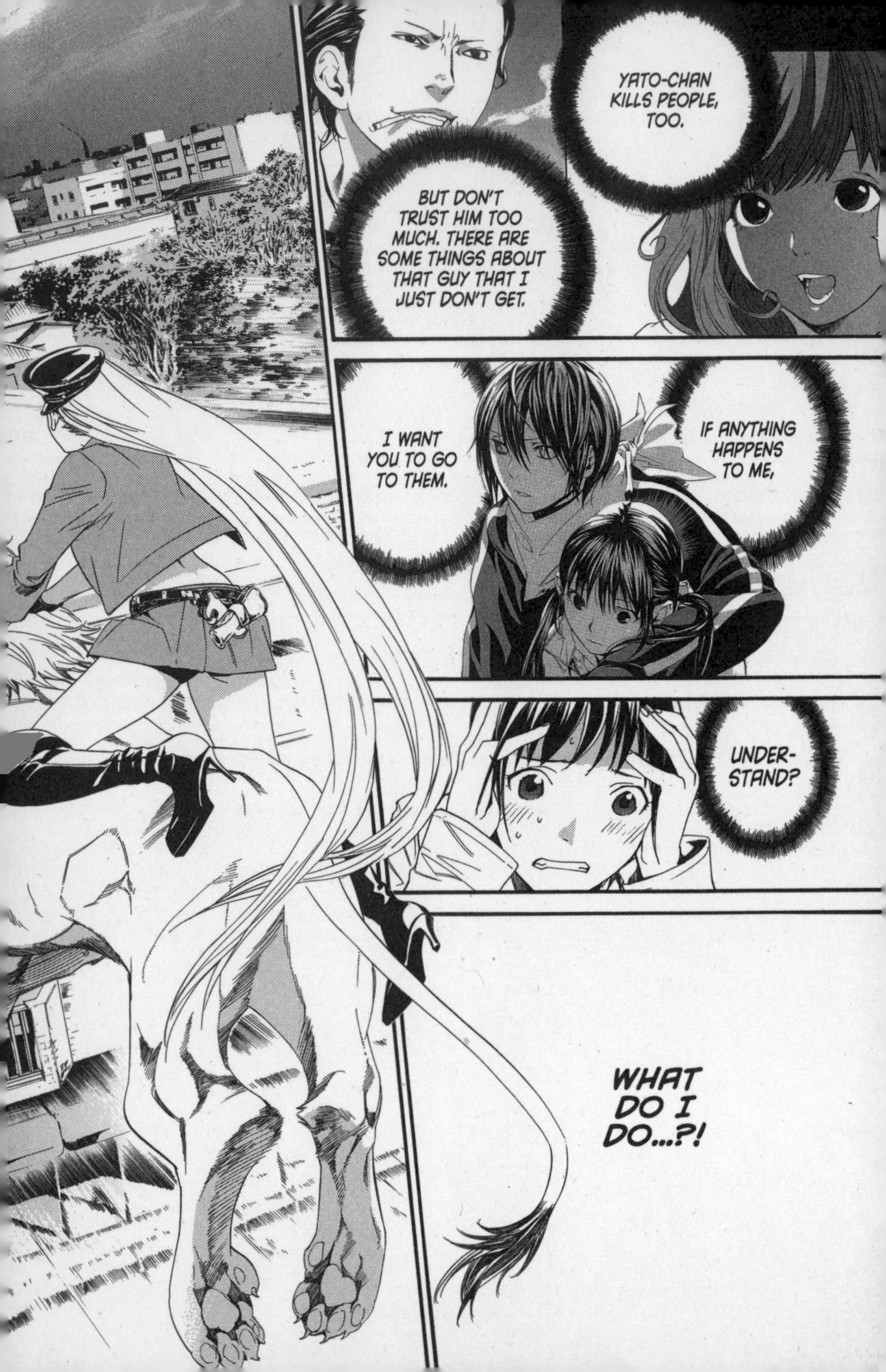
YATO-CHAN KILLS PEOPLE, TOO.
BUT DON'T TRUST HIM TOO MUCH. THERE ARE SOME THINGS ABOUT THAT GUY THAT I JUST DON'T GET.
IF ANYTHING HAPPENS TO ME,
I WANT YOU TO GO TO THEM.
UNDER-STAND?
WHAT DO I DO...?!

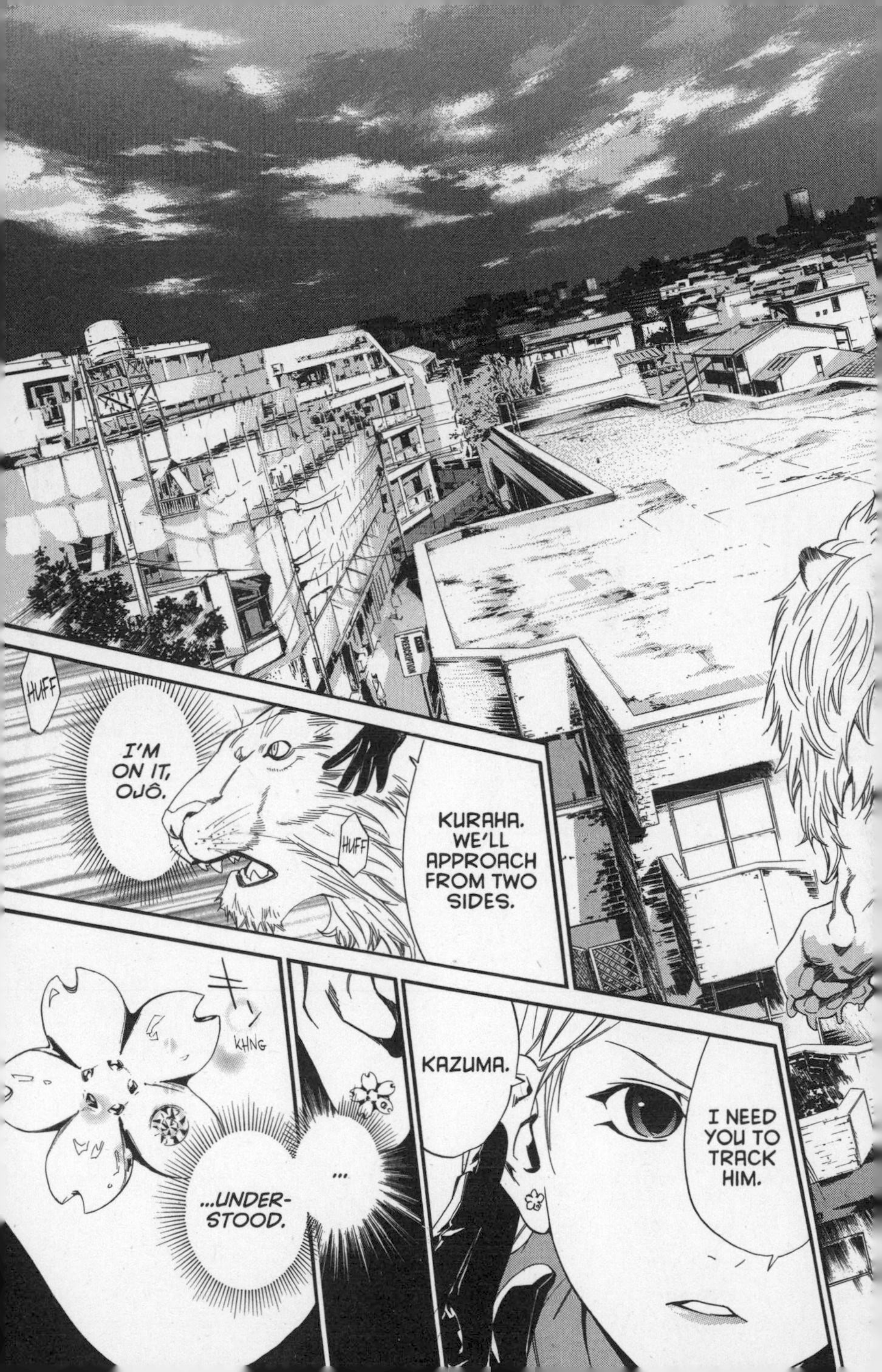
KURAHA. WE'LL APPROACH FROM TWO SIDES.
HUFF
I'M ON IT, OJÔ.
HUFF
KAZUMA.
I NEED YOU TO TRACK HIM.
...
KHNG
...UNDER-STOOD.

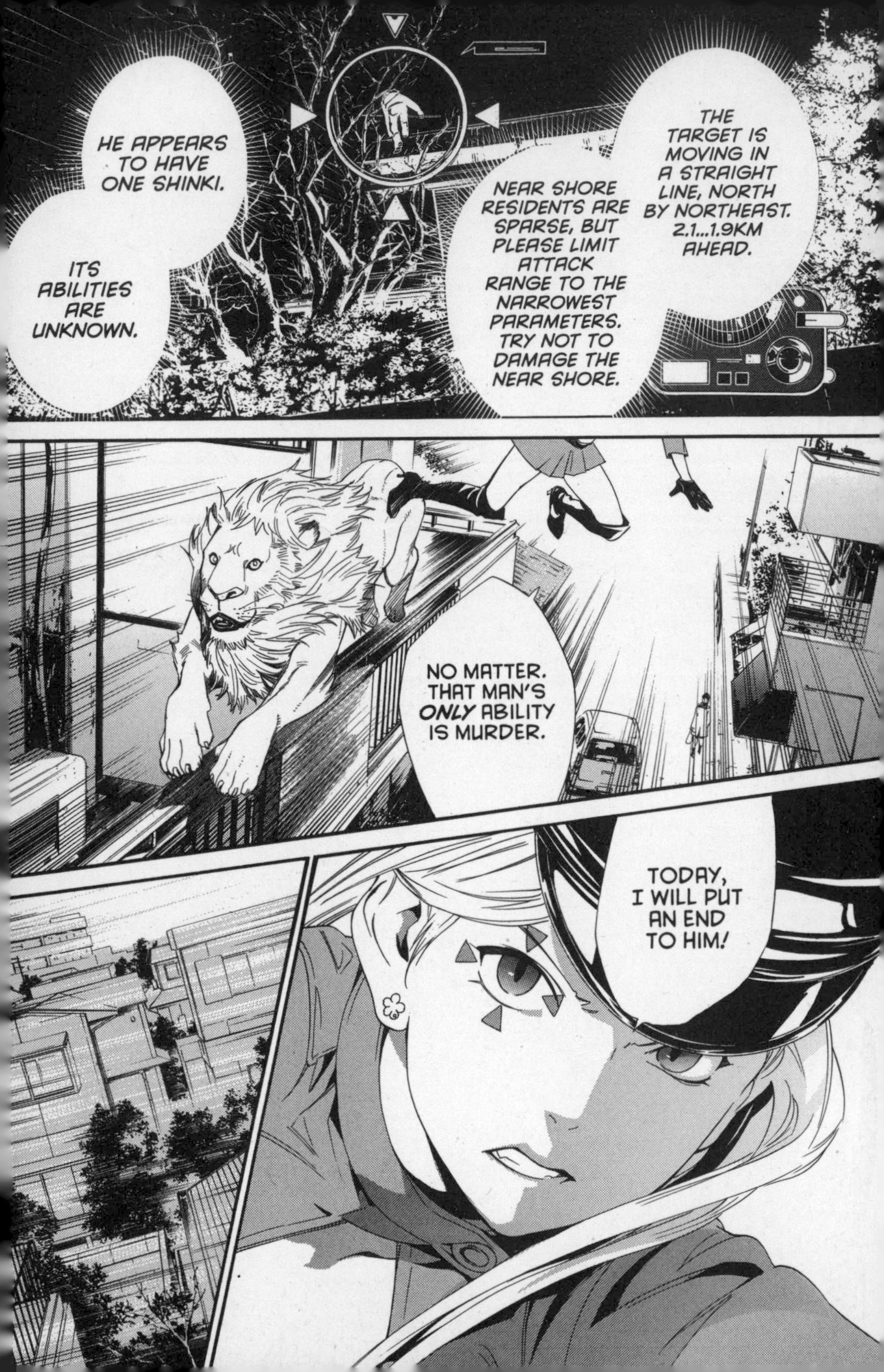
THE TARGET IS MOVING IN A STRAIGHT LINE, NORTH BY NORTHEAST. 2.1...1.9KM AHEAD.
NEAR SHORE RESIDENTS ARE SPARSE, BUT PLEASE LIMIT ATTACK RANGE TO THE NARROWEST PARAMETERS. TRY NOT TO DAMAGE THE NEAR SHORE.
HE APPEARS TO HAVE ONE SHINKI.
ITS ABILITIES ARE UNKNOWN.
NO MATTER. THAT MAN'S *ONLY* ABILITY IS MURDER.
TODAY, I WILL PUT AN END TO HIM!

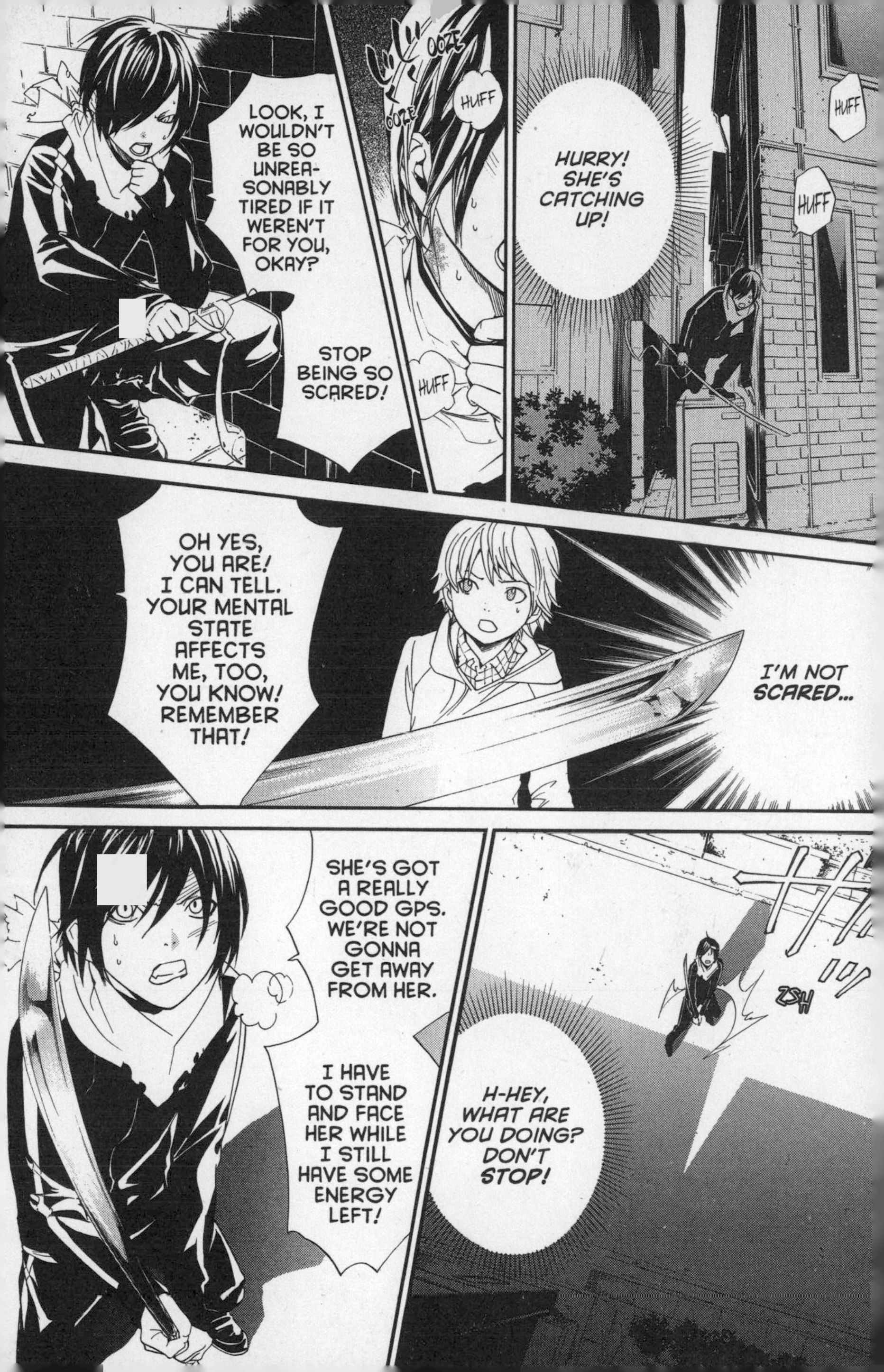
HUFF
HURRY! SHE'S CATCHING UP!
HUFF
OOZE
HUFF
OOZE
HUFF
STOP BEING SO SCARED!
LOOK, I WOULDN'T BE SO UNREASONABLY TIRED IF IT WEREN'T FOR YOU, OKAY?
I'M NOT SCARED...
OH YES, YOU ARE! I CAN TELL. YOUR MENTAL STATE AFFECTS ME, TOO, YOU KNOW! REMEMBER THAT!
ZSH
H-HEY, WHAT ARE YOU DOING? DON'T STOP!
SHE'S GOT A REALLY GOOD GPS. WE'RE NOT GONNA GET AWAY FROM HER.
I HAVE TO STAND AND FACE HER WHILE I STILL HAVE SOME ENERGY LEFT!

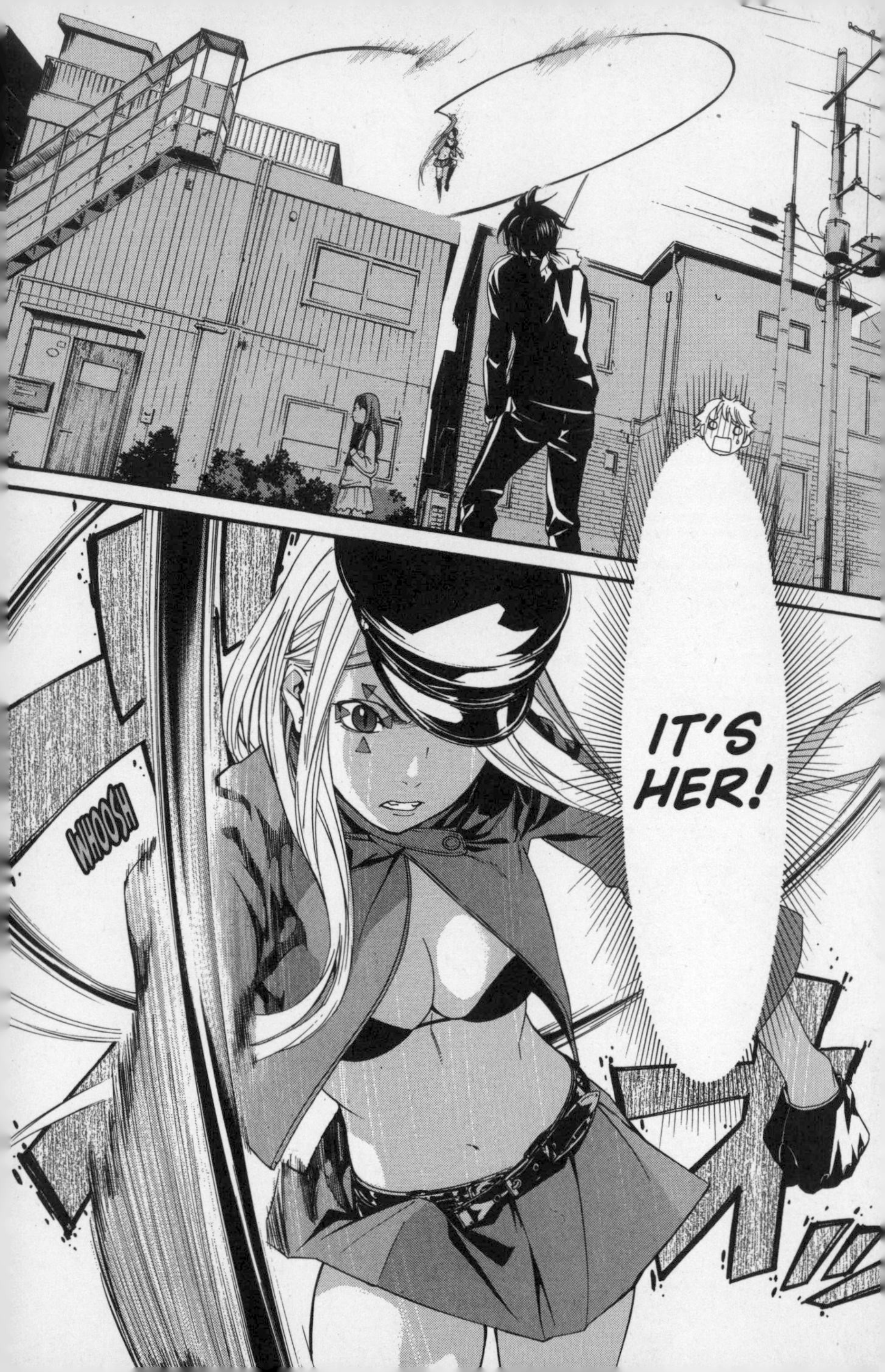
IT'S HER!
WHOOSH

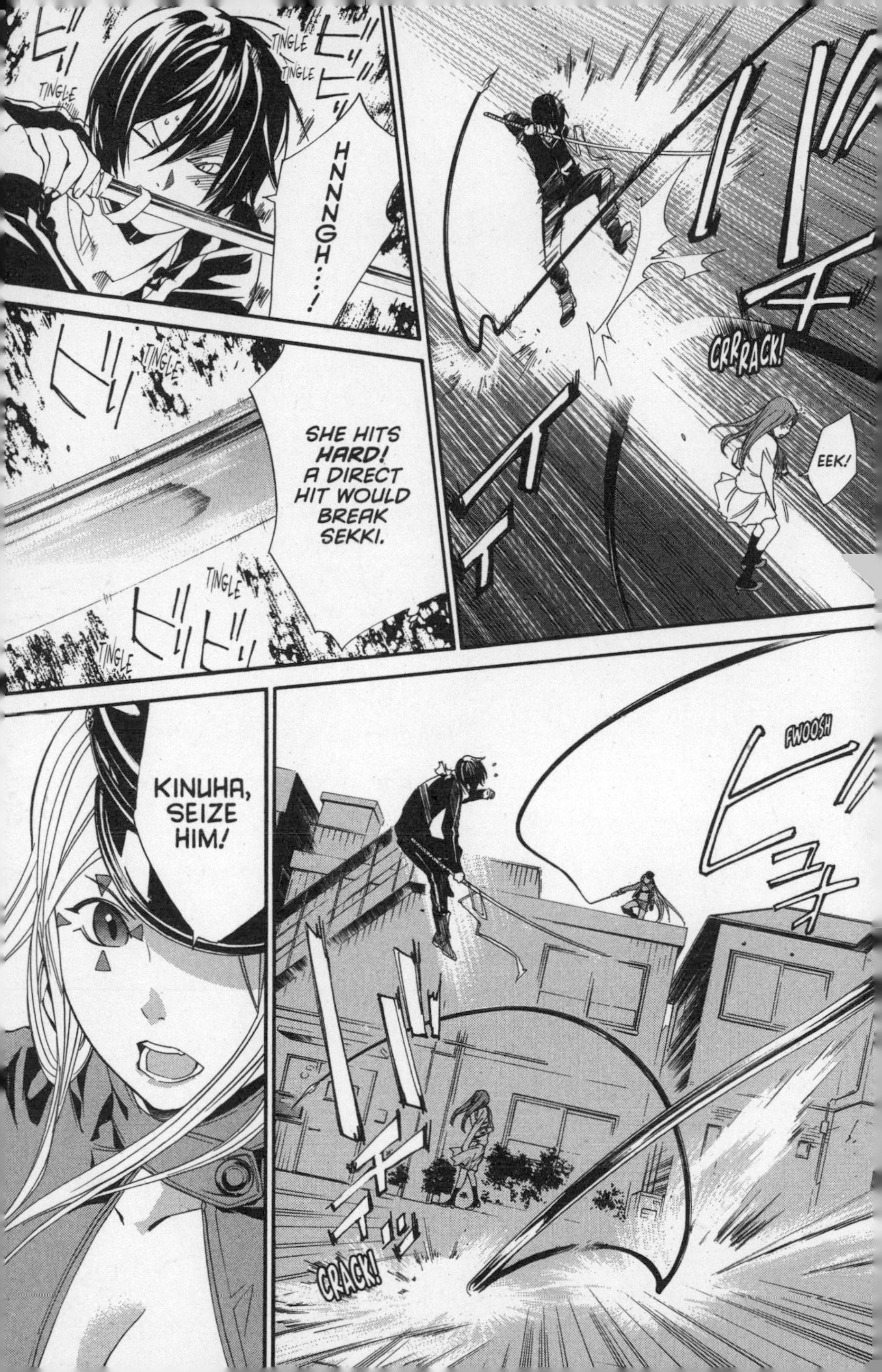
CRRRACK!
EEK!
TINGLE
TINGLE
TINGLE
HNNNGH...!
TINGLE
SHE HITS HARD! A DIRECT HIT WOULD BREAK SEKKI.
TINGLE
TINGLE
FWOOSH
CRACK!
KINUHA, SEIZE HIM!

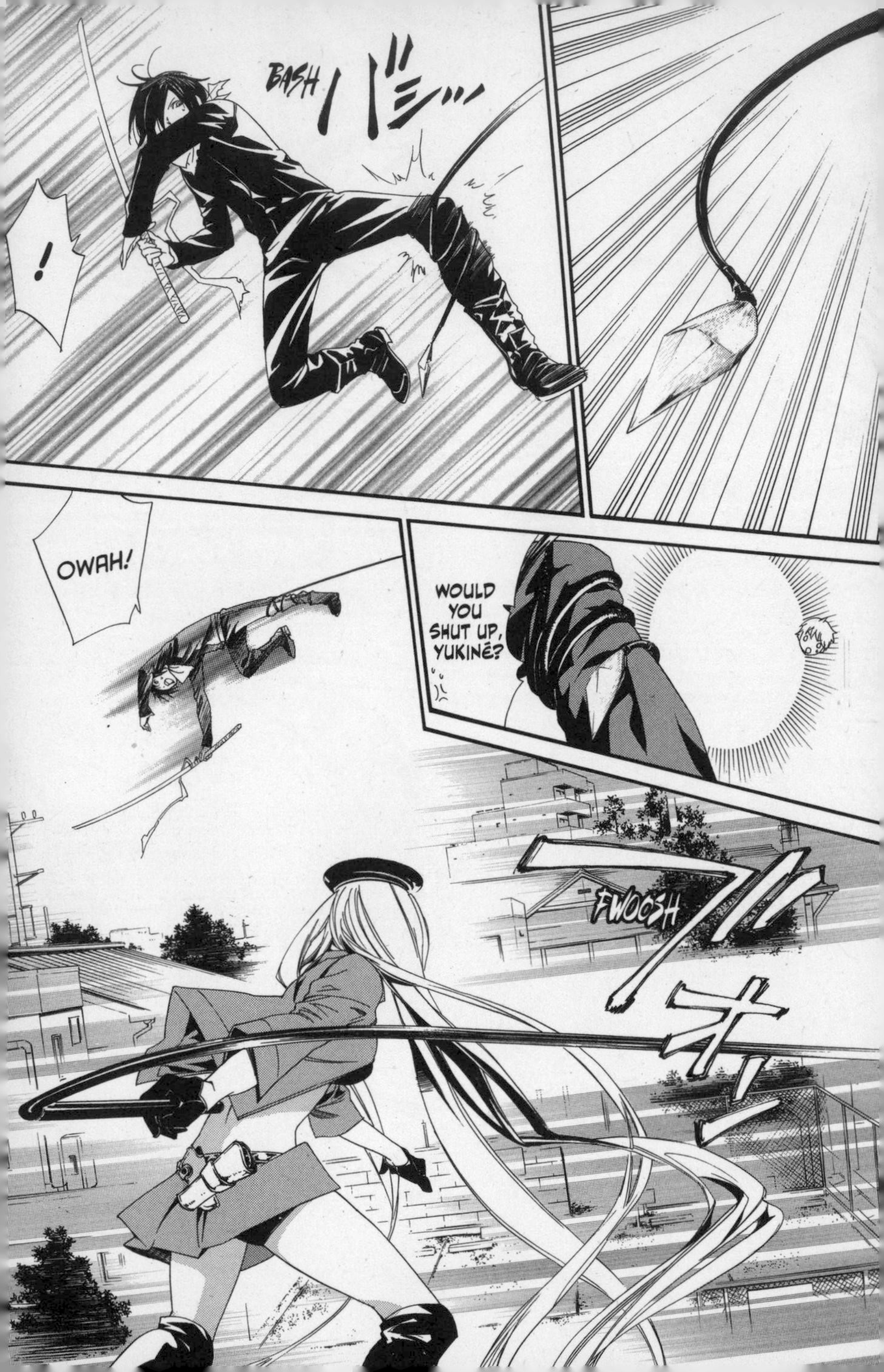
BASH
!
WOULD YOU SHUT UP, YUKINĒ?
OWAH!
FWOOSH

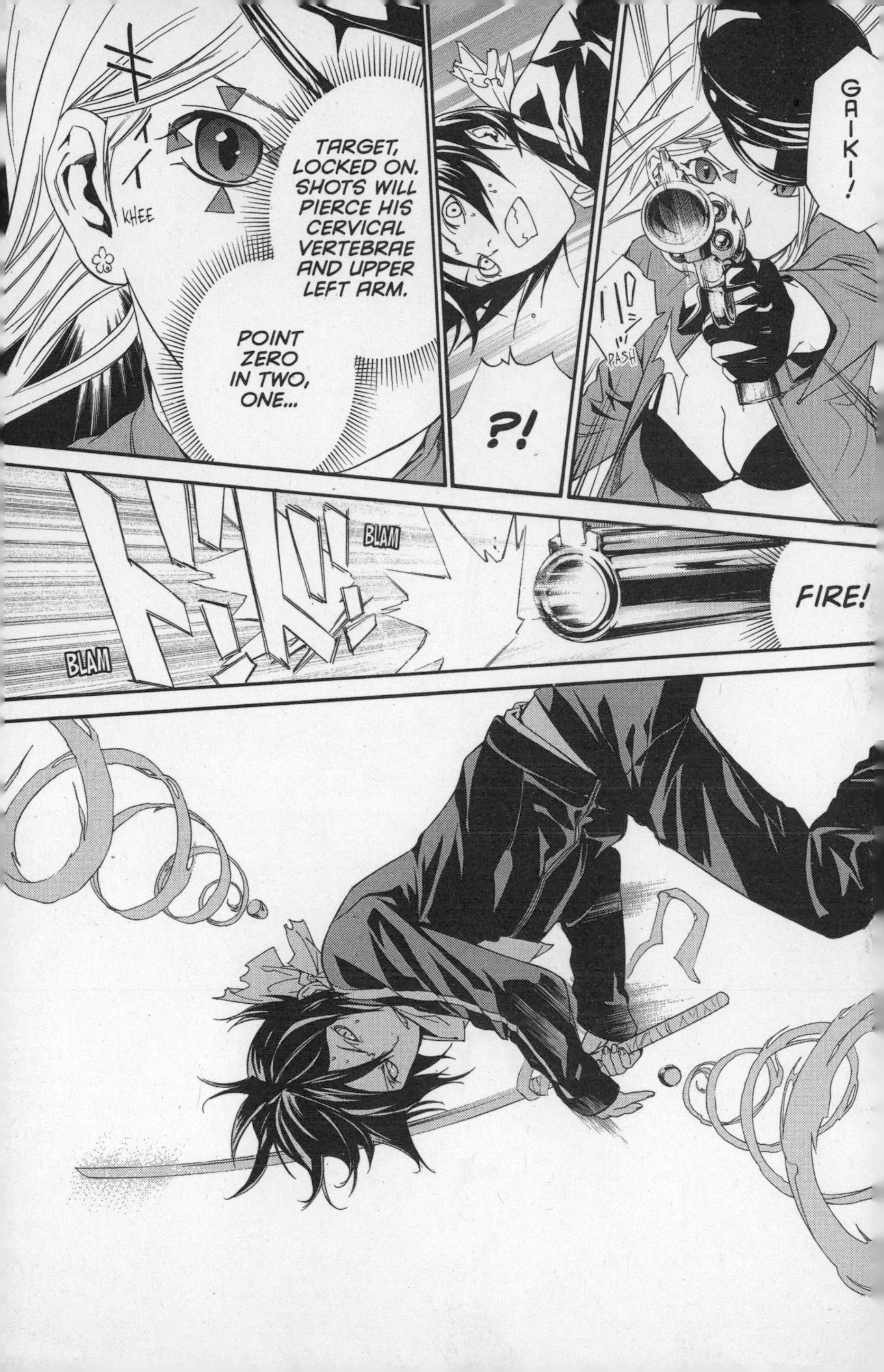
GAIKI!
?!
KHEE
TARGET, LOCKED ON. SHOTS WILL PIERCE HIS CERVICAL VERTEBRAE AND UPPER LEFT ARM.
POINT ZERO IN TWO, ONE...
FIRE!
BLAM
BLAM

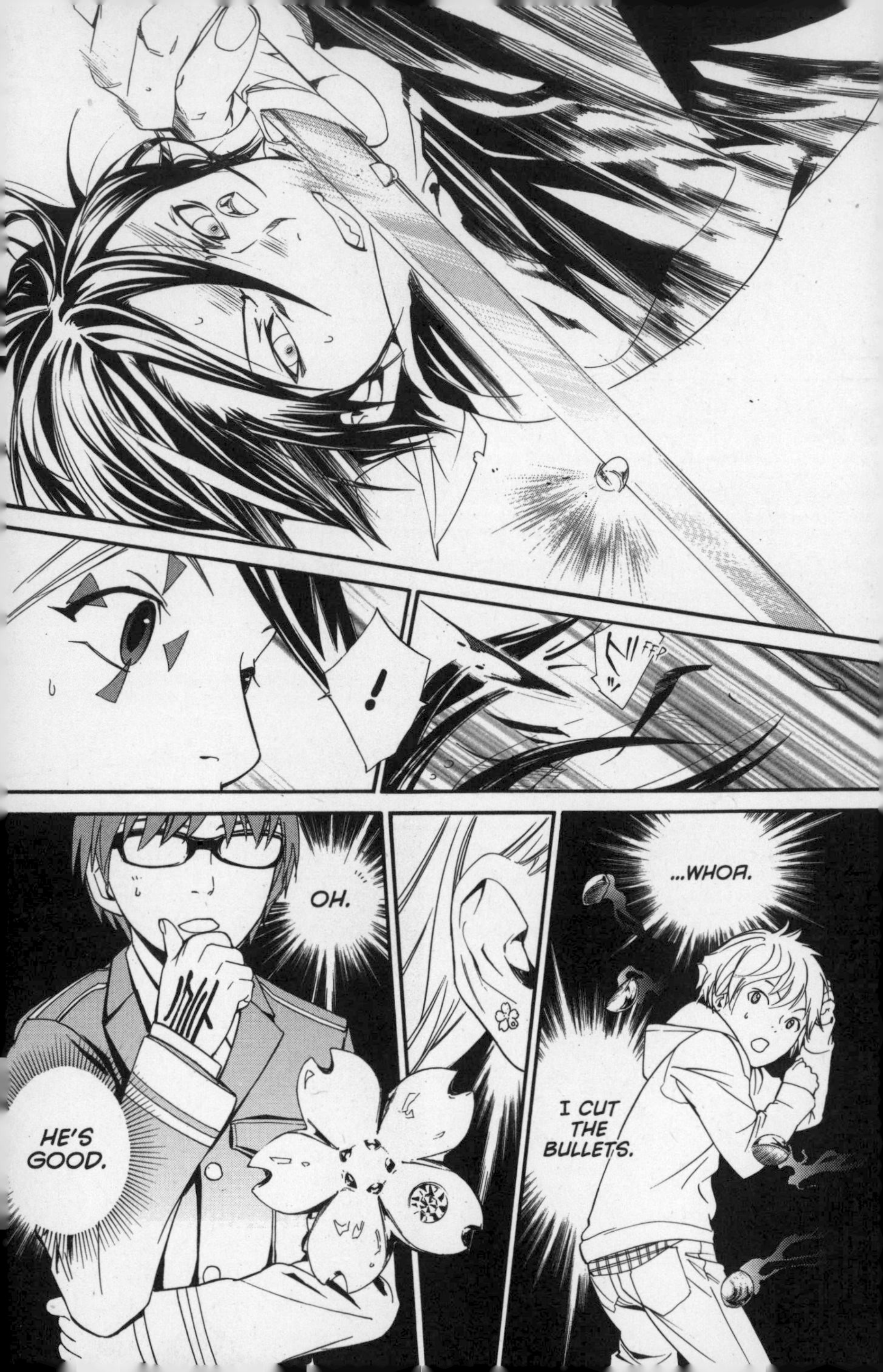
FFP
!
...WHOA.
I CUT THE BULLETS.
OH.
HE'S GOOD.

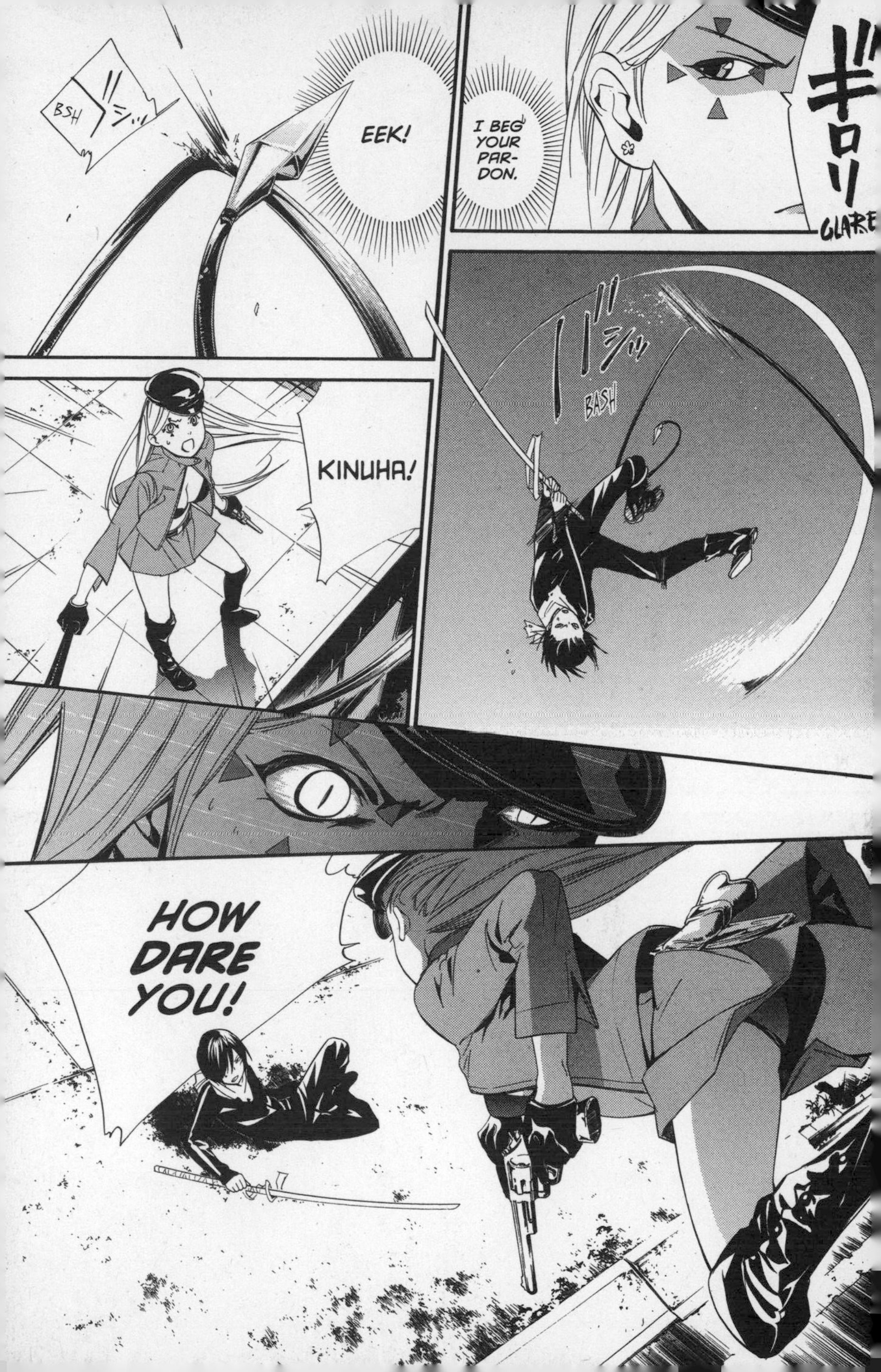
ギロリ
GLARE
I BEG YOUR PAR-DON.
EEK!
BSH
BASH
KINUHA!
HOW DARE YOU!

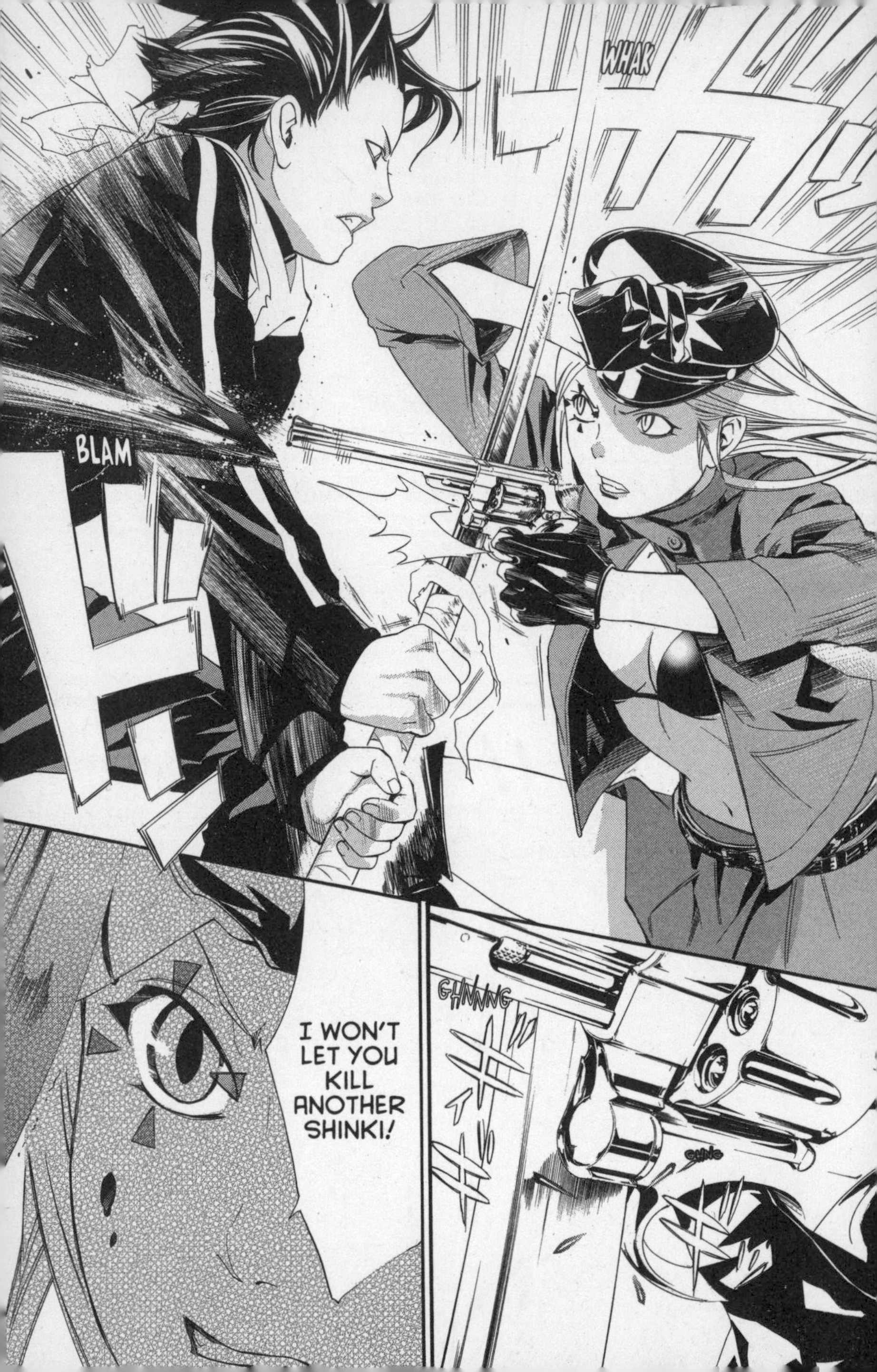
WHAK
BLAM
GHNNNG
GHNG
I WON'T LET YOU KILL ANOTHER SHINKI!

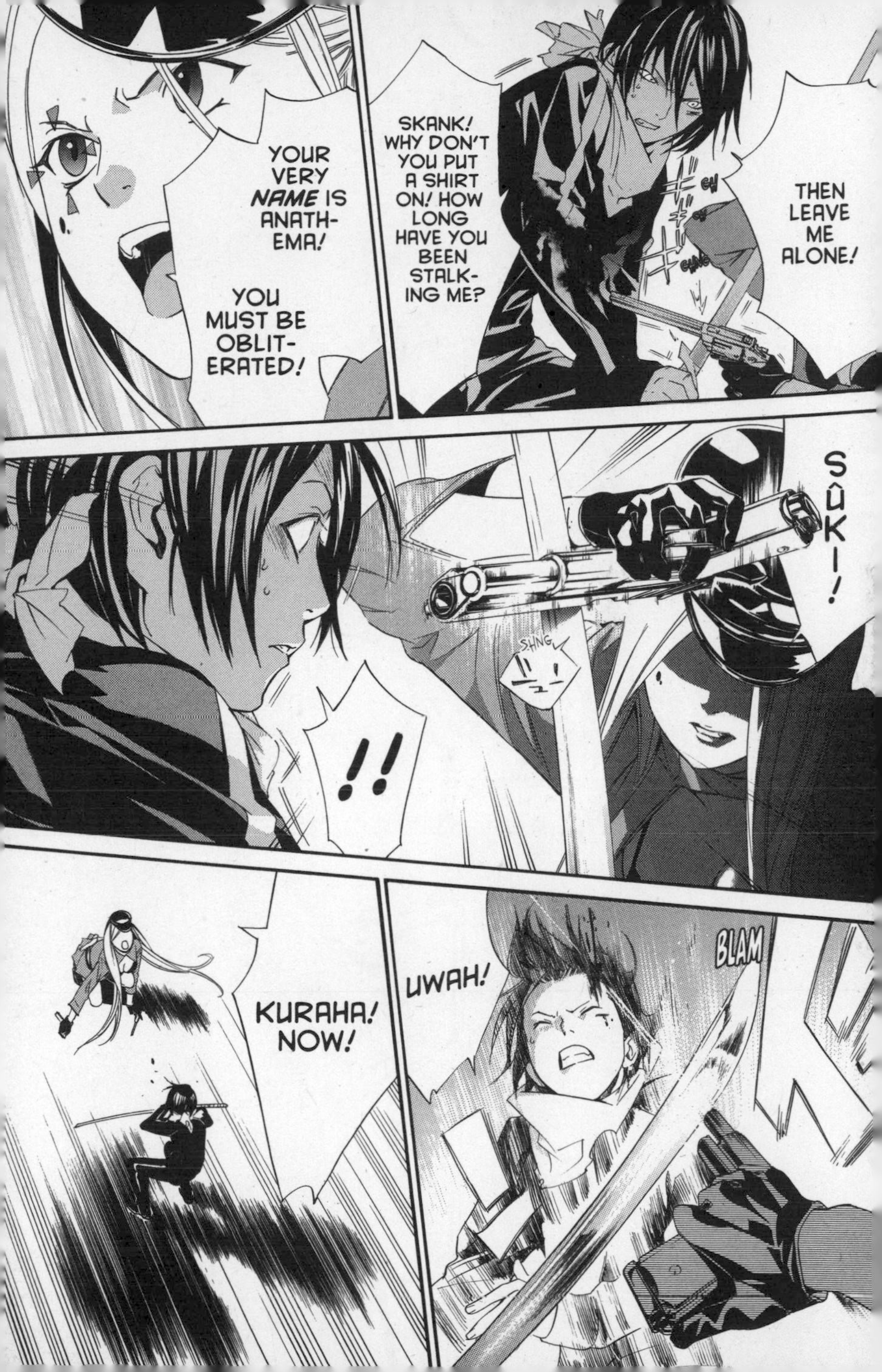
THEN LEAVE ME ALONE!
SKANK! WHY DON'T YOU PUT A SHIRT ON! HOW LONG HAVE YOU BEEN STALKING ME?
YOUR VERY ***NAME*** IS ANATHEMA!
YOU MUST BE OBLITERATED!
SÛKI!
SHING
!!
BLAM
UWAH!
KURAHA! NOW!

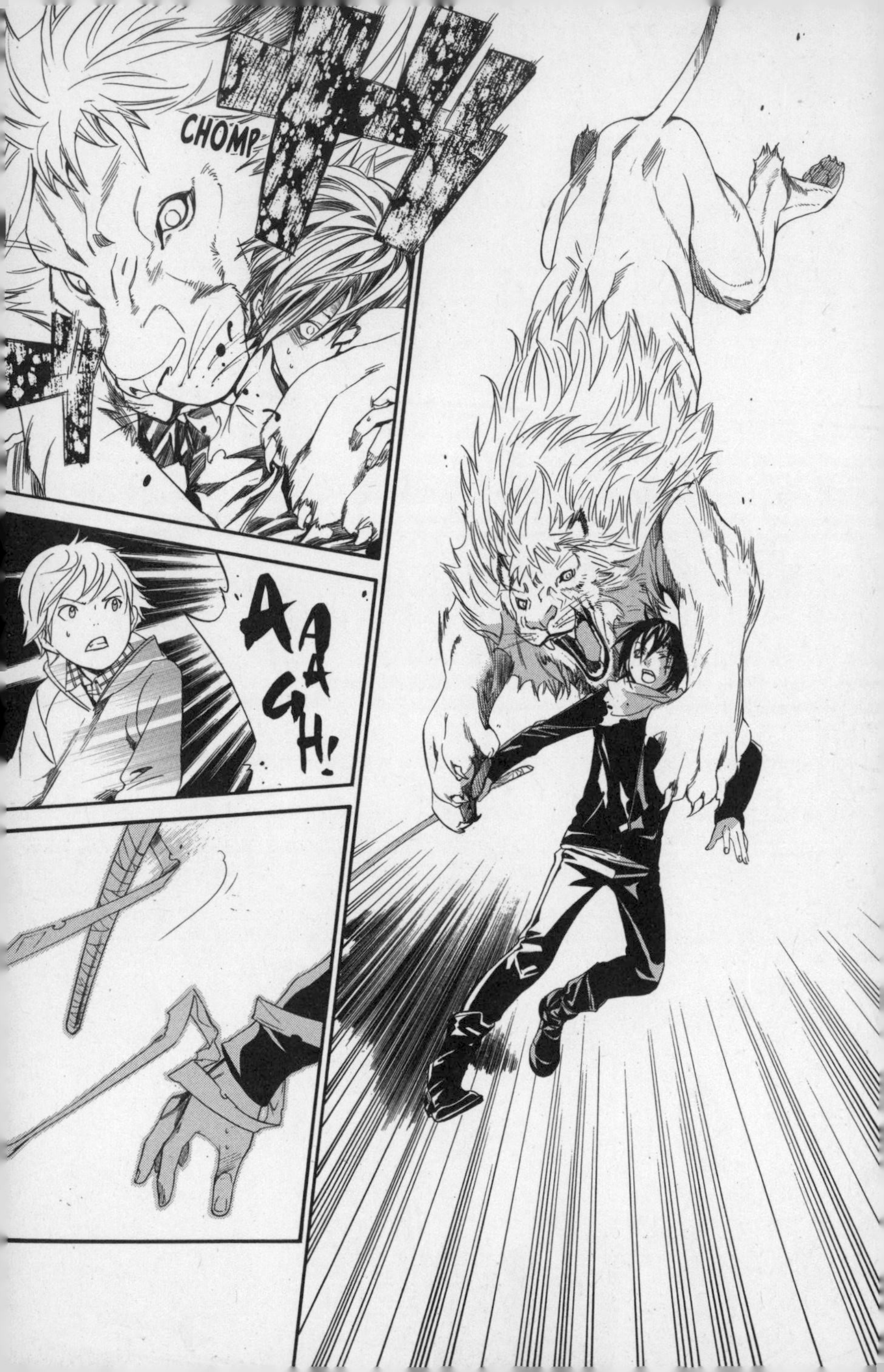
CHOMP
AAAGH!

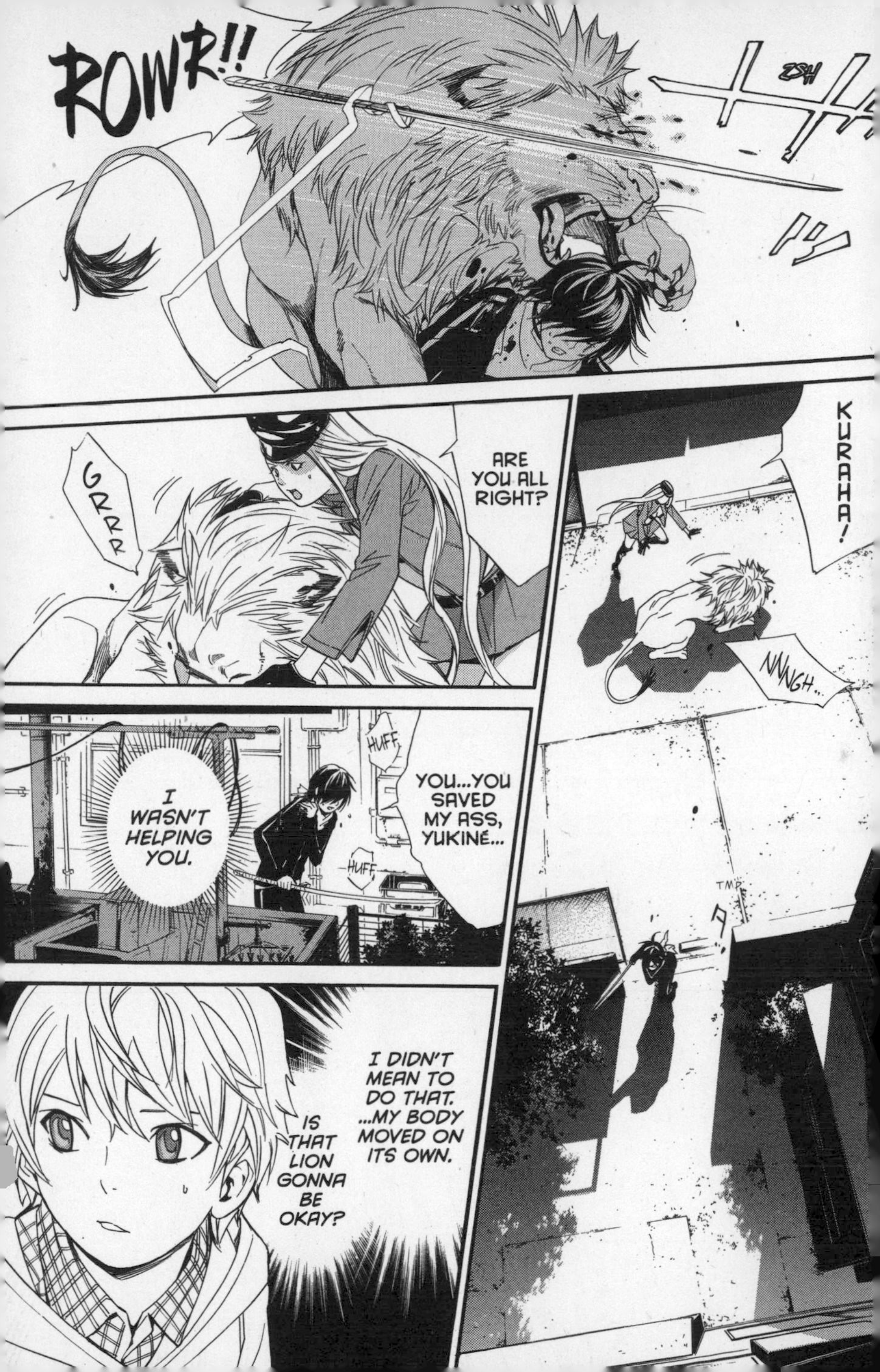
ZSH
ROWR!!
KURAHA!
NNNGH...
TMP
ARE YOU ALL RIGHT?
GRRR
YOU...YOU SAVED MY ASS, YUKINE...
HUFF
HUFF
I WASN'T HELPING YOU.
I DIDN'T MEAN TO DO THAT. ...MY BODY MOVED ON ITS OWN.
IS THAT LION GONNA BE OKAY?

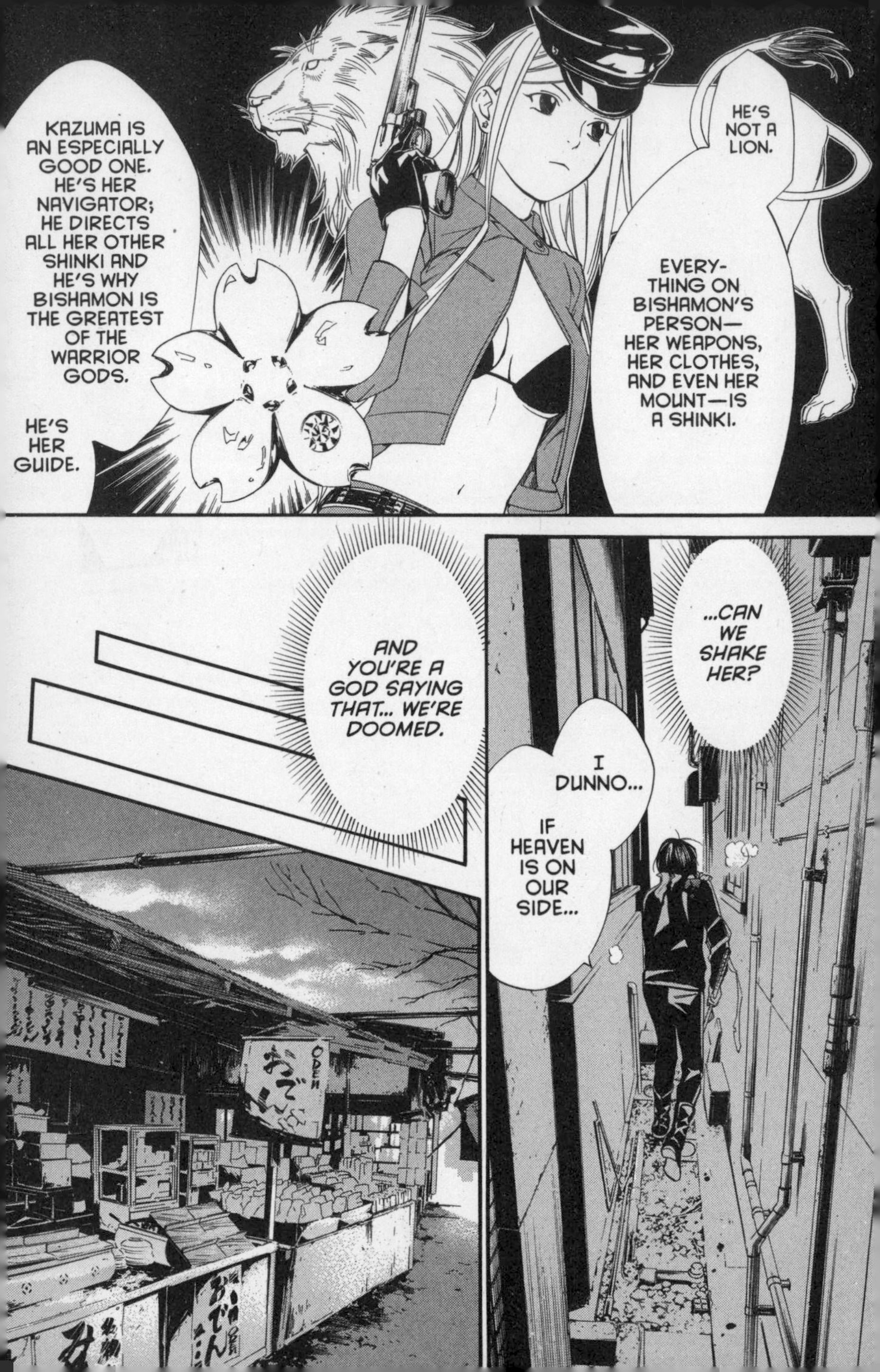
HE'S NOT A LION.
EVERY-THING ON BISHAMON'S PERSON—HER WEAPONS, HER CLOTHES, AND EVEN HER MOUNT—IS A SHINKI.
KAZUMA IS AN ESPECIALLY GOOD ONE. HE'S HER NAVIGATOR; HE DIRECTS ALL HER OTHER SHINKI AND HE'S WHY BISHAMON IS THE GREATEST OF THE WARRIOR GODS.
HE'S HER GUIDE.
...CAN WE SHAKE HER?
I DUNNO...
IF HEAVEN IS ON OUR SIDE...
AND YOU'RE A GOD SAYING THAT... WE'RE DOOMED.
ODEN
おでん

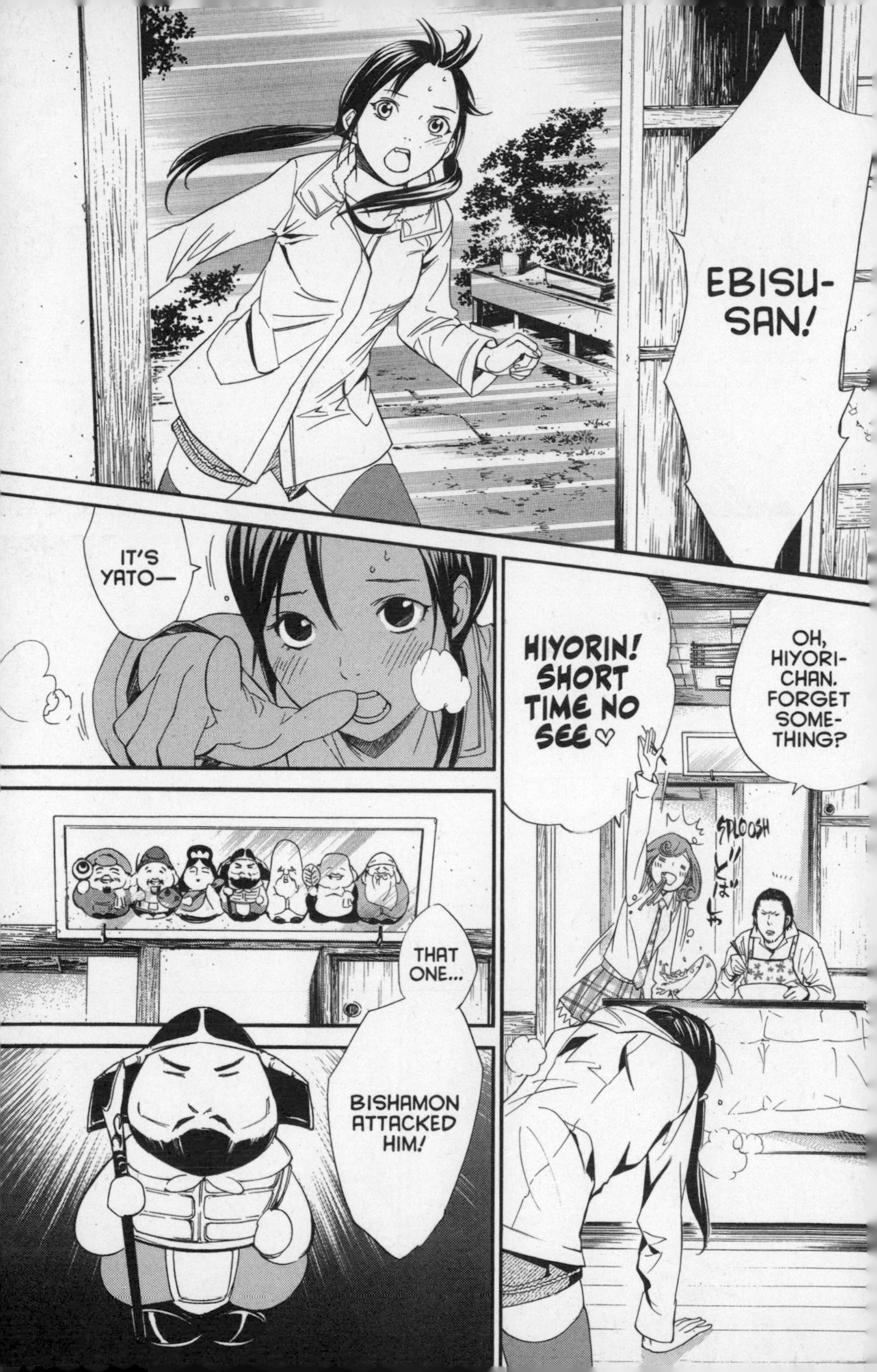
EBISU-SAN!
OH, HIYORI-CHAN. FORGET SOMETHING?
HIYORIN! SHORT TIME NO SEE ♡
SPLOOSH
IT'S YATO—
THAT ONE...
BISHAMON ATTACKED HIM!

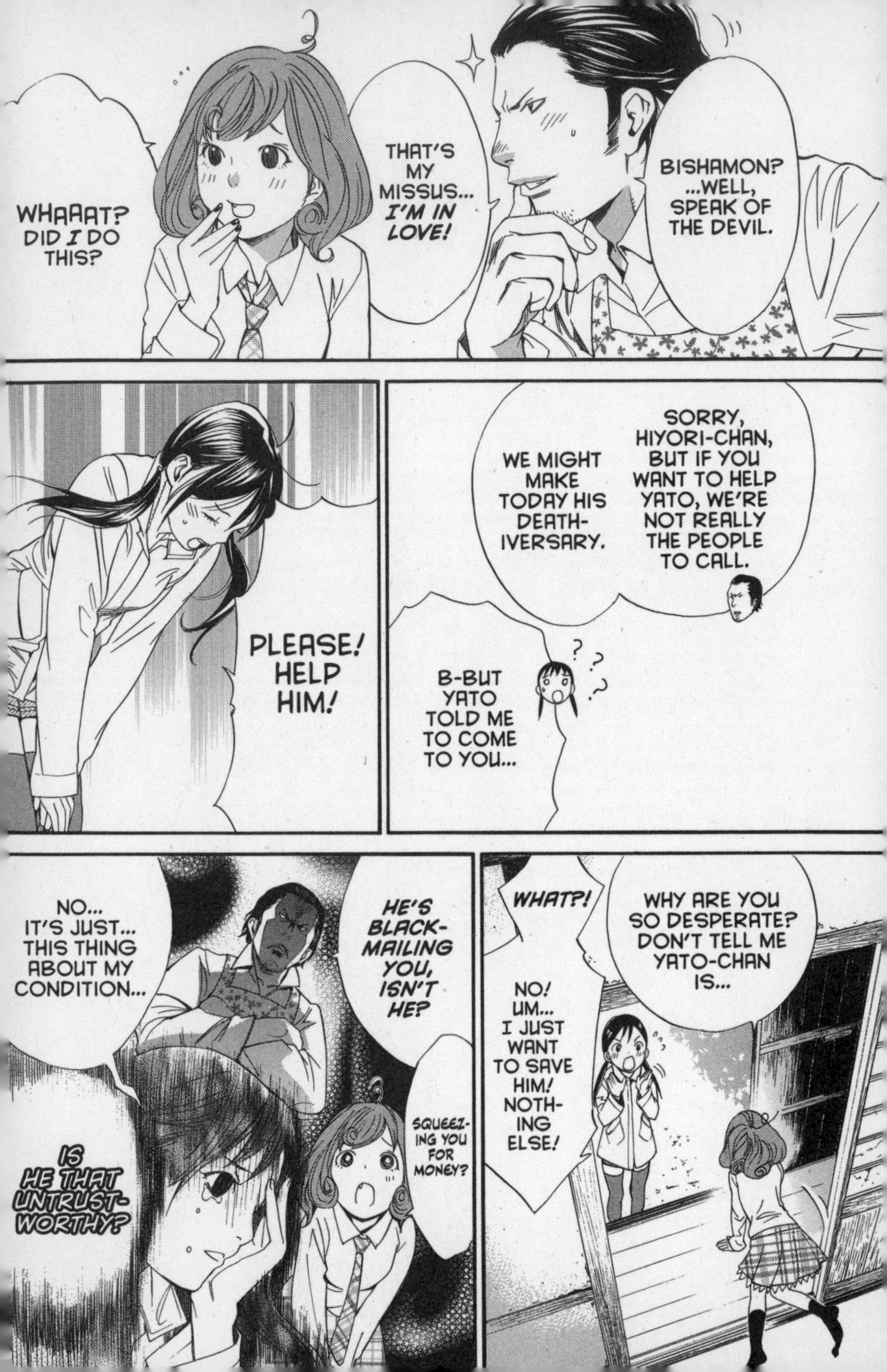
BISHAMON? ...WELL, SPEAK OF THE DEVIL.
THAT'S MY MISSUS... I'M IN LOVE!
WHAAAT? DID I DO THIS?
SORRY, HIYORI-CHAN, BUT IF YOU WANT TO HELP YATO, WE'RE NOT REALLY THE PEOPLE TO CALL.
WE MIGHT MAKE TODAY HIS DEATH-IVERSARY.
B-BUT YATO TOLD ME TO COME TO YOU...
PLEASE! HELP HIM!
WHY ARE YOU SO DESPERATE? DON'T TELL ME YATO-CHAN IS...
WHAT?!
NO! UM... I JUST WANT TO SAVE HIM! NOTHING ELSE!
HE'S BLACKMAILING YOU, ISN'T HE?
SQUEEZING YOU FOR MONEY?
NO... IT'S JUST... THIS THING ABOUT MY CONDITION...
IS HE THAT UNTRUSTWORTHY?

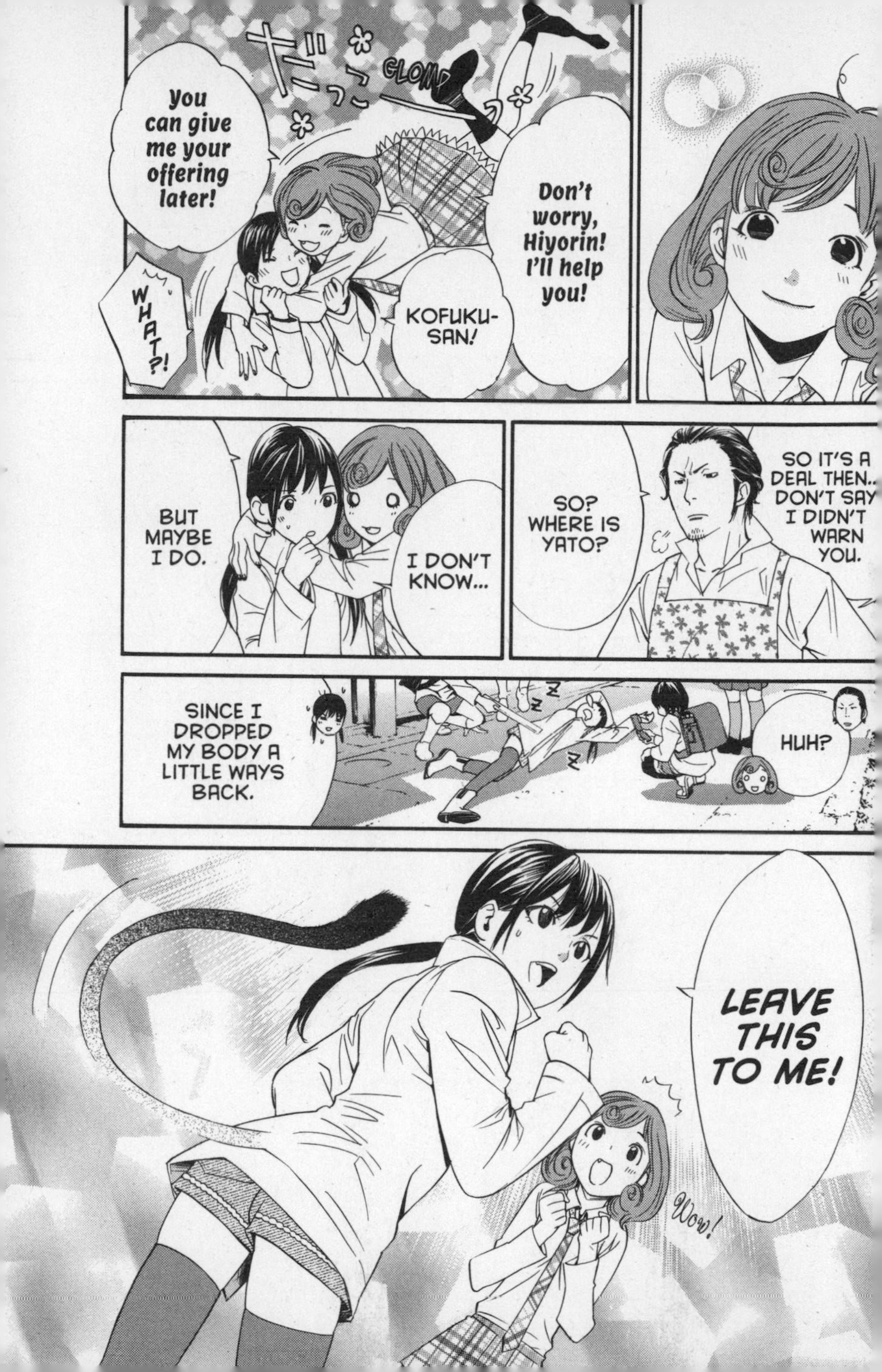
GLOMP
Don't worry, Hiyorin! I'll help you!
KOFUKU-SAN!
You can give me your offering later!
WHAT?!
SO IT'S A DEAL THEN.. DON'T SAY I DIDN'T WARN YOU.
SO? WHERE IS YATO?
I DON'T KNOW...
BUT MAYBE I DO.
HUH?
SINCE I DROPPED MY BODY A LITTLE WAYS BACK.
LEAVE THIS TO ME!
Wow!

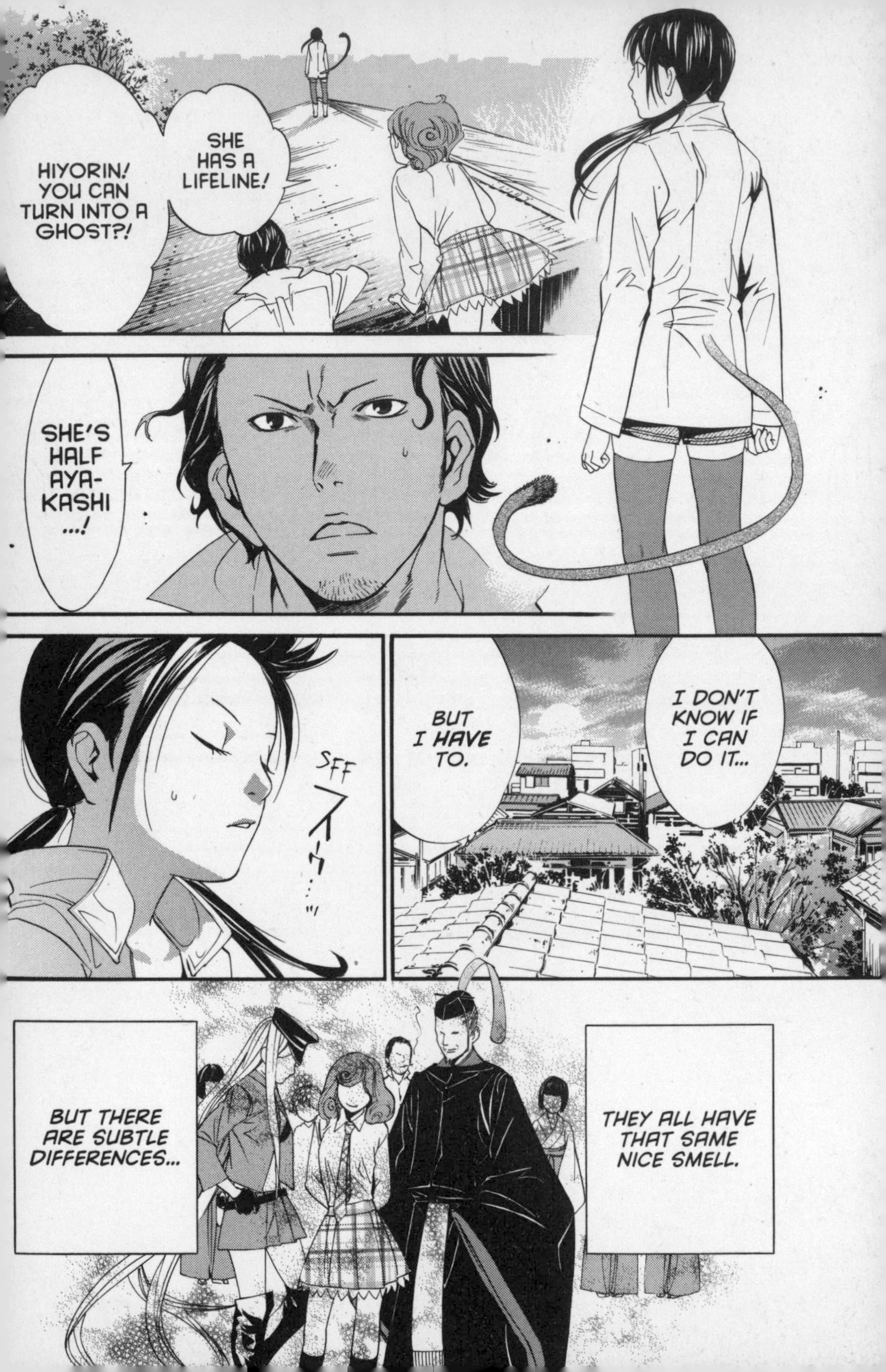
SHE HAS A LIFELINE!
HIYORIN! YOU CAN TURN INTO A GHOST?!
SHE'S HALF AYA-KASHI ...!
I DON'T KNOW IF I CAN DO IT...
BUT I HAVE TO.
SFF
THEY ALL HAVE THAT SAME NICE SMELL.
BUT THERE ARE SUBTLE DIFFERENCES...

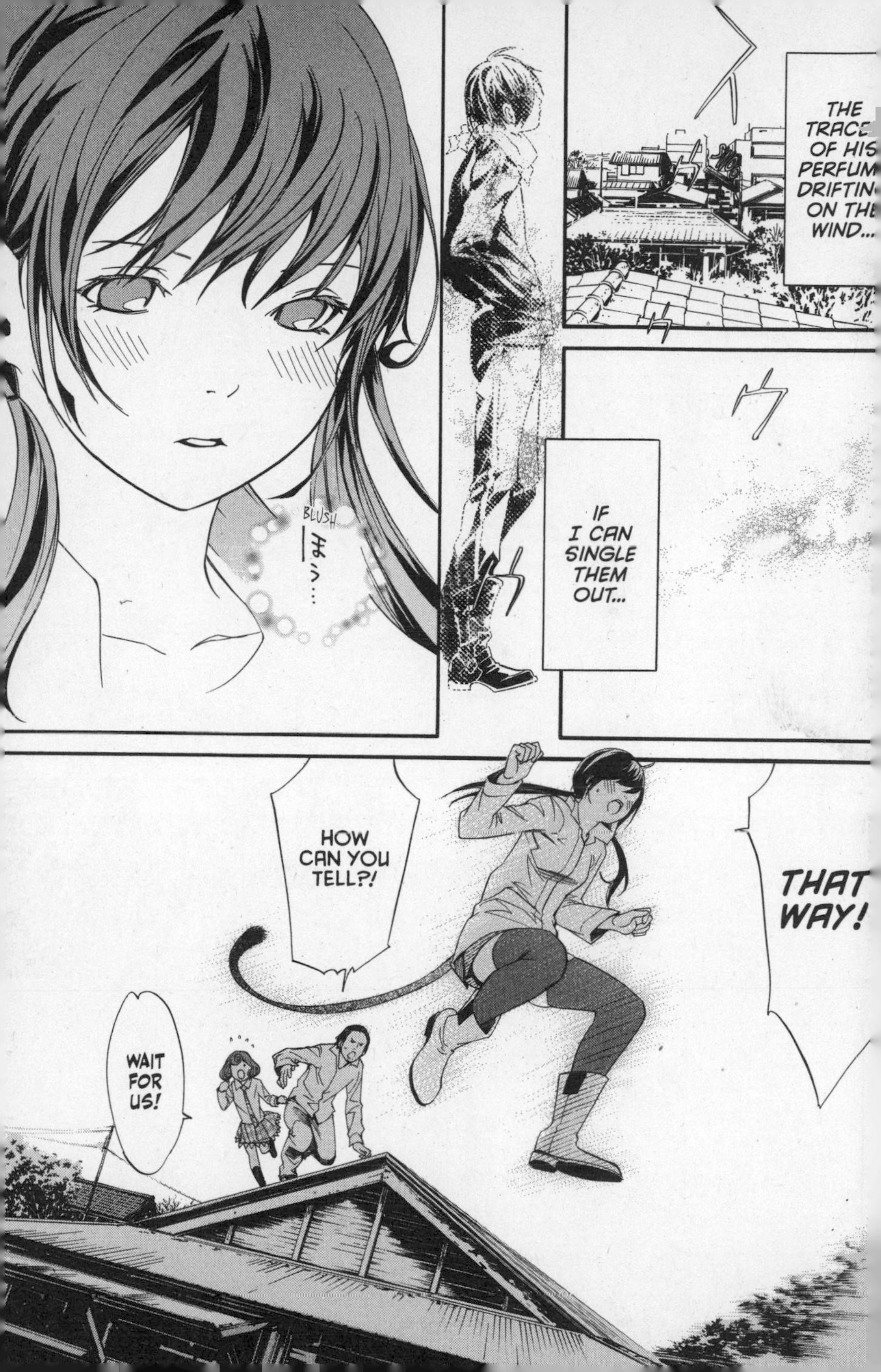
THE TRACE OF HIS PERFUM DRIFTIN ON THE WIND...
IF I CAN SINGLE THEM OUT...
BLUSH
THAT WAY!
HOW CAN YOU TELL?!
WAIT FOR US!

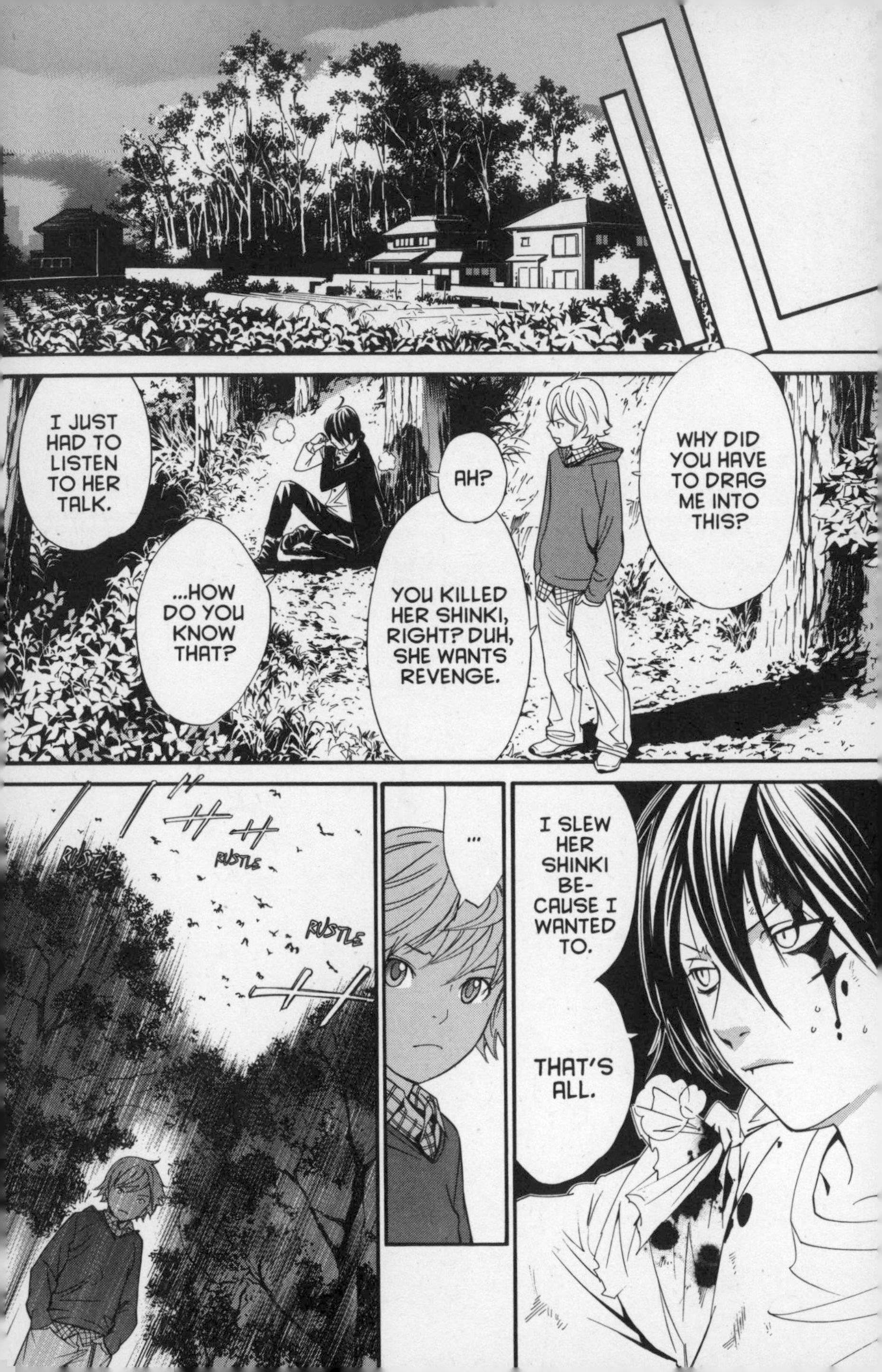
WHY DID YOU HAVE TO DRAG ME INTO THIS?
AH?
YOU KILLED HER SHINKI, RIGHT? DUH, SHE WANTS REVENGE.
...HOW DO YOU KNOW THAT?
I JUST HAD TO LISTEN TO HER TALK.
I SLEW HER SHINKI BE-CAUSE I WANTED TO.
THAT'S ALL.
...
RUSTLE
RUSTLE
RUSTLE

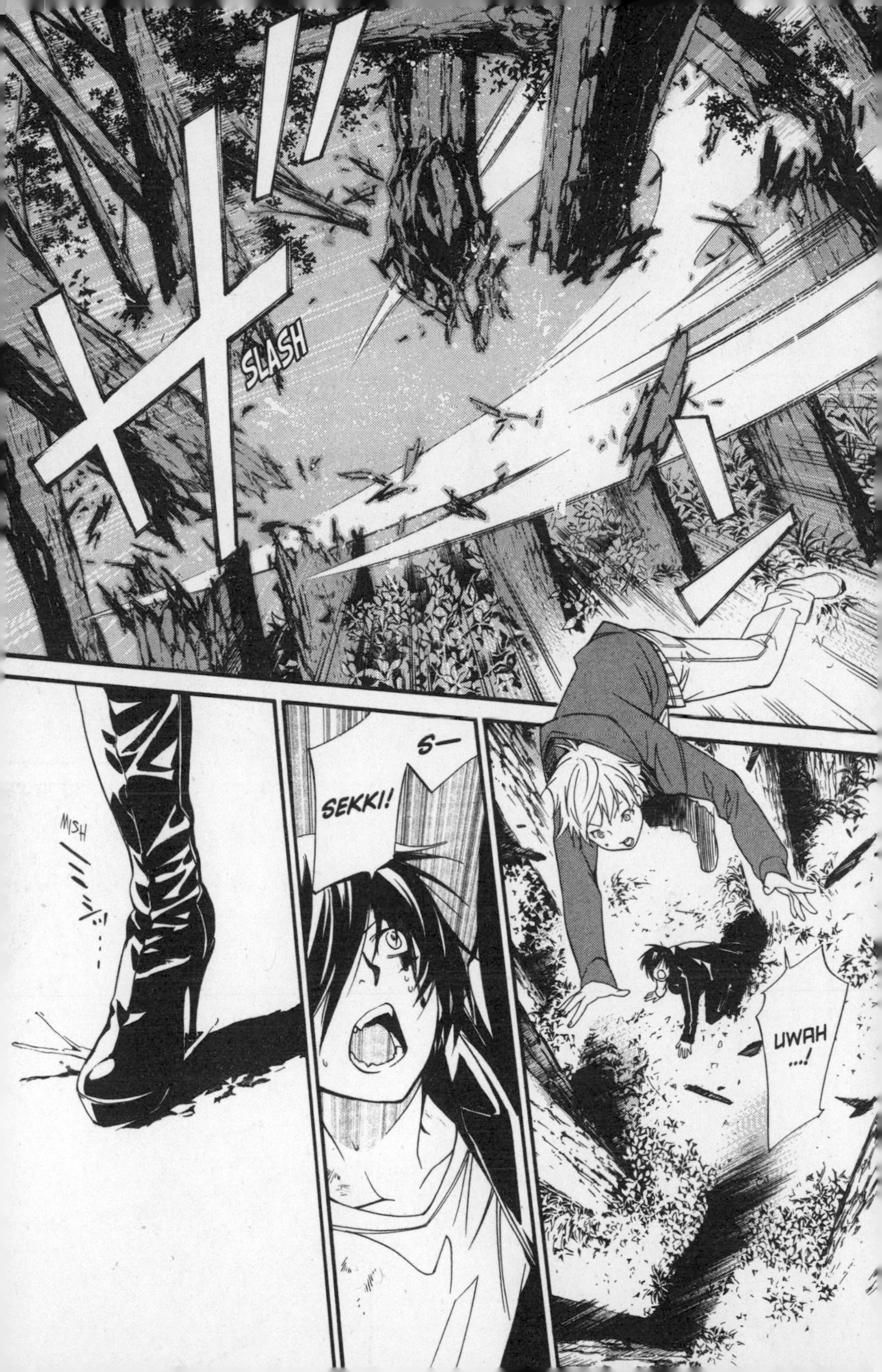
SLASH
UWAH ...!
S—
SEKKI!
MISH

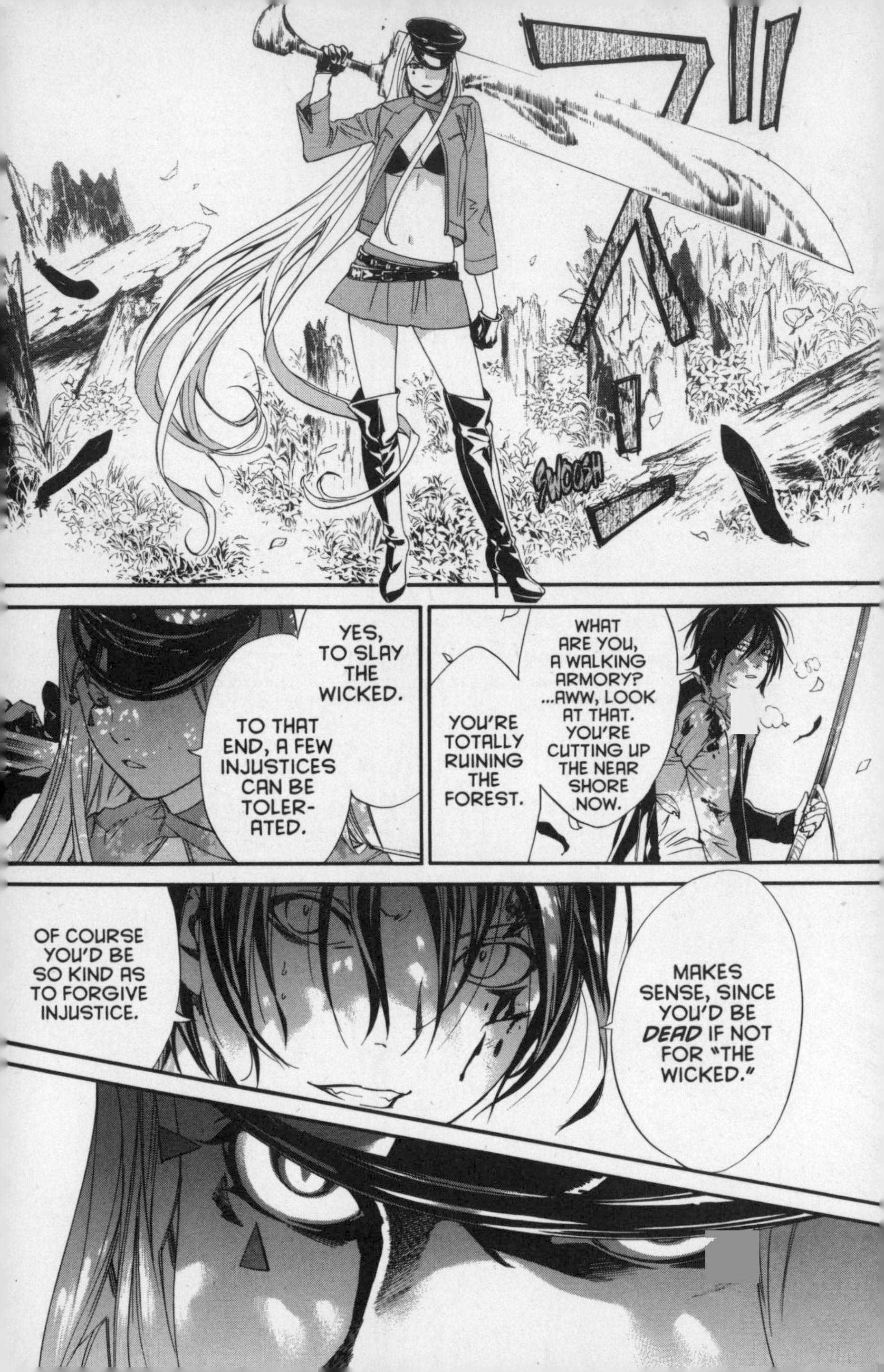
SWOOSH
WHAT ARE YOU, A WALKING ARMORY? ...AWW, LOOK AT THAT. YOU'RE CUTTING UP THE NEAR SHORE NOW.
YOU'RE TOTALLY RUINING THE FOREST.
YES, TO SLAY THE WICKED.
TO THAT END, A FEW INJUSTICES CAN BE TOLER-ATED.
MAKES SENSE, SINCE YOU'D BE *DEAD* IF NOT FOR "THE WICKED."
OF COURSE YOU'D BE SO KIND AS TO FORGIVE INJUSTICE.

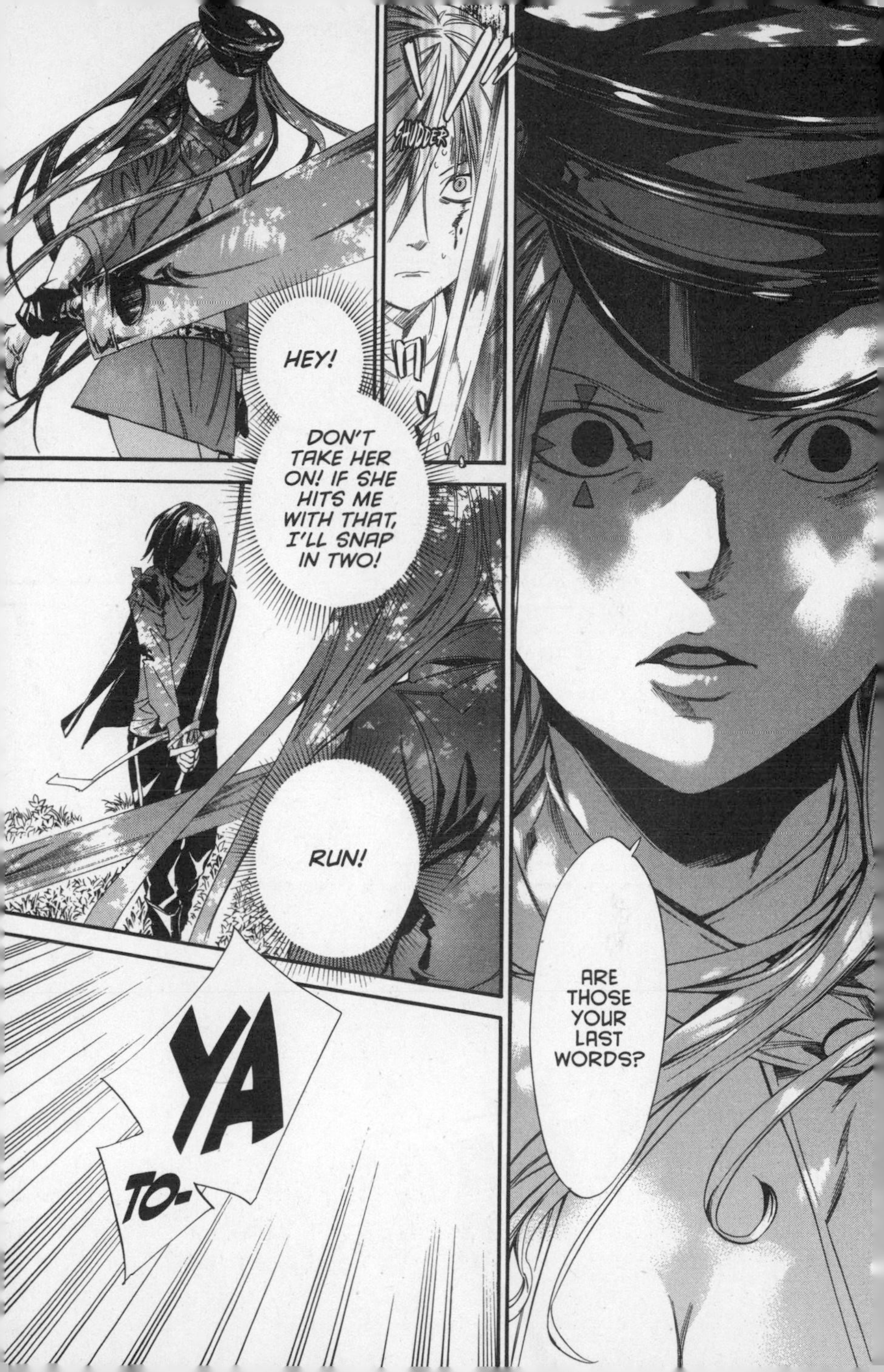
ARE THOSE YOUR LAST WORDS?
SHUDDER
HEY!
DON'T TAKE HER ON! IF SHE HITS ME WITH THAT, I'LL SNAP IN TWO!
RUN!
YA
TO-

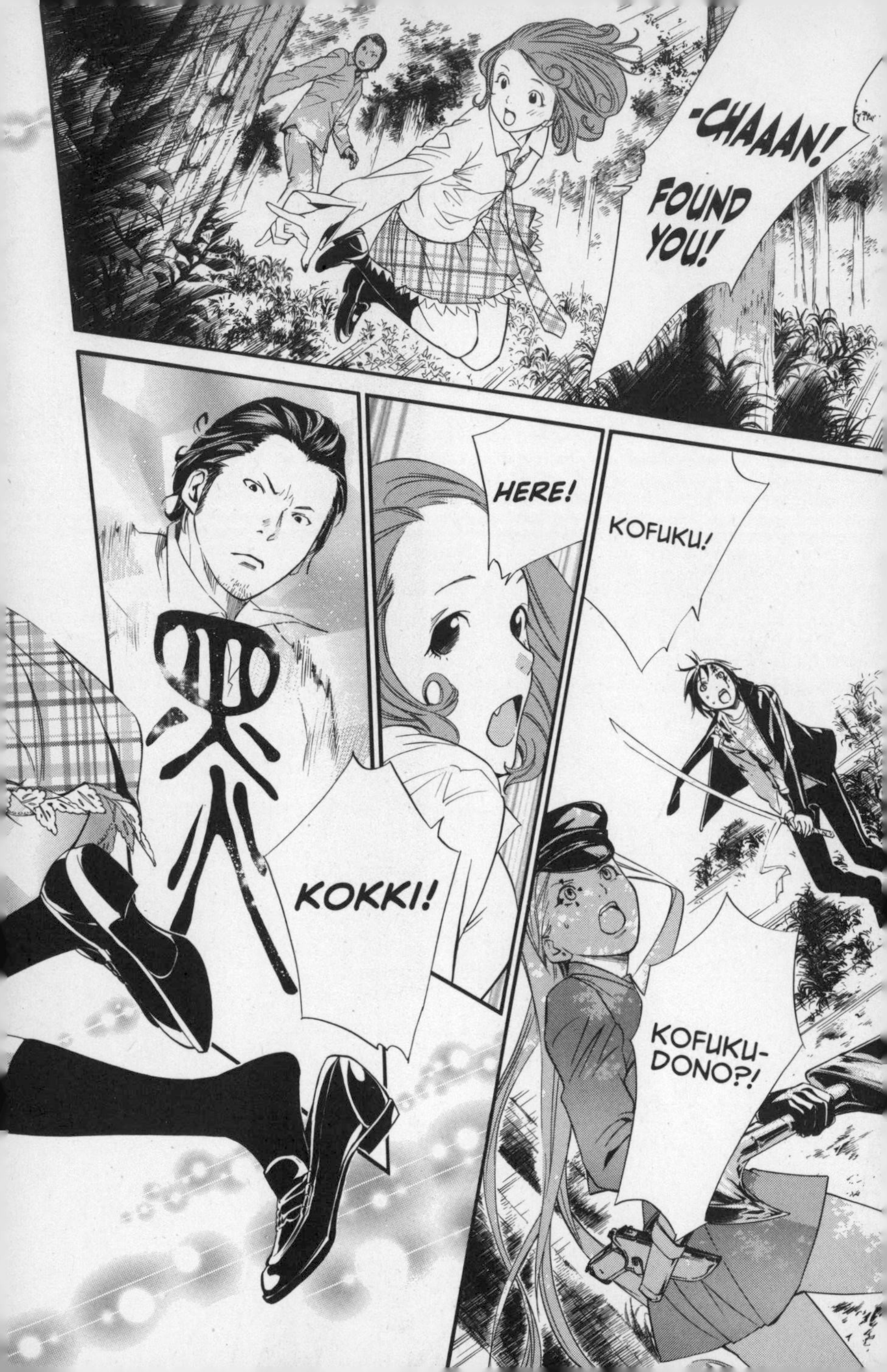
-CHAAAN!
FOUND YOU!
KOFUKU!
KOFUKU-DONO?!
HERE!
KOKKI!

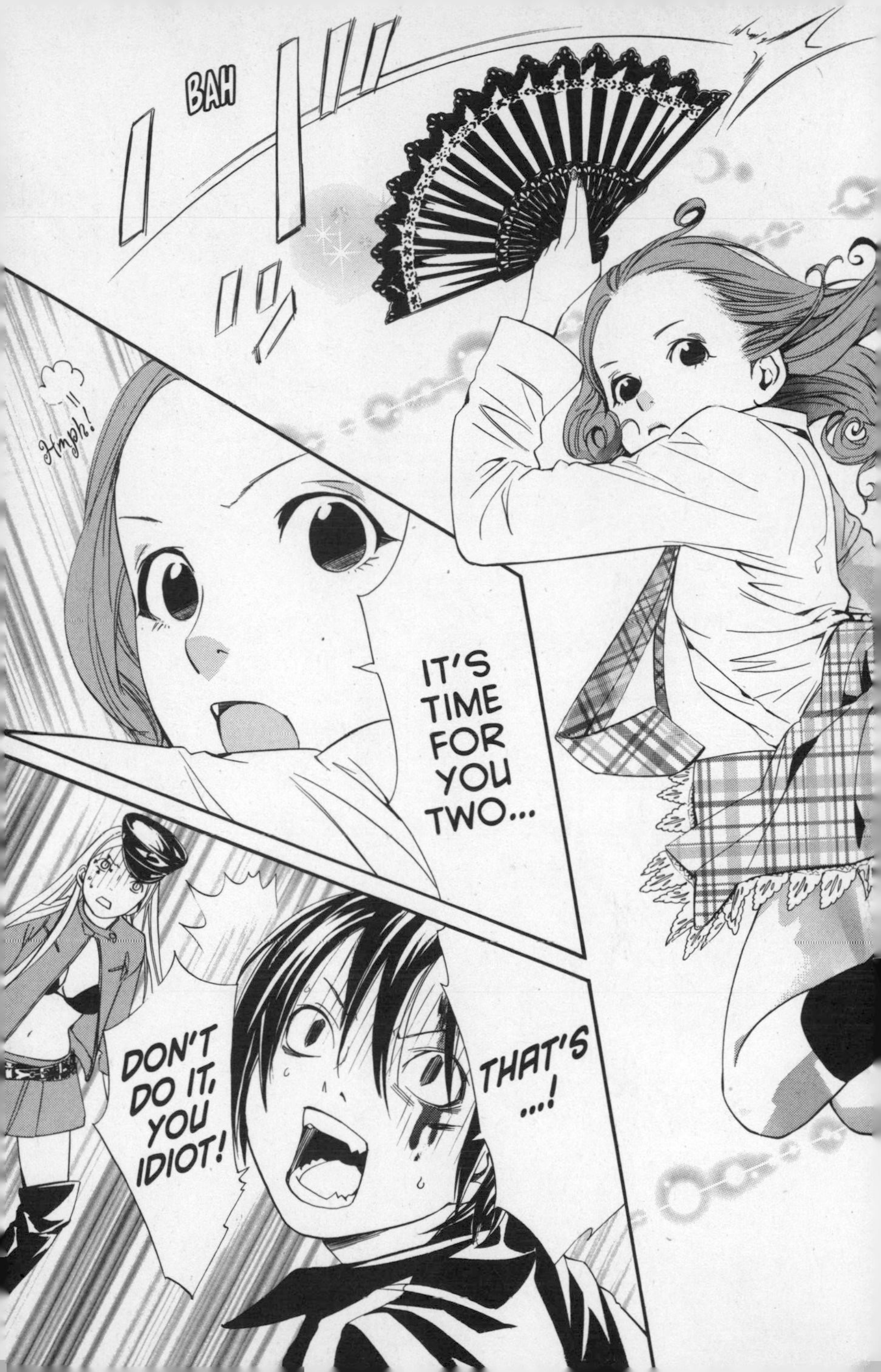
BAH
Hmph!
IT'S TIME FOR YOU TWO...
THAT'S ...!
DON'T DO IT, YOU IDIOT!

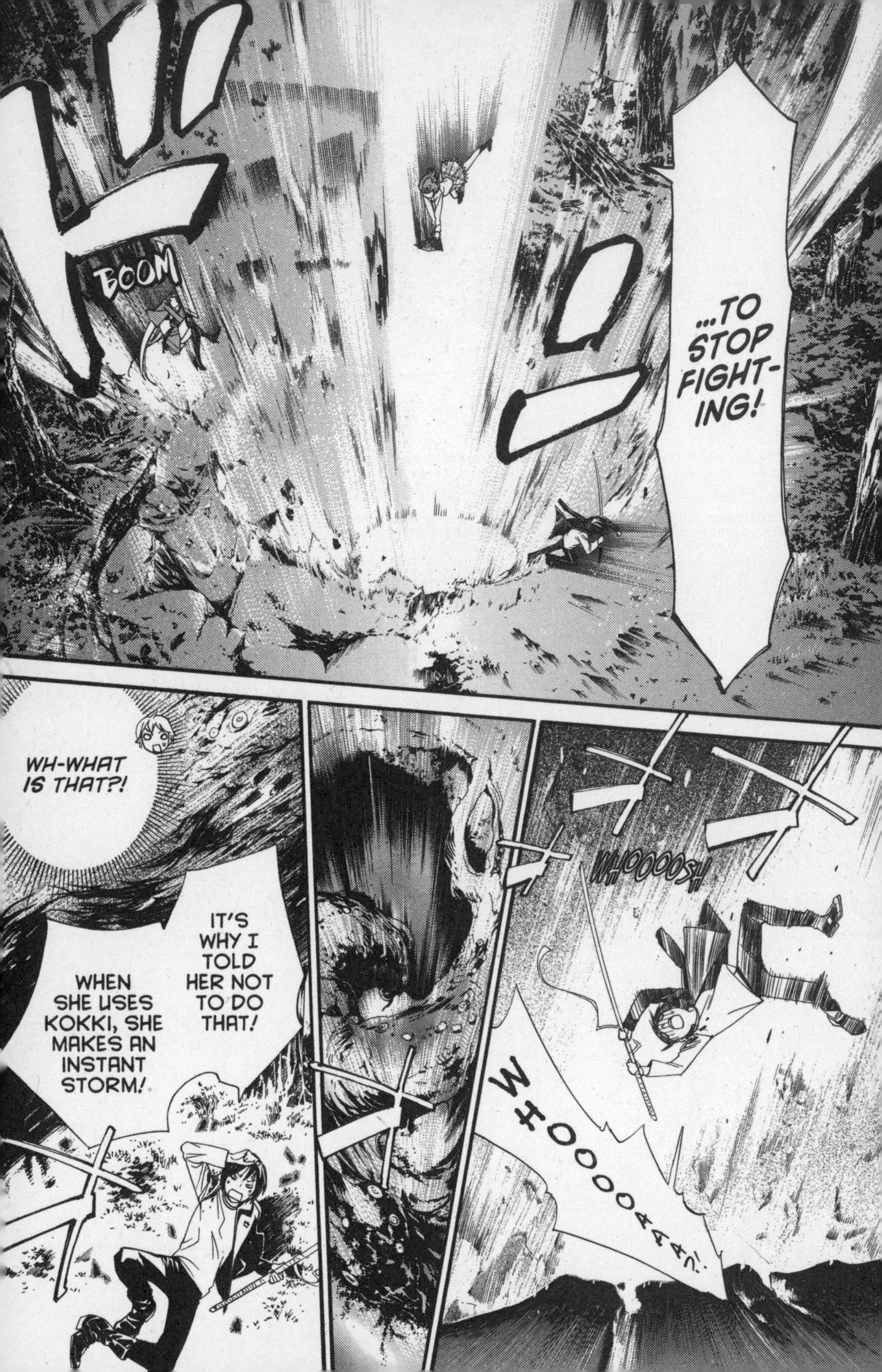
...TO STOP FIGHT-ING!
BOOM
WHOOOOSH
WHOOOOAAAA!
WH-WHAT IS THAT?!
IT'S WHY I TOLD HER NOT TO DO THAT!
WHEN SHE USES KOKKI, SHE MAKES AN INSTANT STORM!

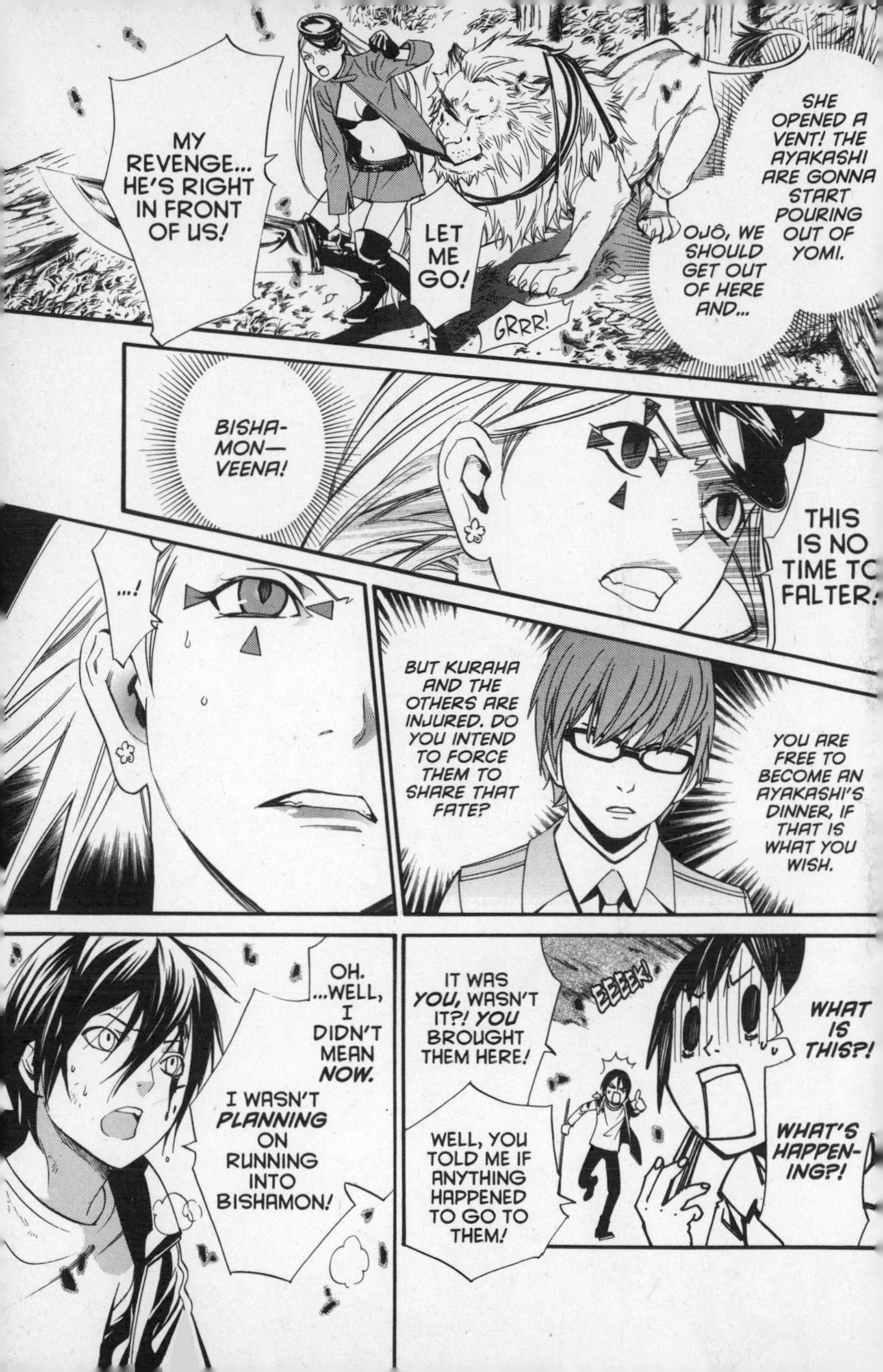
SHE OPENED A VENT! THE AYAKASHI ARE GONNA START POURING OUT OF YOMI.
OJÔ, WE SHOULD GET OUT OF HERE AND...
GRRR!
LET ME GO!
MY REVENGE... HE'S RIGHT IN FRONT OF US!
THIS IS NO TIME TO FALTER!
BISHA-MON—VEENA!
YOU ARE FREE TO BECOME AN AYAKASHI'S DINNER, IF THAT IS WHAT YOU WISH.
BUT KURAHA AND THE OTHERS ARE INJURED. DO YOU INTEND TO FORCE THEM TO SHARE THAT FATE?
...!
WHAT IS THIS?!
EEEEK!
WHAT'S HAPPEN-ING?!
IT WAS *YOU*, WASN'T IT?! *YOU* BROUGHT THEM HERE!
WELL, YOU TOLD ME IF ANYTHING HAPPENED TO GO TO THEM!
OH. ...WELL, I DIDN'T MEAN *NOW*.
I WASN'T *PLANNING* ON RUNNING INTO BISHAMON!

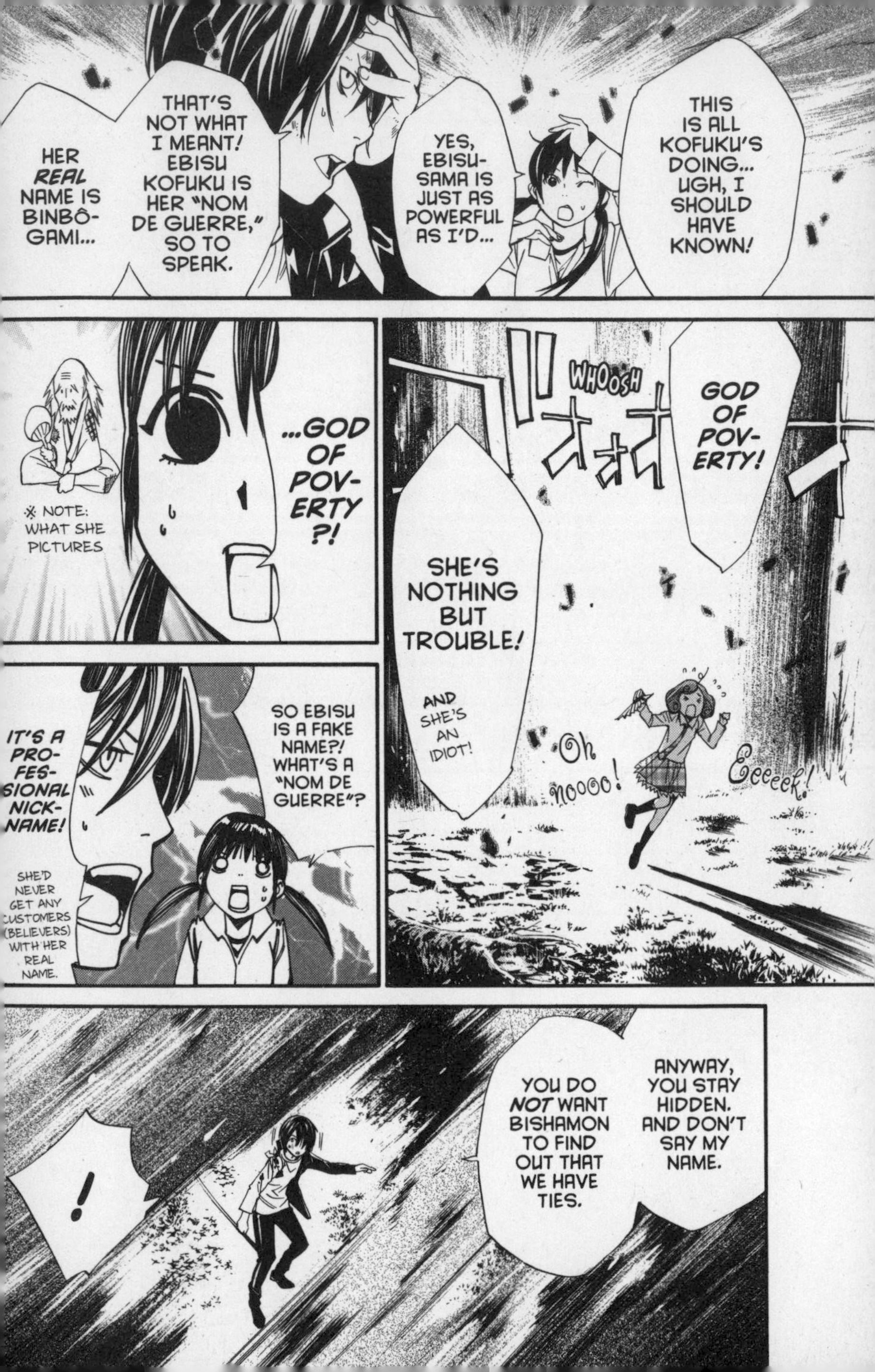
THIS IS ALL KOFUKU'S DOING... UGH, I SHOULD HAVE KNOWN!
YES, EBISU-SAMA IS JUST AS POWERFUL AS I'D...
THAT'S NOT WHAT I MEANT! EBISU KOFUKU IS HER "NOM DE GUERRE," SO TO SPEAK.
HER *REAL* NAME IS BINBÔGAMI...
GOD OF POVERTY!
WHOOSH
SHE'S NOTHING BUT TROUBLE!
AND SHE'S AN IDIOT!
Eeeeek!
Oh noooo!
...GOD OF POVERTY?!
※ NOTE: WHAT SHE PICTURES
SO EBISU IS A FAKE NAME?! WHAT'S A "NOM DE GUERRE"?
IT'S A PROFESSIONAL NICKNAME!
SHE'D NEVER GET ANY CUSTOMERS (BELIEVERS) WITH HER REAL NAME.
ANYWAY, YOU STAY HIDDEN. AND DON'T SAY MY NAME.
YOU DO *NOT* WANT BISHAMON TO FIND OUT THAT WE HAVE TIES.
!

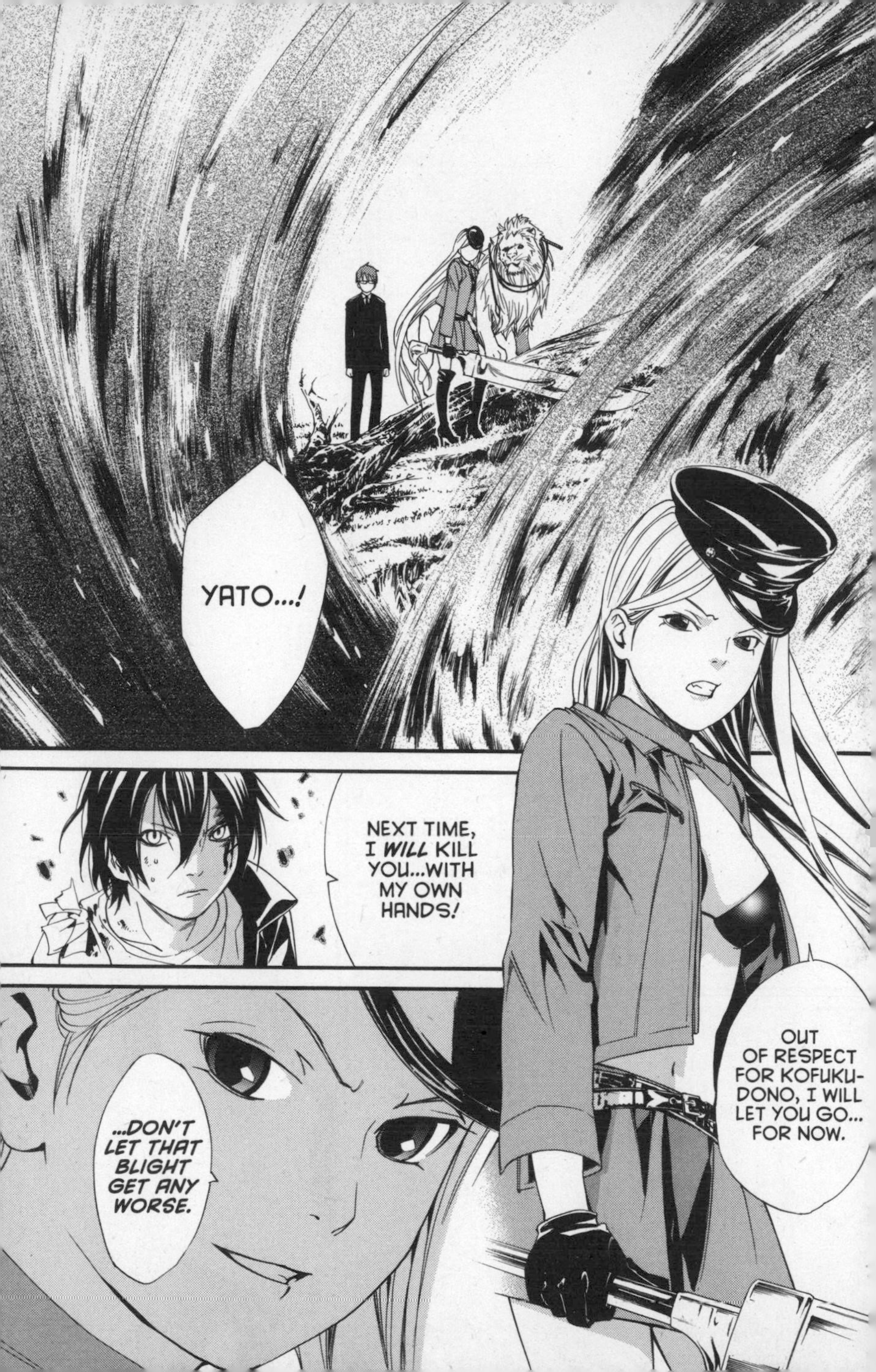
YATO...!
OUT OF RESPECT FOR KOFUKU-DONO, I WILL LET YOU GO... FOR NOW.
NEXT TIME, I *WILL* KILL YOU...WITH MY OWN HANDS!
...DON'T LET THAT BLIGHT GET ANY WORSE.

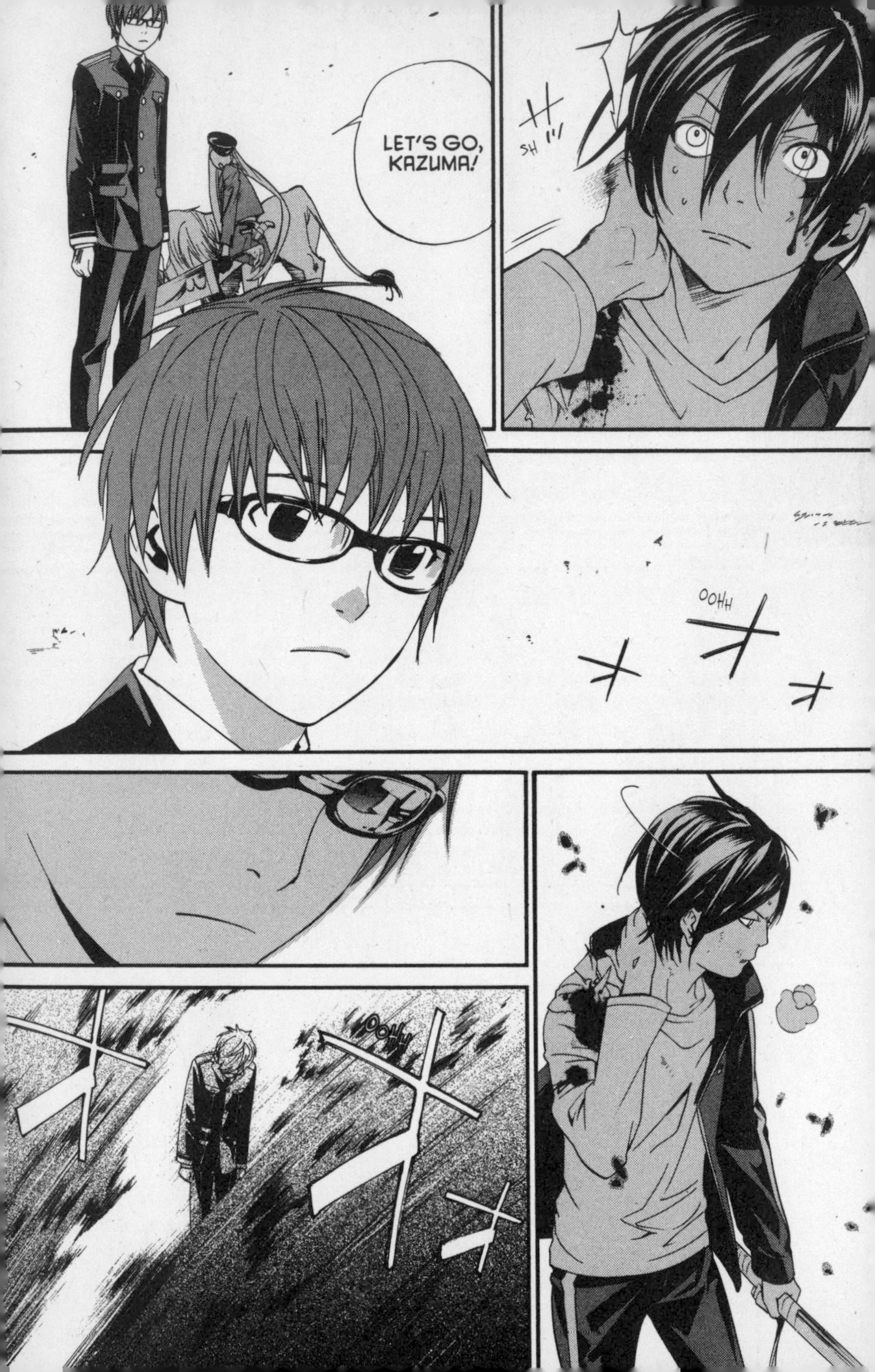
SH
LET'S GO,
KAZUMA!
OOHH
OOHH

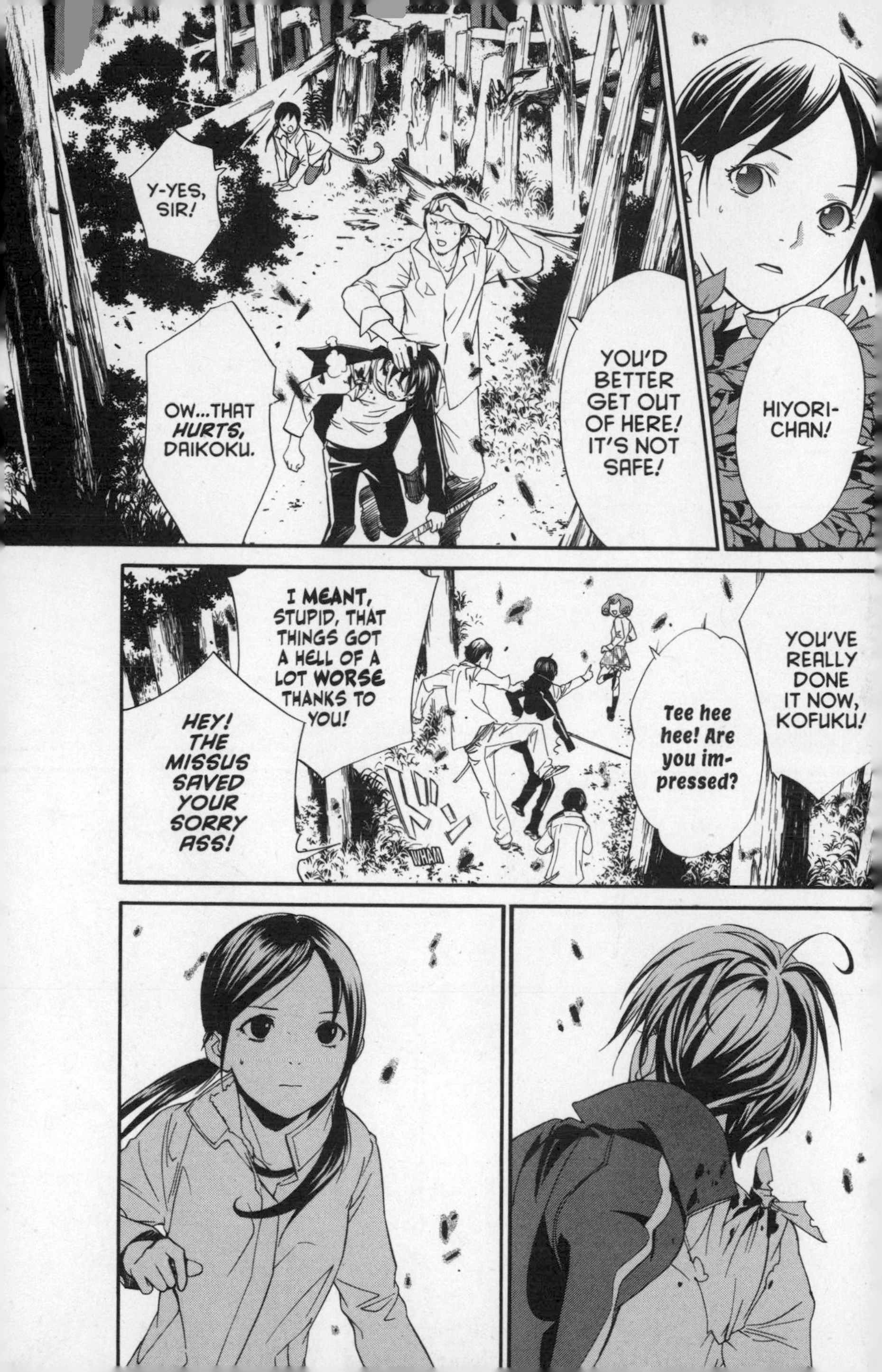
HIYORI-CHAN!
YOU'D BETTER GET OUT OF HERE! IT'S NOT SAFE!
Y-YES, SIR!
OW...THAT *HURTS*, DAIKOKU.
YOU'VE REALLY DONE IT NOW, KOFUKU!
Tee hee hee! Are you im-pressed?
HEY! THE MISSUS SAVED YOUR SORRY ASS!
WHAM
I MEANT, STUPID, THAT THINGS GOT A HELL OF A LOT WORSE THANKS TO YOU!

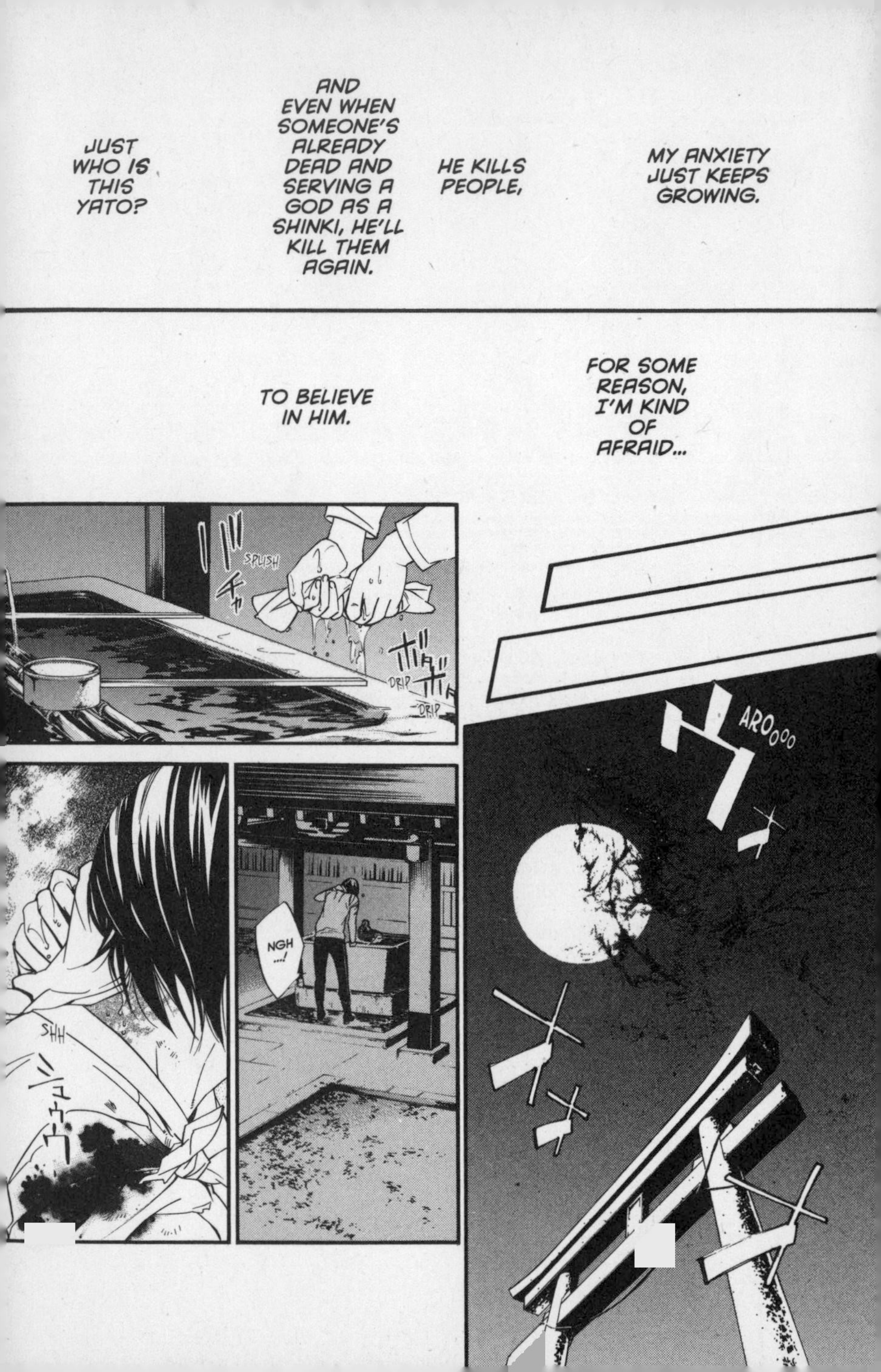
MY ANXIETY JUST KEEPS GROWING.
HE KILLS PEOPLE,
AND EVEN WHEN SOMEONE'S ALREADY DEAD AND SERVING A GOD AS A SHINKI, HE'LL KILL THEM AGAIN.
JUST WHO IS THIS YATO?
FOR SOME REASON, I'M KIND OF AFRAID...
TO BELIEVE IN HIM.
AROooo
SPLISH
DRIP
DRIP
NGH...!
SHH

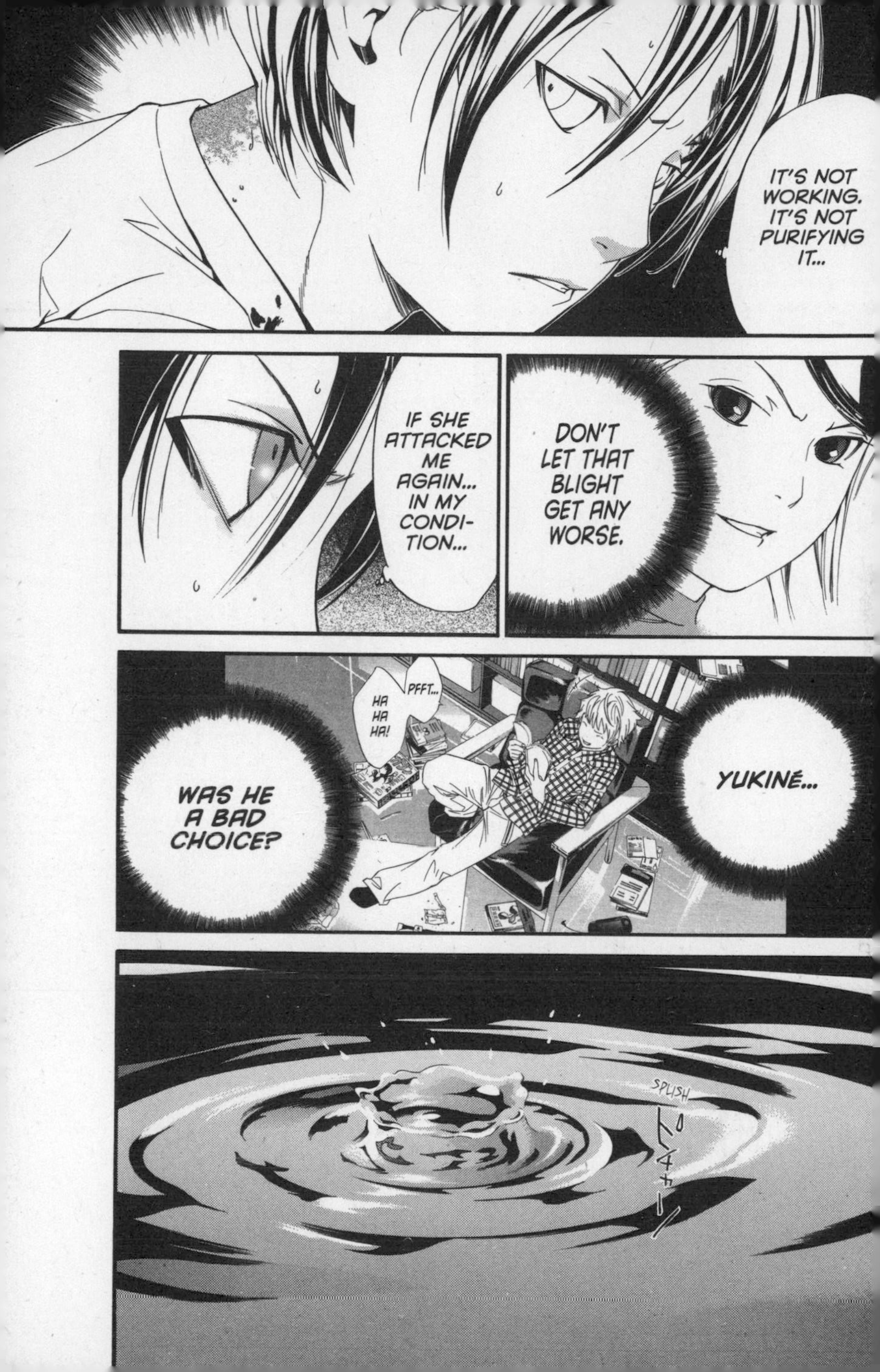
IT'S NOT WORKING. IT'S NOT PURIFYING IT...
DON'T LET THAT BLIGHT GET ANY WORSE.
IF SHE ATTACKED ME AGAIN... IN MY CONDITION...
YUKINÉ...
PFFT...
HA HA HA!
WAS HE A BAD CHOICE?
SPLISH

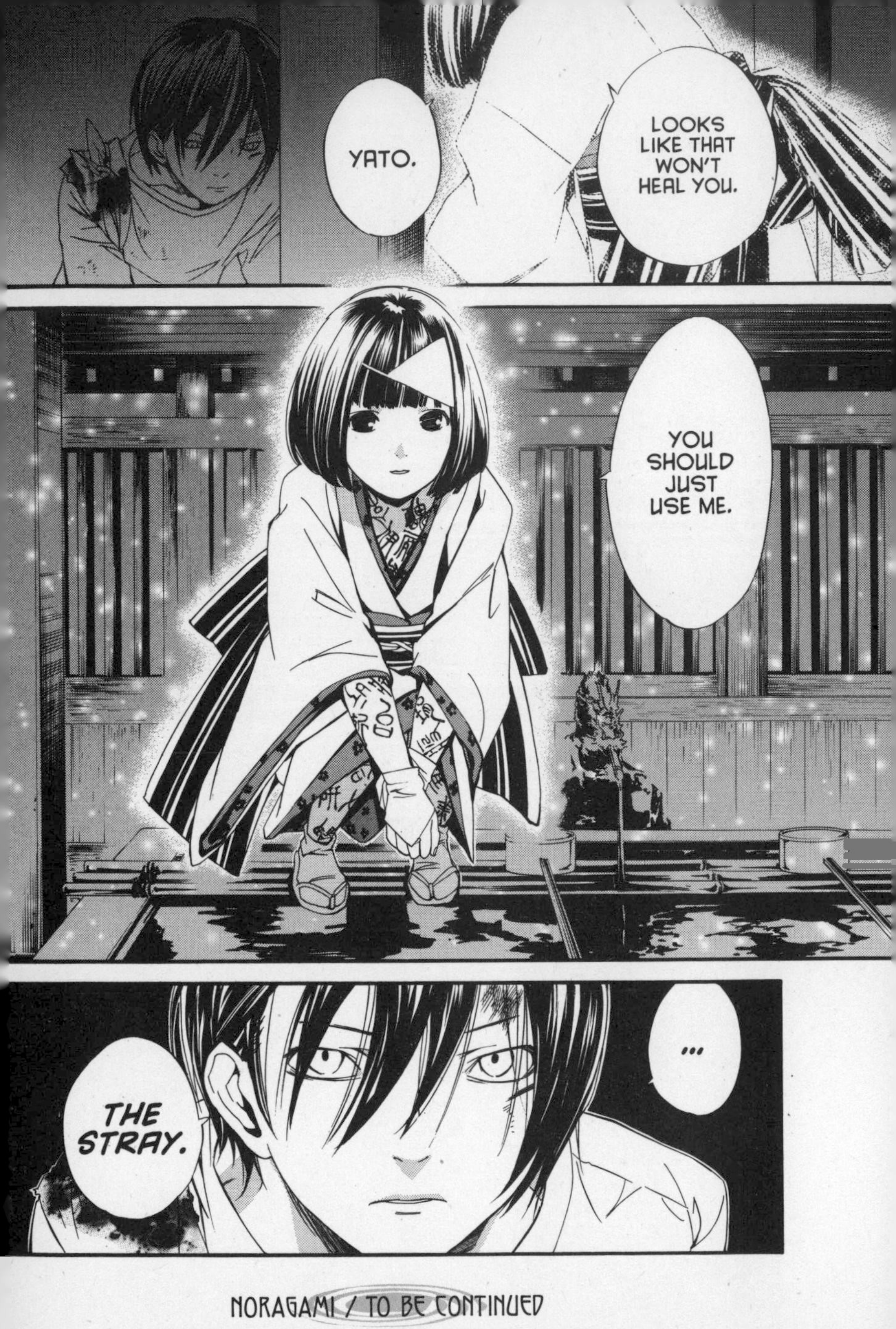
LOOKS LIKE THAT WON'T HEAL YOU.
YATO.
YOU SHOULD JUST USE ME.
...
THE STRAY.

NORAGAMI / TO BE CONTINUED

野

良

神

ATROCIOUS MANGA

GETTING ACQUAINTED

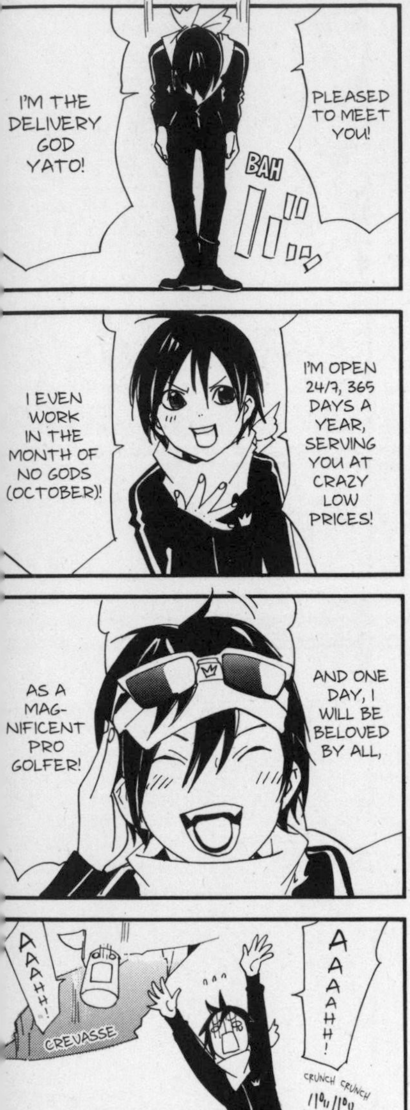
PLEASED TO MEET YOU!
I'M THE DELIVERY GOD YATO!
BAH
I'M OPEN 24/7, 365 DAYS A YEAR, SERVING YOU AT CRAZY LOW PRICES!
I EVEN WORK IN THE MONTH OF NO GODS (OCTOBER)!
AND ONE DAY, I WILL BE BELOVED BY ALL,
AS A MAGNIFICENT PRO GOLFER!
AAAAHH!
AAAHH!
CREVASSE
CRUNCH CRUNCH
NORAGAMI: FIN
GOAT

YATO HELPLINE

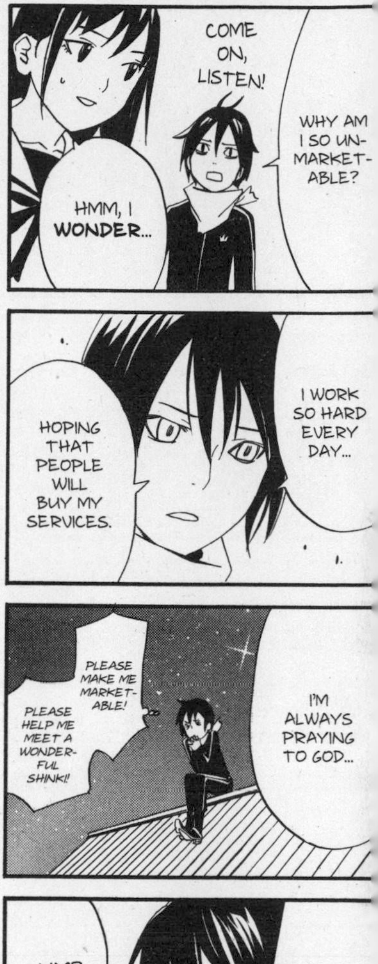
WHY AM I SO UN-MARKET-ABLE?
COME ON, LISTEN!
HMM, I WONDER...
I WORK SO HARD EVERY DAY...
HOPING THAT PEOPLE WILL BUY MY SERVICES.
I'M ALWAYS PRAYING TO GOD...
PLEASE MAKE ME MARKET-ABLE!
PLEASE HELP ME MEET A WONDER-FUL SHINKI!
I DON'T BELIEVE IN GOD ANY-MORE!
...UM?
WHAT?

REBELLIOUS PHASE

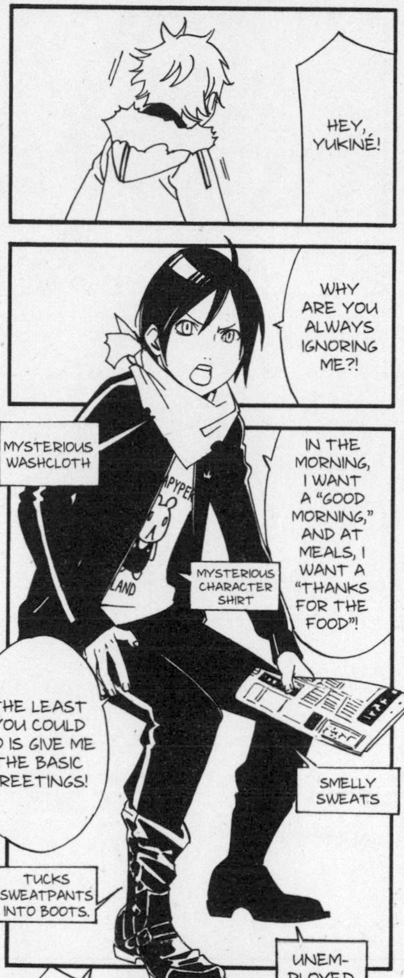
HEY, YUKINÉ!
WHY ARE YOU ALWAYS IGNORING ME?!
IN THE MORNING, I WANT A "GOOD MORNING," AND AT MEALS, I WANT A "THANKS FOR THE FOOD"!
MYSTERIOUS WASHCLOTH
MYSTERIOUS CHARACTER SHIRT
THE LEAST YOU COULD DO IS GIVE ME THE BASIC GREETINGS!
SMELLY SWEATS
TUCKS SWEATPANTS INTO BOOTS.
UNEM-PLOYED
HOW DARE YOU LOOK AT YOUR MASTER LIKE THAT!!
RRRK

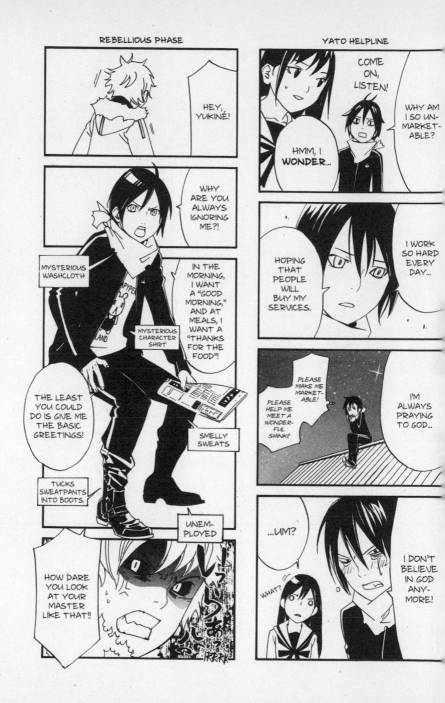

THE MAYU FORMERLY KNOWN AS TOMONÉ

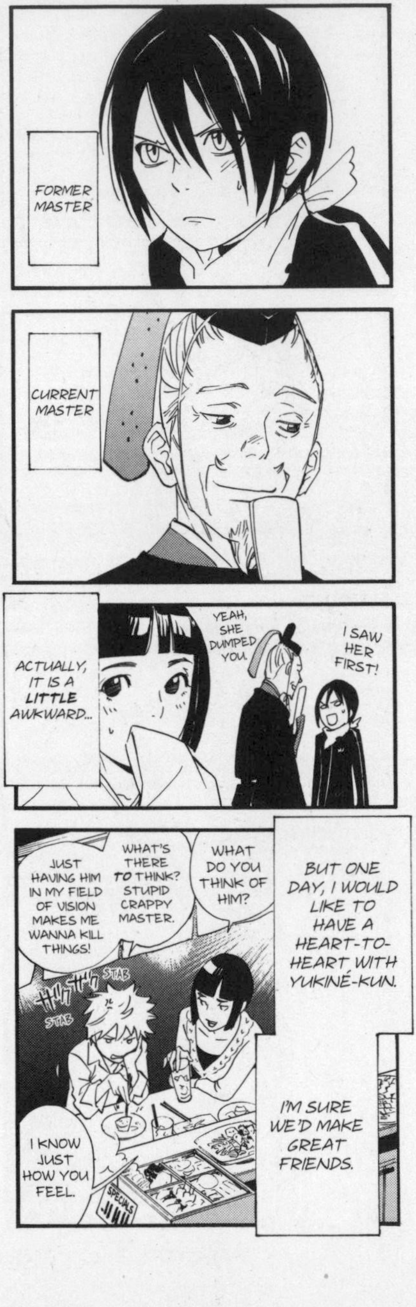
FORMER MASTER
CURRENT MASTER
I SAW HER FIRST!
YEAH, SHE DUMPED YOU.
ACTUALLY, IT IS A LITTLE AWKWARD...
BUT ONE DAY, I WOULD LIKE TO HAVE A HEART-TO-HEART WITH YUKINÉ-KUN.
WHAT DO YOU THINK OF HIM?
WHAT'S THERE TO THINK? STUPID CRAPPY MASTER.
JUST HAVING HIM IN MY FIELD OF VISION MAKES ME WANNA KILL THINGS!
STAB
STAB
I'M SURE WE'D MAKE GREAT FRIENDS.
I KNOW JUST HOW YOU FEEL.
SPECIALS

SKANK!

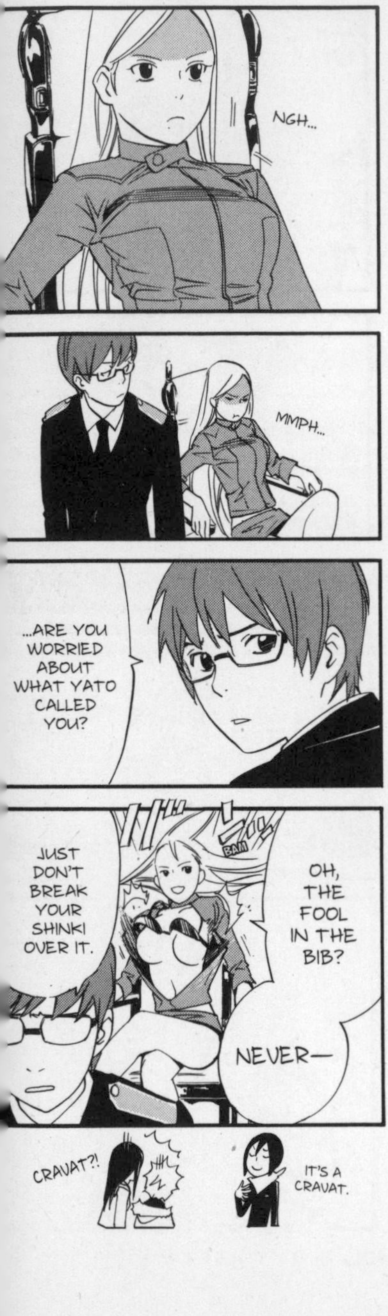
NGH...
MMPH...
...ARE YOU WORRIED ABOUT WHAT YATO CALLED YOU?
OH, THE FOOL IN THE BIB?
BAM
JUST DON'T BREAK YOUR SHINKI OVER IT.
NEVER—
IT'S A CRAVAT.
CRAVAT?!

ANY PROBLEM, SOLVED ☆ INSTANTLY!

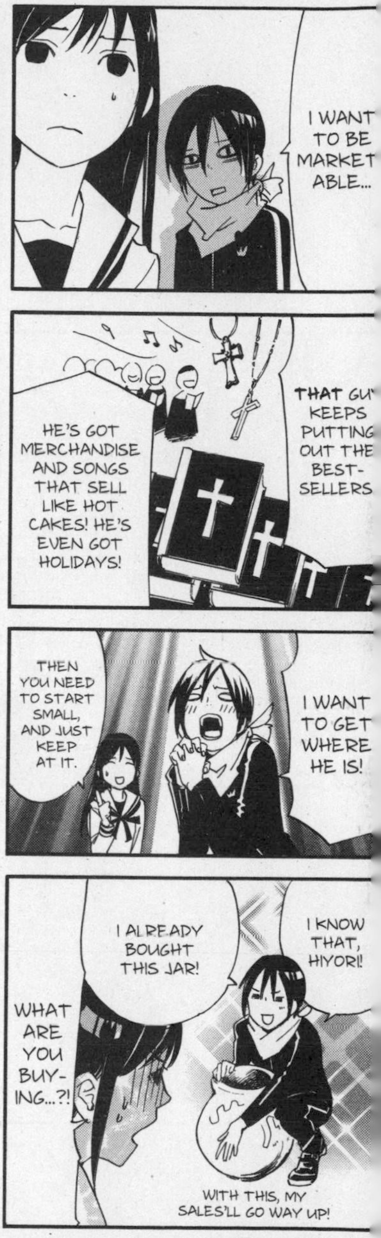

I WANT TO BE MARKET ABLE...
THAT GU KEEPS PUTTING OUT THE BEST-SELLERS
HE'S GOT MERCHANDISE AND SONGS THAT SELL LIKE HOT CAKES! HE'S EVEN GOT HOLIDAYS!
I WANT TO GET WHERE HE IS!
THEN YOU NEED TO START SMALL, AND JUST KEEP AT IT.
I KNOW THAT, HIYORI!
I ALREADY BOUGHT THIS JAR!
WHAT ARE YOU BUYING...?!
WITH THIS, MY SALES'LL GO WAY UP!

ANY PROBLEM, SOLVED ☆ INSTANTLY!

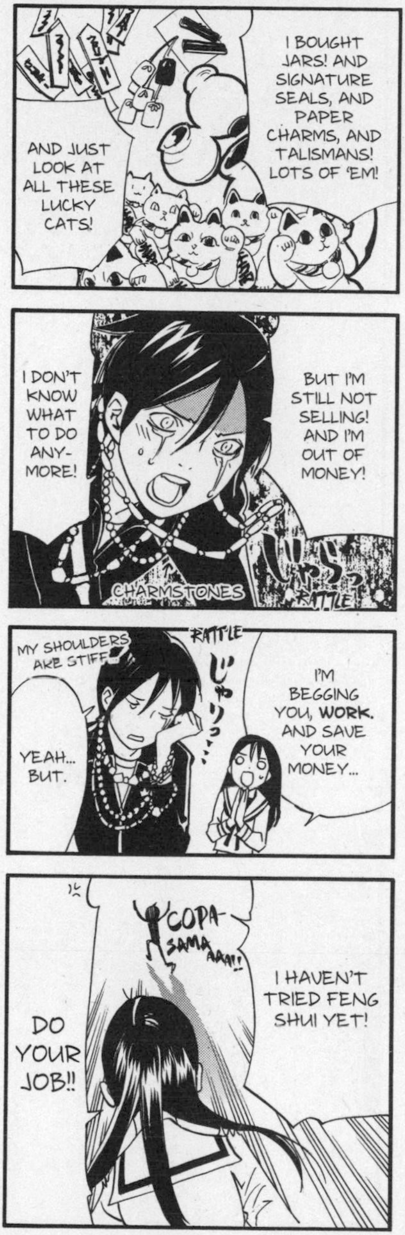

I BOUGHT JARS! AND SIGNATURE SEALS, AND PAPER CHARMS, AND TALISMANS! LOTS OF 'EM!
AND JUST LOOK AT ALL THESE LUCKY CATS!
BUT I'M STILL NOT SELLING! AND I'M OUT OF MONEY!
I DON'T KNOW WHAT TO DO ANY-MORE!
CHARMSTONES
RATTLE
RATTLE
I'M BEGGING YOU, WORK. AND SAVE YOUR MONEY...
MY SHOULDERS ARE STIFF
YEAH... BUT.
COPA-SAMA AAA!!
I HAVEN'T TRIED FENG SHUI YET!
DO YOUR JOB!!

THANK YOU, EVERYONE WHO'S READ THIS FAR!

TRANSLATION NOTES

Japanese is a tricky language for most Westerners, and translation is often more art than science. For your edification and reading pleasure, here are notes on some of the places where we could have gone in a different direction in our translation of the work, or where a Japanese cultural reference is used.

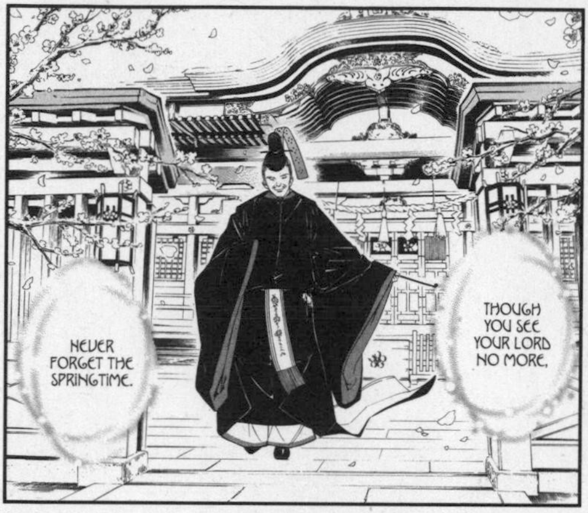
THOUGH YOU SEE YOUR LORD NO MORE,
NEVER FORGET THE SPRINGTIME.

The god of learning, page 21

Readers may remember that Yato slept at Tenjin's shrine in the previous volume, and now we see Tenjin, also known as Tenman Tenjin, himself. The name Tenjin, meaning "sky deity," originally applied to a category of gods associated with natural disasters. Several natural disasters occurred after the death of Sugawara no Michizane, so to placate his angry spirit, he was worshiped as a god and named Tenjin. Centuries later, scholars remembered his great scholastic achievements and came to see him as a patron of learning, and that is what he is mainly worshiped for today. He is especially popular when students are preparing to take entrance exams. Sugawara no Michizane was also a famous poet, and the poem he recites is one of his most well known. It was composed as a farewell to his favorite plum tree, when politics forced him to leave his Kyoto home. Legend has it, the plum tree loved him so much, it flew to his new home in Dazaifu.
Including his main shrine at Dazaifu, Tenjin has a network of more than ten thousand shrines all over Japan.

Yukiné's names, page 22

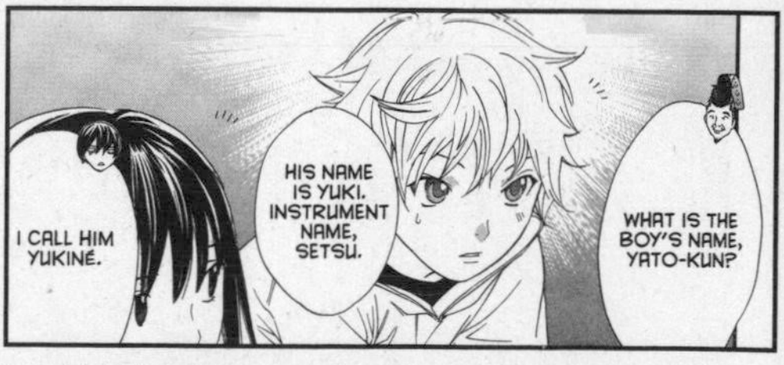
WHAT IS THE BOY'S NAME, YATO-KUN?
HIS NAME IS YUKI. INSTRUMENT NAME, SETSU.
I CALL HIM YUKINÉ.

Every time a shinki is introduced to another Far Shore denizen, three names are provided. The first name is the "true name" assigned by the deity, represented by the Chinese character written somewhere on the shinki's person. The second is the sound-reading of that character, as applied to the shinki's instrument-form. Finally, the *yobina* (called name) is provided—the name by which the shinki is called to avoid too much repetition of the true name.

Pay my respects, page 23

Presented with a respectable god like Tenjin-sama, Hiyori feels the need to worship him properly. The Shinto way to do this is to bow twice, clap twice, and bow again. The bowing shows respect, the clapping invites the deity to you, and the last bow is to respectfully send the deity off after offering your prayer. Of course, Hiyori doesn't need to invite Tenjin to her, but she's following the procedure, just in case.

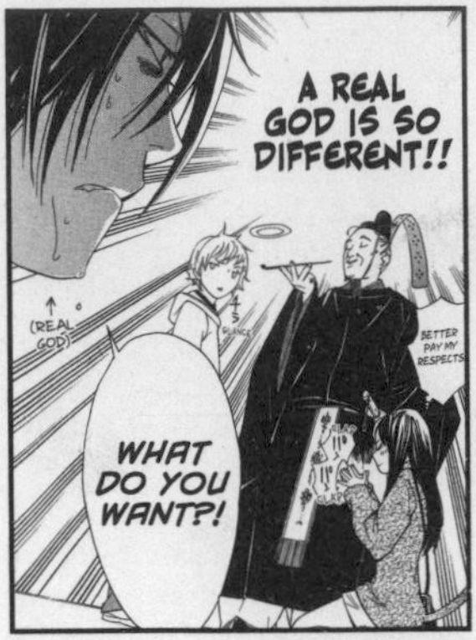
A REAL GOD IS SO DIFFERENT!!
BETTER PAY MY RESPECTS
(REAL GOD)
WHAT DO YOU WANT?!

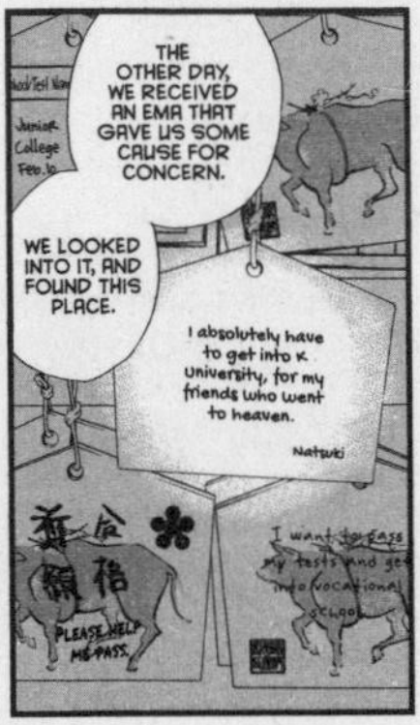
THE OTHER DAY, WE RECEIVED AN EMA THAT GAVE US SOME CAUSE FOR CONCERN.
WE LOOKED INTO IT, AND FOUND THIS PLACE.
I absolutely have to get into K University, for my friends who went to heaven.
Natsuki
I want to pass my tests and get into vocational school
PLEASE HELP ME PASS.

Ema, page 28

An *ema*, literally meaning "pictured horse," is a wooden plaque on which Shinto worshipers write a prayer or wish. They then offer the *ema* up to the shrine, in the hopes that their wish will be granted. Originally, *ema* had pictures of horses on them, hence the name. In the case of Tenjin, some of the *ema* have pictures of bulls on them instead, because the bull is a symbol of Tenjin.

Protective barriers, page 29

The word Mayu uses here for "protective barrier" is *kekkai*, literally "bound world." Often translated to "barrier," a *kekkai* is a boundary marking off the border between the sacred and the profane. The area inside the barrier is supposed to be off-limits to ayakashi—they can't cross the line unless a human takes them across.

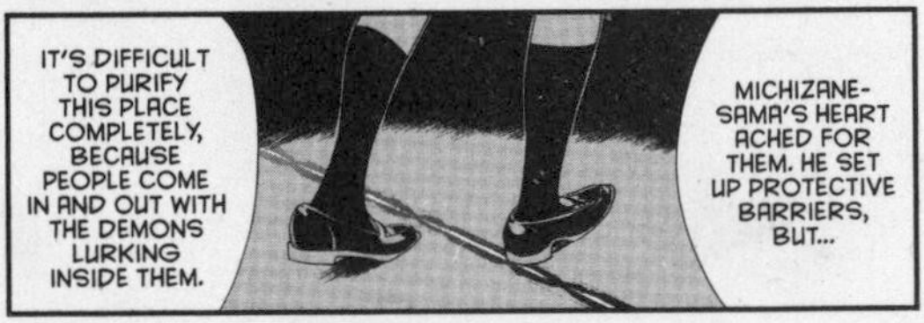
MICHIZANE-SAMA'S HEART ACHED FOR THEM. HE SET UP PROTECTIVE BARRIERS, BUT...
IT'S DIFFICULT TO PURIFY THIS PLACE COMPLETELY, BECAUSE PEOPLE COME IN AND OUT WITH THE DEMONS LURKING INSIDE THEM.

Thanks, son, page 51

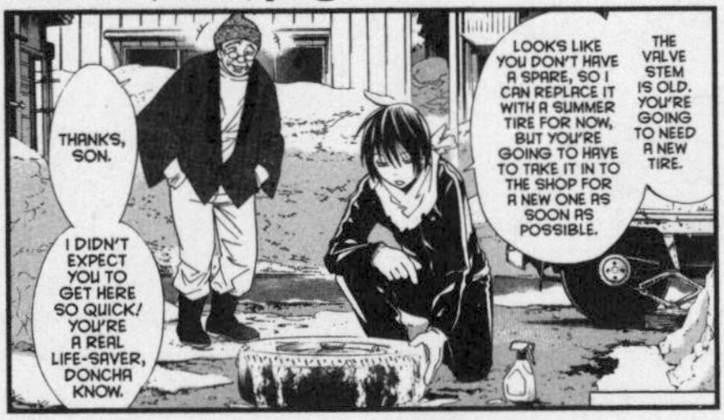
THE VALVE STEM IS OLD. YOU'RE GOING TO NEED A NEW TIRE.
LOOKS LIKE YOU DON'T HAVE A SPARE, SO I CAN REPLACE IT WITH A SUMMER TIRE FOR NOW, BUT YOU'RE GOING TO HAVE TO TAKE IT IN TO THE SHOP FOR A NEW ONE AS SOON AS POSSIBLE.
THANKS, SON.
I DIDN'T EXPECT YOU TO GET HERE SO QUICK! YOU'RE A REAL LIFE-SAVER, DONCHA KNOW.

This old man speaks with what appears to be a Yamagata dialect. That, and the piles of snow behind him indicate that Yato has teleported farther north than where we usually see him with Hiyori. So if nothing else, Yato has the ability to go anywhere in Japan at a moment's notice. He can't get all of Japan to worship him if he stays local, after all.